Saint Paul's Epistle to the EPHESIANS

Saint Paul's Epistle to the EPHESIANS

Brooke Foss Westcott

A CANTERBURY BOOK

BAKER BOOK HOUSE
Grand Rapids, Michigan

Reprinted 1979 by
Baker Book House Company
from the 1906 edition by
Macmillan and Co., Ltd.
ISBN: 0-8010-9623-5

Introduction by Philip Edgcumbe Hughes
copyrighted 1979 by
Baker Book House Company

Canterbury Books (series editor, Philip E. Hughes) are written by Anglican (Episcopalian) authors and offered as contributions of authentic Anglican thought and theology. The series will include important reprints as well as works by contemporary scholars. The significance of the subject matter, together with the quality of the writing and the reputation of the writers, is expected to ensure a wide readership for **Canterbury Books** not only among Episcopalians, but also among Christians of all denominations.

Philip Edgcumbe Hughes, Anglican scholar and author, is currently Associate Rector of St. John's Episcopal Church, Huntingdon Valley, Pennsylvania, and Visiting Professor at Westminster Theological Seminary, Philadelphia. Previously, he served in England as Vice-Principal of Tyndale Hall, Bristol; Executive Secretary of the Church Society; and Editor of *The Churchman.*

PHOTOLITHOPRINTED BY CUSHING - MALLOY, INC.
ANN ARBOR, MICHIGAN, UNITED STATES OF AMERICA
1979

INTRODUCTION

BROOKE FOSS WESTCOTT (1825-1901) was, with J. B. Lightfoot and F. J. A. Hort, one of the famous 'triumvirate' of Anglican New Testament scholars of the last century. All three had been at Trinity College, Cambridge, together, and in 1890 Westcott succeeded Lightfoot as Bishop of Durham. *The New Testament in Greek,* which was produced by Westcott and Hort and first published in 1881 in two volumes (one giving the Greek text and the other containing an extensive introduction and notes), remains a monument to their labors in the field of textual criticism.

Westcott was the author of numerous other works. His commentaries on the Gospel of St. John, the Epistles of St. John, and the Epistle to the Hebrews, which appeared in 1881, 1883, and 1889 respectively, won immediate acclaim and maintain their value as they continue to be widely used by students of these New Testament writings.

This commentary on St. Paul's Epistle to the Ephesians was published posthumously in 1906. Its re-issue as a Canterbury Book will be welcomed not only by Bishop Westcott's fellow Anglicans but also by all who have a serious interest in the study of the Greek text of this important New Testament letter.

Philip Edgcumbe Hughes
Rydal, Pennsylvania

The materials for this edition of the Epistle to the Ephesians were left by my Father in a condition which called for very careful editing. This task I entrusted to my friend the Rev. J. M. Schulhof, M.A., of Clare College, Cambridge, Fellow of St Augustine's College, Canterbury, and sometime Scholar of Trinity College, Cambridge: who has brought to bear on the work not only the loyal zeal of a very faithful disciple, who for long years has studied my Father's writings and, while it was still given, sat at his feet; but also a care and discrimination truly worthy of the best Cambridge traditions. To him all readers of the book will owe a deep debt of gratitude for the infinite pains that he has bestowed on this labour of love.

F. B. WESTCOTT

PREFACE

A DELAY of four years—which have elapsed since the duty was committed to me of preparing for the press the late Bishop Westcott's work on the Epistle to the Ephesians—may be thought to demand some explanation.

My original mandate, as given by the Bishop's Executors, involved a twofold responsibility,—first that of editing the Commentary on the Epistle, left in manuscript by Dr Westcott, and secondly that of constructing, on the basis of such materials as might be found among his papers, an Introduction, and an Appendix of Essays and Additional Notes.

The former task appeared to present no other difficulties than those which attach to the determination, here and there, of the purport of an unfinished sentence, the treatment of an occasional lacuna in the notes, and the verification of references. But it was early interrupted, and for the space of some eighteen months, by the discovery that the notes on Chapter II were missing: a circumstance which was variously interpreted; one opinion, very confidently expressed, being that for some cause no notes had ever been written by Dr Westcott on that portion of the Epistle,—in other words, that the expected posthumous Commentary was after all in no sense complete. I make no apology for having obstinately resisted an urgent recommendation, addressed to me at that time, to presume the non-existence of these notes and publish the Commentary 'as it was.'

Eventually the missing notes were discovered by the Reverend Henry Westcott between the pages of a volume which he had inherited from his father's library.

Meanwhile the heavier and more delicate task of constructing an Introduction, and an Appendix, had been begun on the lines proposed.

It was attended, however, with unusual difficulties owing to the unexpected scantiness of the materials actually extant from the hand of the Bishop. In point of fact those materials consisted mainly of fragmentary notes and jottings, a few summary analyses of projected sections or dissertations, lists of occurrences in the New Testament or elsewhere of words or phrases requiring investigation, and other brief indications of topics to be discussed. Accordingly it soon became evident that only a very small proportion of the language or argument of any such Introduction and supplementary Essays would be of Dr Westcott's workmanship. And the immediate question came to be whether the pen of a disciple might usefully and acceptably provide the desired Prolegomena and Appendix, incorporating all that could be found of Dr Westcott's own conclusions and hints, but without pretence of offering anything less or more than a disciple's elucidation of problems opened, but not continuously treated or always finally resolved, by the departed master.

At this point and on the issue thus declared the judgment of four or five representative exponents of academic opinion in Cambridge was emphatically adverse to the plan originally proposed.

That plan was accordingly abandoned.

The book, as now published, may probably be less useful to the general student than it might otherwise have been; Dr Westcott's unfinished work being, like a classic document, of a quality to need, and to justify, ancillary interpretation and focussing. But, if less generally useful, the book, as it stands, will, we have reason to hope, be specifically more acceptable to scholars, at any rate in the University which owes so much to the great teacher, whose 'vanished hand' no other can simulate, even as no pupil, or follower, can re-awaken, however he may yearn once again to hear, the tones of the 'voice that is still.'

It remains to indicate, as briefly as may be, the lines on which the present volume has been compiled.

In place of the full Introduction originally contemplated, I have prefixed to the Text and Notes a nominal Introduction, formally analogous to that which Dr Westcott has given us in his edition of the Epistle to the Hebrews, but, as regards matter, essentially, though unequally, defective in every part.

The section on 'Text' reproduces, with such modification as was necessary or appropriate, the statistical matter of the corresponding section in Hebrews.

Under the section-headings 'Title and Destination' and 'Date and Place of Writing,' a few relevant paragraphs, from original authorities or from Dr Westcott's papers, are printed, and, for the rest, reference is made to Lightfoot's 'Colossians' and 'Biblical Essays,' Hort's 'Prolegomena' and Professor T. K. Abbott's 'Introduction.'

For the section on 'Canonicity and External Evidence' it has seemed reasonable, and sufficient, to print in parallel columns the chief early patristic passages and the portions of the text of Ephesians, which they appear to presuppose; leaving it to the reader to estimate, as he may, in each instance, the alternative probabilities of purposed citation, reminiscence or coincidence. For guidance he can always refer to the published views of the scholars above named or others.

But in so far as the parallel presentation of the canonical

and patristic texts may be held to imply the view, that the Epistle was known to and used by the early Christian witnesses adduced, the section, thus regarded, has Dr Westcott's authority: all the patristic passages given being cited in the footnotes and appendix to his History of the Canon; of which, therefore, this section may be accounted an excerpt printed '*in extenso.*'

The Section 'Internal Evidence of Authorship' is made up almost entirely of matter drawn from Dr Hort's *Prolegomena*, and arranged under the subdivisions adopted in the 'Abstract of Lectures on Ephesians' printed at the end of that volume.

In view of the long and memorable service of collaboration which has linked together indissolubly the names of Westcott and of Hort, it will, I hope, be felt to be fitting that where in this Epistle the one is silent and the other happily has left a record, already published, of his conclusions, appeal should be made to the latter to supplement the unfinished work, now edited, of the former.

With regard to the Section 'Style and Language' I regret that, owing to an error of marking on my part, the fragmentary notes left by Dr Westcott appear in smaller, instead of in larger, type than the lexical statistics appended. The oversight, however, when discovered, did not seem to me of sufficiently grave importance to demand correction, which would have meant disturbance of several pages of proof.

The three following Sections on the relation of this Epistle to the Colossian Letter, to other Pauline documents, and to certain other, non-Pauline, Apostolic writings respectively, will, I think, speak for themselves.

The 'References to the Gospel History' constituting the tenth Section are Dr Westcott's own.

For Section XI, 'Characteristics' of the Epistle, I have ventured to bring together the judgments of four writers, all sometime (and at the same time) Fellows of Trinity College,

Cambridge, namely, Dr Westcott himself, and his three lifelong friends, Bishop Lightfoot, Dr Hort, and Dr Llewelyn Davies—of whom now the last alone survives.

The twelfth and last Section, exhibiting the 'Plan of the Epistle,' is, again, Dr Westcott's own, and is printed exactly as it stands in his manuscript.

The Text of the Epistle is reprinted from the last edition of Westcott and Hort's 'New Testament.'

The few critical notes are gathered mainly from the 'Notes on Select Readings' in the Appendix to Westcott and Hort's *Introduction*; a small residue being adapted from Dr Sanday's *Delectus Lectionum* in the Clarendon Press *Appendices ad Novum Testamentum*, or from Tregelles's Apparatus Criticus.

One note, partly critical, partly exegetical (on iv. 21), is taken, at the instance and by the kind cooperation of Dr Murray, Warden of St Augustine's College, Canterbury, from the private correspondence of Dr Westcott with Dr Hort.

After the Greek Text and Notes, and before the Appendix, I have printed the texts of the Latin Vulgate version of the Epistle and of two early English versions, namely, those of Wiclif, as revised by Purvey (*c.* 1386), and of Tyndale (1525).

The English versions will, I think, be felt to be an appropriate addition to a volume containing the latest exegetical labours of a theologian who is also the author of the 'History of the English Bible.' Both versions are reprinted from Messrs Bagster's English Hexapla, and as regards the earlier I have ventured, for the sake of brevity, to retain in the title-heading the inexact description, 'Wiclif, 1380,' although it is now the opinion of, I believe, all expert authorities· that the version here given is Purvey's revision, made in or about 1386 (after Wiclif's death), of Wiclif's own translation of 1380. The technical inaccuracy is lessened by the fact that in 'Ephesians' the difference between Wiclif and his reviser amounted to very little.

The Appendix is made up of (i) an analytical conspectus of the theology of the Epistle, (ii) a series of Additional Notes on particular words or topics, (iii) a Greek Vocabulary of the Epistle.

The title 'Heads of Doctrine,' given to the first of these divisions, is taken from a Summary, or Table of proposed Contents, prepared by Dr Westcott for a projected work, which he eventually abandoned, on 'Christian Doctrine.' And nearly all the subject-headings given are selected from that Summary ; that is to say, those subjects in the list have been taken, which admitted of illustration from the Epistle to the Ephesians. But in the treatment of them no uniform rule has been observed. In some cases nothing has been set down beyond the mere words of those verses of the Letter which contain reference to the subject in hand. In other cases brief comment has been interposed either by repetition from one or more of the notes in the text or by citation from one or other of Dr Westcott's published works. And in a few cases, when this was suggested by anything from Dr Westcott's pen, the occurrence of a term or topic has been traced through other Pauline Epistles or even throughout the New Testament.

But for the most part any such treatment of a subject has been reserved for the Additional Notes.

In these, with the exception of a few sentences from Dr Hort's posthumously edited works and a few editorial observations enclosed in square brackets, nothing has been introduced which is not either (a) Biblical Text, (β) statistical matter drawn and digested from Text and Concordance, (γ) express quotation from works actually cited, or used, by Dr Westcott in connexion with this Epistle, or (δ) comment of his own, gathered partly from extant manuscript material, partly from relevant passages in his published Commentaries and other writings.

With regard to the several subjects treated the facts are these. In most cases an Additional Note on the subject was definitely projected by Dr Westcott. In many cases prospective reference to the intended Note had been made in the Commentary. More often than not the general outline of the Note existed in the form of classified groups of instances or brief summary statements with or without accessory matter. In no case had it been brought into a form that could be regarded as final.

It thus became necessary either to leave these collectanea infertile or to supplement them. In adopting the latter course I have observed the restrictions stated above. Scriptural and other testimonies, cited by reference, have been verified and given in full: outlines left by Dr Westcott have been filled in and illustrated, where this was practicable, from his own writings or from sources quoted by him elsewhere.

The few titles not expressly emanating from Dr Westcott cover topics which he has indicated as calling for separate treatment. There is therefore no need to specify or defend them.

For the Vocabulary or Index of Greek Words used in the Epistle, and also for the short Index of Subjects, I am solely responsible.

The foregoing explanation may, I am inclined to hope, suffice to justify the Introduction and the Appendix.

But, if not, it is no great matter. Disapproval signifies merely that, in the judgment of those who disapprove, the 'Addenda' would have been better unpublished than thus arranged, filled in, and edited. It may be so.

After all, it is the Commentary which matters. And in this none can fail to recognise the unalloyed expression of the author's mind and heart; a last, clear word of consolation, strong and unfaltering, from one who through many years had ever, in the intervals of official work, turned with loving joy to the task of the interpretation of this Epistle.

In conclusion I desire to make grateful acknowledgment to those who in one way or another have helped me to make this book less imperfect than otherwise it would have been and less unworthy of him whose name it bears. More particularly I am indebted to the Rev. Professor T. K. Abbott, Litt.D., of Trinity College, Dublin, for kind permission to use a note (*v. inf.* p. 194) from his Commentary on the Epistle ; to the Rev. J. Llewelyn Davies, D.D., Vicar of Kirkby Lonsdale, and sometime Fellow of Trinity College, Cambridge, for a most courteous letter cordially assenting to the incorporation in this edition of the Epistle of some paragraphs from his own Introduction ; to the Rev. J. H. Moulton, Lit.D., late Fellow of King's College, Cambridge, and now Tutor of Didsbury College, Manchester, for assistance in verifying a reference to the works of the late Dr Dale; to H. M. Chadwick, Esq., M.A., Fellow and Librarian of Clare College, Cambridge, for facilities, kindly accorded me, of access to and use of books from the College Library, as well as for advice regarding early English versions ; to the Rev. J. O. F. Murray, D.D., Warden of St Augustine's College, Canterbury, formerly Fellow and Dean of Emmanuel College, Cambridge, for valuable aid and counsel in several points of detail; to the Rev. Arthur Westcott, M.A., Rector of Crayke, for information regarding papers left by the Bishop; to the Rev. F. B. Westcott, M.A., Head Master of Sherborne School and Hon. Canon of Salisbury, for his prolonged forbearance and patience with the slowness of my handiwork ; to my relative, the Rev. H. Brereton Jones, M.A., Senior Curate of St Giles-in-the-Fields, for his kindness and extreme care in reading great part of the proofs; and, not least, to the officials of the Pitt Press for the unfailing courtesy with which they have met my requests and fulfilled their part in the printing of the book.

And last of all there is one to whom my purposed word of thanks can never now be rendered.

After long delays, due largely to causes explained above, though partly to pressure of other work, I had at length, in the early autumn of last year, fully determined that nothing should prevent the immediate completion of the book with a view to its publication at latest by the day of the Feast of St John the Evangelist. So I proposed. But the Angel of Death forbade.

For in the meantime the gentle hand, which not long since had copied out for me with a mother's wonted care two passages from Ruskin now printed in the Appendix, had ceased to write; and the beloved voice, which had so often made kindly enquiry as to the progress of the work, had been stilled for ever. And so it befell that other and sadder thoughts and duties intervened, disabling me from these, and compelling me to relinquish for a while the task of final revision.

Now that I have been enabled to resume and in a manner finish this work of editing, I can but trust that, notwithstanding the many faults by which (as I am deeply conscious) it is marred, it may yet, by the mercy of God, not wholly fail of the end to which it has been directed, that of presenting, clearly and truthfully, the total ascertainable result of Bishop Westcott's meditation on 'the Epistle of Paul the Apostle to the Ephesians.'

J. M. S.

Ascension Day, 1906

POSTSCRIPT TO PREFACE

TO the foregoing acknowledgments of help received I have now, on the eve of publication, to add my very sincere thanks to two eminent Cambridge scholars, who have given me the benefit of their judgment on certain parts of the section 'Text,' as printed in the proof, of the Introduction; namely, to the Regius Professor of Divinity, Dr Swete, for a valuable criticism of my reference to Theodore of Mopsuestia, which I have amended accordingly; and to Professor Burkitt for a note which he has most kindly contributed on the lost text of the Old Syriac and also for information regarding the Sahidic Version.

One other avowal I would make in anticipation of a comparison that may not improbably be instituted.

I have purposely refrained from looking at the Dean of Westminster's edition of the Epistle, published since the death of Bishop Westcott.

J. M. S.

June 1906

CONTENTS

APPENDIX

INTRODUCTION TO THE EPISTLE

I. TEXT.

THE Epistle is contained in whole or in part in the following sources :

1. GREEK MSS.

(i) *Primary uncials :*

ℵ, Cod. Sin., saec. IV. Complete.

A, Cod. Alex., saec. V. Complete.

B, Cod. Vatic., saec. IV. Complete.

C, Cod. Ephraemi, saec. V. Contains ii. 18—iv. 17.

D₂, Cod. Claromontanus, saec. VI. Complete. (Graeco-Latin.)

[E₃, Cod. Sangermanensis, saec. IX. A transcript of D₂.]

[F₂, Cod. Augiensis, saec. IX. A transcript of G₃.]

G₃, Cod. Boernerianus, saec. IX. Complete. (Graeco-Latin.)

(ii) *Secondary uncials :*

K₂, Cod. Mosquensis, saec. IX. Complete.

L₂, Cod. Angelicus, saec. IX. Complete.

P₂, Cod. Porphyrianus, saec. IX. Complete.

O^b, Cod. Mosquensis, saec. VI. Contains Eph. iv. 1—18.

Ψ, Cod. Athous Laurae, saec. VIII.—IX. Complete.

[To these must be added the Damascus Palimpsest of Eph. iv. 21 ἀλήθεια—v. 4, described by Von Soden, *Schr. d. N. T.* I. 244.]

The following unique readings of the chief MSS. illustrate their character.

Unique readings:

(a) Of ℵ.

   i. 18 τῆς κληρονομίας τῆς δόξης.
   ii. 1 τ. ἁμαρτίαις ἑαυτῶν.
      4 om. ἐν.
      7 θεοῦ γάρ ἐσμεν.
   v. 7 τὸ φρόνημα τ. κυρίου.

(b) Of A.

   i. 10 κατὰ τὴν οἰκονομίαν.
   vi. 23 κ. ἔλεος.

(c) Of B.

   i. 13 ἐσφραγίσθη.
     21 ἐξουσίας κ. ἀρχῆς.
   ii. 1 κ. τ. ἐπιθυμίαις ὑμῶν.
     5 τ. παραπτώμασιν + καὶ ταῖς ἐπιθυμίαις.
   v. 17 τ. κυρίου + ἡμῶν.

(d) Of D.

   i. 6 δόξης praef. τῆς.
     16 παύσομαι.
   ii. 15 καταρτίσας.
   iii. 12 ἐν τῷ ἐλευθερωθῆναι.

(iii) *Cursives*:

Some four hundred [Von Soden, *Schr. d. N.T.* I. 102 ff.] are known more or less completely, including 17 (Cod. Colb., saec. XI., = 33 Gosp.), 37 (Cod. Leicestr., saec. XIV., = 69 Gosp.), 47 (Cod. Bodl., saec. XI.), 67** (saec. XI.).

2. VERSIONS.

i. *Latin:*

The Epistle is preserved in two Latin texts.

(a) *Old Latin.*

   d_2, lat.[1] of Cod. Claromontanus, saec. VI. Complete.

   g_3, lat.[1] of Cod. Boernerianus, saec. IX. Complete.

---

[1] Which have 'a genuine Old Latin Text' as basis, 'but altered through- out into verbal conformity with the Greek text.' Hort, *Intr.* p. 82.

> r, Fragm. Freisingensia, saec. v. vel vi. Contain i.
> 1—13, i. 16—ii. 3, ii. 5—16, vi. 24.
>
> m, 'Speculum' pseudo-Augustini, saec. ix. Contains
> excerpts.

(b) *The Vulgate.*

[v. inf. pp. 103 ff.]

ii. *Syriac:*

(a) The *Peshito.*

(b) The *Harclean (Philoxenian) Syriac.*

['A Version which if it survived would be among our most valuable authorities is the *Old Syriac.* For the Old Syriac text of the Pauline Epistles our chief extant authority is the running Commentary of *S. Ephraim,* preserved only in an Armenian translation: a Latin translation of this Armenian was issued by the Mechitarists in 1893. In using this text for critical purposes allowance must always be made for the influence of the Armenian Vulgate upon the Armenian translator of S. Ephraim[1].' F. C. B.]

iii. *Egyptian:*

(a) *Memphitic* or *Bohairic.*

Complete.

(b) *Thebaic* or *Sahidic.*

Complete save for minor lacunae in *c.* vi.

(c) *Bashmuric.*

The Epistle is found in the later versions, *Armenian, Ethiopic,* and (with lacunae v. 11—16, v. 30—vi. 8) *Gothic.*

3. PATRISTIC COMMENTARIES AND QUOTATIONS.

Ante-Nicene Commentaries.

'A small portion of Origen's Commentaries is virtually all that remains to us of the continuous commentaries on the New Testament belonging to this period; they include—many verses of—Ephesians.' (Westcott and Hort, *Introduction,* p. 88.)

---

[1] [For this note on the lost text of the Old Syriac Version I am indebted to the kindness of Professor Burkitt, who adds: '*Ephesians* will be found in the Armenian edition of S. Ephraim's Works, vol. iii. pp. 138—153.' J. M. S.]

Post-Nicene Commentaries and continuous series of homilies written before the middle of the fifth century:—

'Theodore of Mopsuestia'—'in a Latin translation.'
'Chrysostom's Homilies.'
'Theodoret':—founded on Theodore and Chrysostom.
'Cyril of Alexandria':—fragments.
'Fragments by other writers'—in Catenae.   (id. *ib.*)

Account is also taken of *Quotations* made by Marcion (as reported by Tertullian or Epiphanius); Irenaeus, Hippolytus, Clement of Alexandria, and Origen; Tertullian, Cyprian and Novatian; Peter of Alexandria, Methodius, and Eusebius; Lucifer, Hilary, and Victorinus Afer.

[The Latin version of the Epistle incorporated in the Latin translation of the Commentary of Theodore of Mopsuestia contains many 'ante-Hieronymian renderings' (Swete, *Theodore of Mopsuestia on the Minor Epistles of St Paul*, vol. I. Intr. p. xliv), and is illustrated by the following 'Old Latin renderings' collected by Dr Swete.

			Vulg.	
i.	4	coram eo.		in conspectu eius.
	13	audientes.	„	cum audissetis.
	15	propter hoc.	„	propterea.
	18	inluminatos habere oculos.	„	inluminatos oculos.
	19	fortitudinis.	„	virtutis.
ii.	3	voluntates τὰ θελήματα.	„	voluntatem.
	4	multam.	„	nimiam.
	12	abalienati.	„	alienati.
		peregrini.	„	hospites.
	20	existente ὄντος.		—
iii.	3, 9	mysterium.	„	sacramentum.
	16	confortari.	„	corroborari.
	19	cognoscere.	„	scire.
iv.	2	sustinentes.	„	subportantes.
	14	remedium.	„	circumventionem.
	16	partis.	„	membri.
	19	et avaritiae.	„	in avaritia.
	22	concupiscentiam.	„	desideria.
	25	alterutrum.	„	invicem.
v.	5	fornicarius.	„	fornicator.
vi.	4	nutrite.	„	educate.
	9	haec eadem facite ad eos.	„	eadem facite illis.
	12	principatus.	„	principes.
	16	super omnibus = ἐπὶ πᾶσιν.	„	in omnibus = ἐν π.
		ignita.	„	ignea.

To these may be added

iii.	18	profundum et altitudo.	„	sublimitas et profundum.
iv.	16	incrementum.	„	augmentum.]

II. TITLE AND DESTINATION.

[On the subject of the Title and Destination of the Epistle reference may be made to : *Additional Note on* i. 1. *The words* ἐν Ἐφέσῳ (inf. p. 19); Lightfoot, *Biblical Essays*; Hort, *Prolegomena to St Paul's Epistles to the Romans and the Ephesians* (pp. 75—98); T. K. Abbott, *Introduction to the Epistle to the Ephesians*, § 1, pp. i—ix (in International Critical Commentary); Lightfoot, *Destination of the Epistle to the Ephesians* in *Biblical Essays*, pp. 377 sq.].

Origen († A.D. 253) :

Ἐπὶ μόνων Ἐφεσίων εὕρομεν κείμενον τὸ τοῖς ἁγίοις τοῖς οὖσι· καὶ ζητοῦμεν, εἰ μὴ παρέλκει προσκείμενον τὸ τοῖς ἁγίοις τοῖς οὖσι, τί δύναται σημαίνειν· ὅρα οὖν εἰ μὴ ὥσπερ ἐν τῇ Ἐξόδῳ ὄνομα φησὶν ἑαυτῷ ὁ χρηματίζων Μωσεῖ τὸ ὤν, οὕτως οἱ μετέχοντες τοῦ ὄντος γίγνονται ὄντες, καλούμενοι οἰονεὶ ἐκ τοῦ μὴ εἶναι εἰς τὸ εἶναι· ἐξεδέξατο γὰρ ὁ θεὸς τὸ μὴ ὄντα, φησὶν ὁ αὐτὰ Παῦλος, ἵνα τὰ ὄντα καταργήσῃ κ.τ.λ.

Should the position of τὸ be altered—προσκ. τοῖς ἁγίοις τὸ τοῖς οὖσι? At all events Origen's reasoning seems to be 'unless τοῖς οὖσι attached to τοῖς ἁγίοις is redundant or superfluous.' (Lightfoot, *Biblical Essays*, p. 378 n.)

'Origen could not possibly have said that this statement is made of the Ephesians alone, if he had read the words as they stand in the common texts. In this case he would have found several parallels in the Epistles of St Paul. Cf. Rom. i. 7, 1 Cor. i. 2, 2 Cor. i. 1, Phil. i. 1.' (Lightfoot, *B. E.*, p. 378.)

Basil, *contr. Eunom.* ii. 19 (ed. Gam. i. p. 254) :

ἀλλὰ καὶ τοῖς Ἐφεσίοις ἐπιστέλλων ὡς γνησίως ἡνωμένοις τῷ ὄντι δι' ἐπιγνώσεως, ὄντας αὐτοὺς ἰδιαζόντως ὠνόμασεν, εἰπών, τοῖς ἁγίοις τοῖς οὖσι καὶ πιστοῖς ἐν Χριστῷ Ἰησοῦ. οὕτω γὰρ καὶ οἱ πρὸ ἡμῶν παραδεδώκασι, καὶ ἡμεῖς ἐν τοῖς παλαιοῖς τῶν ἀντιγράφων εὑρήκαμεν.

Tertullian, *adv. Marc.* v. 11 (A.D. 207) :

'Praetereo hic et de alia epistola, quam nos ad Ephesios praescriptam habemus, haeretici vero ad Laodicenos.'

ib. v. 17 : 'Ecclesiae quidem veritate epistulam istam ad Ephesios habemus emissam, non ad Laodicenos, sed Marcion ei titulum aliquando interpolare gestiit, quasi et in isto diligentissimus explorator. Nihil autem de titulis interest, cum ad omnes apostolus scripsit, dum ad quosdam.'

Epiphan. (*Haeres.* xlix.) :

οὐ γὰρ ἔδοξε τῷ ἐλεεινοτάτῳ Μαρκίωνι ἀπὸ τῆς πρὸς Ἐφεσίους ταύτην τὴν μαρτυρίαν λέγειν, ἀλλὰ τῆς πρὸς Λαοδικέας, τῆς μὴ οὔσης ἐν τῷ ἀποστόλῳ.

'Of all St Paul's letters it is the most general, the least personal. In this respect it more nearly resembles the Epistle to the Romans than any other.' (Lightf. *B. E.* p. 388.)

'Scribit Ephesiis hanc epistulam beatus Paulus eo modo quo et Romanis dudum scripserat quos necdum ante viderat.' (Theod. Mops., *Argum. ad Eph.* i. p. 112, ed. Swete.)

'Yet though this Epistle so little fulfils our expectation of what St Paul would have written to his converts, it is beyond a question that the early Church universally regarded it as an Epistle to the Ephesians. It is distinctly referred to as such by the writer of the Muratorian Canon, by Irenaeus, by Tertullian, by Clement of Alexandria, even by Origen himself, in whose text, as we have seen, there was no direct mention of Ephesus.'

'Murat. Canon, p. 148 (ed. Credner); Iren. *Haeres.* i. 3, i. 4, pp. 14, 16, i. 8. 4, p. 40, v. 2. 36, p. 294 (ed. Stieren); Tert. *adv. Marc.* v. 17, *de Praescr.* 36, *de monogam.* 5 ; Clem. Alex. *Strom.* iv. 65, p. 592, *Paedag.* i. 18, p. 108 (ed. Potter); Orig. *c. Cels.* iii. 28 (xviii, p. 273, ed. Lomm.).' (Id. *ib.*)

III. DATE AND PLACE OF WRITING.

[For discussion see Lightfoot, *Philippians*, Introd. pp. 29—45. 'Order of the Epistles of the Captivity'; Hort, *Prolegomena*, pp. 99—110; T. K. Abbott, *Introduction to the Epistle to the Ephesians* (International Critical Commentary), § 6, pp. xxix—xxxi.]

THE HISTORICAL SITUATION IMPLIED BY THE LANGUAGE OF THE EPISTLE TO THE EPHESIANS.

There is in the Epistle no charge to spread, no sign of anxiety for spreading the message of the Gospel.

That message, it is felt here as in the First Epistle of St John, will vindicate itself.

Again there is no sign of persecution of Christians by the Roman power. St Paul's 'bonds' were due to Jewish hostility evoked by his activity on behalf of Gentiles (ἐγὼ Παῦλος ὁ δέσμιος τοῦ χριστοῦ Ἰησοῦ ὑπὲρ ὑμῶν τῶν ἐθνῶν, iii. 1). His afflictions (iii. 13) were all connected with his preaching to the Gentiles.

In this respect the Epistle presents a contrast to the situation implied in the First Epistle of St Peter.

IV. CANONICITY AND EXTERNAL EVIDENCE OF AUTHORSHIP.

(Westcott, *Canon of the New Testament*, 4th edn., pp. 48, 91, 199, 225, 280, 292, 296, 305 f., 308, 335, 585.)

Clemens Romanus.	Ephesians.
c. 36. ἠνεῴχθησαν ἡμῶν οἱ ὀφθαλ-μοὶ τῆς καρδίας.	i. 18. πεφωτισμένους τ. ὀφθαλ-μοὺς τῆς καρδίας [ὑμῶν].
c. 38. Σωζέσθω...ἡμῶν ὅλον τὸ σῶμα ἐν Χρ. Ἰησοῦ, καὶ ὑπο-τασσέσθω ἕκαστος τῷ πλησίον αὐτοῦ.	v. 21. ὑποτασσόμενοι ἀλλήλοις ἐν φόβῳ Χριστοῦ. iv. 3 f. σπουδάζοντες τηρεῖν τὴν ἑνότητα τοῦ πνεύματος...ἐν σῶμα κ. ἐν πνεῦμα.
ib. ἐν ἔργοις ἀγαθοῖς.	ii. 10. ἐπὶ ἔργοις ἀγαθοῖς.
c. 46. ἢ οὐχὶ ἕνα θεὸν ἔχομεν καὶ ἕνα Χριστὸν καὶ ἐν πνεῦμα τῆς χάριτος τὸ ἐκχυθὲν ἐφ᾽ ἡμᾶς; καὶ μία κλῆσις ἐν Χριστῷ;	iv. 4. ἐν σῶμα κ. ἐν πνεῦμα, καθὼς [καὶ] ἐκλήθητε ἐν μιᾷ ἐλπίδι τῆς κλήσεως ὑμῶν· εἷς κύριος, μία πίστις, ἐν βάπτισμα· εἷς θεὸς κ.τ.λ.
c. 64. ὁ παντεπόπτης θεὸς κ. δεσπότης τ. πνευμάτων κ. κύριος πάσης σαρκός, ὁ ἐκλεξάμενος τὸν κύριον Ἰησοῦν Χριστὸν κ. ἡμᾶς δι᾽ αὐτὸν εἰς λαὸν περιούσιον.	i. 3, 4. ὁ θεὸς κ. πατὴρ τ. κυρίου ἡμῶν Ἰησοῦ Χριστοῦ, ὁ εὐλογήσας ἡμᾶς ἐν πάσῃ εὐλογίᾳ πνευματικῇ ἐν τ. ἐπουρανίοις ἐν Χριστῷ, καθὼς ἐξελέ-ξατο ἡμᾶς ἐν αὐτῷ...εἶναι ἡμᾶς ἁγίους κ. ἀμώμους...προορίσας ἡμᾶς εἰς υἱο-θεσίαν δι᾽ Ἰησοῦ Χρ. εἰς αὐτόν.

Ignatius, ad *Ephesios*.

The 'opening address contains several obvious reminiscences of Eph. i. 3 f.' (Lightfoot, *Apostolic Fathers*, Pt. II. p. 22 note.)

τῇ εὐλογημένῃ ἐν μεγέθει θεοῦ πατρὸς πληρώματι τῇ προωρισ-μένῃ πρὸ αἰώνων εἶναι διὰ παντὸς εἰς δόξαν παράμονον ἄτρεπτον, ἡνω-μένῃ καὶ ἐκλελεγμένῃ ἐν πάθει ἀλη-θινῷ ἐν θελήματι τοῦ πατρὸς καὶ Ἰησοῦ Χριστοῦ τοῦ θεοῦ ἡμῶν, τῇ ἐκκλησίᾳ τῇ ἀξιομακαρίστῳ τῇ οὔσῃ	Eph. i. 3 f. ὁ θεὸς καὶ πατήρ... τοῦ κ. ἡ. Ἰ. Χρ. ὁ εὐλογήσας ἡμᾶς ἐν πάσῃ εὐλογίᾳ...καθὼς ἐξελέξατο ...πρὸ καταβολῆς κόσμου, εἶναι ἡμᾶς...ἀμώμους...προορίσας ἡμᾶς ...κατὰ τὴν εὐδοκίαν τοῦ θελήματος αὐτοῦ...διὰ τοῦ αἵματος αὐτοῦ... προορισθέντες κατὰ τὴν βουλὴν

Ignatius, *ad Ephesios.*

ἐν Ἐφέσῳ [τῆς Ἀσίας], πλεῖστα ἐν Ἰ. Χρ. καὶ ἐν ἀμώμῳ χαρᾷ χαίρειν.
'The direct *mention* of the Epistle to the Ephesians, which is supposed to occur at a later point in this letter (§ 12 Παύλου...ὃς ἐν πάσῃ ἐπιστολῇ μνημονεύει ὑμῶν) is extremely doubtful;—but the *acquaintance* of Ignatius with that Epistle appears from other passages besides this exordium.'

c. i. μιμηταὶ ὄντες θεοῦ.
'The expression is borrowed from St Paul, Eph. v. 1, thus exhibiting another coincidence with this same Epistle.' (Lightfoot, *ib.* p. 29.)

c. iv. μέλη ὄντας τοῦ υἱοῦ αὐτοῦ.

c. viii. Μὴ οὖν τις ὑμᾶς ἐξαπατάτω, ὥσπερ οὐδὲ ἐξαπατᾶσθε, ὅλοι ὄντες θεοῦ...ὅταν γὰρ μηδεμία ἐπιθυμία ἐνήρεισται ἐν ὑμῖν ἡ δυναμένη ὑμᾶς βασανίσαι, ἄρα κατὰ θεὸν ζῆτε.

c. ix. ὡς ὄντες λίθοι ναοῦ· προητοιμασμένοι εἰς οἰκοδομὴν θεοῦ πατρός, ἀναφερόμενοι εἰς τὰ ὕψη διὰ τῆς μηχανῆς Ἰησοῦ Χριστοῦ, ὅς ἐστιν σταυρός, σχοινίῳ χρώμενοι τῷ πνεύματι τῷ ἁγίῳ· ἡ δὲ πίστις ὑμῶν ἀναγωγεὺς ὑμῶν, ἡ δὲ ἀγάπη ὁδὸς ἡ ἀναφέρουσα εἰς θεόν.
'The metaphor (λίθοι ναοῦ), and in part even its language, is suggested by Eph. ii. 20—22; cf. 1 Pet. ii. 5.' (Lightfoot, *ad loc.*)
'The metaphor [μηχανῆς...σχοινίῳ ...ἀναγωγεὺς...κ.τ.λ.] is extravagant but not otherwise ill-conceived. The framework, or crane, is the Cross of Christ, the connecting instrument, the rope, is the Holy Spirit; the

Ephesians.

τοῦ θελήματος αὐτοῦ...εἰς τὸ εἶναι ἡμᾶς εἰς ἔπαινον δόξης αὐτοῦ. (Cf. iii. 21. κατὰ πρόθεσιν τῶν αἰώνων.)

Eph. v. 1. γίνεσθε οὖν μιμηταὶ τοῦ θεοῦ.

? Eph. v. 30. ὅτι μέλη ἐσμὲν τοῦ σώματος αὐτοῦ.

Eph. iv. 22 ff. ἀποθέσθαι ὑμᾶς... τ. παλαιὸν ἄνθρωπον τ. φθειρόμενον κατὰ τὰς ἐπιθυμίας τῆς ἀπάτης, ἀνανεοῦσθαι δὲ τῷ πνεύματι τοῦ νοὸς ὑμῶν καὶ ἐνδύσασθαι τὸν καινὸν ἄνθρωπον τὸν κατὰ θεὸν κτισθέντα κ.τ.λ.... and *ib.* v. 6, μηδεὶς ὑμᾶς ἀπατάτω κ.τ.λ.

Eph. ii. 20 ff. ἐποικοδομηθέντες ἐπὶ τῷ θεμελίῳ τ. ἀποστόλων κ. προφητῶν, ὄντος ἀκρογωνιαίου αὐτοῦ Χρ. Ἰ., ἐν ᾧ πᾶσα οἰκοδομὴ συναρμολογουμένη αὔξει εἰς ναὸν ἅγιον ἐν κυρίῳ, ἐν ᾧ καὶ ὑμεῖς συνοικοδομεῖσθε εἰς κατοικητήριον τ. θεοῦ ἐν πνεύματι.
Cf. *ib.* v. 10. αὐτοῦ γάρ ἐσμεν ποίημα, κτισθέντες ἐν Χρ. Ἰ. ἐπὶ ἔργοις ἀγαθοῖς οἷς προητοίμασεν ὁ θεὸς ἵνα ἐν αὐτοῖς περιπατήσωμεν, and v. 16, κ. ἀποκαταλλάξῃ ἐν ἑνὶ σώματι τῷ θεῷ διὰ τοῦ σταυροῦ: also v. 18, ὅτι δι᾽ αὐτοῦ ἔχομεν τὴν προσαγωγὴν...ἐν ἑνὶ πνεύματι πρὸς τὸν πατέρα.
In iii. 12, ἐν ᾧ ἔχομεν τ. παρρησίαν

Ignatius, *ad Ephesios.*

Ephesians.

motive power, which acts and keeps the machinery in motion, is faith ; the path (conceived here apparently as an inclined plane) up which the spiritual stones are raised that they may be fitted into the building, is love' (*id. inf.* on ἀναγωγεύς 'a lifting-engine').

κ. προσαγωγὴν ἐν πεποιθήσει διὰ τῆς πίστεως αὐτοῦ, freedom of *access* (St Paul says) is ours *through our faith* in Christ :—in v. 2 περιπατεῖτε ἐν ἀγάπῃ [he bids the 'Ephesians'] *walk in love* ; and in vi. 23 εἰρήνη τ. ἀδελφοῖς κ. ἀγάπη μετὰ πίστεως *faith* is the condition of appropriating peace and *love*.

c. xii. Παύλου συμμύσται τοῦ ἡγιασμένου, τοῦ μεμαρτυρημένου, ἀξιομακαρίστου, οὗ γένοιτό μοι ὑπὸ τὰ ἴχνη εὑρεθῆναι, ὅταν θεοῦ ἐπιτύχω· ὃς ἐν πάσῃ ἐπιστολῇ μνημονεύει ὑμῶν ἐν Χριστῷ Ἰησοῦ.
'i.e. fellow-recipients, fellow-students, of the mysteries, with Paul' !

This was signally true of the Ephesians, among whom St Paul resided for an exceptionally long time (Acts xix. 10 sq., xx. 31), with whom he was on terms of the most affectionate intimacy,—and who were the chief, though probably not the sole, recipients of the most profound of all his epistles. The propriety of the language here is still further enhanced by the fact that St Paul, in the Epistle to the Ephesians more especially dwells on the Gospel dispensation as μυστήριον (i. 9, iii. 3, 4, 9, v. 32, vi. 19). Elsewhere (Phil. iv. 12) he speaks of himself as μεμυημένος (Lightfoot, *ad loc.*).

c. xvii. ἵνα πνέῃ τῇ ἐκκλησίᾳ ἀφθαρσίαν.

Eph. vi. 24. ἐν ἀφθαρσίᾳ. But ἀφθαρσία occurs also in Rom. ii. 7 ; 1 Cor. xv. 42, 50, 53, 54 ; 2 Tim. i. 10, Tit. ii. 7.

c. xviii. ὁ γὰρ θεὸς ἡμῶν Ἰ. ὁ χρ. ἐκυοφορήθη ὑπὸ Μαρίας κατ' οἰκονομίαν ἐκ σπέρματος μὲν Δαυεὶδ, πνεύματος δὲ ἁγίου.

'The word οἰκονομία came to be applied more especially to the Incarnation (as here and below, § 20, ἧς ἠρξάμην οἰκονομίας κ.τ.λ.) because this was *par excellence* the system or plan which God had ordained for the government of His household and the dispensation of His stores.' (Lightfoot, *ad loc.*)

Eph. i. 10. εἰς οἰκονομίαν τοῦ πληρώματος τῶν καιρῶν, ἀνακεφαλαιώσασθαι τὰ πάντα ἐν τῷ χρίστῳ [v. note *ad loc.*].

'The first step towards this special appropriation of οἰκονομία to the Incarnation is found in St Paul: e.g. Eph. i. 10 εἰς οἰκονομίαν κ.τ.λ.' (Lightfoot, *Apostolic Fathers*, II. ii. p. 75.)

Ignatius, *ad Ephesios.*

c. xix. καὶ ἔλαθεν τὸν ἄρχοντα τοῦ αἰῶνος τούτου ἡ παρθενία Μαρίας καὶ ὁ τοκετὸς αὐτῆς, ὁμοίως καὶ ὁ θάνατος τοῦ κυρίου· τρία μυστήρια κραυγῆς, ἅτινα ἐν ἡσυχίᾳ θεοῦ ἐπράχθη. πῶς οὖν ἐφανερώθη τοῖς αἰῶσιν; 'Here κραυγή is the correlative to ἡσυχία, as revelation is to mystery. "These mysteries" Ignatius would say "were preordained and prepared in silence by God, that they might be proclaimed aloud to a startled world." It is an exaggerated expression of the truth stated in Rom. xvi. 25 τὸ κήρυγμα Ἰησοῦ Χριστοῦ κατὰ ἀποκάλυψιν μυστηρίου χρόνοις αἰωνίοις σεσιγημένου, φανερωθέντος δὲ νῦν.... τοῖς αἰῶσιν—'to the ages,' past and future, which are here personified. It seems probable that in St Paul's expression, μυστήριον ἀποκεκρυμμένον ἀπὸ τῶν αἰώνων (Eph. iii. 9, Col. i. 26), the preposition should be taken as temporal (see the note on the latter passage); but Ignatius may have understood it otherwise.' (Lightfoot.)

Ephesians.

Eph. iii. 9. τοῦ μυστηρίου τοῦ ἀποκεκρυμμένου ἀπὸ τῶν αἰώνων ἐν τῷ θεῷ...ἵνα γνωρισθῇ νῦν ταῖς ἀρχαῖς κ. ταῖς ἐξουσίαις ἐν τοῖς ἐπουρανίοις.

Col. i. 26. τὸ μυστήριον τὸ ἀποκεκρυμμένον ἀπὸ τῶν αἰώνων καὶ ἀπὸ τῶν γενεῶν, νῦν δὲ ἐφανερώθη τοῖς ἁγίοις αὐτοῦ.

c. xx. εἰς τὸν καινὸν ἄνθρωπον Ἰησοῦν Χριστόν, ἐν τῇ αὐτοῦ πίστει καὶ ἐν τῇ αὐτοῦ ἀγάπῃ. 'The καινὸς ἄνθρωπος of Ignatius is equivalent to the ἔσχατος Ἀδάμ, the δεύτερος ἄνθρωπος of St Paul (1 Cor. xvi. 45, 47). The Apostle himself seems to use ὁ καινὸς ἄνθρωπος in a different sense, Eph. iv. 24.' (But see note there.)

Eph. iv. 24. κ. ἐνδύσασθαι τὸν καινὸν ἄνθρωπον τὸν κατὰ θεὸν κτισθέντα ἐν δικαιοσύνῃ κ. ὁσιότητι τ. ἀληθείας [v. note *ad loc.*].

Ignat. *ad Polycarpum*, § 5, ἀγαπᾶν τὰς συμβίους, ὡς ὁ κύριος τὴν ἐκκλησίαν 'a reminiscence of Eph. v. 29.' (Lightfoot.)

Eph. v. 29. καθὼς καὶ ὁ χριστὸς τὴν ἐκκλησίαν. [Cf. *v.* 25. ἀγαπᾶτε τὰς γυναῖκας, καθὼς καὶ ὁ χριστὸς ἠγάπησεν τὴν ἐκκλησίαν.]

Polycarp.

c. i. εἰδότες ὅτι χάριτί ἐστε σεσωσμένοι, οὐκ ἐξ ἔργων, ἀλλὰ θελήματι θεοῦ διὰ Ἰησοῦ Χριστοῦ.

c. xii. modo, ut his scripturis dictum est, *irascimini et nolite peccare* et *sol non occidat super iracundiam vestram.*

Ephesians.

ii. 8. τῇ γὰρ χάριτί ἐστε σεσωσμένοι διὰ πίστεως· καὶ τοῦτο οὐκ ἐξ ὑμῶν, θεοῦ τὸ δῶρον· οὐκ ἐξ ἔργων, ἵνα μή τις καυχήσηται.

iv. 26. ὀργίζεσθε κ. μὴ ἁμαρτάνετε (Ps. iv. 5)· ὁ ἥλιος μὴ ἐπιδυέτω ἐπὶ παροργισμῷ ὑμῶν.

('The Two Ways.')
Διδαχὴ τ. ἀποστόλων.

iv. 10, 11. οὐκ ἐπιτάξεις δούλῳ σου ἢ παιδίσκῃ, τοῖς ἐπὶ τ. αὐτὸν θεὸν ἐλπίζουσιν, ἐν πικρίᾳ σου... ὑμεῖς δὲ οἱ δοῦλοι ὑποταγήσεσθε τοῖς κυρίοις ὑμῶν ὡς τύπῳ θεοῦ ἐν αἰσχύνῃ καὶ φόβῳ.

Barnabas.

xix. c. 7. ὑποταγήσῃ κυρίοις ὡς τύπῳ θεοῦ ἐν αἰσχύνῃ καὶ φόβῳ. οὐ μὴ ἐπιτάξῃς δούλῳ σου ἢ παιδίσκῃ ἐν πικρίᾳ, τοῖς ἐπὶ τὸν αὐτὸν θεὸν ἐλπίζουσιν.

Ephesians.

vi. 5, 9. Οἱ δοῦλοι, ὑπακούετε τοῖς κατὰ σάρκα κυρίοις μετὰ φόβου καὶ τρόμου ἐν ἁπλότητι τ. καρδίας ὑμῶν ὡς τῷ χριστῷ...ὡς τῷ κυρίῳ καὶ οὐκ ἀνθρώποις....Καὶ οἱ κύριοι τὰ αὐτὰ ποιεῖτε πρὸς αὐτούς, ἀνιέντες τὴν ἀπειλήν, εἰδότες ὅτι καὶ αὐτῶν καὶ ὑμῶν ὁ κύριός ἐστιν ἐν οὐρανοῖς.

Hermae *Pastor.*

Mand. iii. § 1. Ἀλήθειαν ἀγάπα, καὶ πᾶσα ἀλήθεια ἐκ τοῦ στόματός σου ἐκπορευέσθω...ὅτι ὁ κύριος ἀληθινὸς ἐν παντὶ ῥήματι καὶ οὐδὲν παρ' αὐτῷ ψεῦδος....

ib. § 4. ἔδει γάρ σε ὡς θεοῦ δοῦλον ἐν ἀλ. πορεύεσθαι...μηδὲ λύπην ἐπάγειν τῷ πνεύματι τῷ σεμνῷ καὶ ἀληθεῖ.

(Cf. x. § 2. ἡ λύπη...ἐκτρίβει το πνεῦμα τὸ ἅγιον.)

Sim. ix. c. 13. οὕτω καὶ οἱ πιστεύσαντες τῷ κυρίῳ διὰ τοῦ υἱοῦ αὐτοῦ... ἔσονται εἰς ἓν πνεῦμα, εἰς ἓν σῶμα, καὶ μία χρόα τ. ἱματισμῶν αὐτῶν....

ib. c. 17. λαβόντες οὖν τὴν σφραγῖδα μίαν φρόνησιν ἔσχον καὶ ἕνα νοῦν, καὶ μία πίστις αὐτῶν ἐγένετο καὶ μία ἀγάπη.

(Cf. *inf.* ἓν πνεῦμα κ. ἓν σῶμα κ. ἓν ἔνδυμα.)

Ephesians.

iv. 25. Διὸ ἀποθέμενοι τὸ ψεῦδος λαλεῖτε ἀλήθειαν ἕκαστος μετὰ τοῦ πλησίον αὐτοῦ....

ib. 29. πᾶς λόγος σαπρὸς ἐκ τοῦ στόματος ὑμῶν μὴ ἐκπορευέσθω.

ib. 30. κ. μὴ λυπεῖτε τὸ πνεῦμα τὸ ἅγιον τοῦ θεοῦ (whereas in Is. lxiii. 10 it is παρώξυναν τὸ πνεῦμα τὸ ἅγιον αὐτοῦ).

ib. 3—6. ἀνεχόμενοι ἀλλήλων ἐν ἀγάπῃ, σπουδάζοντες τηρεῖν τ. ἑνότητα τοῦ πνεύματος ἐν τῷ συνδέσμῳ τῆς εἰρήνης· ἓν σῶμα καὶ ἓν πνεῦμα...εἷς κύριος, μία πίστις, ἓν βάπτισμα.

Epist. ad Diognetum.

c. ii. Ἄγε δὴ καθάρας σεαυτὸν ἀπὸ
πάντων τῶν προκατεχόντων σου
τὴν διάνοιαν λογισμῶν καὶ τὴν ἀπα-
τῶσάν σε συνήθειαν ἀποσκευασά-
μενος, καὶ γενόμενος ὥσπερ ἐξ ἀρχῆς
καινὸς ἄνθρωπος, ὡς ἂν καὶ λόγου
καινοῦ...ἀκροατὴς ἐσόμενος, ἴδε κ.τ.λ.

Ephesians.

iv. 21 f. ὑμεῖς δὲ οὐχ οὕτως ἐμάθετε τ. χριστόν, εἴ γε ἠκούσατε, κ.
ἐδιδάχθητε...ἀποθέσθαι ὑμᾶς κατὰ
τὴν προτέραν ἀναστροφὴν τὸν παλαιὸν ἄνθρωπον τὸν φθειρόμενον κατὰ
τὰς ἐπιθυμίας τῆς ἀπάτης, ἀνανεοῦσθαι δὲ τῷ πνεύματι τοῦ νοὸς ὑμῶν
καὶ ἐνδύσασθαι τὸν καινὸν ἄνθρωπον
τ. κατὰ θεὸν κτισθέντα ἐν δικαιοσύνῃ κ.
ὁσιότητι τῆς ἀληθείας.

Theophilus Antiochenus, *ad
Autolycum.*

ii. p. 102. ἅμα δὲ καὶ ἐπὶ πλείονα
χρόνον, ἠβούλετο ἁπλοῦν καὶ ἀκέραιον
διαμεῖναι τὸν ἄνθρωπον νηπιάζοντα·
τοῦτο γὰρ ὅσιόν ἐστι, οὐ μόνον παρὰ
θεῷ, ἀλλὰ καὶ παρὰ ἀνθρώποις, τὸ ἐν
ἁπλότητι καὶ ἀκακίᾳ ὑποτάσσεσθαι
τοῖς γονεῦσιν· ἔτι δὲ χρὴ τὰ τέκνα
τοῖς γονεῦσιν ὑποτάσσεσθαι, εἰ
δὲ χρὴ τ. τέκνα τ. γονεῦσιν ὑποτάσσεσθαι, πόσῳ μᾶλλον τῷ θεῷ καὶ
πατρὶ τῶν ὅλων.

Ephesians.

v. 20. εὐχαριστοῦντες πάντοτε...
τῷ θεῷ κ. πατρὶ (cf. iv. 6 θ. κ. π.
πάντων), ὑποτασσόμενοι ἀλλήλοις
ἐν φόβῳ Χριστοῦ.

vi. 1. τὰ τέκνα, ὑπακούετε τοῖς
γονεῦσιν ὑμῶν ἐν κυρίῳ· τοῦτο γάρ
ἐστιν δίκαιον.

ib. 5. οἱ δοῦλοι, ὑπακούετε τοῖς κατὰ
σάρκα κυρίοις μετὰ φόβου κ. τρόμου ἐν
ἁπλότητι τῆς καρδίας ὑμῶν ὡς τ.
χριστῷ.

Ophitae, ap. Hippol. *adv.
Haeres.* v. 7 f.

p. 97 (ed. Miller), p. 136 (ed.
Duncker). ἵν᾽ οὖν τελέως ᾖ κεκρατη-
μένος ὁ μέγας ἄνθρωπος ἄνωθεν, ἀφ᾽
οὗ, καθὼς λέγουσι, πᾶσα πατρία
ὀνομαζομένη ἐπὶ γῆς καὶ ἐν τοῖς
οὐρανοῖς συνέστηκεν, ἐδόθη αὐτῷ καὶ
ψυχή κ.τ.λ.

Ephesians.

iii. 15. ἐξ οὗ πᾶσα πατρία ἐν
οὐρανοῖς καὶ ἐπὶ γῆς ὀνομάζεται
followed by (*v.* 16)
ἵνα δῷ ὑμῖν κατὰ τὸ πλοῦτος τ.
δόξης αὐτοῦ δυνάμει κραταιωθῆναι διὰ
τ. πνεύματος εἰς τὸν ἔσω ἄνθρωπον.

p. 104 (M.), p. 146 (D.). περὶ τούτων,
φησίν, ἡ γραφὴ λέγει· Ἔγειραι ὁ
καθεύδων καὶ ἐξεγέρθητι, καὶ ἐπιφαύσει σοι ὁ χριστός.

v. 14. διὸ λέγει
Ἔγειρε, ὁ καθεύδων
καὶ ἀνάστα ἐκ τῶν νεκρῶν,
καὶ ἐπιφαύσει σοι ὁ χριστός.

p. 107 (M.), p. 156 (D.). παῦε, παῦε
τὴν ἀσυμφωνίαν τοῦ κόσμου καὶ ποίησον εἰρήνην τοῖς μακράν, τούτεστι
τοῖς ὑλικοῖς καὶ χοϊκοῖς, καὶ εἰρήνην
τοῖς ἐγγύς, τούτεστι τοῖς πνευματι-
κοῖς κ. νοεροῖς, τελείοις ἀνθρώποις.

ii. 17. καὶ ἐλθὼν εὐηγγελίσατο
εἰρήνην ὑμῖν τοῖς μακρὰν καὶ εἰρήνην τοῖς ἐγγύς.

Basilides, ap. Hippol. *adv.*
Haeres. vii. 25.

p. 239 (M.), p. 370 (D.). ἦλθε τὸ
εὐαγγέλιον εἰς τὸν κόσμον, καὶ διῆλθε
διὰ πάσης ἀρχῆς καὶ ἐξουσίας
καὶ κυριότητος καὶ παντὸς ὀνόματος ὀνομαζομένου.

p. 241 (M.), p. 374 (D.). ἀποκαλυφθῆναι τὸ μυστήριον, ὃ ταῖς
προτέραις γενεαῖς οὐκ ἐγνωρίσθη,
καθὼς γέγραπται, φησί· Κατὰ ἀποκάλυψιν ἐγνωρίσθη μοι τὸ μυστήριον.

Valentinus (? seu Valentiniani),
ap. Hippol. vi. 3.

p. 193 (M.), p. 284 (D.). Τοῦτο
ἐστί, φησί, τὸ γεγραμμένον ἐν τῇ
γραφῇ. Τούτου χάριν κάμπτω τὰ
γόνατά μου πρὸς τὸν θεὸν καὶ πατέρα καὶ κύριον τοῦ κυρίου ἡμῶν Ἰ.
Χρ., ἵνα δῴη ὑμῖν ὁ θεὸς κατοικῆσαι τὸν χριστὸν εἰς τὸν ἔσω ἄνθρωπον, τουτέστι τὸν ψυχικόν, οὐ τὸν
σωματικόν, ἵνα ἐξισχύσητε νοῆσαι
τί τὸ βάθος, ὅπερ ἐστὶν ὁ πατὴρ τῶν
ὅλων, καὶ τί τὸ πλάτος, ὅπερ ἐστὶν
ὁ σταυρος, ὁ ὅρος τοῦ πληρώματος, ἢ
τί τὸ μῆκος, τουτέστι τὸ πλήρωμα
τῶν αἰώνων.

Ptolemaeus[1], ap. Irenaeum.

i. 8. 5 (ed. Massuet). Τοῦτο δὲ καὶ
ὁ Παῦλος λέγει· Πᾶν γὰρ τὰ φανερούμενον φῶς ἐστιν. Ἐπεὶ τοίνυν
ἐφανέρωσε κ. ἐγέννησε τὸν τε ᾽Ανθρω-
πον καὶ τὴν Ἐκκλησίαν ἡ Ζωὴ, φῶς
εἰρῆσθαι αὐτῶν.

ib. 8. 4. Καὶ τὰς συζυγίας δὲ τὰς
ἐντὸς πληρώματος τὸν Παῦλον εἰρη-
κέναι φάσκουσιν ἐπὶ ἑνὸς δείξαντα.
περὶ γὰρ τῆς περὶ τὸν βίον συζυγίας
γράφων ἔφη· Τὸ μυστήριον τοῦτο
μέγα ἐστίν, ἐγὼ δὲ λέγω εἰς
Χριστὸν καὶ τὴν Ἐκκλησίαν.

Ephesians.

i. 21. ὑπεράνω πάσης ἀρχῆς καὶ
ἐξουσίας καὶ δυνάμεως καὶ κυριότητος καὶ παντὸς ὀνόματος ὀνομαζομένου οὐ μόνον ἐν τῷ αἰῶνι
τούτῳ ἀλλὰ καὶ ἐν τῷ μέλλοντι.

iii. 3 f. κατὰ ἀποκάλυψιν ἐγνωρίσθη
μοι τὸ μυστήριον...ὃ ἑτέραις γενεαῖς οὐκ ἐγνωρίσθη τοῖς υἱοῖς τ.
ἀνθρώπων.

Ephesians.

iii. 14 ff. Τούτου χάριν κάμπτω
τὰ γόνατά μου πρὸς τὸν πατέρα,
ἐξ οὗ κ.τ.λ....ἵνα δῷ ὑμῖν...κραταιω-
θῆναι...εἰς τὸν ἔσω ἄνθρωπον κατοικῆσαι τὸν χριστὸν διὰ τῆς πίστεως
ἐν τ. καρδίαις ὑμῶν...ἵνα ἐξισχύσητε καταλαβέσθαι...τί τὸ πλάτος
καὶ μῆκος καὶ ὕψος καὶ βάθος κ.τ.λ.

Ephesians.

v. 13. πᾶν γὰρ τὸ φανερούμενον
φῶς ἐστιν. διὸ κ.τ.λ.

v. 32. τὸ μυστήριον τοῦτο μέγα
ἐστίν, ἐγὼ δὲ λέγω εἰς Χριστὸν καὶ
[εἰς] τὴν ἐκκλησίαν.

[1] 'Ptolemaeus was a disciple of Valentinus...and it appears that he reduced the Valentinian system to order and presented it under its most attractive aspect' (Westcott, *Canon of the N. T.* p. 313).

Theodotus¹, ad calc. Clem. Alex.

§ 7. φησὶ γὰρ ὁ ἀπόστολος "ὁ γὰρ ἀναβὰς αὐτός ἐστι καὶ ὁ καταβάς" (cf. § 43).

§ 19. καὶ ὁ Παῦλος "ἔνδυσαι τὸν καινὸν ἄνθρωπον τὸν κατὰ θεὸν κτισθέντα."

§ 48. διὸ καὶ λέγει ὁ ἀπόστολος "καὶ μὴ λυπεῖτε τὸ πνεῦμα τὸ ἅγιον τοῦ θεοῦ, ἐν ᾧ ἐσφραγίσθητε."

ib. πνεύματα τῆς πονηρίας, πρὸς ἃ ἡ πάλη ἡμῖν.

Ephesians.

iv. 10. ὁ καταβὰς αὐτός ἐστιν καὶ ὁ ἀναβὰς ὑπεράνω πάντων τ. οὐρανῶν.

iv. 24. καὶ ἐνδύσασθαι τὸν καινὸν ἄνθρωπον τὸν κατὰ θεὸν κτισθέντα.

iv. 30. καὶ μὴ λυπεῖτε τὸ πνεῦμα τὸ ἅγιον τοῦ θεοῦ, ἐν ᾧ ἐσφραγίσθητε κ.τ.λ.

vi. 12. ὅτι οὐκ ἔστιν ἡμῖν ἡ πάλη πρὸς...ἀλλὰ...πρὸς τὰ πνευματικὰ τῆς πονηρίας....

Irenaeus, adv. Haer. i. 8, 5.

Τοῦτο δὲ καὶ ὁ Παῦλος λέγει· πᾶν γὰρ τὸ φανερούμενον φῶς ἐστίν.

id. ib. v. 2, 3. Καθὼς ὁ μακάριος Παῦλός φησιν ἐν τῇ πρὸς Ἐφεσίους ἐπιστολῇ· ὅτι μέλη ἐσμὲν τοῦ σώματος.

Clemens Alexandrinus, Paedag. i. 18.

σαφέστατα δὲ Ἐφεσίοις γράφων (ὁ ἀπόστολος) ἀπεκάλυψε τὸ ζητούμενον λέγων· μέχρι καταντήσωμεν ἅπαντες εἰς τὴν ἑνότητα τῆς πίστεως.

id. Strom. iv. 65. διὸ καὶ ἐν τῇ πρὸς Ἐφεσίους γράφει· ὑποτασσόμενοι ἀλλήλοις ἐν φόβῳ θεοῦ.

Tertullian, adv. Marc. v. 11 (v. supra, p. xxiii):

Praetereo hic et de alia epistola, quam nos ad Ephesios praescriptam habemus.

---

¹ 'At the end of the works of Clement of Alexandria is usually published a series of fragments entitled Short Notes from the Writings of Theodotus and the so-called Eastern School at the time of Valentinus (ἐκ τῶν Θεοδότου καὶ τῆς ἀνατολικῆς διδασκαλίας κατὰ τοὺς Οὐαλεντίνου χρόνους ἐπιτομαί)....The books of the New Testament to which they contain allusions...are these: the Four Gospels; the Epistles of St Paul to the Romans, 1 Corinthians, Ephesians, Galatians, Philippians, Colossians, 1 Timothy; the First Epistle of St Peter' (Canon, p. 317 n.).

V.   INTERNAL EVIDENCE OF AUTHORSHIP.

Theories, which find in the Epistle indications of (a) Montanist or (β) pseudo-Gnostic influence, being discarded, 'a view' of the Epistle 'which has...to be considered' is that maintained by Holtzmann, Pfleiderer, and Von Soden, who 'ascribe it to an advanced disciple of St Paul.' Also 'it is...alleged that there are marks of simply different authorship, differences of language, style, and the like.' (Hort, *Prolegomena*, pp. 120 f.)

A. *Doctrine.*

'Is the Paulinism later than St Paul?' 'No one who carefully reads the Epistle to the Ephesians can doubt that its doctrinal contents do differ considerably from those of any one of St Paul's earlier Epistles or of all of them taken together....What we have to ask is whether the differences are incompatible with identity of authorship.' (*Prolegomena*, p. 123.)

'Some of the chief combinations of identity and difference between St Paul's earlier recorded theology and that of the Epistle to the Ephesians.' (*ib.* p. 125.)

(i)   Relation of Jews to Gentiles as Christians.

(a)   In *Ephesians* 'the duty of Jewish and Gentile fellowship is deduced from the eternal purpose of God and the very idea of the Christian faith, not, as in earlier Epistles, from arguments about the Law and the Promise. Yet this is only the teaching of the Epistle to the Romans a little more unfolded.' (*ib.* p. 126.)

(b)   'In both Epistles alike' (*Romans* and *Ephesians*) 'the need for the universal salvation is made to rest on the universality of the previous corruption.' Eph. ii. 1—3 answers to Rom. i. 18—32, ii. 17—29, iii. 9.

(c)   As to 'Circumcision,' with Eph. ii. 11 compare Rom. ii. 28 f.

(ii)   The Church.

In *Ephesians* 'we for the first time hear Christians throughout the world described as together making up a single Ecclesia, i.e. assembly of God, or Church; and here for the first time we find the relation of Christ to *the* or *a* Church conceived as that of a Head to a Body.' (*Prolegomena*, p. 128.)

But these thoughts stand in closest connexion with what preceded.

(a)   An 'impulse towards laying stress on the unity of the society of Christians throughout the world doubtless came from the position of St Paul as writing from Rome.'

'Nor...would it be strange that he should use the name Ecclesia in this new and extended sense, although hitherto...applied only to the Christian community of Jerusalem or Judaea or to individual local Christian communities outside the Holy Land.' (*ib.* p. 129.)

(β)   Though the language of Eph. i. 22, iv. 15 f. (and Col. i. 18), compared with that of 1 Cor. xii. 12 and Rom. xii. 4 f. 'is new,' the new image is Pauline (cf. 1 Cor. xi. 3); also the image of the Corner-stone (cf. Mt. xxi. 42, Mk. xii. 10 f., Lk. xx. 17, Acts iv. 11) cannot have been 'either unknown to St Paul...or rejected by him.' (*ib.* p. 134.)

(iii)   Person and Office of Christ.

(a)   'Earlier Epistles imply His Pre-existence' (cf. 2 Cor. viii. 9, Gal. iv. 4, Rom. viii. 3).

'Colossians (i. 16 f.) carries back His Lordship to the beginning of things.'

'Ephesians (i. 10) makes the reconciliation—effected by His death—include all things, and carries back His Headship of the Ecclesia to a primordial choosing of its members "in him" (iii. 14).' But of this there is anticipation in 1 Cor. viii. 6, xv. 45 f.

(β)   'In Eph. ii. 16 it is Christ'—whereas in 2 Cor. v. 28 f. it is God "through Christ"—'who appears as the Reconciler.'—'But the two forms of language are consistent.'

(γ)   So also variation of language of Eph. iv. 11 from 1 Cor. xii. 28, as to the source of gifts, is due to context.   (*ib.* pp. 134 ff., 190.)

(iv)   The Holy Spirit.

'The contrast with the Epistle to the Colossians is great in this respect; but there is no similar contrast with the earlier Epistles' (e.g. Rom., 1 Cor.).

'In the First Epistle to the Corinthians and in that to the Ephesians alike St Paul is anxiously insisting on the mutual duties of members of the Christian community and therefore has need to go back to the inner principle of its life, the one uniting Spirit' (*id. ib.* pp. 140 f.).

(v)   The Present and the Future.

In *Ephesians* 'the immediate imminence of the Coming of the Lord has faded out of view': and 'a sense of present blessedness has arisen' (i. 3 ff., iv. 11—16) and of 'a long and gradual growth reaching far out into the future from age to age.'

But 'in the earlier Epistles themselves there is a certain gradation in this respect:—Romans suggests the ordering of the ages': and it was 'natural...that a change like this should come over St Paul's mind' in view of 'the spread of the faith through the Roman Empire.'

(vi)   'Apostles and Prophets.'

'The two names represent the two types of guidance specially given to that earliest age' (*Prolegomena*, p. 145).

Eph. iii. 5.   ἀπεκαλύφθη τ. ἁγίοις ἀποστόλοις αὐτοῦ καὶ προφήταις ἐν πνεύματι, εἶναι τὰ ἔθνη συνκληρονόμα κ.τ.λ. 'does but sum up in a pregnant form what had been the real course of things' (cf. e.g. Acts xiii. 1—4).

Eph. ii. 20.   ἐποικοδομηθέντες ἐπὶ τῷ θεμελίῳ τῶν ἀποστόλων καὶ προφητῶν gives 'the historical order of the actual structure and growth of the Ecclesia itself, not any authority over the Ecclesia.' 'And St Paul himself could fitly...speak thus; and use the special image of the *foundation*.' 'Nor would he by so using it...contradict...1 Cor. iii. 10 f.   For there he is not speaking of the Christian society, but of the Christian faith' (*ib.* p. 147).

Again 'Apostles and prophets stand first in list of gifts' in 1 Cor. xii. 28 as in Eph. iv. 11.

(vii) St Paul himself.

Language of Eph. iii. 1 f., iv. 1, vi. 20 paralleled by Rom. xi. 13, xv. 16. With Eph. iii. 8 cf. (besides 1 Cor. xv. 9) Gal. i. 13—16.

B. Style, Vocabulary, and Phraseology.

(*a*) Causes of difference of *style*—as compared with earlier Epistles.

(1) 'Sense of dangers surmounted, aspirations satisfied, and a vantage ground gained for the world-wide harmonious development of the Christian community under the government of God'

(2) 'that now for the first time St Paul is free, as it were, to pour forth his own thoughts in a positive form instead of carrying on an argument' (*ib*. p. 153).

(*b*) 'The bulk of the *vocabulary* is in accordance with Pauline usage' (*ib*. p. 158).

'Unique words are due to quotation, context, brevity, or accident' (*ib*. p. 156).

(*c*) 'Unique *phrases* prove little, being common elsewhere in St Paul' (*ib*. p. 192).

'Those who cannot read the Epistle to the Ephesians without being awed by the peculiar loftiness, by the grandeur of conception, by the profound insight, by the eucharistic inspiration, which they recognise in it, will require strong evidence to persuade them that it was written by some other man who wished it to pass as St Paul's. Apart from the question of the morality of the act, imitators do not pour out their thoughts in the free and fervid style of this Epistle. Nor can we easily imagine how such an imitation could have been successful either near the time of St Paul or at any subsequent period. It is not conceivable that it should have made its appearance without exciting wonder and inquiry. In the lifetime of St Paul the pious fraud would not have been attempted. Within a few years after his death the difficulty of deceiving his friends and the Church in such a matter must have been very great. At a later time the estimation in which St Paul's writings were held would have ensured the careful scrutiny of any previously unknown work put forward in his name.' (Llewelyn Davies : *Introduction to Ephesians*, p. 9.)

VI. STYLE AND LANGUAGE.

Words characteristic of the Ephesian Epistle:

μυστήριον [v. inf. p. 180].
δόξα [v. inf. p. 187].
ἐνέργεια [v. inf. p. 155].
προσαγωγή [see note on ii. 18].
πληροῦν [see notes on i. 23, v. 18].
πλήρωμα [see notes on i. 10, 23].
μεθοδεία [see note on vi. 11].

Also the expressions:

ἐν πνεύματι.
τὰ ἐπουράνια [v. inf. p. 152].

Among words, which do not occur in this Epistle, are, it is to be remarked, the following:

θάνατος,
χάρα, ⎰
χαίρειν. ⎱

[All these words occur in the Epistle to the Colossians and frequently in that to the Philippians.]

The various grammatical modes of expressing end or purpose, used in the Epistle, may be noted.

(1) The Simple Infinitive:

    i. 4.   εἶναι ἡμᾶς ἁγίους κ.τ.λ. after ἐξελέξατο ἡμᾶς (cf. iii. 6).
    iii. 17. κατοικῆσαι τ. χριστὸν...ἐν τ. καρδίαις ὑμῶν.
    vi. 19. γνωρίσαι.

(2) εἰς τὸ c. inf.

    i. 12.   εἰς τὸ εἶναι ἡμᾶς... after προορισθέντες.
    18.   εἰς τὸ εἰδέναι ἡμᾶς... after πεφωτισμένους.

    πρὸς τὸ c. inf.

    vi. 11. ἐνδύσασθε...πρὸς τὸ δύνασθαι ὑμᾶς.

(3) ἵνα.

    i. 17. ἵνα δῴη... after μνείαν ποιούμενος.
    ii. 7, 10, 15.
    iii. 9 f., 14 ff., 18.
    iv. 14, 28 (bis).
    v. 25 ff., 33.
    vi. 3, 13, 19, 20, 21, 22.

Repetition of phrases—in one context—is found at:

i. 6, 12, 14. εἰς ἔπαινον δόξης (bis)...εἰς ἔ. τῆς δόξης....

ii. 1, 5. καὶ ὑμᾶς ὄντας νεκρούς...καὶ ὄντας ἡμᾶς νεκρούς....

iii. 2, 7. τῆς χάριτος τοῦ θεοῦ τῆς δοθείσης μοι (bis).

Interrupted constructions occur:

 ii. 3, 11 f.
 iii. 1.

Aorist and Present tenses [in near conjunction or sequence] are found:

 i. 13. πιστεύσαντες, 19 πιστεύοντας.
 ii. 20. ἐποικοδομηθέντες, 22 συνοικοδομεῖσθε.
 iv. 1. περιπατῆσαι, 17 περιπατεῖν.
 v. 29. ἐμίσησεν, ἐκτρέφει κ. θάλπει.
 vi. 10. ἐνδυναμοῦσθε, 11 ἐνδύσασθε.

Perfect Participles are frequent:

 i. 12. προηλπικότας, 18 πεφωτισμένους.
 ii. 5, 8. σεσωσμένοι, 12 ἀπηλλοτριωμένοι.
 iii. 9. ἀποκεκρυμμένου, 17 ἐρριζωμένοι κ. τεθεμελιωμένοι.
 iv. 17. ἐσκοτωμένοι, 18 ἀπηλλοτριωμένοι, 19 ἀπηλγηκότες.
 vi. 16. πεπυρωμένα.

Parallel Clauses occur:

 i. 11, 13. ἐν ᾧ καὶ ἐκληρώθημεν...,
    ἐν ᾧ καὶ ὑμεῖς ἀκούσαντες...ἐν ᾧ καὶ πιστεύσαντες, ἐσφρα-
    γίσθητε.

 ii. 2. κατὰ τὸν αἰῶνα τοῦ κόσμου τούτου,
    κατὰ τὸν ἄρχοντα τῆς ἐξουσίας τοῦ ἀέρος.

 21 f. ἐν ᾧ πᾶσα οἰκοδομὴ...αὔξει...ἐν κυρίῳ,
    ἐν ᾧ καὶ ὑμεῖς συνοικοδομεῖσθε...ἐν πνεύματι.

 iii. 7. κατὰ τ. δωρεὰν τ. χάριτος τ. θεοῦ,
    κατὰ τ. ἐνέργειαν τ. δυνάμεως αὐτοῦ.

 iv. 13. εἰς τ. ἑνότητα τ. πίστεως κ. τ. ἐπιγνώσεως,
    εἰς ἄνδρα τέλειον,
    εἰς μέτρον ἡλικίας.

 18. διὰ τὴν ἄγνοιαν ἐν αὐτοῖς,
    διὰ τὴν πώρωσιν τ. καρδίας αὐτῶν.

[The foregoing notes on Style and Language are those actually left by Dr Westcott. The following statistics have been editorially compiled.]

Words found nowhere in the New Testament except in the Epistle to the Ephesians.

 (a) *Nouns.*   ἑνότης.

αἰσχρότης.   ἑτοιμασία.

ἄνοιξις.   εὔνοια.

βέλος.   εὐτραπελία.

θυρεός.
καταρτισμός.
κοσμοκράτωρ.
κυβεία.
μέγεθος.
μεθοδεία.
μεσότοιχον.
μωρολογία.
πάλη.
παροργισμός.
προσκαρτέρησις.
ῥυτίς.
συμπολίτης.

(b)   Adjectives.

ἄθεος.
ἄσοφος.
ἐλαχιστότερος.
κατώτερος.
μακροχρόνιος.

πολυποίκιλος.
συμμέτοχος.
σύσσωμος.

(c)   Verbs.

αἰχμαλωτεύειν.
ἀνανεοῦν.
ἀπαλγεῖν.
ἐκτρέφειν.
ἐξισχύειν.
ἐπιδύειν.
ἐπιφαύσκειν.
κληροῦν.
κλυδωνίζεσθαι.
προελπίζειν.
συναρμολογεῖν.
συνοικοδομεῖν.

(d)   Adverb.

κρυφῇ.

Words common to 'Ephesians' and 'Colossians,' but not used elsewhere in the New Testament.

(a)   Nouns.

αὔξησις.
ἀφή.
ὀφθαλμοδουλεία.
ὕμνος.

(b)   Adjective.

ἀνθρωπάρεσκος.

(c)   Verbs.

ἀπαλλοτριοῦσθαι.
ἀποκαταλλάσσειν.
αὔξειν.
ῥιζοῦν.
συζωοποιεῖν.
συμβιβάζειν.
συνεγείρειν.

Common and peculiar to 'Ephesians,' 'Colossians' and 'Philemon' is ἀνῆκεν (v. τὸ ἀνῆκον).

*Words peculiar to the Pauline Epistles, occurring in 'Ephesians'
and also in some Epistle other than 'Colossians.'*

(i)   Common to 'Ephesians' and 'Philippians.'

ἐπιχορηγία (but ἐπιχορηγεῖν 2 Cor., Gal., Col., 2 Pet.).

κάμπτειν (also twice in O. T. quotations in Rom.).

(ii)   Common to 'Ephesians' and one or more of the six earlier
Epistles (1 and 2 Thess., 1 and 2 Cor., Gal., Rom.).

ἀγαθωσύνη (2 Th., Gal., Rom.,	ποίημα (Rom., Eph.).
ἀληθεύειν (Gal., Eph.). [Eph.).	πρεσβεύειν (2 Cor., Eph.).
ἀνακεφαλαιοῦσθαι (Rom., Eph.).	προετοιμάζειν (Rom., Eph.).
ἀνεξιχνίαστος (Rom., Eph.).	προσαγωγή (Rom., Eph.).
ἀρραβών (2 Cor., Eph.).	προτίθεσθαι (Rom., Eph.).
θάλπειν (1 Th., Eph.).	υἱοθεσία (Gal., Rom., Eph.).
περικεφαλαία (1 Th., Eph.).	ὑπερβάλλειν (2 Cor., Eph.).
πλεονέκτης (1 Cor., Eph.).	ὑπερεκπερισσοῦ (1 Th., Eph.).

Also the connective ἄρα οὖν (1 Th., 2 Th., Gal., Rom., Eph.).

(iii)   Common to 'Ephesians,' 'Philippians,' and one earlier
Epistle.

εὐωδία (2 Cor., Phil., Eph.).

πεποίθησις (2 Cor., Phil., Eph.).

(iv)   Common to 'Ephesians,' 'Colossians,' and one or more of
the earlier Epistles.

ἁπλότης (2 Cor., Rom., Col., Eph.).

ἐξαγοράζειν (Gal., Col., Eph.).

(v)   Common to 'Ephesians,' 'Colossians,' 'Philippians,' and earlier
Epistles.

ἐνέργεια (2 Th., Phil., Col., Eph.).

(vi)   Common to 'Ephesians,' the 'Pastorals' and one or more
of the earlier Epistles.

αἰσχρός (1 Cor., Eph., Tit.).

ἀφθαρσία (1 Cor., Rom., Eph., 2 Tim., Tit.).

νουθεσία (1 Cor., Eph., Tit.).

οἰκεῖος (Gal., Eph., 1 Tim.).

(vii) Common, and peculiar, to the Epistles of the Captivity and the 'Pastorals,' and occurring in 'Ephesians.'

λουτρόν (Eph. v. 36, Tit. iii. 5 only).

(viii) Common to 'Ephesians' with 'Colossians,' 'Philemon,' or 'Philippians,' earlier Epistles, and the 'Pastorals.'

μνεία (1 Th., 2 Th., Rom., Phil., Philem., Eph., 2 Tim.).

πραότης (1 Cor., 2 Cor., Gal., Col., Eph., 1 Tim., 2 Tim., Tit.).

χρηστότης (2 Cor., Gal., Rom., Col., Eph., Tit.).

Words occurring in 'Ephesians,' common, and peculiar, to Pauline Epistles, and Speeches of St Paul in 'Acts.'

μαρτύρομαι (Acts xx. 26, Gal. v. 3, Eph. iv. 17).

νυνί (Acts xxii. 1, xxiv. 13, 1 Cor., 2 Cor., Rom., Col., Philem., Eph., and *v.l.* in Heb. viii. 6).

Words common to 'Ephesians,' other Pauline Epistles, and the Gospel of St Luke or 'Acts.'

ἔνδοξος (Lk. vii. 25, xiii. 17, 1 Cor., Eph.).

εὐαγγελίστης (Acts xxi. 8, Eph., 2 Tim.).

μεταδιδόναι (Lk. iii. 11, 1 Th., Rom. i. 11, xii. 8, Eph.).

οἰκονομία (Lk. xvi. 2, 3, 4, 1 Cor., Col., Eph., 1 Tim.).

ὀνομάζειν (Lk. vi. 13, 14, Acts xix. 13, 1 Cor., Rom., Eph., 2 Tim.).

πανουργία (Lk. xx. 23, 1 Cor., 2 Cor., Eph.).

προορίζειν (Acts iv. 28, 1 Cor., Rom., Eph.).

συμβιβάζειν (Acts, 1 Cor. LXX., Col., Eph.).

σύνδεσμος (Acts viii. 23, Col., Eph.).

Words common, and peculiar, to 'Ephesians' and the Gospel of St Luke or 'Acts.'

ἀπειλή, ἀπελπίζειν (*v.l.*), ὁσιότης, πανοπλία, πολιτεία, ⚫υγκαθίζειν, σωτήριον, φρόνησις, χαριτοῦν.

VII. RELATION TO THE COLOSSIAN EPISTLE.

Parallel passages in 'Colossians' and 'Ephesians.'

Colossians.	Ephesians.

Colossians.

i. 14. ἐν ᾧ ἔχομεν τὴν ἀπολύτρωσιν, τὴν ἄφεσιν τῶν ἁμαρτιῶν.

ib. 20. κ. δι᾽ αὐτοῦ ἀποκαταλλάξαι τὰ πάντα εἰς αὐτόν, εἰρηνοποιήσας διὰ τοῦ αἵματος τοῦ σταυροῦ αὐτοῦ, δι᾽ αὐτοῦ εἴτε τὰ ἐπὶ τῆς γῆς εἴτε τὰ ἐν τοῖς οὐρανοῖς.

ib. 3, 4. εὐχαριστοῦμεν τῷ θεῷ πατρὶ τοῦ κυρίου ἡμῶν Ἰησοῦ Χριστοῦ πάντοτε περὶ ὑμῶν προσευχόμενοι· ἀκούσαντες τὴν πίστιν ὑμῶν ἐν Χρ. Ἰ. καὶ τὴν ἀγάπην ἣν ἔχετε εἰς πάντας τοὺς ἁγίους.

ib. 27. οἷς ἠθέλησεν ὁ θεὸς γνωρίσαι τί τὸ πλοῦτος τῆς δόξης τοῦ μυστηρίου τούτου ἐν τοῖς ἔθνεσιν, ὅ ἐστιν Χριστὸς ἐν ὑμῖν, ἡ ἐλπὶς τῆς δόξης.

ii. 12. διὰ τῆς πίστεως τῆς ἐνεργείας τοῦ θεοῦ τοῦ ἐγείραντος αὐτὸν ἐκ νεκρῶν.

i. 16—19. ὅτι ἐν αὐτῷ ἐκτίσθη τὰ πάντα ἐν τοῖς οὐρανοῖς καὶ ἐπὶ τῆς γῆς, τὰ ὁρατὰ καὶ τὰ ἀόρατα, εἴτε θρόνοι εἴτε κυριότητες εἴτε ἀρχαὶ εἴτε ἐξουσίαι· τὰ πάντα δι᾽ αὐτοῦ καὶ εἰς αὐτὸν ἔκτισται· καὶ αὐτός ἐστιν πρὸ πάντων, καὶ τὰ πάντα ἐν αὐτῷ συνέστηκεν, καὶ αὐτός ἐστιν ἡ κεφαλὴ τοῦ σώματος, τῆς ἐκκλησίας· ὅς ἐστιν ἀρχή, πρωτότοκος ἐκ τῶν νεκρῶν, ἵνα γένηται ἐν πᾶσιν αὐτὸς πρωτεύων· ὅτι ἐν αὐτῷ εὐδόκησεν πᾶν τὸ πλήρωμα κατοικῆσαι.

Ephesians.

i. 7. ἐν ᾧ ἔχομεν τὴν ἀπολύτρωσιν διὰ τοῦ αἵματος αὐτοῦ, τὴν ἄφεσιν τῶν παραπτωμάτων.

ib. 10. ἀνακεφαλαιώσασθαι τὰ πάντα ἐν τῷ χριστῷ, τὰ ἐπὶ τοῖς οὐρανοῖς καὶ τὰ ἐπὶ τῆς γῆς.

ib. 15—17. διὰ τοῦτο κἀγώ, ἀκούσας τὴν καθ᾽ ὑμᾶς πίστιν ἐν τῷ κυρίῳ Ἰησοῦ καὶ τὴν εἰς πάντας τοὺς ἁγίους, οὐ παύομαι εὐχαριστῶν ὑπὲρ ὑμῶν μνείαν ποιούμενος ἐπὶ τῶν προσευχῶν μου, ἵνα ὁ θεὸς τοῦ κυρίου ἡμῶν Ἰ. Χρ., ὁ πατὴρ τῆς δόξης, δῴη ὑμῖν κ.τ.λ.

ib. 18. εἰς τὸ εἰδέναι ὑμᾶς τίς ἐστιν ἡ ἐλπὶς τῆς κλήσεως αὐτοῦ, τίς ὁ πλοῦτος τῆς δόξης τῆς κληρονομίας αὐτοῦ ἐν τοῖς ἁγίοις.

ib. 19. τὸ ὑπερβάλλον μέγεθος τ. δυνάμεως αὐτοῦ εἰς ἡμᾶς τοὺς πιστεύοντας κατὰ τὴν ἐνέργειαν τ. κράτους τ. ἰσχύος αὐτοῦ ἣν ἐνήργηκεν ἐν τῷ χριστῷ ἐγείρας αὐτὸν ἐκ νεκρῶν.

ib. 21—23. ὑπεράνω πάσης ἀρχῆς καὶ ἐξουσίας καὶ δυνάμεως καὶ κυριότητος καὶ παντὸς ὀνόματος ὀνομαζομένου οὐ μόνον ἐν τῷ αἰῶνι τούτῳ ἀλλὰ καὶ ἐν τῷ μέλλοντι· καὶ πάντα ὑπέταξεν ὑπὸ τοὺς πόδας αὐτοῦ, καὶ αὐτὸν ἔδωκεν κεφαλὴν ὑπὲρ πάντα τῇ ἐκκλησίᾳ, ἥτις ἐστὶ τὸ σῶμα αὐτοῦ, τὸ πλήρωμα τοῦ τὰ πάντα ἐν πᾶσιν πληρουμένου.

Colossians.	Ephesians.

ib. 21. καὶ ὑμᾶς ποτὲ ὄντας κ.τ.λ.

    ii. 1. καὶ ὑμᾶς ὄντας κ.τ.λ.

ii. 13. καὶ ὑμᾶς νεκροὺς ὄντας τοῖς παραπτώμασιν κ. τῇ ἀκροβυστίᾳ τ. σαρκὸς ὑμῶν συνεζωοποίησεν ὑμᾶς σὺν αὐτῷ.

    ib. 5. καὶ ὄντας ἡμᾶς νεκροὺς τοῖς παραπτώμασιν συνεζωοποίησεν τῷ χριστῷ.

ib. 12. ἐν ᾧ καὶ συνηγέρθητε (cf. iii. 1).

    ib. 6. καὶ συνήγειρεν.

i. 21. καὶ ὑμᾶς ποτὲ ὄντας ἀπηλλοτριωμένους.

    ib. 12. ὅτι ἦτε τῷ καιρῷ ἐκείνῳ (cf. *v.* 11 ὅτι ποτὲ ὑμεῖς) χωρὶς Χριστοῦ ἀπηλλοτριωμένοι τ. πολιτείας τ. Ἰσραήλ.

ii. 14. ἐξαλείψας τὸ καθ᾽ ἡμῶν χειρόγραφον τοῖς δόγμασιν, ὃ ἦν ὑπεναντίον ἡμῖν.

    ib. 15 f. τὴν ἔχθραν ἐν τῇ σαρκὶ αὐτοῦ, τὸν νόμον τῶν ἐντολῶν ἐν δόγμασιν, καταργήσας ἵνα τ. δύο κτίσῃ ἐν αὐτῷ εἰς ἕνα καινὸν ἄνθρωπον ποιῶν εἰρήνην, καὶ ἀποκαταλλάξῃ τοὺς ἀμφοτέρους ἐν ἑνὶ σώματι τῷ θεῷ διὰ τοῦ σταυροῦ.

i. 20. κ. δι᾽ αὐτοῦ ἀποκαταλλάξαι τ. πάντα εἰς αὐτόν, εἰρηνοποιήσας διὰ τοῦ αἵματος τοῦ σταυροῦ αὐτοῦ.

ii. 7. ἐρριζωμένοι κ. ἐποικοδομούμενοι ἐν αὐτῷ καὶ βεβαιούμενοι τῇ πίστει.

    ib. 20 f. ἐποικοδομηθέντες...ὄντος ἀκρογωνιαίου αὐτοῦ Χρ. Ἰ., ἐν ᾧ πᾶσα οἰκοδομὴ κ.τ.λ....(cf. iii. 17 ἐρριζωμένοι κ. τεθεμελιωμένοι).

i. 23—26. οὗ ἐγενόμην ἐγὼ Παῦλος διάκονος. Νῦν χαίρω ἐν τ. παθήμασιν ὑπὲρ ὑμῶν, κ. ἀνταναπληρῶ τ. ὑστερήματα τ. θλίψεων τ. χριστοῦ ἐν τ. σαρκί μου ὑπὲρ τ. σώματος αὐτοῦ, ὅ ἐστιν ἡ ἐκκλησία· ἧς ἐγενόμην ἐγὼ διάκονος κατὰ τὴν οἰκονομίαν τοῦ θεοῦ τὴν δοθεῖσάν μοι εἰς ὑμᾶς, πληρῶσαι τ. λόγον τ. θεοῦ, τὸ μυστήριον τὸ ἀποκεκρυμμένον ἀπὸ τ. αἰώνων κ. ἀπὸ τ. γενεῶν, νῦν δὲ ἐφανερώθη τοῖς ἁγίοις αὐτοῦ.

    iii. 1—3, 5. Τούτου χάριν ἐγὼ Παῦλος ὁ δέσμιος τοῦ χριστοῦ Ἰησοῦ ὑπὲρ ὑμῶν τῶν ἐθνῶν,...εἴ γε ἠκούσατε τὴν οἰκονομίαν τῆς χάριτος τοῦ θεοῦ τῆς δοθείσης μοι εἰς ὑμᾶς, ὅτι κατὰ ἀποκάλυψιν ἐγνωρίσθη μοι τὸ μυστήριον...ὃ ἑτέραις γενεαῖς οὐκ ἐγνωρίσθη τ. υἱοῖς τ. ἀνθρώπων ὡς νῦν ἀπεκαλύφθη τοῖς ἁγίοις ἀποστόλοις αὐτοῦ κ. προφήταις ἐν πνεύματι.

ib. 29. εἰς ὃ καὶ κοπιῶ ἀγωνιζόμενος κατὰ τὴν ἐνέργειαν αὐτοῦ τὴν ἐνεργουμένην ἐν ἐμοὶ ἐν δυνάμει.

    ib. 7. οὗ ἐγενήθην διάκονος κατὰ τὴν δωρεὰν τ. χάριτος τ. θεοῦ τ. δοθείσης μοι κατὰ τὴν ἐνέργειαν τῆς δυνάμεως αὐτοῦ.

ib. 27. τὸ πλοῦτος τ. δόξης τ. μυστηρίου τούτου ἐν τ. ἔθνεσιν, ὅ ἐστιν Χριστὸς ἐν ὑμῖν.

    ib. 8 f. τοῖς ἔθνεσιν εὐαγγελίσασθαι τὸ ἀνεξιχνίαστον πλοῦτος τ. χριστοῦ, κ. φωτίσαι τίς ἡ οἰκονομία τ. μυστηρίου τ. ἀποκεκρυμμένου ἀπὸ τ. αἰώνων.

Colossians.	Ephesians.

iii. 12 ff. ταπεινοφροσύνην, πραΰτητα, μακροθυμίαν· ἀνεχόμενοι ἀλλήλων...ἐπὶ πᾶσιν δὲ τούτοις τὴν ἀγάπην, ὅ ἐστιν σύνδεσμος τῆς τελειότητος. καὶ ἡ εἰρήνη τοῦ χριστοῦ βραβευέτω ἐν τ. καρδίαις ὑμῶν· εἰς ἣν καὶ ἐκλήθητε ἐν ἑνὶ σώματι.

iv. 2—4. μετὰ πάσης ταπεινοφροσύνης κ. πραΰτητος, μετὰ μακροθυμίας, ἀνεχόμενοι ἀλλήλων ἐν ἀγάπῃ, σπουδάζοντες τηρεῖν τὴν ἑνότητα τοῦ πνεύματος ἐν τῷ συνδέσμῳ τῆς εἰρήνης· ἓν σῶμα καὶ ἓν πνεῦμα, καθὼς καὶ ἐκλήθητε ἐν μιᾷ ἐλπίδι τῆς κλήσεως ὑμῶν.

ii. 19. οὐ κρατῶν τὴν κεφαλήν, ἐξ οὗ πᾶν τὸ σῶμα διὰ τῶν ἁφῶν καὶ συνδέσμων ἐπιχορηγούμενον καὶ συνβιβαζόμενον αὔξει τὴν αὔξησιν τοῦ θεοῦ.

ib. 15 f. αὐξήσωμεν εἰς αὐτὸν τὰ πάντα, ὅς ἐστιν ἡ κεφαλή, Χριστός, ἐξ οὗ πᾶν τὸ σῶμα συναρμολογούμενον καὶ συνβιβαζόμενον διὰ πάσης ἁφῆς τ. ἐπιχορηγίας κατ᾽ ἐνέργειαν ἐν μέτρῳ ἑνὸς ἑκάστου μέρους τ. αὔξησιν τοῦ σώματος ποιεῖται.

i. 21. ὄντας ἀπηλλοτριωμένους καὶ ἐχθροὺς τῇ διανοίᾳ ἐν τ. ἔργοις τ. πονηροῖς.

ib. 18. ἐσκοτωμένοι τῇ διανοίᾳ ὄντες, ἀπηλλοτριωμένοι τῆς ζωῆς τοῦ θεοῦ.

iii. 8 ff. νυνὶ δὲ ἀπόθεσθε καὶ ὑμεῖς τὰ πάντα, ὀργήν, θυμόν, κακίαν, βλασφημίαν, αἰσχρολογίαν ἐκ τοῦ στόματος ὑμῶν· μὴ ψεύδεσθε εἰς ἀλλήλους· ἀπεκδυσάμενοι τὸν παλαιὸν ἄνθρωπον σὺν ταῖς πράξεσιν αὐτοῦ, καὶ ἐνδυσάμενοι τὸν νέον, τὸν ἀνακαινούμενον εἰς ἐπίγνωσιν κατ᾽ εἰκόνα τοῦ κτίσαντος αὐτόν.

ib. 22 ff. ἀποθέσθαι ὑμᾶς κατὰ τὴν προτέραν ἀναστροφὴν τὸν παλαιὸν ἄνθρωπον τὸν φθειρόμενον κατὰ τ. ἐπιθυμίας τ. ἀπάτης, ἀνανεοῦσθαι δὲ τῷ πνεύματι τοῦ νοὸς ὑμῶν, καὶ ἐνδύσασθαι τὸν καινὸν ἄνθρωπον τὸν κατὰ θεὸν κτισθέντα ἐν δικαιοσύνῃ κ. ὁσιότητι τ. ἀληθείας.
Διὸ ἀποθέμενοι τὸ ψεῦδος λαλεῖτε ἀλήθειαν ἕκαστος μετὰ τοῦ πλησίον αὐτοῦ....

ib. 29. πᾶς λόγος σαπρὸς ἐκ τοῦ στόματος ὑμῶν μὴ ἐκπορευέσθω....

ib. 31. πᾶσα πικρία καὶ θυμὸς καὶ ὀργὴ καὶ κραυγὴ καὶ βλασφημία ἀρθήτω ἀφ᾽ ὑμῶν σὺν πάσῃ κακίᾳ.

ib. 12 f. ἐνδύσασθε οὖν, ὡς ἐκλεκτοὶ τοῦ θεοῦ, ἅγιοι κ. ἠγαπημένοι, σπλάγχνα οἰκτιρμοῦ, χρηστότητα, ταπεινοφροσύνην, πραΰτητα, μακροθυμίαν, ἀνεχόμενοι ἀλλήλων καὶ χαριζόμενοι ἑαυτοῖς, ἐάν τις πρός τινα ἔχῃ μομφήν· καθὼς καὶ ὁ κύριος ἐχαρίσατο ὑμῖν, οὕτως καὶ ὑμεῖς.

ib. 32—v. 1. γίνεσθε δὲ εἰς ἀλλήλους χρηστοί, εὔσπλαγχνοι, χαριζόμενοι ἑαυτοῖς καθὼς καὶ ὁ θεὸς ἐν Χριστῷ ἐχαρίσατο ὑμῖν. γίνεσθε οὖν μιμηταὶ τοῦ θεοῦ, ὡς τέκνα ἀγαπητά.

ib. 5 f. νεκρώσατε οὖν τὰ μέλη τὰ ἐπὶ τῆς γῆς· πορνείαν, ἀκαθαρσίαν,

v. 3—6. πορνεία δὲ καὶ ἀκαθαρσία πᾶσα ἢ πλεονεξία μηδὲ ὀνομαζέσθω

Colossians.

πάθος, ἐπιθυμίαν κακήν, καὶ τὴν πλεο
νεξίαν, ἥτις ἐστὶν εἰδωλολατρεία, δι᾽ ἃ
ἔρχεται ἡ ὀργὴ τοῦ θεοῦ.

iv. 5. ἐν σοφίᾳ περιπατεῖτε πρὸς
τοὺς ἔξω, τὸν καιρὸν ἐξαγοραζόμενοι.

iii. 16 ff. διδάσκοντες καὶ νουθε
τοῦντες ἑαυτοὺς ψαλμοῖς, ὕμνοις, ᾠδαῖς
πνευματικαῖς ἐν τῇ χάριτι, ᾄδοντες ἐν
ταῖς καρδίαις ὑμῶν τῷ θεῷ, καὶ πᾶν
ὅτι ἐὰν ποιῆτε ἐν λόγῳ ἢ ἐν ἔργῳ,
πάντα ἐν ὀνόματι κυρίου Ἰησοῦ, εὐχα
ριστοῦντες τῷ θεῷ πατρὶ δι᾽ αὐτοῦ.
Αἱ γυναῖκες, ὑποτάσσεσθε τοῖς ἀν
δράσιν, ὡς ἀνῆκεν ἐν κυρίῳ. Οἱ ἄνδρες,
ἀγαπᾶτε τὰς γυναῖκας....τὰ τέκνα, ὑπα
κούετε τοῖς γονεῦσιν κατὰ πάντα· τοῦτο
γὰρ εὐάρεστόν ἐστιν ἐν κυρίῳ. Οἱ
πατέρες, μὴ ἐρεθίζετε τὰ τέκνα ὑμῶν,
ἵνα μὴ ἀθυμῶσιν. Οἱ δοῦλοι, ὑπακούετε
κατὰ πάντα τοῖς κατὰ σάρκα κυρίοις,
μὴ ἐν ὀφθαλμοδουλείᾳ ὡς ἀνθρω
πάρεσκοι, ἀλλ᾽ ἐν ἁπλότητι καρδίας,
φοβούμενοι τὸν κύριον, ὃ ἐὰν ποιῆτε,
ἐκ ψυχῆς ἐργάζεσθε ὡς τῷ κυρίῳ καὶ
οὐκ ἀνθρώποις, εἰδότες ὅτι ἀπὸ κυρίου
ἀπολήμψεσθε τὴν ἀνταπόδοσιν τῆς
κληρονομίας· τῷ κυρίῳ Χριστῷ δου
λεύετε· ὁ γὰρ ἀδικῶν κομίσεται ὃ
ἠδίκησεν, καὶ οὐκ ἔστι προσωπολημψία.

iv. 1. Οἱ κύριοι, τὸ δίκαιον καὶ τὴν
ἰσότητα τοῖς δούλοις παρέχεσθε,
εἰδότες ὅτι καὶ ὑμεῖς ἔχετε κύριον ἐν
οὐρανῷ.

ib. 2. Τῇ προσευχῇ προσκαρτερεῖτε,
γρηγοροῦντες ἐν αὐτῇ ἐν εὐχαριστίᾳ·
προσευχόμενοι ἅμα καὶ περὶ ἡμῶν, ἵνα

Ephesians.

ἐν ὑμῖν...κ. αἰσχρότης κ. μωρολογία...
ὅτι πᾶς πόρνος ἢ ἀκάθαρτος ἢ πλεο
νέκτης, ὅ ἐστιν εἰδωλολάτρης, οὐκ ἔχει
κληρονομίαν ἐν τ. βασιλείᾳ τ. χριστοῦ
κ. θεοῦ....διὰ ταῦτα γὰρ ἔρχεται ἡ ὀργὴ
τοῦ θεοῦ ἐπὶ τοὺς υἱοὺς τῆς ἀπειθείας.

ib. 15 f. βλέπετε οὖν ἀκριβῶς πῶς
περιπατεῖτε, μὴ ὡς ἄσοφοι ἀλλ᾽ ὡς
σοφοί, ἐξαγοραζόμενοι τὸν καιρόν.

ib. 19. λαλοῦντες ἑαυτοῖς ψαλμοῖς
καὶ ὕμνοις καὶ ᾠδαῖς πνευματικαῖς,
ᾄδοντες καὶ ψάλλοντες τῇ καρδίᾳ ὑμῶν
τῷ κυρίῳ, εὐχαριστοῦντες πάντοτε ὑπὲρ
πάντων ἐν ὀνόματι τοῦ κυρίου ἡμῶν
Ἰησοῦ Χριστοῦ τῷ θεῷ καὶ πατρί,
ὑποτασσόμενοι ἀλλήλοις ἐν φόβῳ
Χριστοῦ.
Αἱ γυναῖκες, τοῖς ἰδίοις ἀνδράσιν ὡς
τῷ κυρίῳ, ὅτι κ.τ.λ.

ib. 24. Οἱ ἄνδρες, ἀγαπᾶτε τὰς
γυναῖκας, καθὼς κ.τ.λ....

vi. 1—9. Τὰ τέκνα, ὑπακούετε τοῖς
γονεῦσιν ὑμῶν ἐν κυρίῳ. τοῦτο γάρ
ἐστι δίκαιον· τίμα κ.τ.λ....Καὶ οἱ
πατέρες, μὴ παροργίζετε τὰ᾽ τέκνα
ὑμῶν, ἀλλὰ ἐκτρέφετε αὐτὰ ἐν παιδείᾳ
καὶ νουθεσίᾳ Κυρίου. Οἱ δοῦλοι ὑπα
κούετε τοῖς κατὰ σάρκα κυρίοις μετὰ
φόβου καὶ τρόμου ἐν ἁπλότητι τ.
καρδίας ὑμῶν ὡς τῷ χριστῷ, μὴ κατ᾽
ὀφθαλμοδουλίαν ὡς ἀνθρωπάρεσκοι,
ἀλλ᾽ ὡς δοῦλοι Χριστοῦ ποιοῦντες τὸ
θέλημα τοῦ θεοῦ, ἐκ ψυχῆς μετ᾽
εὐνοίας δουλεύοντες, ὡς τῷ κυρίῳ καὶ
οὐκ ἀνθρώποις, εἰδότες ὅτι ἕκαστος,
ἐάν τι ποιήσῃ ἀγαθόν, τοῦτο κομίσεται
παρὰ κυρίου, εἴτε δοῦλος εἴτε ἐλεύθερος.
Καὶ οἱ κύριοι, τὰ αὐτὰ ποιεῖτε πρὸς
αὐτοὺς ἀνιέντες τὴν ἀπειλήν, εἰδότες
ὅτι καὶ αὐτῶν καὶ ὑμῶν ὁ κύριός ἐστιν
ἐν οὐρανοῖς, καὶ προσωπολημψία οὐκ
ἔστιν παρ᾽ αὐτῷ.

ib. 18—20. διὰ πάσης προσευχῆς
καὶ δεήσεως προσευχόμενοι ἐν παντὶ
καιρῷ ἐν πνεύματι, καὶ εἰς αὐτὸ ἀ

Colossians.

ὁ θεὸς ἀνοίξῃ ἡμῖν θύραν τοῦ λόγου, λαλῆσαι τὸ μυστήριον τοῦ χριστοῦ, δι᾿ ὃ καὶ δέδεμαι, ἵνα φανερώσω αὐτὸ ὡς δεῖ με λαλῆσαι.

Ephesians.

γρυπνοῦντες ἐν πάσῃ προσκαρτερήσει καὶ δεήσει περὶ πάντων τῶν ἁγίων, καὶ ὑπὲρ ἐμοῦ, ἵνα μοι δοθῇ λόγος ἐν ἀνοίξει τοῦ στόματός μου, ἐν παρρησίᾳ γνωρίσαι τὸ μυστήριον τ. εὐαγγελίου, ὑπὲρ οὗ πρεσβεύω ἐν ἁλύσει, ἵνα ἐν αὐτῷ παρρησιάσωμαι ὡς δεῖ με λαλῆσαι.

ib. 7. Τὰ κατ᾿ ἐμὲ πάντα γνωρίσει ὑμῖν Τύχικος ὁ ἀγαπητὸς ἀδελφὸς καὶ πιστὸς διάκονος καὶ σύνδουλος ἐν κυρίῳ· ὃν ἔπεμψα πρὸς ὑμᾶς εἰς αὐτὸ τοῦτο, ἵνα γνῶτε τὰ περὶ ἡμῶν καὶ παρακαλέσῃ τὰς καρδίας ὑμῶν.

ib. 21. Ἵνα δὲ εἰδῆτε καὶ ὑμεῖς τὰ κατ᾿ ἐμέ, τί πράσσω, πάντα γνωρίσει ὑμῖν Τύχικος ὁ ἀγαπητὸς ἀδελφὸς καὶ πιστὸς διάκονος ἐν κυρίῳ· ὃν ἔπεμψα πρὸς ὑμᾶς εἰς αὐτὸ τοῦτο ἵνα γνῶτε τὰ περὶ ἡμῶν καὶ παρακαλέσῃ τὰς καρδίας ὑμῶν.

Parallel phrases in passages otherwise not parallel.

Colossians.

i. 22. ἁγίους καὶ ἀμώμους κ. ἀνεγκλήτους κατενώπιον αὐτοῦ.

ib. 10. ·περιπατῆσαι ἀξίως τοῦ κυρίου.

Ephesians.

i. 4. ἁγίους καὶ ἀμώμους κατενώπιον αὐτοῦ.

iv. 1. ἀξίως περιπατῆσαι τ. κλήσεως ἧς ἐκλήθητε.

'It is difficult indeed to say, considering the patent coincidences of expression in the two Epistles, whether the points of likeness or of unlikeness between them are the more remarkable.   No one can doubt that either one Epistle was an intentional copy of the other or else that both were written at very nearly the same time by the same author.   It is when we are considering the doctrinal substance of the Epistles that the latter conclusion forces itself upon us most irresistibly as the true one.   These two letters are twins, singularly like one another in face, like also in character, but not so identical as to be without a strongly marked individuality.'   (Davies: *The Epistles of St Paul to the Ephesians, the Colossians and Philemon*, p. 7.)

'The Epistle to the Ephesians stands to the Epistle to the Colossians in very much the same relation as the Romans to the Galatians.   The one is the general and systematic exposition of the same truths which appear in a special bearing in the other.' (Lightfoot: *Biblical Essays*, p. 395.)

VIII.   RELATION TO OTHER PAULINE DOCUMENTS.

(a)   'Ephesians' and the Epistle to Philemon.

Philemon.	Ephesians.
v. 1. Παῦλος, δέσμιος Χριστοῦ Ἰησοῦ.	iii. 1. ἐγὼ Παῦλος ὁ δέσμιος τοῦ χριστοῦ Ἰησοῦ.
v. 9. Παῦλος, πρεσβύτης νυνὶ δὲ καὶ δέσμιος Χριστοῦ Ἰησοῦ.	vi. 20. ὑπὲρ οὗ πρεσβεύω ἐν ἁλύσει.
v. 5. τὴν πίστιν ἣν ἔχεις πρὸς τὸν κύριον Ἰησοῦν καὶ εἰς πάντας τοὺς ἁγίους.	i. 15. τὴν καθ' ὑμᾶς πίστιν ἐν τῷ κυρίῳ Ἰησοῦ καὶ τὴν εἰς πάντας τοὺς ἁγίους.
v. 4. εὐχαριστῶ τῷ θεῷ μου πάντοτε μνείαν σου ποιούμενος ἐπὶ τῶν προσευχῶν μου.	*ib.* 16. οὐ παύομαι εὐχαριστῶν ὑπὲρ ὑμῶν μνείαν ποιούμενος ἐπὶ τῶν προσευχῶν μου.
v. 6. ὅπως ἡ κοινωνία τῆς πίστεώς σου ἐνεργὴς γένηται ἐν ἐπιγνώσει παντὸς ἀγαθοῦ τοῦ ἐν ἡμῖν εἰς Χριστόν.	*ib.* 17. ἐν ἐπιγνώσει αὐτοῦ. iv. 13. εἰς τ. ἑνότητα τῆς πίστεως καὶ τῆς ἐπιγνώσεως τ. υἱοῦ τ. θεοῦ.
v. 16. ἀδελφὸν ἀγαπητόν.	vi. 1. ὁ ἀγαπητὸς ἀδελφός (cf. Col. iv. 7).

(b)   'Ephesians' and the Epistle to the Philippians.

Philippians.	Ephesians.
i. 1 f. (a) Παῦλος καὶ Τιμόθεος, δοῦλοι Χρ. Ἰ.	i. 1 f. (a) Παῦλος ἀπόστολος Χρ. Ἰ. διὰ θελήματος θεοῦ
(b) πᾶσιν τοῖς ἁγίοις ἐν Χριστῷ Ἰησοῦ τοῖς οὖσιν ἐν Φιλίπποις σὺν ἐπισκόποις καὶ διακόνοις·	(b) τοῖς ἁγίοις τοῖς οὖσιν [ἐν Ἐφέσῳ] καὶ πιστοῖς ἐν Χριστῷ Ἰησοῦ·
(c) χάρις ὑμῖν κ. εἰρήνη ἀπὸ θεοῦ πατρὸς ἡμῶν κ. κυρίου Ἰησοῦ Χριστοῦ.	(c) χάρις ὑμῖν κ. εἰρήνη ἀπὸ θεοῦ πατρὸς ἡμῶν κ. κυρίου Ἰησοῦ Χριστοῦ.
ib. 3. εὐχαριστῶ τῷ θεῷ ἐπὶ πάσῃ τῇ μνείᾳ ὑμῶν πάντοτε ἐν πάσῃ δεήσει μου ὑπὲρ πάντων ὑμῶν.	*ib.* 16. οὐ παύομαι εὐχαριστῶν ὑπὲρ ὑμῶν μνείαν ποιούμενος ἐπὶ τῶν προσευχῶν μου.
ib. 9. ἵνα ἡ ἀγάπη ὑμῶν...περισσεύῃ ἐν ἐπιγνώσει καὶ πάσῃ αἰσθήσει, εἰς τὸ δοκιμάζειν ὑμᾶς τὰ διαφέροντα....	*ib.* 17. ἵνα...δῴη ὑμῖν πνεῦμα σοφίας κ. ἀποκαλύψεως ἐν ἐπιγνώσει... εἰς τὸ εἰδέναι ὑμᾶς τίς ὁ πλοῦτος...κ. τί τὸ ὑπερβάλλον μέγεθος....

Philippians.	Ephesians.

Philippians.

ib. 11. καρπὸν δικαιωσύνης (cf. Amos vi. 12, Ja. iii. 18).

ib. 27. ἀξίως τ. εὐαγγ. τ. χ. πολιτεύεσθε (cf. iii. 20 ἡμῶν τὸ πολίτευμα ἐν οὐρανοῖς ὑπάρχει).

ib. 27 f. ὅτι στήκετε ἐν ἑνὶ πνεύματι, μιᾷ ψυχῇ συναθλοῦντες...μὴ πτυρόμενοι ὑπὸ τῶν ἀντικειμένων....

ii. 2. τὸ ἓν φρονοῦντες.

ib. 3. τῇ ταπεινοφροσύνῃ ἀλλήλους ἡγούμενοι ὑπερέχοντας ἑαυτῶν.

ib. 9. ὁ θεὸς αὐτὸν ὑπερύψωσεν κ. ἐχαρίσατο αὐτῷ τὸ ὄνομα τὸ ὑπὲρ πᾶν ὄνομα.

ib. 10. ἐπουρανίων κ. ἐπιγείων κ. καταχθονίων.

ib. 12. μετὰ φόβου καὶ τρόμου.

iii. 3. ἡμεῖς γάρ ἐσμεν ἡ περιτομή, οἱ πνεύματι θεοῦ λατρεύοντες καὶ καυχώμενοι ἐν Χρ. Ἰ. καὶ οὐκ ἐν σαρκὶ πεποιθότες.

ib. 10. τοῦ γνῶναι αὐτὸν καὶ τὴν δύναμιν τῆς ἀναστάσεως αὐτοῦ κ.τ.λ....

ib. 21. κατὰ τὴν ἐνέργειαν τοῦ δύνασθαι αὐτὸν κ.τ.λ....

iv. 6. ἐν παντὶ τῇ προσευχῇ καὶ τῇ δεήσει τὰ αἰτήματα ὑμῶν γνωριζέσθω.

ib. 18. ὀσμὴν εὐωδίας, θυσίαν δεκτὴν εὐάρεστον τῷ θεῷ.

Ephesians.

v. 9. ὁ...καρπὸς τ. φωτὸς ἐν πάσῃ ἀγαθωσύνῃ κ. δικαιοσύνῃ.

ii. 12. τ. πολιτείας τ. Ἰσραήλ.

ib. 19. συμπολῖται τ. ἁγίων κ. οἰκεῖοι τ. θεοῦ.

vi. 13. ἵνα δυνηθῆτε ἀντιστῆναι... στῆναι. στήκετε οὖν κ.τ.λ....

ii. 18. ἐν ἑνὶ πνεύματι.

iv. 3. σπουδάζοντες τηρεῖν τ. ἑνότητα τ. πνεύματος.

ib. 4. ἓν σῶμα κ. ἓν πνεῦμα.

ib. 2. μετὰ πάσης ταπεινοφροσύνης...ἀνεχόμενοι ἀλλήλων ἐν ἀγάπῃ.

i. 20 f. καθίσας ἐν δεξιᾷ αὐτοῦ ἐν τ. ἐπουρανίοις ὑπεράνω πάσης ἀρχῆς κ.τ.λ....κ. παντὸς ὀνόματος ὀνομαζομένου.

ib. 10. τὰ ἐπὶ τ. οὐρανοῖς κ. τὰ ἐπὶ τ. γῆς.

vi. 5. μετὰ φόβου καὶ τρόμου.

ii. 11. οἱ λεγόμενοι ἀκροβυστία ὑπὸ τῆς λεγομένης περιτομῆς ἐν σαρκὶ χειροποιήτου.

i. 18 f. τὸ εἰδέναι...τί τὸ...μέγεθος τ. δυνάμεως αὐτοῦ εἰς ἡμᾶς τ. πιστεύοντας κατὰ τὴν ἐνέργειαν τοῦ κράτους τῆς ἰσχύος αὐτοῦ, ἣν ἐνήργηκεν ἐν τ. χριστῷ ἐγείρας αὐτὸν ἐκ νεκρῶν.

vi. 18. διὰ πάσης προσευχῆς καὶ δεήσεως προσευχόμενοι ἐν παντὶ καιρῷ.

v. 2. προσφορὰν καὶ θυσίαν τῷ θεῷ εἰς ὀσμὴν εὐωδίας.

(c) Comparison with the Address at Miletus.

Address at Miletus
(Acts xx. 18—25).

Ephesians.

xx. 19. δουλεύων τῷ κυρίῳ μετὰ
πάσης ταπεινοφροσύνης.

vi. 7. δουλεύοντες ὡς τῷ κυρίῳ
καὶ οὐκ ἀνθρώποις.

iv. 2. μετὰ πάσης ταπεινοφροσύνης.

ib. 20. τὴν εἰς θεὸν μετάνοιαν καὶ
πίστιν εἰς τὸν κύριον ἡμῶν Ἰησοῦν.

i. 15. τὴν καθ᾽ ὑμᾶς πίστιν ἐν τῷ
κυρίῳ Ἰησοῦ καὶ τὴν εἰς πάντας τοὺς
ἁγίους.

ib. 23. τὸ πνεῦμα τὸ ἅγιον...δια-
μαρτύρεταί μοι λέγον ὅτι δεσμὰ καὶ
θλίψεις με μένουσιν.

iii. 13. ἐν ταῖς θλίψεσίν μου
ὑπὲρ ὑμῶν.

iv. 1. ἐγὼ ὁ δέσμιος.

ib. 24. τὴν διακονίαν ἣν ἔλαβον
παρὰ τοῦ κυρίου Ἰησοῦ, διαμαρτύ-
ρασθαι τὸ εὐαγγέλιον τῆς χάριτος
τοῦ θεοῦ.

i. 15. ἐν τῷ κυρίῳ Ἰησοῦ.

iii. 6, 7. διὰ τοῦ εὐαγγελίου, οὗ
ἐγενήθην διάκονος κατὰ τὴν δωρεὰν
τῆς χάριτος τοῦ θεοῦ τῆς δοθείσης
μοι.

ib. 26. ἐν οἷς διῆλθον κηρύσσων
τὴν βασιλείαν.

v. 5. οὐκ ἔχει κληρονομίαν ἐν τῇ
βασιλείᾳ τοῦ χριστοῦ καὶ θεοῦ.

ib. 27. ἀναγγεῖλαι πᾶσαν τὴν
βουλὴν τοῦ θεοῦ.

i. 11. κατὰ τὴν βουλὴν τοῦ θελήματος αὐτοῦ.

ib. 28. παντὶ τῷ ποιμνίῳ, ἐν ᾧ ὑμᾶς
τὸ πνεῦμα τὸ ἅγιον ἔθετο ἐπισκό-
πους, ποιμαίνειν τὴν ἐκκλησίαν
τοῦ θεοῦ.

iii. 20. αὐτῷ ἡ δόξα ἐν τῇ ἐκκλησίᾳ ἐν Χριστῷ Ἰησοῦ.

iv. 3. τὴν ἑνότητα τοῦ πνεύματος.

ib. 4. ἓν σῶμα, ἓν πνεῦμα.

ib. 11. κ. αὐτὸς ἔδωκεν τοὺς μὲν
ἀποστόλους...τοὺς δὲ ποιμένας καὶ
διδασκάλους.

ib. 30. τὸ πνεῦμα τὸ ἅγιον τοῦ
θεοῦ.

ib. 29. ἣν περιεποιήσατο διὰ
τοῦ αἵματος τοῦ ἰδίου.

i. 6 f. ἐν τῷ ἠγαπημένῳ, ἐν ᾧ
ἔχομεν τὴν ἀπολύτρωσιν διὰ τοῦ
αἵματος αὐτοῦ.

ib. 14. εἰς ἀπολύτρωσιν τῆς περιποιήσεως.

Address at Miletus.	Ephesians.

ib. 32. καὶ τὰ νῦν παρατίθεμαι ὑμᾶς τῷ κυρίῳ καὶ τῷ λόγῳ τῆς χάριτος αὐτοῦ τῷ δυναμένῳ οἰκο-δομῆσαι καὶ δοῦναι τὴν κληρονομίαν ἐν τοῖς ἡγιασμένοις πᾶσιν.

ib. 16 f. μνείαν ποιούμενος ἐπὶ τῶν προσευχῶν μου, ἵνα ὁ θεὸς τ. κυρίου ἡμῶν 'Ι. δῴη ὑμῖν...εἰς τὸ εἰδέναι ὑμᾶς...τίς ὁ πλοῦτος τ. δόξης τῆς κληρονομίας αὐτοῦ ἐν τοῖς ἁγίοις.

iv. 12. πρὸς τ. καταρτισμὸν τ. ἁγίων..., εἰς οἰκοδομὴν τοῦ σώματος τ. χριστοῦ (cf. *v.* 29 πρὸς οἰκοδομὴν τ. χρείας).

(d) 'Ephesians' and 'Romans.'

'St Paul has two comparatively general Epistles, the Epistle to the Romans and the Epistle to the Ephesians and the contrast between them illustrates both.   Both are full of the especially Pauline Gospel that the Gentiles are fellow-heirs, but the one glances chiefly to the past, the other to the future.   The unity at which the former Epistle seems to arrive by slow and painful steps, is assumed in the latter as a starting-point with a vista of wondrous possibilities beyond.'

(Hort, *Prolegomena to the Epistle to the Romans*, p. 49.)

With Rom. i. 18 ff. Ἀποκαλύπτεται γὰρ ὀργὴ θεοῦ κ.τ.λ.
compare Eph. v. 6.

„   Rom. v. 1 ff. Δικαιωθέντες οὖν...εἰρήνην ἔχωμεν κ.τ.λ.
compare Eph. ii. 17 f.

„   Rom. viii. 28—30 —προέγνω...προώρισεν—κ.τ.λ.
compare Eph. i. 11—14.

„   Rom. xi. 15 —μὴ ζωὴ ἐκ νεκρῶν ;—
compare Eph. ii. 1 ff.

„   Rom. xi. 33 ff. ὦ βάθος πλούτου κ.τ.λ.   }
„   Rom. xii. 1—8 παρακαλῶ οὖν ὑμᾶς κ.τ.λ.   }
compare { Eph. iii. 16—19.
        „   iv. 1—6.

„   Rom. xiii. 11—14   compare { Eph. v. 7—11.
        „   vi. 10—13.

(e) 'Ephesians' and the 'Pastorals.'

Ephesians.

(a) vi. 10 f. Τοῦ λοιποῦ ἐνδυναμοῦσθε ἐν κυρίῳ κ. ἐν τῷ κράτει τ.
ἰσχύος αὐτοῦ. ἐνδύσασθε τ. πανοπλίαν
τ. θεοῦ πρὸς τὸ δύνασθαι ὑμᾶς στῆναι
πρὸς…· ὅτι οὐκ ἔστιν ἡμῖν ἡ πάλη πρὸς
…ἀλλὰ πρὸς…· διὰ τοῦτο ἀναλάβετε
τὴν πανοπλίαν τ. θεοῦ, ἵνα δυνηθῆτε
ἀντιστῆναι…στῆτε οὖν…ἐνδυσάμενοι
τ. θώρακα τ. δικαιοσύνης…ἐν πᾶσιν
ἀναλαβόντες τὸν θυρεὸν τῆς πίστεως,
ἐν ᾧ δυνήσεσθε πάντα τὰ βέλη τ. πονηροῦ…σβέσαι κ.τ.λ.

ib. 11. τὰς μεθοδίας τοῦ διαβόλου.

(b) iv. 13. μέχρι καταντήσωμεν οἱ
πάντες εἰς τὴν ἑνότητα τῆς πίστεως κ.
τ. ἐπιγνώσεως τ. υἱοῦ τ. θεοῦ….

ib. 5. εἷς κύριος…εἷς θεὸς κ.
πατὴρ πάντων….

i. 6 f. εἰς ἔπαινον δόξης τ. χάριτος
αὐτοῦ, ἧς ἐχαρίτωσεν ἡμᾶς ἐν τῷ
ἠγαπημένῳ, ἐν ᾧ ἔχομεν τὴν ἀπολύτρωσιν….

v. 2. κ. παρέδωκεν ἑαυτὸν ὑπὲρ
ἡμῶν….

ib. 25 f. ὁ χριστὸς ἠγάπησεν τ. ἐκκλησίαν κ. ἑαυτὸν παρέδωκεν ὑπὲρ
αὐτῆς· ἵνα αὐτὴν ἁγιάσῃ καθαρίσας
τῷ λουτρῷ τ. ὕδατος.

Pastorals.

1 Tim. i. 18. ἵνα στρατεύῃ ἐν
αὐταῖς τ. καλὴν στρατείαν, ἔχων πίστιν.

ib. vi. 12. ἀγωνίζου τ. καλὸν ἀγῶνα
τῆς πίστεως.

ib. 11. δίωκε δικαιοσύνην, πίστιν, ἀγάπην, ὑπομονήν, πραϋπαθείαν.

2 Tim. ii. 1. ἐνδυναμοῦ ἐν τῇ
χάριτι τῇ ἐν Χρ. Ἰ.

ib. 3. συνκακοπάθησον ὡς καλὸς
στρατιώτης Χριστοῦ Ἰησοῦ.

ib. 5. ἐὰν δὲ καὶ ἀθλῇ τις οὐ
στεφανοῦται ἐὰν μὴ νομίμως ἀθλήσῃ.

iv. 7. τὸν καλὸν ἀγῶνα ἠγώνισ-
μαι, τὸν δρόμον τετέλεκα, τὴν πίστιν
τετήρηκα.

1 Tim. iii. 7. παγίδα τοῦ διαβόλου.

2 Tim. ii. 26. ἐκ τῆς τ. διαβόλου
παγίδος.

1 Tim. ii. 4. τοῦτο γὰρ καλὸν καὶ
ἀπόδεκτον ἐνώπιον τοῦ σωτῆρος ἡμῶν
θεοῦ, ὃς πάντας ἀνθρώπους θέλει
σωθῆναι κ. εἰς ἐπίγνωσιν ἀληθείας
ἐλθεῖν. εἰς γὰρ θεός, εἷς μεσίτης θεοῦ
κ. ἀνθρώπων, ἄνθρωπος Χρ. Ἰησοῦς, ὁ
δοὺς ἑαυτὸν ἀντίλυτρον ὑπὲρ πάντων.

2 Tim. ii. 25. μή ποτε δῴη αὐτοῖς
ὁ θεὸς μετάνοιαν εἰς ἐπίγνωσιν ἀληθείας.

Tit. ii. 13 f. προσδεχόμενοι τ.
μακαρίαν ἐλπίδα κ. ἐπιφάνειαν τ.
δόξης τ. μεγάλου θεοῦ καὶ σωτῆρος
ἡμῶν Ἰ. Χριστοῦ, ὃς ἔδωκεν ἑαυτὸν
ὑπὲρ ἡμῶν, ἵνα λυτρώσηται ἡμᾶς
ἀπὸ πάσης ἀνομίας κ. καθαρίσῃ ἑαυτῷ
λαόν….

iii. 5. ἔσωσεν ἡμᾶς διὰ λουτροῦ
παλινγενεσίας.

Ephesians.	Pastorals.

ii. 7 f. ἵνα ἐνδείξηται ἐν τ. αἰῶσιν τ. ἐπερχομένοις τὸ ὑπερβάλλον πλοῦτος τ. χάριτος αὐτοῦ ἐν χρηστότητι ἐφ᾽ ἡμᾶς ἐν Χρ. Ἰησοῦ. τῇ γὰρ χάριτί ἐστε σεσωσμένοι διὰ πίστεως· καὶ τοῦτο οὐκ ἐξ ὑμῶν, θεοῦ τὸ δῶρον· οὐκ ἐξ ἔργων, ἵνα μή τις καυχήσηται. αὐτοῦ γάρ ἐσμεν ποίημα, κτισθέντες ἐν Χρ. Ἰ. ἐπὶ ἔργοις ἀγαθοῖς οἷς προητοίμασεν ὁ θεὸς ἵνα ἐν αὐτοῖς περιπατήσωμεν.

ib. 12. ὅτι ἦτε τῷ καιρῷ ἐκείνῳ χωρὶς Χριστοῦ.

ib. 13. νυνὶ δὲ ἐν Χρ. Ἰησοῦ ὑμεῖς οἵ ποτε ὄντες μακράν....

ib. 1 ff. τ. ἁμαρτίαις, ἐν αἷς ποτὲ περιεπατήσατε κατὰ τὸν αἰῶνα τοῦ κόσμου τούτου...τ. υἱοῖς τῆς ἀπειθείας· ἐν οἷς καὶ ἡμεῖς πάντες ἀνεστράφημέν ποτε ἐν ταῖς ἐπιθυμίαις τ. σαρκὸς ἡμῶν.

ib. 1—4. ὑπομίμνησκε αὐτοὺς ἀρχαῖς ἐξουσίαις ὑποτάσσεσθαι πειθαρχεῖν, πρὸς πᾶν ἔργον ἀγαθὸν ἑτοίμους εἶναι, μηδένα βλασφημεῖν, ἀμάχους εἶναι ἐπιεικεῖς, πᾶσαν ἐνδεικνυμένους πραΰτητα πρὸς πάντας ἀνθρώπους. ἦμεν γάρ ποτε καὶ ἡμεῖς ἀνόητοι, ἀπειθεῖς, πλανώμενοι, δουλεύοντες ἐπιθυμίαις κ. ἡδοναῖς ποικίλαις....ὅτε δὲ ἡ χρηστότης κ. ἡ φιλανθρωπία ἐπεφάνη τ. σωτῆρος ἡμῶν θεοῦ, οὐκ ἐξ ἔργων τ. ἐν δικαιοσύνῃ ἃ ἐποιήσαμεν ἡμεῖς, ἀλλὰ κατὰ τὸ αὐτοῦ ἔλεος....

ii. 12. ἵνα ἀρνησάμενοι τ. ἀσέβειαν κ. τὰς κοσμικὰς ἐπιθυμίας σωφρόνως κ. δικαίως κ. εὐσεβῶς ζήσωμεν ἐν τῷ νῦν αἰῶνι.

iv. 22. κατὰ τὰς ἐπιθυμίας τῆς ἀπάτης.

2 Tim. iv. 3. κατὰ τὰς ἰδίας ἐπιθυμίας...κ. ἀπὸ τ. ἀληθείας τ. ἀκοὴν ἀποστρέψουσιν, ἐπὶ δὲ τ. μύθους ἐκτραπήσονται.

ib. 11. τοὺς δὲ εὐαγγελιστάς.

ib. 5. ἔργον ποίησον εὐαγγελιστοῦ.

i. 13. ἀκούσαντες τὸν λόγον τῆς ἀληθείας.

ii. 15. ὀρθοτομοῦντα τὸν λόγον τῆς ἀληθείας.

(c) ii. 19 ff. ἀλλὰ ἐστὲ συμπολῖται τ. ἁγίων καὶ οἰκεῖοι τοῦ θεοῦ, ἐποικοδομηθέντες ἐπὶ τῷ θεμελίῳ τῶν ἀποστόλων κ. προφητῶν, ὄντος ἀκρογωνιαίου αὐτοῦ Χριστοῦ Ἰησοῦ, ἐν ᾧ πᾶσα οἰκοδομὴ συναρμ. αὔξει εἰς ναὸν ἅγιον ἐν κυρίῳ, ἐν ᾧ καὶ ὑμεῖς συνοικοδομεῖσθε εἰς κατοικητήριον θεοῦ ἐν πνεύματι.

1 Tim. iii. 15. ἵνα εἰδῇς πῶς δεῖ ἐν οἴκῳ θεοῦ ἀναστρέφεσθαι, ἥτις ἐστὶν ἐκκλησία θεοῦ ζῶντος, στύλος καὶ ἑδραίωμα τῆς ἀληθείας.

2 Tim. ii. 19. ὁ μέντοι στερεὸς θεμέλιος τοῦ θεοῦ ἕστηκεν, ἔχων τὴν σφραγῖδα ταύτην Ἔγνω Κύριος τοὺς ὄντας αὐτοῦ, καὶ Ἀποστήτω ἀπὸ ἀδικίας πᾶς ὁ ὀνομάζων τὸ ὄνομα Κυρίου.

iii. 17. κ. τεθεμελιωμένοι.

iv. 3. σπουδάζοντες τηρεῖν τ. ἑνότητα τ. πνεύματος ἐν τῷ συνδέσμῳ τῆς εἰρήνης.

ib. 15. σπούδασον σεαυτὸν δόκιμον παραστῆσαι τῷ θεῷ.

Ephesians.

Pastorals.

ib. 2. μετὰ πάσης ταπεινοφροσύνης κ. πραΰτητος, μετὰ μακροθυμίας, ἀνεχόμενοι ἀλλήλων ἐν ἀγάπῃ.

ib. 22. δίωκε δὲ δικαιοσύνην, πίστιν, ἀγάπην, εἰρήνην μετὰ τ. ἐπικαλουμένων τ. κύριον ἐκ καθαρᾶς καρδίας.

v. 27. ἵνα παραστήσῃ αὐτὸς ἑαυτῷ ἔνδοξον τ. ἐκκλησίαν, μὴ ἔχουσαν σπίλον ἢ ῥυτίδα ἤ τι τῶν τοιούτων, ἀλλ᾽ ἵνα ᾖ ἁγία καὶ ἄμωμος.

ib. 24. ἀνεξίκακον, ἐν πραΰτητι παιδεύοντα τοὺς ἀντιδιατιθεμένους.

iii. 10. τῇ πίστει, τῇ μακροθυμίᾳ, τῇ ἀγάπῃ, τῇ ὑπομονῇ.

1 Tim. v. 14. τηρῆσαί σε τὴν ἐντολὴν ἄσπιλον ἀνεπίλημπτον μέχρι τῆς ἐπιφανείας τ. κυρίου ἡμῶν Ἰ. Χρ.

(*d*) i. 15. τὴν καθ᾽ ὑμᾶς πίστιν ἐν τῷ κυρίῳ Ἰησοῦ.

iii. 13. ἐν πίστει τῇ ἐν Χριστῷ Ἰησοῦ.

2 Tim. iii. 19. διὰ πίστεως τῆς ἐν Χριστῷ Ἰησοῦ.

(*e*) vi. 4. ἐκτρέφετε αὐτὰ ἐν παιδείᾳ κ. νουθεσίᾳ κυρίου.

iv. 11 f. τοὺς δὲ ποιμένας καὶ διδασκάλους, πρὸς τὸν καταρτισμὸν τ. ἁγίων εἰς ἔργον διακονίας.

ib. 16. ὠφέλιμος πρὸς διδασκαλίαν, πρὸς ἐλεγμόν, πρὸς ἐπανόρθωσιν, πρὸς παιδείαν τὴν ἐν δικαιοσύνῃ, ἵνα ἄρτιος ᾖ ὁ τοῦ θεοῦ ἄνθρωπος, πρὸς πᾶν ἔργον ἀγαθὸν ἐξηρτισμένος.

vi. 5 f. Οἱ δοῦλοι, ὑπακούετε τοῖς κατὰ σάρκα κυρίοις...ἐν ἁπλότητι τῆς καρδίας ὑμῶν...ἐκ ψυχῆς μετ᾽ εὐνοίας δουλεύοντες.

1 Tim. vi. 1. Ὅσοι εἰσὶν ὑπὸ ζυγὸν δοῦλοι, τοὺς ἰδίους δεσπότας πάσης τιμῆς ἀξίους ἡγείσθωσαν.

v. 21. ὑποτασσόμενοι ἀλλήλοις.

Tit. ii. 9. δούλους ἰδίοις δεσπόταις ὑποτάσσεσθαι ἐν πᾶσιν, εὐαρέστους εἶναι.

'In the Epistle to the Ephesians the great mystery of the Christian Society is set forth under two images which include the essential truths of all later speculations. It is the Body of Christ in virtue of the one life which it derives from *Him who is its Head,* and it is the Temple of God, so far as it is built up in various ages and of various elements on the foundations which Christ laid, and of which He is *the corner-stone.* In the Pastoral Epistles this teaching is realised in the outlines of a visible society.'

(*History of the Canon of the N. T.,* p. 32.)

IX.   RELATION TO OTHER APOSTOLIC WRITINGS.

(a)   The Epistle to the Ephesians and the First Epistle
of St Peter.

'The connexion, though close, does not lie on the surface.   It is
shewn more by identities of thought and similarity in the structure
of the two Epistles as wholes than by identities of phrase.'
(Hort, *Introductory Lecture to First Epistle of St Peter*, p. 5.)

'The truth is that in the First Epistle of St Peter many
thoughts are derived from the Epistle to the Ephesians, as others
are from that to the Romans ; but St Peter makes them fully his
own by the form into which he casts them, a form for the most part
unlike what we find in any Epistle of St Paul's.'
(id. *Prolegomena to Ephesians*, p. 169.)

[The 'parallelisms,' as here exhibited, are for the most part noted either
in Dr Westcott's Commentary itself or in Hort's notes on 1 Pet. i. 1—ii. 17
or in Prof. Abbott's Introduction, pp. xxiv ff., if not in all of these works.]

Ephesians.

i. 3.   Εὐλογητὸς ὁ θεὸς καὶ
πατὴρ τοῦ κυρίου ἡμῶν Ἰησοῦ
Χριστοῦ, ὁ εὐλογήσας ἡμᾶς ἐν
πάσῃ εὐλογίᾳ πνευματικῇ ἐν τοῖς
ἐπουρανίοις ἐν Χριστῷ, καθὼς ἐξελέξατο...πρὸ καταβολῆς κόσμου...
προορίσας ἡμᾶς εἰς υἱοθεσίαν διὰ Ἰ.
Χρ....εἰς ἔπαινον δόξης τ. χάριτος
αὐτοῦ...ἐν τῷ ἠγαπημένῳ, ἐν ᾧ ἔχομεν
τ. ἀπολύτρωσιν διὰ τ. αἵματος
αὐτοῦ....

ib. 12.   εἰς τὸ εἶναι ἡμᾶς εἰς ἔπαινον
δόξης αὐτοῦ...ἐν τ. χρ.

ib. 13.   ἐν ᾧ καὶ ὑμεῖς ἀκούσαντες
τ. λόγον τῆς ἀληθείας, τὸ εὐαγγέλιον
τῆς σωτηρίας ὑμῶν, ἐν ᾧ καὶ πιστεύσαντες ἐσφραγίσθητε τῷ πνεύματι

1 Peter.

i. 3.   Εὐλογητὸς ὁ θεὸς καὶ πατὴρ
τοῦ κυρίου ἡμῶν Ἰησοῦ Χριστοῦ,
ὁ κατὰ τὸ πολὺ αὐτοῦ ἔλεος ἀναγεννήσας ἡμᾶς εἰς ἐλπίδα ζῶσαν δι'
ἀναστάσεως Ἰησοῦ Χριστοῦ ἐκ
νεκρῶν, εἰς κληρονομίαν ἄφθαρτον
καὶ ἀμίαντον καὶ ἀμάραντον, τετηρη-
μένην ἐν οὐρανοῖς εἰς ὑμᾶς τοὺς
ἐν δυνάμει θεοῦ φρουρουμένους διὰ
πίστεως εἰς σωτηρίαν ἑτοίμην ἀποκαλυφθῆναι ἐν καιρῷ ἐσχάτῳ. ἐν ᾧ
ἀγαλλιᾶσθε, ὀλίγον...λυπηθέντες...ἵνα
τὸ δοκίμιον ὑμῶν τ. πίστεως...εὑρεθῇ
εἰς ἔπαινον καὶ δόξαν καὶ τιμὴν ἐν
ἀποκαλύψει Ἰησοῦ Χριστοῦ. ὃν οὐκ
ἰδόντες ἀγαπᾶτε, εἰς ὃν ἄρτι μὴ ὁρῶντες
πιστεύοντες δὲ ἀγαλλιᾶτε χαρᾷ ἀνεκ-
λαλήτῳ καὶ δεδοξασμένῃ, κομιζό-

Ephesians.

τῆς ἐπαγγελίας τῷ ἁγίῳ, ὅ ἐστιν
ἀρραβὼν τ. κληρονομίας ἡμῶν...εἰς
ἔπαινον τ. δόξης αὐτοῦ.

ib. 15. Διὰ τοῦτο....

ib. 18 f. εἰς τὸ εἰδέναι ὑμᾶς τίς ἐστιν
ἡ ἐλπὶς τῆς κλήσεως ὑμῶν, τίς ὁ
πλοῦτος τ. δόξης τ. κληρονομίας
αὐτοῦ ἐν τοῖς ἁγίοις, καὶ τί τὸ ὑπερβάλλον μέγεθος τῆς δυνάμεως αὐτοῦ
εἰς ἡμᾶς τ. πιστεύοντας κατὰ τ.
ἐνέργειαν τ. κράτους τ. ἰσχύος αὐτοῦ
ἣν ἐνήργηκεν ἐν τ. χριστῷ ἐγείρας
αὐτὸν ἐκ νεκρῶν καθίσας ἐν δεξιᾷ
αὐτοῦ ἐν τ. ἐπουρανίοις ὑπεράνω
πάσης ἀρχῆς καὶ ἐξουσίας καὶ
δυνάμεως...κ. πάντα ὑπέταξεν.

ii. 2 f. ἐν αἷς ποτὲ περιεπατήσατε
κατὰ τὸν αἰῶνα τ. κόσμου τούτου,
κατὰ τὸν ἄρχοντα τ. ἐξουσίας τ. ἀέρος,
τ. πνεύματος τ. νῦν ἐνεργοῦντος ἐν
τ. υἱοῖς τῆς ἀπειθείας· ἐν οἷς καὶ
ἡμεῖς πάντες ἀνεστράφημέν ποτε
ἐν ταῖς ἐπιθυμίαις τ. σαρκὸς ἡμῶν.

ii. 18. ὅτι δι' αὐτοῦ ἔχομεν τὴν
προσαγωγὴν οἱ ἀμφότεροι ἐν ἑνὶ
πνεύματι πρὸς τὸν πατέρα.

ib. 19 f. οἰκεῖοι τοῦ θεοῦ, ἐποικοδομηθέντες ἐπὶ τῷ θεμελίῳ...ὄντος
ἀκρογωνιαίου αὐτοῦ Χριστοῦ Ἰησοῦ,
ἐν ᾧ πᾶσα οἰκοδομὴ...αὔξει εἰς ναὸν
ἅγιον ἐν κυρίῳ, ἐν ᾧ καὶ ὑμεῖς
συνοικοδομεῖσθε εἰς κατοικητήριον τοῦ θεοῦ ἐν πνεύματι.

i. 20. καθίσας ἐν δεξιᾷ κ.τ.λ. (*v.*
supr.)

1 Peter.

μενοι τὸ τέλος τῆς πίστεως σωτηρίαν
ψυχῶν. Περὶ ἧς σωτηρίας ἐξεζή-
τησαν...προφῆται...οἷς ἀπεκαλύφθη
ὅτι οὐχ ἑαυτοῖς ὑμῖν δὲ διηκόνουν
αὐτά, ἃ νῦν ἀνηγγέλη ὑμῖν διὰ τῶν
εὐαγγελισαμένων ὑμᾶς πνεύματι
ἁγίῳ ἀποσταλέντι ἀπ' οὐρανοῦ.

ib. 13. Διὸ....

ib. 14. ὡς τέκνα ὑπακοῆς, μὴ
συνσχηματιζόμενοι ταῖς πρότερον ἐν
τῇ ἀγνοίᾳ ὑμῶν ἐπιθυμίαις, ἀλλὰ
κατὰ τὸν καλέσαντα ὑμᾶς ἅγιον καὶ
αὐτοὶ ἅγιοι ἐν πάσῃ ἀναστροφῇ
γενήθητε....

ib. 17. καὶ...ἐν φόβῳ...ἀναστρά-
φητε· εἰδότες ὅτι οὐ φθαρτοῖς...
ἐλυτρώθητε ἐκ τῆς ματαίας ὑμῶν
ἀναστροφῆς..., ἀλλὰ...αἵματι...
Χριστοῦ, προεγνωσμένου μὲν πρὸ
καταβολῆς κόσμου, φανερωθέντος
δὲ ἐπ' ἐσχάτου τῶν χρόνων δι' ὑμᾶς,
τ. δι' αὐτοῦ πιστοὺς εἰς θεὸν τὸν
ἐγείραντα αὐτὸν ἐκ νεκρῶν κ. δόξαν
αὐτῷ δόντα.

ii. 3. ἵνα ἐν αὐτῷ αὐξηθῆτε εἰς
σωτηρίαν....

ib. 4—6. πρὸς ὃν προσερχόμενοι,
λίθον ζῶντα...καὶ αὐτοὶ ὡς λίθοι
ζῶντες οἰκοδομεῖσθε οἶκος πνευματικὸς εἰς ἱεράτευμα ἅγιον.

iii. 18. ἵνα ἡμᾶς προσαγάγῃ τῷ
θεῷ.

ib. 22. ὅς ἐστιν ἐν δεξιᾷ θεοῦ
πορευθεὶς εἰς οὐρανὸν ὑποταγέντων
αὐτῷ ἀγγέλων καὶ ἐξουσιῶν καὶ
δυνάμεων.

Ephesians.	1 Peter.
iv. 2. μετὰ...ταπεινοφροσύνης.	ii. 1. Ἀποθέμενοι οὖν πᾶσαν κακίαν κ. πάντα δόλον κ. ὑποκρίσεις κ. φθόνους κ. καταλαλιάς.
ib. 22. ἀποθέσθαι ὑμᾶς...τ. παλαιὸν ἄνθρωπον.	
ib. 25. διὸ ἀποθέμενοι τὸ ψεῦδος.	iii. 18. ὁμόφρονες, συμπαθεῖς, φιλάδελφοι, εὔσπλαγχνοι, ταπεινόφρονες.
ib. 31 f. πᾶσα πικρία...καὶ θυμὸς καὶ ὀργὴ...καὶ βλασφημία ἀρθήτω ἀφ᾽ ὑμῶν σὺν πάσῃ κακίᾳ. γίνεσθε δὲ εἰς ἀλλήλους χρηστοί, εὔσπλαγχνοι.	
v. 22. Αἱ γυναῖκες τοῖς ἰδίοις ἀνδράσιν (ὑποτασσ.).	*ib.* 1. Ὁμοίως γυναῖκες ὑποτασσόμεναι τοῖς ἰδίοις ἀνδράσιν.
ib. 25. Οἱ ἄνδρες, ἀγαπᾶτε τ. γυναῖκας.	*ib.* 7. Οἱ ἄνδρες ὁμοίως...ὡς ἀσθενεστέρῳ σκεύει τῷ γυναικείῳ ἀπονέμοντες τιμήν.
vi. 5. Οἱ δοῦλοι, ὑπακούετε τοῖς κατὰ σάρκα κυρίοις μετὰ φόβου κ. τρόμου.	ii. 18. Οἱ οἰκέται ὑποτασσόμενοι ἐν παντὶ φόβῳ τοῖς δεσπόταις.

Words common, and peculiar, to Ephesians and 1 Peter.

ἀκρογωνιαῖος, εὔσπλαγχνος.

(b) Relation to Johannine Books.

(1) 'Ephesians' and the Apocalypse.

(a) The Church as the Bride of Christ.

Ephesians.	Apocalypse.
v. 25. Οἱ ἄνδρες ἀγαπᾶτε τὰς γυναῖκας, καθὼς καὶ ὁ χριστὸς ἠγάπησεν τὴν ἐκκλησίαν καὶ ἑαυτὸν παρέδωκεν ὑπὲρ αὐτῆς, ἵνα αὐτὴν ἁγιάσῃ καθαρίσας..., ἵνα παραστήσῃ...ἔνδοξον τὴν ἐκκλησίαν.	xix. 7. ὅτι ἦλθεν ὁ γάμος τοῦ ἀρνίου, καὶ ἡ γυνὴ αὐτοῦ ἡτοίμασεν ἑαυτήν, καὶ ἐδόθη αὐτῇ ἵνα περιβάληται βύσσινον λαμπρὸν καθαρόν· τὸ γὰρ βύσσινον τὰ δικαιώματα τῶν ἁγίων ἐστίν.
	xxi. 2. καὶ τὴν πόλιν τὴν ἁγίαν Ἰερουσαλὴμ καινὴν εἶδον...ἡτοιμασμένην ὡς νύμφην κεκοσμημένην τῷ ἀνδρὶ αὐτῆς.
ib. 29. ἐκτρέφει κ. θάλπει αὐτήν, καθὼς καὶ ὁ χριστὸς τὴν ἐκκλησίαν.	
ib. 32. τὸ μυστήριον τοῦτο μέγα ἐστίν, ἐγὼ δὲ λέγω εἰς Χριστὸν καὶ [εἰς] τὴν ἐκκλησίαν.	*ib.* 9. δείξω σοι τὴν νύμφην τὴν γυναῖκα τοῦ ἀρνίου.
	xxii. 17. καὶ τὸ πνεῦμα καὶ ἡ νύμφη λέγουσιν Ἔρχου.

(β)   The Apostles as foundation-stones of the Church.

Ephesians.   Apocalypse.

ii. 20.   ἐποικοδομηθέντες ἐπὶ τῷ
θεμελίῳ τῶν ἀποστόλων καὶ προφητῶν.

ib. 21.   ἐν ᾧ πᾶσα οἰκοδομὴ συναρμολογουμένη αὔξει εἰς ναὸν ἅγιον ἐν
κυρίῳ, ἐν ᾧ καὶ ὑμεῖς συνοικοδομεῖσθε
εἰς κατοικητήριον τοῦ θεοῦ ἐν
πνεύματι.

xxi. 14.   καὶ τὸ τεῖχος τῆς πόλεως
ἔχων θεμελίους δώδεκα καὶ ἐπ᾽ αὐτῶν
δώδεκα ὀνόματα τῶν δώδεκα ἀποστόλων τοῦ ἀρνίου.

ib. 10.   τὴν πόλιν ΄τ. ἁγίαν Ἰερουσαλήμ...ἔχουσαν τὴν δόξαν τοῦ θεοῦ.

ib. 22.   καὶ ναὸν οὐκ εἶδον ἐν αὐτῇ,
ὁ γὰρ κύριος, ὁ θεός, ὁ παντοκράτωρ,
ναὸς αὐτῆς ἐστίν.

xxii. 3.   κ. ὁ θρόνος τ. θεοῦ κ. τ.
ἀρνίου ἐν αὐτῇ ἔσται.

[It has been more than once observed that there is little in common
between St Paul's Epistle 'to the Ephesians' and the Epistle, in the
Apocalypse, addressed 'to the Angel of the Church in Ephesus.' Regarded
as a Pastoral, written to the Churches of the province of Asia generally,
the Pauline Epistle may naturally be compared rather with the Seven
Letters in the Apocalypse taken together.   The following are possible
parallelisms, suggested by such comparison.]

Ephesians.   Apocalypse i.—iii.

(Conflict with powers of evil,
steadfastness and victory.)

vi. 10—13.   ἐνδυναμοῦσθε ἐν κυρίῳ.
ἐνδύσασθε τ. πανοπλίαν τ. θεοῦ.
στῆναι πρὸς τ. μεθοδίας τ. διαβόλου.
ὅτι...ἡμῖν ἡ πάλη κ.τ.λ.
ἵνα δυνηθῆτε ἀντιστῆναι.

ib. 14.   στῆτε οὖν κ.τ.λ.

ib. 15.   ἀναλαβόντες τὸν θυρεὸν τ.
πίστεως.

ib. 18.   τὴν μάχαιραν τοῦ πνεύματος, ὅ ἐστιν ῥῆμα θεοῦ.

(Ephesus.)

ii. 3.   κ. ὑπομονὴν ἔχεις κ. ἐβάστασας
διὰ τὸ ὄνομά μου.

ib. 5.   τὴν ἀγάπην σου τ. πρώτην
ἀφῆκες.

ib. 7.   τῷ νικῶντι.

(Smyrna.)

ib. 10.   γίνου πιστὸς ἄχρι θανάτου.

ib. 11.   ὁ νικῶν.

(Pergamum.)

ib. 16.   κ. πολεμήσω μετ᾽ αὐτῶν ἐν
τῇ ῥομφαίᾳ τοῦ στόματός μου (cf.
i. 16).

ib. 17.   τῷ δὲ νικῶντι...ὄνομα καινόν.

(Faithfulness and love.)

i. 1. τ. ἁγίοις τοῖς οὖσιν [ἐν Ἐφέσῳ] καὶ πιστοῖς ἐν Χριστῷ Ἰησοῦ.

vi. 21. ὁ ἀγαπητὸς ἀδελφὸς καὶ πιστὸς διάκονος ἐν κυρίῳ.

ib. 23. ἀγάπη μετὰ πίστεως.

v. 25. καθὼς καὶ ὁ χριστὸς ἠγάπησεν τ. ἐκκλησίαν.

(The new Society and Temple of God.)

ii. 15. ἵνα τ. δύο κτίσῃ ἐν αὐτῷ εἰς ἕνα καινὸν ἄνθρωπον.

ib. 19. συμπολῖται τ. ἁγίων κ. οἰκεῖοι τ. θεοῦ.

ib. 20 f. ἐποικοδομηθέντες κ.τ.λ.... ναὸν ἅγιον.

(Eyes of the heart.)

i. 17. πεφωτισμένους τοὺς ὀφθαλμοὺς τ. καρδίας.

(Exaltation of the Ascended Christ and of His own with Him.)

ib. 20. κ. καθίσας ἐν δεξιᾷ αὐτοῦ ἐν τ. ἐπουρανίοις.

ii. 4 f. ὁ δὲ θεὸς...ἡμᾶς...συνεκάθισεν ἐν τ. ἐπουρανίοις ἐν Χριστῷ Ἰησοῦ.

(Thyatira.)

ii. 19. τὰ ἔργα σου κ. τ. ἀγάπην κ. τ. πίστιν κ. τ. διακονίαν κ. τ. ὑπομονήν σου.

ib. 26. ὁ νικῶν.

(Sardis.)

iii. 2. οὐ γὰρ εὕρηκά σου ἔργα πεπληρωμένα.

ib. 5. ὁ νικῶν.

(Philadelphia.)

ib. 7. ὁ νικῶν...ποιήσω αὐτὸν στύλον ἐν τῷ ναῷ τ. θεοῦ μου.

ib. 9. κ. γνῶσιν ὅτι ἠγάπησά σε.

ib. 12. γράψω ἐπ' αὐτὸν τὸ ὄνομα τ. θεοῦ μου κ. τ. ὄνομα τῆς πόλεως τοῦ θεοῦ μου, τ. καινῆς Ἰερουσαλήμ.

(Laodicea.)

ib. 18. ἐγχρῖσαι τοὺς ὀφθαλμούς σου ἵνα βλέπῃς.

ib. 21. ὁ νικῶν, δώσω αὐτῷ καθίσαι μετ' ἐμοῦ ἐν τῷ θρόνῳ μου, ὡς κἀγὼ ἐνίκησα καὶ ἐκάθισα μετὰ τοῦ πατρός μου ἐν τῷ θρόνῳ αὐτοῦ.

(2) 'Ephesians' and the Gospel of St John.

Ephesians.

i. 12 f. ἐν τῷ χριστῷ, ἐν ᾧ καὶ ὑμεῖς ἀκούσαντες τὸν λόγον τῆς ἀληθείας.

iv. 9 f. τὸ δὲ Ἀνέβη τί ἐστιν εἰ μὴ ὅτι καὶ κατέβη...; ὁ καταβὰς αὐτός ἐστιν καὶ ὁ ἀναβὰς κ.τ.λ.

St John.

i. 17. ἡ χάρις καὶ ἡ ἀλήθεια διὰ Ἰησοῦ Χριστοῦ ἐγένετο.

iii. 13. καὶ οὐδεὶς ἀναβέβηκεν εἰς τὸν οὐρανὸν εἰ μὴ ὁ ἐκ τοῦ οὐρανοῦ καταβάς.

Ephesians.

St John.

v. 11. κ. μὴ συνκοινωνεῖτε τ. ἔργοις τ. ἀκάρποις τ. σκότους, μᾶλλον δὲ καὶ ἐλέγχετε.

iii. 19. ἠγάπησαν οἱ ἄνθρωποι μᾶλλον τὸ σκότος ἢ τὸ φῶς.

ib. 13. τὰ δὲ πάντα ἐλεγχόμενα ὑπὸ τοῦ φωτὸς φανεροῦται, πᾶν γὰρ τὸ φανερούμενον φῶς ἐστίν (v. note ad loc.).

ib. 9. νῦν δὲ φῶς ἐν κυρίῳ.

ib. 20. πᾶς γὰρ ὁ φαῦλα πράσσων μισεῖ τὸ φῶς καὶ οὐκ ἔρχεται πρὸς τὸ φῶς ἵνα μὴ ἐλεγχθῇ τὰ ἔργα αὐτοῦ· ὁ δὲ ποιῶν τὴν ἀλήθειαν ἔρχεται πρὸς τὸ φῶς, ἵνα φανερωθῇ αὐτοῦ τὰ ἔργα ὅτι ἐν θεῷ ἐστὶν εἰργασμένα.

iv. 4, 7. ἐν σῶμα κ. ἐν πνεῦμα κ.τ.λ. ἐνὶ δὲ ἑκάστῳ ἡμῶν ἐδόθη ἡ χάρις κατὰ τὸ μέτρον τῆς δωρεᾶς τοῦ χριστοῦ.

ib. 34. ὃν γὰρ ἀπέστειλεν ὁ θεὸς τὰ ῥήματα τ. θεοῦ λαλεῖ, οὐ γὰρ ἐκ μέτρου δίδωσιν τὸ πνεῦμα (cp. vii. 39).

i. 6. τ. χάριτος αὐτοῦ, ἧς ἐχαρίτωσεν ἡμᾶς ἐν τῷ ἠγαπημένῳ.

ib. 35. ὁ πατὴρ ἀγαπᾷ τὸν υἱὸν καὶ πάντα δέδωκεν ἐν τῇ χειρὶ αὐτοῦ (cp. x. 17).

v. 6. διὰ ταῦτα γὰρ ἔρχεται ἡ ὀργὴ τοῦ θεοῦ ἐπὶ τοὺς υἱοὺς τῆς ἀπειθείας.

ib. 36. ὁ δὲ ἀπειθῶν τῷ υἱῷ οὐκ ὄψεται ζωήν, ἀλλ᾽ ἡ ὀργὴ τοῦ θεοῦ μένει ἐπ᾽ αὐτόν.

ii. 5, 6. κ. ὄντας ἡμᾶς νεκροὺς... συνεζωοποίησεν τῷ χριστῷ...καὶ συνήγειρεν.

v. 21. ὥσπερ γὰρ ὁ πατὴρ ἐγείρει τοὺς νεκροὺς καὶ ζωοποιεῖ, οὕτως καὶ ὁ υἱὸς οὓς θέλει ζωοποιεῖ.

ib. 25. ἔρχεται ὥρα καὶ νῦν ἐστὶν ὅτε οἱ νεκροὶ ἀκούσουσιν τ. φωνῆς τ. υἱοῦ τ. θεοῦ καὶ οἱ ἀκούσαντες ζήσουσιν.

iv. 4 f. ἐν σῶμα...καθὼς...ἐκλήθητε ἐν μιᾷ ἐλπίδι τῆς κλήσεως ὑμῶν· εἷς κύριος, μία πίστις.

x. 16. καὶ ἄλλα πρόβατα ἔχω ἃ οὐκ ἔστιν ἐκ τῆς αὐλῆς ταύτης· κἀ‑κεῖνα δεῖ με ἀγαγεῖν, καὶ τῆς φωνῆς μου ἀκούσουσιν, καὶ γενήσονται μία ποίμνη, εἷς ποιμήν.

xvii. 20. ἵνα πάντες ἓν ὦσιν.

(3) 'Ephesians' and the Epistles of St John.

Ephesians.

1 John.

v. 8 f. ἦτε γάρ ποτε σκότος, νῦν δὲ φῶς ἐν κυρίῳ· ὡς τέκνα φωτὸς περιπατεῖτε.

iv. 5. ἀληθεύοντες...ἐν ἀγάπῃ.

i. 6. ἐὰν εἴπωμεν ὅτι κοινωνίαν ἔχομεν μετ᾽ αὐτοῦ καὶ ἐν τῷ σκότει περιπατῶμεν, ψευδόμεθα καὶ οὐ ποιοῦμεν τὴν ἀλήθειαν· ἐὰν δὲ ἐν τῷ φωτὶ περιπατῶμεν ὡς αὐτὸς ἔστιν ἐν τῷ φωτί....

Ephesians.

1 John.

v. 26. ἵνα αὐτὴν ἁγιάσῃ καθαρίσας τῷ λουτρῷ.

i. 7. ἐν ᾧ ἔχομεν τ. ἀπολύτρωσιν διὰ τοῦ αἵματος αὐτοῦ, τὴν ἄφεσιν τ. παραπτωμάτων.

i. 9. ἵνα ἀφῇ ἡμῖν τὰς ἁμαρτίας καὶ καθαρίσῃ ἡμᾶς ἀπὸ πάσης ἀδικίας (cp. v. 7, τὸ αἷμα Ἰ....καθαρίζει ἡμᾶς ἀπὸ πάσης ἁμαρτίας).

iv. 25. ἀποθέμενοι τὸ ψεῦδος λαλεῖτε ἀλήθειαν.

ii. 21. πᾶν ψεῦδος ἐκ τῆς ἀληθείας οὐκ ἔστιν.

v. 8. τέκνα φωτός (v. supra).

iii. 2. ἀγαπητοί, νῦν τέκνα θεοῦ ἐσμέν (cp. i. 5, ὁ θεὸς φῶς ἐστίν).

ib. 6. μηδεὶς ὑμᾶς ἀπατάτω.

ib. 9. ὁ καρπὸς τοῦ φωτὸς ἐν πάσῃ ἀγαθωσύνῃ καὶ δικαιοσύνῃ κ. ἀληθείᾳ.

ib. 13. τὰ...πάντα...ὑπὸ τοῦ φωτὸς φανεροῦται.

ib. 7 f. τεκνία, μηδεὶς πλανάτω ὑμᾶς· ὁ ποιῶν δικαιοσύνην δίκαιός ἐστιν· ὁ ποιῶν τ. ἁμαρτίαν ἐκ τ. διαβόλου ἐστίν.

ib. 10. ἐν τούτῳ φανερά ἐστιν τὰ τέκνα τοῦ θεοῦ καὶ τὰ τέκνα τ. διαβόλου· πᾶς ὁ μὴ ποιῶν τὴν δικαιοσύνην οὐκ ἔστιν ἐκ τοῦ θεοῦ.

ii. 3. κ. ἦμεθα τέκνα φύσει ὀργῆς.

v. 10. δοκιμάζοντες τί ἐστιν εὐάρεστον τῷ κυρίῳ (cp. Rom. xii. 2).

iv. 1. δοκιμάζετε τὰ πνεύματα εἰ ἐκ τοῦ θεοῦ ἐστίν.

ii. 2. ἐν αἷς ποτὲ περιεπατήσατε κατὰ τὸν αἰῶνα τοῦ κόσμου τούτου, κατὰ τὸν ἄρχοντα τ. ἐξουσίας τ. ἀέρος, τ. πνεύματος τοῦ νῦν ἐνεργοῦντος ἐν τ. υἱοῖς τῆς ἀπειθίας.

iv. 13. πρὸς τ. μεθοδίαν τῆς πλάνης.

ib. 4 ff. ὅτι μείζων ἐστὶν ὁ ἐν ὑμῖν ἢ ὁ ἐν τῷ κόσμῳ· αὐτοὶ ἐκ τ. κόσμου εἰσίν.

ἡμεῖς ἐκ τοῦ θεοῦ ἐσμέν.

γινώσκομεν τὸ πνεῦμα τῆς ἀληθείας κ. τὸ πνεῦμα τῆς πλάνης.

2 John.

ib. 15. ἀληθεύοντες ἐν ἀγάπῃ.

v. 2. περιπατεῖτε ἐν ἀγάπῃ.

v. 3. ἐν ἀληθείᾳ καὶ ἀγάπῃ.

v. 6. κ. αὕτη ἐστὶν ἡ ἀγάπη ἵνα περιπατῶμεν κατὰ τ. ἐντολὰς αὐτοῦ· αὕτη ἡ ἐντολή ἐστιν...ἵνα ἐν αὐτῇ περιπατῆτε.

'St Paul had brought home to believers the divine majesty of the glorified Christ: St John laid open the unchanged majesty of "Jesus Christ come in the flesh".'

(*Introduction to Gospel of St John*, p. xv.)

X. HISTORIC FACTS OF THE GOSPEL TO WHICH REFERENCE IS MADE IN 'EPHESIANS.'

The Incarnation and life of Christ on earth.

ii. 15. 'having abolished the enmity...the law of commandments in ordinances...*in His flesh,*' i.e. under the conditions of our mortal life.

The Passion.

i. 7. 'in Whom we have our redemption through His blood (διὰ τοῦ αἵματος αὐτοῦ).'

ii. 13. 'were made near (ἐγενήθητε ἐγγὺς) in the blood of the Christ'—the reference being "to the—redemption of the Gentiles once for all accomplished by Christ's— Passion."

ib. 16. 'and reconcile them...to God *through the cross* (διὰ τοῦ σταυροῦ).'

v. 2. 'even as Christ also loved you and gave Himself up (παρέδωκεν ἑαυτὸν) for us.'

ib. 25. 'even as Christ loved the Church and gave Himself up for it.'

The Descent into Hades is probably [included in that] which is described in the words κατέβη εἰς τὰ κατώτερα τῆς γῆς (iv. 9) and ὁ καταβάς (v. 10) [*v.* notes *ad loc.*].

The Resurrection.

i. 19, 20. 'according to the working of the might of His strength, which He wrought in the Christ, *when He raised Him from the dead*' (ἐγείρας αὐτὸν ἐκ νεκρῶν).

ii. 6. 'and *raised us up with* Him (συνήγειρεν).'

The Ascension.

i. 20.   'and made Him to sit at His right hand in the heavenly order.'

iv. 8, 10.   'When He ascended up on high (ἀναβὰς εἰς ὕψος)... Now this He ascended (τὸ δέ 'Ανέβη)...He that descended He Himself is also He that ascended far above all the Heavens.'

The absence from the Epistle of any clear reference to the 'Return' is to be noted. (But cf. iv. 30 εἰς ἡμέραν ἀπολυτρώσεως and notes on i. 14; also i. 18.)

The descent of the Holy Spirit at Pentecost as a special gift to the Church is implied in i. 13 f., 'in Whom ye also, having heard the word of the truth, the gospel of your salvation,—in Whom, having also believed, ye were sealed with the Spirit of promise, the Holy Spirit, which is an earnest of our inheritance' [*v. not. ad loc.*].

With iv. 11 'pastors (ποιμένας) and teachers,' the only place [in the N.T.] in which ποιμήν is the definite title of an office [*v. not. ad loc.*] may be compared Jo. xxi. 16 'He saith unto him, Tend (ποίμαινε) my sheep.'

XI. CHARACTERISTICS.

'In this Epistle St Paul still dwells on the same class of truths as in the Epistle to the Colossians. Only whereas in the Colossians he combats error directly, he here combats it indirectly; whereas there he is special, distinct, personal, here he speaks broadly and generally.' (Lightfoot, *Biblical Essays*, p. 395.)

'Besides this, St Paul has given to his teaching a new centre. In this Epistle it revolves about the doctrine of the Church. The same truths which in the Epistle to the Colossians are advanced to combat a peculiar phase of false doctrine, have here a place as leading up to the doctrine of the Church. Compare, for example, the treatment of the subject of Christ the Logos in Col. i. 1, ii. 9 with Eph. i. 22, or of the law of ordinances in Col. ii. 14 with Eph. ii. 14, 15, or again the practical lessons of the relations of husbands and wives in Col. iii. 18, 19 with Eph. v. 25 f., 32. The propriety of this new centre of teaching is obvious when we remember that it is addressed not in a special letter to an individual Church, but in an encyclical to several Churches.' (*id. ib.*)

The Epistle to the Ephesians 'conducts us from the two peoples who are so prominent in the Epistle to the Romans to the one people, or one man, which in that Epistle is nowhere explicitly set forth, though it is implied in its teachings and aspirations..., but now in the Epistle to the Ephesians is to be brought into clear prominence.' (Hort, *Prolegomena*, p. 179.)

'This idea—of the unity of Christians as forming a single society with Christ for its invisible Head—which in different forms dominates the whole Epistle, was the natural outflow of the Apostle's mind at this time, as determined by the course of outward and inward history on the basis of his primary faith. It was needed to be set forth for the completion of his Gospel. On the other

hand it was equally needed for the instruction of the no longer
infant churches of Western Asia Minor.' (*id. ib.*)

In reading the Epistle we all feel the grandeur of the vision,
which it opens, of the unity of Creation.

Experience more and more shews us that we were born to strive
for it. It is brought ever nearer.

St Paul enforces this truth when he tells of the 'mystery'
entrusted to him—the incorporation of the Gentiles in the Body of
Christ.

Having set forth the truth—unsearchable, inexhaustible, and
extending 'unto all the ages of the ages,' he goes on to shew that it
yet finds its application in the commonest virtues.

'Walk worthily,' he says, 'of the calling wherewith ye are called.'

The consummation depends on the co-operation of all to whom
the truth has been made known.

'There is one God and Father of all, Who is over all and through
all and in all.'

Here is our sufficient, and unfailing hope.

'But to each of us'—here is our strength and our responsibility
—'was given'—not 'will be' in the future, but '*was*' given—the
grace which we severally need for the fulfilment of our specific
functions.

While we keep in mind the whole, we must do our part.

And our part is determined for us, that we may contribute to
the great whole.

Our grace—the Divine help accorded us—is proportional to the
place which our part has in the great unity.

The unity of life, of all life, nay of all being, of the seen and the
unseen : and, specially the fellowship of man with men and of man
with God.

The Epistle to the Ephesians...in the fewest words commends
this aspect of Creation to us, and it is...of intense practical
significance.

If we believe in the unity shewn under three different aspects in
Eph. ii. 14—18, hope and confidence will return, when we look on
the unfathomable sadnesses of life ; if we believe that for each of us
a work is prepared which we can do, if we surrender ourselves to
God (ii. 10), we shall be saved from the restless anxiety of
self-chosen plans ; if we believe that all the details of ordinary life
have a spiritual side and opportunities of service (v. 20 f.: cf.
Col. iii. 17), we shall be enabled perhaps to preach our Gospel a
little more effectually in life.

[Part of the foregoing is taken from a letter, published in the
'Life and Letters' of Bishop Westcott, vol. ii. p. 232, the rest from
notes for an unpublished sermon.]

'The forces of Nature, so to speak, are revealed to us as
gathered together and crowned in man, and the diversities of men
as gathered together and crowned in the Son of Man; and so we
are encouraged to look forward to the end, to a unity of which
every imaginary unity on earth is a phantom or a symbol, when the
will of the Father shall be accomplished and He shall *sum up all
things in Christ*—all things and not simply all persons—both *the
things in the heavens and the things upon the earth* (Eph. i. 10).'
(*Christus Consummator*, p. 103.)

'Men, so to speak, furnish the manifold elements through which
(in the language of St Paul) a body of Christ (Eph. i. 23) is shaped ;
just as the world furnishes the elements through which man himself
finds expression for his character.' (*ib.* p. 106.)

'In the Epistle to the Ephesians St Paul lays open a vision of
the spiritual origins and influences and issues of things temporal,
and confirms the truth which lies in the bold surmise of the poet
that earth is in some sense a shadow of heaven.

'Now he sees in the fabric of the material Temple with its "wall
of partition" a figure of the state of the world before the Advent,
and then passes to the contemplation of its living antitype, built on
the foundation of apostles and prophets with Christ for its head

corner-stone. Now he traces in the organisation of the natural body the pattern of a glorious society fitly framed together by the ministries of every part, and guided by the animating energy of a Divine Head.

'Now he shews how through the experience of the Church on earth the manifold wisdom of God is made known to the heavenly hierarchy. Now he declares that marriage, in which the distinctive gifts and graces of divided humanity are brought together in harmonious fellowship is a sign, a sacrament in his own language, of that perfect union in which the Incarnate Word takes to Himself His Bride, the firstfruits of creation.' (*The Incarnation and Common Life*, p. 161.)

'The concluding appeal or peroration (vi. 10—20), breathing a very lofty and eloquent tone, contains a carefully-wrought account of the warfare between the Church and the powers of darkness and evil which brood over the world. It is to be observed that here as generally throughout the Apostolic writings, the imagery is borrowed from the poetical books of the Old Testament. Most of it may be found in the book of Isaiah. The warfare described is not the battle of the individual Christian for his own salvation, but the greater conflict in which Christ leads His forces against the enemy, the war of the Gospel against the powers which keep mankind in slavery. But individual Christians are the soldiers in this war, and the armour mentioned is such as individual Christians must put on.

'The sentences with which the Epistle closes,—the mention and commendation of the messenger who was to carry it, and the usual benedictory prayer,—remind us that this was a *bonâ fide* pastoral letter, addressed to Christians, who looked up to St Paul as their teacher.' (Llewelyn Davies, *Introduction to the Ephesians*, p. 25.)

XII. PLAN OF THE EPISTLE.

A. THE CHRISTIAN DISPENSATION.

THE UNITY AND UNIVERSALITY OF THE CHURCH, ETERNAL FACTS NOW AT LAST REVEALED (i.—iii.).

SALUTATION (i. 1, 2).

I. A HYMN OF PRAISE TO GOD FOR THE REDEMPTION AND CONSUMMATION OF THINGS CREATED IN CHRIST (i. 3—14).

1. The work of the Divine love: the fulness of the Divine blessing realised 'in Christ' (v. 3).

2. The bestowal of the blessing (4—14)

(a) wrought out before time in the eternal order according to the Divine idea (4—6),

(b) and realised in time in spite of man's fall (7—14).

II. THANKSGIVING FOR FAITH REALISED: PRAYER FOR DEEPER KNOWLEDGE: GENERAL EXPOSITION OF THE WORK OF CHRIST FOR MEN (i. 15—ii. 22).

1. Thanksgiving for the faith of the Ephesians (i. 15, 16 a).

2. Prayer for their fuller enlightenment (i. 16 b—21).

3. The work of God for men in Christ,—overcoming personal disqualifications (i. 22—ii. 10).

4. Union of Jews and Gentiles in one Divine Body (ii. 11—22).

III. THE GRANDEUR OF THE REVELATION MADE TO ST PAUL. PRAYER FOR FULLER UNDERSTANDING IN THOSE WHO RECEIVE IT (iii.)

1. Revelation to St Paul of the central truth, or 'mystery,' of the universality of the Gospel (1—13).

2. Prayer that those who receive it may be enabled to apprehend its lessons (14—19).

Doxology (20, 21).

B. THE CHRISTIAN LIFE (iv. 1—vi. 20).

I. THE GROUND, THE GROWTH, THE CHARACTER OF THE CHRISTIAN LIFE (iv. 1—24).

1. The correspondence of life and faith (1—3).

2. The unity and harmonious growth of the Christian Society, that Body of which Christ is the Head (4—16).

3. Contrast of the old life and the new (17—24):

(a) the old life (17—19),

(b) the new life (20—24).

II. THE OUTWARD MANIFESTATION OF THE CHRISTIAN LIFE, PERSONAL AND SOCIAL (iv. 25—vi. 9).

1. Special features in the Christian character (iv. 25—v. 14): truth (v. 25), control of anger (26 f.), honest labour (28), good language (29 f.), tenderheartedness (32), lovingkindness (v. 1 f.), as opposed to impure and selfish indulgence. The Christian life the life of a child of light (7—14).

2. Cardinal social relationships (v. 15—vi. 9).

(a) Social conduct and temper in general (15—21).

(b) Wives and husbands (22—33).

(c) Children and parents (vi. 1—4).

(d) Servants and masters (5—9).

III. THE CHRISTIAN WARFARE (vi. 10—20).

EPILOGUE.

Personal message (vi. 21, 22).
Benediction (23, 24).

ΠΡΟΣ ΕΦΕΣΙΟΥΣ

THE CHRISTIAN DISPENSATION

A. THE UNITY AND UNIVERSALITY OF THE CHURCH, ETERNAL
FACTS NOW AT LAST REVEALED (i.—iii.).

SALUTATION: i. 1, 2.

I. A HYMN OF PRAISE TO GOD FOR THE REDEMPTION AND
CONSUMMATION OF THINGS CREATED IN CHRIST (i. 3—14).

II. THANKSGIVING FOR FAITH REALISED: PRAYER FOR DEEPER
KNOWLEDGE: GENERAL EXPOSITION OF THE WORK OF CHRIST
FOR MEN (i. 15—ii. 22).

III. THE GRANDEUR OF THE REVELATION MADE TO ST PAUL.
PRAYER FOR FULLER UNDERSTANDING IN THOSE WHO
RECEIVE IT (iii.).

ΠΡΟΣ ΕΦΕΣΙΟΥΣ

*ΠΑΥΛΟΣ ΑΠΟΣΤΟΛΟΣ Χριστοῦ Ἰησοῦ διὰ θελή-
ματος θεοῦ τοῖς ἁγίοις τοῖς οὖσιν* [*ἐν Ἐφέσῳ*] *καὶ*

1 om. ἐν Ἐφέσῳ ℵ*B 67** codd vet ap Bas.

I, 2. SALUTATION.

[1] *Paul, an apostle of Christ
Jesus through the will of* GOD, *to
the saints which are at Ephesus and
faithful in Christ Jesus:* [2] *Grace
to you and peace from* GOD *our
Father and the Lord Jesus Christ.*

1. Παῦλος] In the cognate letters
to the Colossians and Philemon, St
Paul joins with himself 'Timothy our
brother.' The Epistles to the Romans,
Galatians and the Pastoral Epistles
are written in his own name alone.

ἀπόστολος Χ. Ἰ.] Compare Tit. i. 1
δοῦλος θεοῦ ἀπόστολος δὲ Ἰ. Χ.; Philemon 1 δέσμιος Χ. Ἰ. The title marks
the writer as the accredited envoy of
his Lord : comp. John xvii. 18.

διὰ θελ. θεοῦ] 1 Cor. i. 1; 2 Cor.
i. 1; Col. i. 1. The thought is ex-
panded in Gal. i. 1 and Rom. i. 1, 5,
which form the best commentary on
the phrase, though the controversial
colouring present there has no place
here. Conscious dependence upon
GOD Who had called him is the source
and strength of St Paul's ministry.
Self is lost in GOD (comp. *c.* ii. 10). *Per
voluntatem Dei,* subauditur Patris,
non meis meritis (Primas.). The original Divine call was the foundation
for the Apostle's separation for his
special work: Acts xiii. 2.

The thought finds a somewhat different expression in 1 Tim. i. 1.

Man's freedom lies in the acceptance
of GOD's will as his will. The Apostle
feels GOD's purpose for him and
welcomes it. All he does is (in purpose) the fulfilment of the will of
GOD.

τοῖς ἁγίοις...Ἰησοῦ] St Paul addresses not the organised body 'the
[local] Church' (as in writing to the
Thessalonians and Corinthians, comp.
Acts xx. 17; Apoc. ii. 1 &c.) or
local 'churches' (as in writing to the
Galatians), but 'the saints' (as in the
Epistles to the Romans, Philippians,
Colossians), using the title which was
common to all Christians. The word
suggests the idea of a Catholic Church,
in which 'the saints and faithful'
scattered throughout the world were
united. Even in this slight trait we
can recognise the influence of the
conception of the empire on the
Apostle. Compare *c.* iii. 18.

The clause τοῖς οὖσιν ἐν Ἐφέσῳ is
intercalated naturally in the fundamental phrase τοῖς ἁγίοις καὶ πιστοῖς
to the saints and faithful. The corresponding enlargement in Col. i. 2
τοῖς ἐν Κολοσσαῖς ἁγίοις καὶ πιστοῖς
ἀδελφοῖς brings out the meaning
clearly. The words ἐν Χ. Ἰ. go with
the whole sentence : 'being as you
are in Christ Jesus': incorporated
in Him and living by His life. The
words are not to be taken here or in

πιστοῖς ἐν Χριστῷ Ἰησοῦ· ²χάρις ὑμῖν καὶ εἰρήνη ἀπὸ
θεοῦ πατρὸς ἡμῶν καὶ κυρίου Ἰησοῦ Χριστοῦ.

1 Cor. iv. 17 with πιστός. Comp. c. vi.
21 ; and Addit. Note on ἐν Χριστῷ.
For the sense of ἅγιος see 1 John
ii. 20 and for the absolute use of
πιστός see Acts x. 45 ; 1 Tim. iv. 3,
12 ; v. 16 ; vi. 2 ; Tit. i. 6.

The three characteristics *saints,*
faithful, in Christ Jesus, give a
complete and harmonious view of
those to whom St Paul writes. He
addresses men who are consecrated
to GOD in a Divine Society (*saints*),
who are inspired by a personal devotion towards Him (*faithful*), who are
in Him in Whom the Church finds its
unity and life (*c.* iv. 16). Thus the order
saints, faithful, is seen to be perfectly
natural. The two thoughts are complementary : GOD's will, man's answer.
So the thought of the social consecration to GOD precedes the thought of
the continuous individual faith by
which the members of the body keep
their place in it.

The word πιστοῖς may mean either
(1) 'trustworthy,' or (2) 'believing.'
The rendering 'faithful' contains elements of both and best represents the
meaning here.

The fundamental idea of ἅγιος is
consecration to GOD. Consecration to
GOD implies either in purpose or in
attainment conformity to His will.

The word is found of Christians in
Acts xxvi. 10 (St Paul) ; in all St Paul's
Epistles except that to the Galatians ;
in Hebrews, Jude, Apocalypse ; but
it is not found in the Epistles of
St James, St Peter and St John.

2. χάρις καὶ εἰρήνη] The uniform
salutation of St Paul in his Epistles
to Churches. The words of common
courtesy become words of solemn
blessing. Christ Himself blesses
through the believer.

For εἰρήνη see Phil. iv. 7 ; John xiv.
27 ; Col. iii. 15.

ἀπὸ θεοῦ πατρὸς ἡμῶν...] The ἡμῶν
is omitted in the salutations 2 Thess.

i. 2 ; 1 Tim. i. 2 ; 2 Tim. i. 2 ; Tit. i. 4 ;
and in the corresponding phrase *c.* vi.
23. For the different shade of thought
compare the use of ὁ πατήρ and ὁ
πατήρ μου in St John. (Addit. Note
on 1 John i. 2.)

καὶ κ. Ἰ. Χ.] The Lord Jesus Christ
is united with the Father in all the
salutations of St Paul. The language
in 1 Thess. i. 1, 2 Thess. i. 1—2 and
Tit. i. 4 is specially worthy of notice.

Primasius adds justly : cum ab
utroque gratia optatur, unum (ἕν John
x. 30) esse monstrantur.

I. A HYMN OF PRAISE TO GOD FOR
THE REDEMPTION AND CONSUMMATION
OF THINGS CREATED IN CHRIST (i. 3—
14).

The whole passage is a Psalm of
praise for the redemption and consummation of created things, fulfilled
in Christ through the Spirit according
to the eternal purpose of GOD.

This fulfilment is contemplated
specially in the relation of believers
to Christ, chosen in Him, redeemed,
enlightened, sealed.

That which has been done already
is the pledge of that which shall be.

The general sequence of thought is
clear. The work of the Divine love is
summarily characterised in *v.* 3 ; and
then it is analysed in detail, as it was
wrought beyond time in the eternal
order (*vv.* 4—6), and then historically
realised in time in the experience of
believers, both Jews and Gentiles
(*vv.* 7—14).

From first to last the fulness of the
Divine blessing is shewn to be realised
'in Christ' (*v.* 3).

In Him GOD chose us (*v.* 4).

In the Beloved He graced us (*v.* 6).

In Him we have our redemption
(*v.* 7) ; even as GOD purposed in Him
to sum up all things in the Christ
(*v.* 10).

In Him the faithful of Israel were
made a Divine heritage (*v.* 11).

³Εὐλογητὸς ὁ θεὸς καὶ πατὴρ τοῦ κυρίου ἡμῶν

In Him the Gentiles found a place (*v.* 13). In Him they were sealed by the Spirit (*v.* 13), the pledge of a larger hope (*v.* 14). The rhythmical structure of the passage will be apparent, if it is arranged according to the succession of the principal clauses ; and at the same time some obscurities of construction will be removed when attention is fixed on the dominant finite verbs (as in Phil. ii. 6—11).

3 Εὐλογητὸς ὁ θεὸς καὶ πατὴρ τοῦ κυρίου ἡμῶν Ἰησοῦ Χριστοῦ,
        ὁ εὐλογήσας ἡμᾶς ἐν πάσῃ εὐλογίᾳ πνευματικῇ
            ἐν τοῖς ἐπουρανίοις
                ἐν Χριστῷ,
4 καθὼς ἐξελέξατο ἡμᾶς ἐν αὐτῷ πρὸ καταβολῆς κόσμου,
        εἶναι ἡμᾶς ἁγίους καὶ ἀμώμους κατενώπιον αὐτοῦ ἐν ἀγάπῃ,
5 προορίσας ἡμᾶς εἰς υἱοθεσίαν διὰ Ἰησοῦ Χριστοῦ εἰς αὐτόν,
        κατὰ τὴν εὐδοκίαν τοῦ θελήματος αὐτοῦ,
6   εἰς ἔπαινον δόξης τῆς χάριτος αὐτοῦ
        ἧς ἐχαρίτωσεν ἡμᾶς ἐν τῷ ἠγαπημένῳ,
7 ἐν ᾧ ἔχομεν τὴν ἀπολύτρωσιν διὰ τοῦ αἵματος αὐτοῦ,
        τὴν ἄφεσιν τῶν παραπτωμάτων,
            κατὰ τὸ πλοῦτος τῆς χάριτος αὐτοῦ
8 ἧς ἐπερίσσευσεν εἰς ἡμᾶς ἐν πάσῃ σοφίᾳ καὶ φρονήσει
9   γνωρίσας ἡμῖν τὸ μυστήριον τοῦ θελήματος αὐτοῦ,
            κατὰ τὴν εὐδοκίαν αὐτοῦ ἣν προέθετο ἐν αὐτῷ
10   εἰς οἰκονομίαν τοῦ πληρώματος τῶν καιρῶν,
        ἀνακεφαλαιώσασθαι τὰ πάντα ἐν τῷ χριστῷ,
            τὰ ἐπὶ τοῖς οὐρανοῖς καὶ
                τὰ ἐπὶ τῆς γῆς·
11 ἐν αὐτῷ, ἐν ᾧ καὶ ἐκληρώθημεν
        προορισθέντες
            κατὰ πρόθεσιν τοῦ τὰ πάντα ἐνεργοῦντος
            κατὰ τὴν βουλὴν τοῦ θελήματος αὐτοῦ,
12   εἰς τὸ εἶναι ἡμᾶς εἰς ἔπαινον δόξης αὐτοῦ
            τοὺς προηλπικότας ἐν τῷ χριστῷ·
13 ἐν ᾧ καὶ ὑμεῖς ἀκούσαντες τὸν λόγον τῆς ἀληθείας,
        τὸ εὐαγγέλιον τῆς σωτηρίας ὑμῶν,
    ἐν ᾧ καὶ πιστεύσαντες, ἐσφραγίσθητε τῷ πνεύματι τ. ἐπαγγελίας τ. ἁγίῳ,
14   ὅ ἐστιν ἀρραβὼν τῆς κληρονομίας ἡμῶν,
            εἰς ἀπολύτρωσιν τῆς περιποιήσεως,
                εἰς ἔπαινον τῆς δόξης αὐτοῦ.

(1) The work of the divine love : the blessing of Him Who blessed (*v.* 3).

Blessed be the GOD *and Father of our Lord Jesus Christ, Who blessed us in all spiritual blessing in the heavenly* order *in Christ.*

3. The verse is man's adoring response to GOD for the manifestation of His love.

Εὐλογ....Ἰ. Χ.] The whole phrase is found again in 1 Pet. i. 3, in thanksgiving for the gift of new birth, together with the prospect of an eternal inheritance ; and in 2 Cor. i. 3 in thanksgiving for effective consolation in distress.

The word εὐλογητός expresses the claim to be blessed as of right. In

Ἰησοῦ Χριστοῦ, ὁ εὐλογήσας ἡμᾶς ἐν πάσῃ εὐλογίᾳ

this respect it stands in contrast with εὐλογημένος, which is used of a person who has been visited with blessing (Lk. i. (28), 42 [contrast i. 68]; xiii. 35; xix. 38, &c.; in John xii. 13 D₁ reads εὐλογητός). The distinction is recognised by Philo de migr. Abr. 19. Εὐλογητός is used in the N. T. of GOD only eight times (St Mk xiv. 61 ὁ υἱὸς τοῦ εὐλογητοῦ, St Lk., St Paul, 1 Pet.). In the LXX. it is used of men, but not absolutely (Gen. xxvi. 29 ὑπὸ κυρίου; Deut. vii. 14; Ruth ii. 20; 1 Sam. xv. 13, &c.).

Compare Ezra Abbot, Essays p. 410; Hort on 1 Pet. i. 3.

It is uncertain whether εἴη or ἐστίν is to be supplied with εὐλογητός— whether the phrase is a wish or an affirmation. The other instances in the N. T. give no clear decision. The examples in 2 Cor. i. 3 and 1 Pet. i. 3 are exactly parallel. Luke i. 68 suggests 'be' by the following ὅτι. Rom. ix. 5 is uncertain. The affirmative sense is definitely expressed in Rom. i. 25 (ὅς ἐστιν εὐλ.), and 2 Cor. xi. 31 (ὁ ὢν εὐλ.). On the whole the rendering Blessed be... seems to be the most natural. V. L. benedictus est.

ὁ θεὸς καὶ πατὴρ τ. κ. ἡμ. Ἰ. Χ.] Both titles may be taken with the genitive: 'the GOD and Father of our Lord Jesus Christ.' He Who is 'our GOD and Father' is also 'the GOD and the Father' of the Lord: John xx. 17 πρὸς τὸν πατέρα μου καὶ πατέρα ὑμῶν καὶ θεόν μου καὶ θεὸν ὑμῶν. The title 'the GOD of our Lord Jesus Christ' occurs v. 17 (compare Heb. i. 9; Matt. xxvii. 46); but 'the Father of our Lord Jesus Christ' in c. iii. 14 is a false reading.

On the other hand the corresponding phrase in Col. i. 3 τῷ θεῷ πατρὶ τοῦ κ. ἡ. Ἰ. Χ. is unambiguous—GOD the Father of our Lord Jesus Christ; and the words here can be understood in this sense: GOD Who is also Father of our Lord Jesus Christ. In this

case the article is taken with the whole compound phrase θεὸς καὶ π. τ. κ. Ἰ. Χ.: 'He Who is GOD and is further revealed as Father of our Lord Jesus Christ.'

There is the same ambiguity in the other places where the phrase occurs: 2 Cor. i. 3; xi. 31; Rom. xv. 6; 1 Pet. i. 3. But in Apoc. i. 6 τῷ θεῷ καὶ πατρὶ αὐτοῦ (i.e. Ἰ. Χ.); 1 Cor. xv. 24 ὅταν παραδιδῷ τὴν βασ. τῷ θεῷ καὶ πατρί the sense appears to be clear.

ὁ εὐλογήσας...] Who blessed..., not 'who blesses' or 'who will bless.' The work of GOD for us is potentially complete. Probably the time to which St Paul looks is the call of each believer when he was made partaker of the truth of the Incarnation.

The divine blessing is regarded under three co-ordinate aspects (ἐν, ἐν, ἐν): ἐν· π. εὐλογίᾳ, the atmosphere, as it were, by which it encompasses us; ἐν τοῖς ἐπουρανίοις, the order in which it is realised; ἐν Χριστῷ, the living Person in Whom it is centred. A true personal sense of this blessing, which is a matter of experience and not of testimony, gives the right interpretation of life and duty and service.

For the use of the aorist in regard to the Divine work of redemption in different relations, compare v. 4 ἐξελέξατο, v. 5 προορίσας, v. 6 ἐχαρίτωσεν. 2 Tim. i. 9; Tit. iii. 5.

ἡμᾶς] St Paul unites himself in this respect with his fellow-believers; compare 1 John iii. 1 f. note. He assumes that his own experience is theirs. He is not teaching a new truth, but reminding them of one with which they were familiar. The repetition of ἡμεῖς throughout this section is to be noticed. Elsewhere the passage from the general thought of Christian privileges to the special grace shewn to the Gentiles is most suggestive: vv. 12, 13; cc. i. 18—20; iii. 8—10; iv. 1, 7, 13, 20; vi. 11—20.

ἐν πάσῃ εὐλ. πν.] in all spiritual

blessing, in spiritual blessing of every form (*v.* 8 ἐν πάσῃ σοφίᾳ; iv. 2 μετὰ πάσης ταπεινοφροσύνης note), blessing, that is, which quickens and finds its place in our highest life. All human powers can be spiritually affected. Compare 1 Cor. i. 30; Col. ii. 9 f. 'Spiritual' is opposed to that which is earthly and sensuous (1 Cor. xv. 44 ff.) in its source and form and object; compare 1 Pet. ii. 5. With this exception the word πνευματικός is found (more than twenty times) only in St Paul's Epistles. The temporal blessings of the Old Covenant are contrasted by implication with the spiritual blessings of the New.

ἐν τοῖς ἐπουρανίοις] Vg. *in caelestibus, in the heavenly order.* The phrase (τὰ ἐπουράνια), as it is here used, is peculiar to this Epistle (not in Colossians). It describes the supramundane, supra-sensual, eternal order, or, as we should say, generally 'the spiritual world,' which is perceived by thought and not by sight (2 Cor. iv. 18). This is not distant or future but present, the scene even now of the Christian's struggle (*c.* vi. 12), where (for we are forced by the limitation of our minds to localise the conception) his life is already centred (Phil. iii. 20 ἡμῶν τὸ πολίτευμα ἐν οὐρανοῖς ὑπάρχει; comp. *c.* ii. 19), and his strength is assured to him, and his triumph is already realised (*cc.* i. 20; ii. 6). Nay, even more, the work of the Church is to make known in this region of a higher life the facts of the Lord's Coming (*c.* iii. 10). Comp. Orig. ὅρα εἰ δύναται τὸ ἐν τοῖς ἐπουρανίοις εἶναι ἀντὶ τοῦ ἐν τοῖς νοητοῖς καὶ ἔξω αἰσθήσεων. Elsewhere the adj. ἐπουράνιος is used for that which belongs to the spiritual world : John iii. 12 (of heavenly truths); Heb. viii. 5 note; ix. 23 (of the heavenly archetypes of the Levitical institutions); 2 Tim. iv. 18 (the heavenly kingdom); Phil. ii. 10 (as contrasted with ἐπίγειος and καταχθόνιος). Compare also 1 Cor. xv. 48 f., where this word is applied

to Christ as the 'spiritual,' 'supramundane' man.

ἐν Χριστῷ] In virtue of our union with Him, 'in Whom are all the treasures of knowledge and wisdom hidden' (Col. ii. 3), of which we potentially become partakers. See *v.* 1 and additional note.

Observe the continual reiteration of the thought throughout this section : 4 ἐν αὐτῷ; 6 ἐν τῷ ἠγαπημένῳ; 7 ἐν ᾧ; 9 ἐν αὐτῷ; 10 ἐν τῷ Χριστῷ; 11 ἐν αὐτῷ; ἐν ᾧ; (12 ἐν τῷ Χριστῷ;) 13 ἐν ᾧ, ἐν ᾧ. Contrast διὰ Ἰ. Χ. *v.* 5.

The blessing which GOD has bestowed upon us is, to sum what has been said, spiritual in its essence, spiritual in the sphere of its action, spiritual in its personal realisation. Compare Col. iii. 1—4. The life of the Christian is ideally lived 'in Christ,' 'in the heavenly order.' Contrast the blessing 'in Christ' with the blessing 'in Abraham' (Gen. xii. 3).

The repetition of the cognate forms εὐλογητός, εὐλογήσας, εὐλογίᾳ, though in somewhat different senses, for GOD blesses in deed and we in word, is characteristic of St Paul. Compare 2 Cor. v. 18 ff. So below *v.* 6 τῆς χάριτος...ἧς ἐχαρίτωσεν ἡμᾶς.

(2) The bestowal of the blessing (4—14) (*a*) wrought out before time in the eternal order, according to the Divine idea (4—6), (*b*) and realised in time, in spite of man's fall (7—14).

The blessing described generally in *v.* 3 is now regarded in the details of its bestowal. In describing these, the Apostle brings into sight the work of each person of the Holy Trinity : of the Father in the eternal purpose of His love (*vv.* 4—6); of the Son in His Incarnation (*vv.* 7—12); of the Holy Spirit in giving now to each believer the earnest of His inheritance (*vv.* 13, 14). Compare 1 Cor. xii. 4—6.

The form of the whole section is, as has been already said, that of a lyrical doxology; and the close of each division is marked by the solemn burden, found only here, which de-

πνευματικῇ ἐν τοῖς ἐπουρανίοις ἐν Χριστῷ, ⁴καθὼς ἐξελέξατο ἡμᾶς ἐν αὐτῷ πρὸ καταβολῆς κόσμου, εἶναι ἡμᾶς

clares that the several aspects and
stages of Redemption are *unto the
praise of the glory of GOD* (*vv.* 6,
12, 14).

(*a*) The blessing wrought out before
time in the eternal order according to
the Divine idea (*vv.* 4—6).

In this work we notice:
an election to holiness (*v.* 4),
resting on predestination to sonship (*v.* 5),
followed by the gift of GOD'S grace
whereby we are made meet
for *His* presence (*v.* 6).

⁴ *Even as He chose us in Him before
the foundation of the world, that we
should be holy and without blemish
before Him in love;* ⁵ *having foreordained us unto adoption as sons
through Jesus Christ unto Himself,
according to the good pleasure of His
will,* ⁶ *to the praise of the glory of
His grace, which He freely bestowed
on us in the Beloved.*

4. καθώς...] The several points
which follow display the mode and
the measure of the blessing with
which GOD has blessed us. The
historical fulfilment in time corresponds with the eternal Divine will.
St Paul piles up phrase on phrase
to shew that all is of God's timeless
love.

ἐξελέξατο] *He chose us* (*i.e.* Christians as a body *v.* 3) for Himself out
of the world. The word ἐκλέγεσθαι
is found in the Epistles only in 1 Cor.
i. 27, 28 and James ii. 5 in addition
to this place. The theological sense
of the word is seen most clearly in
the words of the Lord recorded by
St John: vi. 70; xiii. 18; xv. 16—19.
(Compare Mk xiii. 20; Acts xiii. 17.)
The derivatives ἐκλεκτός (Synoptists,
St Paul, 1 Peter, 2 John, Apoc.) and
ἐκλογή (Acts, St Paul, 2 Pet.) must be
considered with ἐκλέξασθαι. The
middle voice emphasises in all the
places, where ἐκλέξασθαι is used in the

N. T., the relation of the person
chosen to the special purpose of him
who chooses. The 'chosen' are regarded not as they stand to others
who are not chosen, but as they stand
to the counsel of GOD Who works
through them. Compare Lightfoot,
Col. iii. 12. The ἐκλογή, like the ἐκκλησία, is preparatory to a wider work
(*vv.* 10, 14).

πρὸ κατ. κ.] Vg. *ante mundi constitutionem, before the foundation of
the world.* As the thought of 'the
heavenly order,' the scene of the
Christian's life, lifts us above the
limits of space, so the origin of his
life is placed beyond the limits of
time. The members of Christ are
placed in an eternal relation to Christ
their Head. The same phrase (πρὸ
κατ. κ.) is used of the love of the
Father for His Son, John xvii. 24,
and of the work of Redemption in
the Son (1 Pet. i. 20). Compare also
1 Cor. ii. 7 πρὸ τῶν αἰώνων, 2 Tim. i. 9
πρὸ χρόνων αἰωνίων ‖ Tit. i. 2. The
Jewish Covenant was from Abraham,
late in time: the Christian Covenant
was before all time: compare John
viii. 56 ff. Contrast with πρὸ κατ. κ.
the corresponding phrase ἀπὸ κατ. κ.
from the foundation of the world,
since time began: Matt. xxv. 34;
Lk. xi. 50; Heb. iv. 3; ix. 26; Apoc.
xiii. 8; xvii. 8. Comp. Rom. xvi. 25
(χρόνοις αἰωνίοις). A like difference
lies between ἐν ἀρχῇ John i. 1 f. and
ἀπ' ἀρχῆς 1 John i. 1.

For καταβολή see 2 Macc. ii. 29. It
is not used elsewhere in LXX. Κατα-
βάλλειν, βάλλεσθαι and καταβολή are
used rarely in classical writers of
'foundation,' literal or metaphorical.

εἶναι ἡμᾶς...] *that we should be
holy* (as devoted to Him) *and without blemish* (as acceptable offerings)
before Him, in whose sight no evil
can stand. For ἅγιος see *v.* 1. Ἄμωμος is properly 'blameless' morally

ἀγίους καὶ ἀμώμους κατενώπιον αὐτοῦ ἐν ἀγάπῃ, ⁵προο-
ρίσας ἡμᾶς εἰς υἱοθεσίαν διὰ Ἰησοῦ Χριστοῦ εἰς αὐτόν,

5 Χριστοῦ Ἰησοῦ B ; text codd rel Or.

but in the LXX. it came to be used for
victims which were 'without blemish,'
and this sense prevails here, and in
1 Pet. i. 19; Heb. ix. 14. The addition of ἀνεγκλήτους in the parallel
passage of the Colossians (i. 22) gives
a moral colour to the word there,
and this meaning is dominant in Jude
24 and Apoc. xiv. 5. The combination
ἅγιοι καὶ ἄμωμοι (comp. c. v. 27) gives
the fulness of the conception positively and negatively. Chrysostom
expresses another aspect of the combination : ἅγιός ἐστιν ὁ τῆς πίστεως
μετέχων, ἄμωμος ὁ ἀνεπίληπτον βίον
μετιών.
For the thought compare 2 Tim. i. 9.
The use of the simple infinitive
(εἶναι) as distinguished from εἰς τὸ
εἶναι (v. 12) marks the purpose as
potentially realised and not simply as
aimed at. So far as Christians are 'in
Christ,' living in Him and He in them
—and so far only do they live—they
are 'holy and blameless' (Gal. ii. 20;
1 John iv. 16). In capite omnia
membra benedixit et elegit, ut nos
faceret sanctos et immaculatos ; non
quia futuri eramus sed ut essemus
(Primas.).
κατενώπιον αὐτοῦ] *before Him, in
His sight* before Whom every fault is
patent (Heb. iv. 13). There appears
to be a reference to the appointed
inspector of victims, the μωμοσκόπος:
comp. Philo i. 320; Clem. Alex. *Strom.*
iv. 18 § 117.
ἐν ἀγάπῃ] These words may be
taken either with what follows or
with what precedes. But the connexion with προορίσας, *having in
love foreordained us*, is against the
rhythm; and the qualification of the
participle generally follows (c. iv. 2,
15, 16; c. iii. 17 is doubtful, see note ;
Col. ii. 2 ; cf. c. v. 2, 1 Thess. v. 13). If
then they are joined with what pre-

cedes (so Vg. *in caritate qua praed.*),
as seems on the whole to be best,
they complete the description of the
Christian character. As Christians
are 'holy and blameless' towards GOD,
so do they bear themselves one toward
another 'in love' (1 Cor. xvi. 14) which
they have appropriated as GOD'S great
gift: 1 John iii. 1. Compare cc. iii. 17;
iv. 15 f. ; v. 2.
A special reference to the love of
GOD, which is indeed the spring of
human love (1 John iv. 10 f.) does not
appear to be called for here. The
actions described are a manifestation
of it.
5. προορίσας...εἰς αὐτόν] For προορίζειν compare v. 11 ; Acts iv. 28 ;
1 Cor. ii. 7 ; Rom. viii. 29 f. The
'choice' of GOD (v. 4) rested on the
fact that He had 'foreordained us
unto adoption as sons.' For υἱοθεσία
compare Gal. iv. 5 ; Rom. viii. 15, 23 ;
ix. 4. This new relation expresses
the special position of Christians.
Υἱός, as distinguished from τέκνον (c.
v. 1), suggests the idea of privilege
and not of nature. Comp. note on
1 John iii. 1. That which was in type
the privilege of Israel was prepared in
spiritual fulness for believers. GOD
not only chose us in Christ—He might
have chosen us as His servants—but
He also destined for us through Christ
the right of sonship, bringing us into
fellowship with Himself (εἰς αὐτόν);
and this not in regard to our merits,
but *according to the good pleasure
of His will*, which is absolute and yet
not arbitrary. His will is directed (as
we apprehend it) to the accomplishment of the highest good (Rom. xii. 2 ;
Hebr. x. 7 ff.; Apoc. iv. 11 ἦσαν).
Out of the privilege of 'sons' grows
the character of sons. In the fullest
sense therefore the realization of the
adoption is still future: Rom. viii. 23.

κατὰ τὴν εὐδοκίαν τοῦ θελήματος αὐτοῦ, ⁶εἰς ἔπαινον
δόξης τῆς χάριτος αὐτοῦ ἧς ἐχαρίτωσεν ἡμᾶς ἐν τῷ

The use of διὰ Ἰησοῦ Χριστοῦ (as contrasted with ἐν Χριστῷ) is significant. The 'many sons' (Hebr. ii. 10) are regarded in their personality and not as incorporated in their Lord. Under this aspect their life comes 'through Him,' and they are brought personally to GOD (εἰς αὐτόν). The phrase does not occur again in the Epistle (c. iii. 9 is a false reading). For εἰς αὐτόν in a wider sense compare Rom. xi. 36; Col. i. 20; and, as applied to the Son, Col. i. 16.

κατὰ τὴν εὐδοκ. τ. θ. αὐ.] Vg. secundum propositum (placitum : Hier. beneplacitum) voluntatis suae. Compare v. 9 τὸ μυστήριον τοῦ θελ. αὐτοῦ and v. 11 τὴν βουλὴν τοῦ θελ. αὐτοῦ. These phrases stand by themselves, and encourage us to see GOD's will as the expression of His gracious purpose, disclosed to us in the Incarnation, and carried to its issue πολυμερῶς καὶ πολυτρόπως in what we with our limited faculties regard as a plan.

Origen notices that εὐδοκία is strange to classical Greek. It occurs not unfrequently in the LXX. (Pss., Ecclus.).

6. εἰς ἔπ. δ. τ. χ. αὐ.] The adoption of men as sons of GOD leads to the praise of the glory of His grace. The grace of GOD is, as is explained in the next clause, the free and bounteous goodness with which He has visited us in His Son. The glory of this grace is the manifestation of its power as men are enabled to perceive it. Each fresh manifestation calls out a fresh acknowledgment of its surpassing excellence. Christians therefore in whom it is effective are set to reveal the perfections of Christ—the Son made known in the many sons— and by revealing them, to call out the thankful adoration of men. Compare Phil. i. 11.

For τῆς χάριτος compare v. 7 τὸ πλοῦτος τῆς χάριτος αὐτοῦ, c. ii. 7 τὸ ὑπερβάλλον πλοῦτος τ. χαρ. αὐτοῦ. So

St Paul reckons his own apostolic commission (ἡ χάρις c. iii. 2, 7, 8) and the endowment of each Christian (ἡ χάρις c. iv. 7) as GOD's bounteous gift.

ἧς ἐχαρίτωσεν ἡμ.] Latt. in qua gratificavit nos. Wherewith He highly favoured us, which He freely bestowed upon us. For ἧς see c. iv. 1; 2 Cor. i. 4. It may represent ἥν (χάριν χαριτοῦν) or ᾗ, though the attraction of the dative is very much rarer. See v. 8. Χαριτοῦν is to affect with χάρις, which may be taken either subjectively 'to endue with grace,' 'to make gracious,' or objectively 'to visit with grace,' 'to treat graciously.' The former sense is found in Ecclus. xviii. 17 παρὰ ἀνδρὶ κεχαριτωμένῳ and Ps. xvii. (xviii.) 26 Symm. μετὰ τοῦ κεχαριτωμένου χαριτωθήσῃ, and is given by Chrysostom here: οὐ μόνον ἁμαρτημάτων ἀπήλλαξεν ἀλλὰ καὶ ἐπεράστους ἐποίησεν. But it appears to be contrary to the context which dwells on the greatness of GOD's gift. Nor does St Paul use χάρις of human grace, not c. iv. 29, nor Col. iv. 6 (yet see Lightfoot l. c.). On κεχαριτωμένη in Lk. i. 28 Bengel remarks truly : non ut mater gratiae sed ut filia gratiae appellatur.

At the same time the working of GOD's gracious gift by incorporating the believer in Christ makes him capable and meet for the presence of GOD.

ἐν τῷ ἠγαπ.] Latt. in dilecto filio suo : in the beloved. There is the same ambiguity in this translation as in blessed (v. 3). Two forms are thus rendered, the verbal ἀγαπητός (answering to εὐλογητός) claiming love by its very nature ; and ἠγαπημένος, which (like εὐλογημένος) suggests in every case some special manifestation of love. Ἀγαπητός is used of Christ by the heavenly Voice : Matt. iii. 17 (Mk i. 11 ; Lk. iii. 22) ; Matt. xvii. 5 (2 Pet. i. 17 ; Mk ix. 7 ; not Lk. ix. 35) ; and it is used of men fre-

ἠγαπημένῳ, ⁷ἐν ᾧ ἔχομεν τὴν ἀπολύτρωσιν διὰ τοῦ

quently. This is the only place in which ἠγαπημένος is used of Christ in the N. T., and it is evident that stress is laid upon the manifestation of GOD's love to His Son which He had even then made in His exaltation to heaven. This was itself the pledge of man's exaltation (*c.* ii. 6). For this reason a unique title is used in place of ἐν Χριστῷ. Ἠγαπημένος is used of men 1 Thess. i. 4; 2 Thess. ii. 13 (LXX.); Rom. ix. 25 (LXX.); Col. iii. 12; and of Christ in Barn. *ep.* iii. 6 (with the note of Gebhardt and Harnack); iv. 3 (8).

(*b*) The blessing realised in time in spite of man's fall (*vv.* 7—14).

So far the Apostle has described the eternal purpose and work of the Father, for with Him purpose and work are one. He now passes on to the historical fulfilment of the Divine counsel after sin entered the world, and shows that the redemption wrought by Christ through His blood (*v.* 7) has been made known in its universal power (8—10), for which glorious consummation Israel had been prepared by a long discipline (11, 12) and in which the Gentiles by faith had found a place (13), receiving the Holy Spirit, the pledge of the final victory of GOD (14).

⁷*In Whom we have our redemption through His blood, the forgiveness of our trespasses, according to the riches of His grace* ⁸*which He made to abound toward us in all wisdom and prudence,* ⁹*having made known unto us the mystery of His will, according to His good pleasure, which He purposed in Him* ¹⁰*unto a dispensation of the fulness of the seasons, to sum up all things in the Christ, the things in the heavens and the things upon the earth; in Him, I say,* ¹¹*in Whom we were also made* GOD's *portion, having been foreordained according to the purpose of Him, Who worketh all things after*

the counsel of His will, ¹²*to the end that we should be to the praise of His glory, we who had before hoped in Christ;* ¹³*in Whom ye also are, having heard the word of the truth, the gospel of your salvation, in Whom, having also believed, ye were sealed with the Holy Spirit of promise* ¹⁴*which is an earnest of our inheritance, unto the redemption of* GOD's *own possession, unto the praise of His glory.*

7. The great counsel of GOD, which was interrupted by man's sin, was accomplished by the redemptive work of Christ.

ἐν ᾧ...παραπτωμάτων] *In Whom,* as incorporated with Him and made members of His Body (Rom. iii. 24 τῆς ἀπολυτρώσεως τῆς ἐν X. 'I.), *we have* and enjoy (*c.* ii. 18; Rom. v. 1) *redemption,* or, more emphatically, *our redemption*—the redemption which is the outcome of our Christian faith—*through His blood,* even *the forgiveness of our trespasses.* Men as sinners are represented under a twofold aspect. They are captives at once and debtors : captives to the devil from whom they are ransomed ; debtors to GOD Who remits what they owe to Him. For ἀπολύτρωσις compare Addit. Note on Hebr. ix. 12.

διὰ τοῦ αἵμ. αὐτ.] On the meaning of 'blood' as essentially distinct from 'death,' see Notes on 1 John i. 7. It may be observed that θάνατος, ἀποθανεῖν (common elsewhere : Col. i. 22 ; ii. 20 ; iii. 3) do not occur in the Epistle.

The various constructions under which 'the blood' of Christ is presented in relation to the redemption and salvation of men should be carefully studied. We have

(1) διά c. gen., *through, by means of.* Acts xx. 28; Eph. i. 7; Hebr. ix. 12.

(2) διά c. acc., *by reason of.* Apoc. xii. 11.

(3) ἐν *in,* implying a living connexion of the believer with the source

αἵματος αὐτοῦ, τὴν ἄφεσιν τῶν παραπτωμάτων, κατὰ
τὸ πλοῦτος τῆς χάριτος αὐτοῦ ⁸ἧς ἐπερίσσευσεν εἰς

of life, the life, as it were, encompassing him.
  Rom. v. 9; Eph. ii. 13; Hebr.
  x. 19; Apoc. i. 5; v. 9; vii. 14.
Compare Rom. iii. 25; 1 Cor. xi. 25;
Hebr. ix. 22, 25; xiii. 20.
  (4) simple dat. of the instrument.
  1 Pet. i. 19.
  Διά and ἐν are used in the same
context : 1 John v. 6 note.
  τὴν ἄφ. τ. παρ.] the forgiveness of
our trespasses.
  The exact phrase does not occur
elsewhere. In the parallel, Col. i. 14,
the commoner phrase τὴν ἄφεσιν τῶν
ἁμαρτιῶν is used, which recurs ten
times in the Synoptists and the Acts,
but not again in the Epistles. The
original of the expression (ἀφιέναι
παραπτ.) is found in Matt. vi. 14 ff.;
Mk xi. 25 f. The difference between
'trespass' and 'sin' seems to be, that
'trespass' brings out the idea of the
violation of a definite law, while 'sin'
expresses the essential estrangement
from God implied in the act whereby
man misses his true end. Compare
Rom. v. 12—21, where the proper
meaning of the two words can be
seen plainly. The parallel of 'forgiveness of trespasses' with 'redemption'
lies in the fact that through forgiveness man is placed in his true relation
to God : he has 'received the atonement' (Rom. v. 11), and is 'atoned'
to Him. The past with its results is
that which holds us in bondage. The
removal of these bands brings freedom. It is not unlikely that some
false interpretation of 'redemption'
as a deliverance from the fetters of
physical law caused the Apostle to
emphasise its moral nature. Comp.
Lightfoot on Col. i. 14.
  κατὰ τὸ πλ. τ. χ. αὐ.] This characteristic form of expression is peculiar to
St Paul : 2 Cor. viii. 2; Rom. ii. 4;
ix. 23; Phil. iv. 19; Col. i. 27; ii. 2;
and below v. 18; cc. ii. 7; iii. 16.

8—10. This revelation of His grace
God has made known to us in its
immeasurable issues.
  8. ἧς ἐπερ....φρονήσει] Latt. quae
superabundavit in nobis, which
(grace) He made to abound toward
us in all wisdom and prudence....
The rhythm of the sentence determines that the words ἐν π. σοφ. καὶ
φρον. are to be joined with ἐπερίσσευσεν
and not with γνωρίσας. The parallel
phrase in Col. i. 9 ἵνα πληρωθῆτε τὴν
ἐπίγνωσιν τοῦ θελήματος αὐτοῦ seems
to be no less decisive for the interpretation of π. σοφία καὶ φρονήσει as describing the manner in which the grace
of God was manifested in those on
whom it was bestowed. The application of 'wisdom and prudence' to God
in Prov. iii. 19 (LXX.) and the use of
πολυποίκιλος σοφία in c. iii. 10 does
not justify the reference of πᾶσα σοφ.
καὶ φρον. to God here. On the other
hand the fact that His grace issued in
such gifts to men implies that they
found exercise in the contemplation
of His working. Through these believers are enabled to trace the connexion between the successive revelations which he made πολυμερῶς καὶ
πολυτρόπως, all leading up to the final
revelation in His Son; and yet more
the complete and harmonious fulfilment of His earthly work in His Birth,
His Death, His Resurrection, His Ascension, followed by the descent of the
Holy Spirit. The same gifts have
also a further application. St Paul's
thoughts necessarily turned to the
contemplation of the special privileges
of the Jews (comp. Rom. ix. 4 f.); but
we can now observe the signs of
God's counsel in the training of 'the
nations' and in the slow realisation
of manifold lessons of the Gospel in
post-Christian history.
  For the transitive sense of ἐπερίσσευσεν see 1 Thess. iii. 12; 2 Cor. iv.
15; ix. 8. The intransitive sense

ἡμᾶς ἐν πάσῃ σοφίᾳ καὶ φρονήσει ⁹γνωρίσας ἡμῖν τὸ
μυστήριον τοῦ θελήματος αὐτοῦ, κατὰ τὴν εὐδοκίαν
αὐτοῦ ἣν προέθετο ἐν αὐτῷ ¹⁰εἰς οἰκονομίαν τοῦ πληρώ-

'*wherewith He abounded*' would require ἧς to be an attraction from ᾗ
which is very much rarer than the
attraction ἥν.
For πάσῃ compare *v.* 3 note. The
distinction of σοφία and φρόνησις is
marked from the time of Aristotle
(*Eth. Nic.* vi. 7).
'Wisdom' deals with principles:
'prudence' with action. In this way
'prudence' may be called 'the child of
wisdom' (Prov. x. 23 LXX. ἡ σοφία
ἀνδρὶ τίκτει φρόνησιν). Φρόνησις occurs
in the N.T. again only in Lk. i. 17,
but the corresponding adjective occurs
frequently (*e.g.* Matt. x. 16; xxv. 2).
9. γνωρίσας...τοῦ θελ. αὐ.] Vg. *ut
notum faceret sacramentum voluntatis suae. Having made known*—in
that He made known—*the mystery*,
the Divine counsel now revealed, which
was the expression *of His will.* The
fact of a revelation is always implied
in the word 'mystery' in the N. T. (see
c. iii. 3 note), even in the Apocalypse,
where the revelation is imminent.
The phrase τὸ μυστ. τῆς βουλῆς occurs
in Judith ii. 2. Compare 2 Tim. i. 9 f.
9, 10. κατὰ τὴν εὐδοκίαν...] *according to His good pleasure*—gracious
purpose—*which He purposed* (set
before Himself) to accomplish *in Him,*
the Beloved, destined *to issue in a
dispensation* belonging to and, as it
were, springing out *of the fulness of
the seasons*—when the full measure of
their appointed course, with all their
lessons of preparation and discipline,
should be accomplished—namely, *to
sum up all things in the Christ....*
προέθετο] Rom. i. 13; iii. 25. See
πρόθεσις *v.* 11.
ἐν αὐτῷ] Latt. *in eo, in the Beloved.*
The Incarnate Son embodied the
purpose of GOD. The end of Creation
was reached in Him through Whom it
had its origin (Hebr. i. 2).

The common text ἐν ἑαυτῷ adds
nothing to the force of προέθετο.
οἰκονομίαν] *dispensation.* The original word describes the function of a
'steward' (οἰκονόμος 1 Cor. iv. 1 f.), as
indeed does the English word according to its derivation. It occurs (in
addition to Lk. xvi. 2 ff.) in 1 Cor. ix.
17; Col. i. 25 (1 Tim. i. 4); *c.* iii. 2, 9.
The exact meaning which it conveys
appears to be in each case that of a
distribution of Divine treasures, which
have been committed by GOD to
chosen representatives, that they may
be faithfully administered by them.
All earlier 'dispensations' were crowned by that of Christ, in Whom are
*all the treasures of wisdom and
knowledge hidden* (Col. ii. 3). These
He dispenses with perfect righteousness and love, giving Himself for and
to 'His brethren.' The act of 'dispensation' passes naturally into the scheme
of dispensation. Compare Lightfoot
Col. l. c.
τοῦ πληρ. τ. καιρῶν] Latt. *plenitudinis*
(Tert. *adimpletionis*) *temporum, the
fulness of the seasons.* The phrase
differs characteristically from that in
Gal. iv. 4 τὸ πλήρωμα τοῦ χρόνου *the
fulness of the time* (contrast Mark i.
15). τὸ πληρ. τ. χρόνου marks the
limit of an appointed term: τὸ πληρ.
τ. καιρῶν, the close of a series of critical periods, each of which had its
peculiar character and was naturally
connected in some way with the final
issue: comp. Mk i. 15; John vii. 8;
Lk. xxi. 24. The words 'times' and
'seasons' are connected in Acts i. 7;
1 Thess. v. 1; Tit. i. 2 f. (a singularly instructive passage as to their
difference): see *c.* v. 16. 'Time'
(χρόνος) expresses simply duration:
'season' (καιρός) a space of time defined with regard to its extent and
character.

μάτος τῶν καιρῶν, ἀνακεφαλαιώσασθαι τὰ πάντα ἐν τῷ
χριστῷ, τὰ ἐπὶ τοῖς οὐρανοῖς καὶ τὰ ἐπὶ τῆς γῆς· ἐν
αὐτῷ, ¹¹ἐν ᾧ καὶ ἐκληρώθημεν προορισθέντες κατὰ πρό-

ἀνακεφαλαιώσασθαι] Latt. instaurare: Tert. (Ir. int.) Hier. recapitulare, to sum up, specially to gather into a brief compass the heads of an argument or statement (Rom. xiii. 9). The word here expresses the typical union of all things in the Messiah, a final harmony answering to the idea of creation, just as the corresponding word ἀποκαταλλάξαι used in Col. i. 20 expresses the reconciliation of the parts of creation one to another and to GOD in view of the separation and estrangement wrought by sin. Even apart from sin the ἀνακεφαλαίωσις of created things was required that they might attain their unity in GOD (Rom. xi. 36); and sin introduced the necessity for an atonement (καταλλαγή Rom. v. 11). Comp. Ps.-Hipp. c. Beron. 2 ἧς (i.e. τῆς αὐτοῦ σωματώσεως) ἔργον ἡ τῶν ὅλων ἐστὶν εἰς αὐτὸν ἀνακεφαλαίωσις. Just. M. ap. Iren. iv. 6 (11), 2...unigenitus Filius venit ad nos, suum plasma in semet ipsum recapitulans... This consummation lies beyond the unity of the Church, the Body of Christ, which contributes towards its realisation.

Οὐ μόνον οἱ κατακερματισμοὶ τῶν οἰκονομουμένων καὶ οἱ καθ' ἕνα λόγοι τῶν διοικουμένων εἰσὶν ἐν τῷ τοῦ θεοῦ Λόγῳ καὶ τῇ σοφίᾳ αὐτοῦ, ἀλλὰ καὶ ἡ ἀνακεφαλαίωσις καὶ, ὡς ἄν εἴποι τις, συγκεφαλαίωσις πάντων (Orig.).

τὰ πάντα...] Whereas πάντα (Jo. i. 3, Heb. iii. 4) denotes all things taken severally, τὰ πάντα properly signifies all things in their unity, actual or ideal —the sum of all things. Compare vv. 11, 23; cc. iii. 9; iv. 10; Col. i. 16, 17, 20; and especially Heb. i. 3, where see note.

ἐν τῷ χριστῷ] in the Christ, in the Messiah. The title appears to be used here with a distinct reference to the Lord as the expected Saviour. With

the article (as in this Epistle: cc. i. 12, 20; ii. 5, 13; iii. 4 (6), 8, 17, 19; iv. 7, 12, 13, 20; v. 2, 5, 14, 23 ff.; vi. 5) 'Christ' is dominantly, if not exclusively, the title of the office and not simply a proper name. Creation was brought under the consequences of sin through man (Gal. iii. 22) and so redemption came to creation through man. Comp. 1 Cor. xv. 28; Rom. viii. 19.

τὰ ἐπὶ τοῖς οὐρ....] the things in the heavens.... This sublime revelation of the extent of redemption as commensurate with the whole creation is brought out especially in the Epistles of the Roman Captivity: Phil. ii. 9, 10; Col. i. 20; v. 21. The solitary prisoner could see farthest into the glory of the Divine counsels, even as the martyr 'saw the heavens opened and the Son of Man standing at the right hand of GOD' (Acts vii. 56). At the same time the outward unity of the Empire furnished an image of the Divine reality.

It is altogether arbitrary to introduce any limitation into the interpretation of τὰ πάντα. The truth transcends our comprehension, but we can see that it answers to the fact and purpose of creation (Apoc. iv. 11 ἦσαν; Rom. xi. 36).

The slight difference of construction between ἐπὶ τοῖς οὐρ. and ἐπὶ τῆς γ. will be noticed. With the dat. ἐπὶ denotes simple position, with the gen. extension over. Ἐπὶ τοῖς οὐρ. is a unique phrase; elsewhere in corresponding connexions ἐν is undisturbed: Matt. vi. 10; xxviii. 18; 1 Cor. viii. 5; Col. i. 16, 20; Apoc. v. 13; c. iii. 15.

11, 12.   For which consummation a preparation had been made by the discipline of Israel.

11.   ἐν αὐ. ἐν ᾧ....] in Him, I say, in Whom we were also made GOD'S portion.... Christians are a new Israel

θεσιν τοῦ τὰ πάντα ἐνεργοῦντος κατὰ τὴν βουλὴν τοῦ

(comp. Deut. xxxii. 9): Gal. vi. 16;
comp. Gal. iv. 28; Matt. iii. 9. It is
through the Church in the New Dispensation, as through Israel in old
time, that the counsel of GOD is
wrought out for the world.
The sense of ἐκληρώθημεν is difficult
to determine. The word is not found
elsewhere in the N. T. The nearest
parallel is in Acts xvii. 4 προσε-
κληρώθησαν τῷ Παύλῳ *were assigned
by* GOD *to Paul*.... So here it may be
'we were assigned,' that is, to GOD;
while the conception of Israel as
GOD's κλῆρος served to define the idea
(Deut. ix. 29). Compare Pind. *Ol.*
viii. 19 ὕμμε δ' ἐκλάρωσε πότμος Ζηνί.
It has also been taken to mean 'we
were made partakers of the Divine
inheritance.' This is in harmony with
Col. i. 12; but it is difficult to obtain
the meaning from the form. The
parallels quoted are not to the point.
Early writers take the simple sense
'we were appointed (Vg. *sorte vocati
sumus*; Ambr. *sorte constituti*; Aug.
sortem consecuti; Ambrst. *sortiti*)...
to the end that....' This is perfectly
legitimate, but the context seems to
require a reference to the Divine
κλῆρος (Acts xxvi. 18; Col. i. 12).
Comp. *v.* 18.

προορισθέντες...] *having been foreordained* (*v.* 5 προορίσας) to occupy
this position...to the end that we
should be....

κατὰ πρόθεσιν] Comp. *c.* iii. 11 κατὰ
πρόθεσιν τῶν αἰώνων; Rom. viii. 28;
2 Tim. i. 9; Rom. ix. 11.
The word πρόθεσις is used of 'purpose' generally: Acts xi. 23; xxvii. 13;
2 Tim. iii. 10.

τοῦ τὰ πάντα ἐνεργ....] *of Him who
worketh all things after the counsel
of His will*. The language which
describes the action of GOD must of
necessity be figurative. The phrase
βουλὴ τοῦ θελήματος, which occurs here
only in the N. T., expresses that His
will is not arbitrary, but, if presented

in terms of human experience, guided
by a settled counsel. Βουλή (only in
the Pauline group of Epistles) expresses counsel with reference to
action: θέλημα (in all groups) will
generally. Comp. Acts ii. 23 τῇ ὡρισ-
μένῃ βουλῇ καὶ προγνώσει τοῦ θεοῦ
ἔκδοτον; iv. 28 ὅσα ἡ χείρ σου καὶ ἡ
βουλὴ προώρισεν γενέσθαι; xx. 27 πᾶσαν
τὴν βουλὴν τοῦ θεοῦ. Hebr. vi. 17 τὸ
ἀμετάθετον τῆς βουλῆς αὐτοῦ. Lk. vii.
30 τὴν βουλὴν τοῦ θεοῦ ἠθέτησαν εἰς
ἑαυτούς. Acts xiii. 36. Comp. Matt.
i. 19.

τὰ π. ἐνεργοῦντος] Comp. 1 Cor. xii. 6
ὁ ἐνεργῶν τὰ πάντα ἐν πᾶσιν; *v.* 11
πάντα δὲ ταῦτα ἐνεργεῖ τὸ ἓν καὶ τὸ
αὐτὸ πνεῦμα. Gal. iii. 5 ὁ...ἐνεργῶν
δυνάμεις ἐν ὑμῖν; ii. 8 ἐνεργήσας ἐν ὑμῖν
Phil. ii. 13 θεός ἐστιν ὁ ἐνεργῶν ἐν ὑμῖν
καὶ τὸ θέλειν καὶ τὸ ἐνεργεῖν. The
verb ἐνεργεῖν brings out the idea of
the personal power which is operative rather than the result produced
(ἐργάζεσθαι *c.* iv. 28). It has reference always to action in the human
sphere.

12 f. The general statement that
Christians as Christians were made
GOD's portion through their incorporation in Christ (ἐκληρώθημεν without ἡμεῖς) is now defined. The new
Israel included both Jews and Gentiles. The Jews with whom St Paul
identifies himself (εἰς τὸ εἶναι ἡμᾶς...)
who had fixed their hopes on the
promises of the Deliverer, were in a
peculiar sense 'for a praise of GOD's
glory' now that their expectations
had found fulfilment, witnessing to
the accomplishment of His purpose
prepared through their national discipline (comp. 1 Pet. i. 12). At the
same time the Gentiles also, of whom
the Ephesians were representatives
(καὶ ὑμεῖς), had found a place in the
same Divine fellowship, when they accepted the message of the truth which
was brought to them and the larger
hope of the prophets was fulfilled.

θελήματος αὐτοῦ, ¹²εἰς τὸ εἶναι ἡμᾶς εἰς ἔπαινον δόξης
αὐτοῦ τοὺς προηλπικότας ἐν τῷ χριστῷ· ¹³ἐν ᾧ καὶ
ὑμεῖς ἀκούσαντες τὸν λόγον τῆς ἀληθείας, τὸ εὐαγγέλιον τῆς σωτηρίας ὑμῶν, ἐν ᾧ καὶ πιστεύσαντες,

12. εἰς τὸ εἶναι ἡμᾶς] Contrast v. 4
εἶναι. See note ad loc.
The ἡμᾶς is emphatic : 'we Jews
who through all delays and disappoint-
ments clung to the teaching of the
prophets.'
εἰς ἔπαινον δόξης αὐτοῦ] see v. 14.
The note of Primasius is worth quoting :
Ut per signa quae facimus laudetur
gloria Dei.
τοὺς προηλπ. ἐν τῷ χρ.] Comp.
1 Cor. xv. 19 ἠλπικότες ἐσμὲν ἐν Χριστῷ
(not Matt. xii. 21 ; Phil. ii. 19 is different); 2 Cor. i. 10 εἰς ὃν ἠλπίκαμεν.
1 Tim. iv. 10 ἤλπ. ἐπὶ θεῷ ζῶντι; vi. 17
ἤλπ. ἐπὶ πλούτου ἀδηλότητι ; v. 5 ἤλπ.
ἐπὶ τὸν θεόν. 1 Pet. iii. 5 ἐλπ. εἰς.
Προελπίζειν occurs here only in the
N. T. The πρό is limited not by the
belief of the Ephesian Gentiles ('believed before you') but by the Advent
('believed before Christ actually came').
The perf. indicates that the spirit of
this faith still remained.

13, 14. And with Israel the Gentiles
were now associated by faith, having
received the Holy Spirit, the pledge
of the victory of GOD.

13. ἐν ᾧ...] in Whom ye also are—
as members of His Body,—having
heard. It appears to be simplest
to take the first ἐν ᾧ as parallel to
the second and not as resumed by it.
Two thoughts are marked, the first
that the Gentiles are included in the
new Israel, and the second that being
included they have received the gift
of the Holy Spirit. These two blessings correspond with the quickening
of the Church with the Divine Life on
the Day of the Resurrection (John xx.
22 f.) and the endowing of the Church
on the day of Pentecost ; and in the
experience of the individual with Baptism and the Laying on of hands.

καὶ ὑμεῖς] Comp. Acts xi. 18 ἄρα
καὶ τοῖς ἔθνεσιν ὁ θεὸς τὴν μετάνοιαν
εἰς ζωὴν ἔδωκεν.
τὸν λόγον τῆς ἀλ.] the word, the
message, of the truth. Comp. 2 Tim.
ii. 15 ὀρθοτομοῦντα τὸν λόγον τῆς ἀλ.
James i. 18 λόγος ἀλ. Christianity as
a message, is essentially 'the truth':
John i. 17 (note); 2 Thess. ii. 12 ;
2 Cor. iv. 2 ; 1 John iii. 19 (note). It
presents the right view of the ultimate
relations of man, the world, and GOD.
Comp. v. 9 note.
The substance of Christ's message
is Christ Himself, Who is the Truth
(John xiv. 6).
Similar phrases are : 2 Cor. v. 19
ὁ λόγος τῆς καταλλαγῆς, Acts xiii. 26
ὁ λόγος τῆς σωτηρίας ταύτης, Acts
xiv. 3, xx. 32 ὁ λόγος τῆς χάριτος
αὐτοῦ.
τὸ εὐαγγέλιον τῆς σωτ. ὑ.] the gospel
—the glad tidings—of your salvation
(Gal. ii. 7 τὸ εὐαγγ. τῆς ἀκροβυστίας),
proclaiming that 'to the Gentiles' also
'was sent the salvation of GOD' (Acts
xxviii. 28 ; xi. 18 ; xv. 7).
The phrase is unique. Comp. Acts
xx. 24 τὸ εὐαγγέλιον τῆς χάριτος τοῦ
θεοῦ, 2 Cor. iv. 4 τὸ εὐαγγέλιον τῆς
δόξης τοῦ χριστοῦ, 1 Tim. i. 11 τὸ
εὐαγγ. τῆς δόξης τοῦ μακαρίου θεοῦ.

13 b. The incorporation of the
Gentiles in the Body of Christ leads
on to the wider thought of the action
of the Spirit through the Church
which brings the consummation of
the Divine will. The relation of man
and of humanity to GOD is essentially
established through the action of the
Word, the Son, in Creation and in
Redemption. The Holy Spirit is a
special gift to the Church and Christians.
ἐν ᾧ καὶ πιστ. ἐσφρ.] in Whom, as

ἐσφραγίσθητε τῷ πνεύματι τῆς ἐπαγγελίας τῷ ἁγίῳ,
¹⁴⸢ὅ⸣ ἐστιν ἀρραβὼν τῆς κληρονομίας ἡμῶν, εἰς ἀπολύτρωσιν τῆς περιποιήσεως, εἰς ἔπαινον τῆς δόξης αὐτοῦ.

14 ὅς
ὅ ABG₃L 47; ὅς אD₂K 17 37

united with Him, *having also believed*
(Acts xix. 2) *ye were sealed*.... It is
possible to take ἐν ᾧ in connexion
with εὐαγγέλιον, '*and when ye believed in it*, as not hearers only, *ye
were sealed*....' This construction is
justified by Mk i. 15, but it seems to
be less natural than that which has
been adopted.

ἐσφραγίσθητε] See *c*. iv. 30 μὴ
λυπεῖτε τὸ πν. τὸ ἅγ. τοῦ θεοῦ ἐν ᾧ
ἐσφραγίσθητε εἰς ἡμέραν ἀπολυτρώσεως.

Σφραγίς is used of a visible attestation of the reality of a spiritual fact :
1 Cor. ix. 2; Rom. iv. 11; 2 Tim. ii. 19.
Comp. Apoc. vii. 3 ff.; ix. 4. The
'seal' openly marked the servants of
God as belonging to Him (2 Cor. i.
22), and assured them of His protection. So they were solemnly recognised as His sons (comp. John vi. 27)
and on the other hand pledged to His
service.

τῷ πν. τῆς ἐπαγγ. τῷ ἁγ.] *with the
Spirit of promise, the Holy* Spirit :
the Spirit who had been the subject
of the promises of God through the
prophets and of the Incarnate Son :
Luke xxiv. 49; Acts i. 4 f.; ii. 17, 33;
John xiv. 15 ff.; xvi. 7 ff.; Gal. iii. 14.
The emphatic order which fixes attention on the characteristic attribute of
the Spirit (τῷ ἁγίῳ) leads on to the
description of His work in *v*. 14.
Comp. 1 Thess. iv. 8 τὸ πν. αὐτοῦ τὸ
ἅγιον.

Here the Spirit is regarded as the
instrument with which (τῷ πν.) believers are sealed : in *c*. iv. 30 as the
element, so to speak, in which they
are immersed (ἐν ᾧ: comp. Matt. iii.
11). Those who are 'in Christ' are
also 'in the Spirit.' Here the thought
of the gift is dominant : there the

thought of the Person. For τὸ πν.
τῆς ἐπαγγ. compare Hebr. xi. 9 εἰς τὴν
γῆν τῆς ἐπαγγελίας.

14. ὅ ἐστιν...] *which is an earnest
of our inheritance, unto the redemption of* God's *own possession* (Vg. *in
redemptionem acquisitionis* (V. L.
adoptionis)), *unto the praise of His
glory*. The partial gift—partial because it is limited by our present
capacity—shews surely that to which
it leads, and in which it will find its
consummation. What we have received is a pledge of that which God
has prepared for us as sons. When we
gain our end, then creation also shall
find deliverance from corruption and
enter on 'the freedom of the glory of
the children of God,' and all things
shall declare the praise of their Maker
and Redeemer. Rom. viii. 18—25 is a
pregnant commentary on the verse.

ἀρραβών] An 'earnest' : 2 Cor. i.
22; v. 5 [ὁ] δοὺς τὸν ἀρραβῶνα τοῦ πνεύματος. Ἀρραβών is properly a deposit
paid as security for the rest of the
purchase money ; and then, by a
natural transference, the first instal-
ment of a treasure given as a pledge
for the delivery of the remainder.

For the thought compare Rom. viii.
15 ff.; 23 (τὴν ἀπαρχὴν τοῦ πνεύματος
ἔχοντες).

εἰς ἀπολύτρωσιν...] *leading unto*....
The temporal sense, *until*... is possible,
but the parallelism of the two clauses
εἰς ἀπολύτρ....εἰς ἔπαινον... is decisive
for the other sense. The redemption
of God's own possession, and the
consequent praise of His glory are, so
to speak, the final cause of the work
of Christ and the Mission of the
Spirit.

τῆς περιποιήσεως] God's *own possession*, all that which God has made

His own in earth and heaven, not men only, who had fallen from Him, and earth which had shared the consequences of man's fall, but all created things, gathered together in the last crisis of their history. 'Creation' held 'in the bondage of corruption' required redemption. GOD has made us His sons 'that we should be a kind of firstfruits of His creation' (James i. 18 ἀπαρχήν τινα τῶν αὐτοῦ κτισμάτων). Our inheritance is preparatory to (εἰς) a larger blessing. The crown of the inheritance of Christians is that their consummation in Christ leads to His complete triumph. Creation waits for their revelation as the sons of GOD (Rom. viii. 19 f.). Then shall it also be 'delivered from the bondage of corruption into the liberty of the glory of the children of GOD.'

The interpretation which has been given to περιποίησις (after the Syriac and Œcumenius) is not without difficulty. Περιποίησις is properly the *acquisition* of something : 1 Thess. v. 9 εἰς περιποίησιν σωτηρίας, 2 Thess. ii. 14 εἰς περιποίησιν δόξης, Hebr. x. 39 εἰς περιπ. ψυχῆς. In 1 Pet. ii. 9 Christians are spoken of as λαὸς εἰς περιποίησιν in words borrowed from the LXX. (Mal. iii. 17 ἔσονταί μοι...εἰς περιποίησιν). GOD in His infinite patience and love wins His creatures to Himself. The αὐτοῦ in the last clause gives colour to τῆς περιποιήσεως. The thought is of the complete fulfilment of GOD's purpose. There is therefore nothing unnatural in the use of ἡ περιποίησις in this widest sense.

Additional Note on i. 1.   *The words* ἐν Ἐφέσῳ.

i 1] <[ἐν Ἐφέσῳ] ℵ*B "the older of the MSS" consulted by Bas. 67**
(Marcion, see below) Orig. *loc.* (distinctly) Bas. (expressly). Orig. interprets
τοῖς οὖσιν absolutely, in the sense of 1 Cor. i. 28, as he could not have done
had he read ἐν Ἐφέσῳ : Bas. probably has Orig. in mind when he refers for
this reading to 'predecessors,' from whom however Bas. manifestly dis-
tinguishes MSS consulted by himself (οὕτω γὰρ καὶ οἱ πρὸ ἡμῶν παραδεδώκασι
καὶ ἡμεῖς ἐν τοῖς παλαιοῖς τῶν ἀντιγράφων εὑρήκαμεν). It is doubtless again to
Orig. that Hier. refers when he speaks of 'certain' as interpreting the passage
in this manner 'with unnecessary refinement' (*curiosius quam necesse est*) :
—a remark which shews on the one hand that Hier. was not himself
acquainted with the reading, and on the other that Orig. in his unabridged
commentary can have made no reference to any MSS as containing ἐν
Ἐφέσῳ, since otherwise Hier. could not have treated the question as though
it affected interpretation alone.   Tert. distinctly states that Marcion retained
this Epistle, but under the title 'To the Laodicenes.'   Epiph. is silent on
this point in his short account of Marcion's readings in the Ep., but after the
conclusion of his remarks on all the epistles (374 A πρὸς Φιλιππησίους ί · οὕτως
γὰρ παρὰ τῷ Μαρκίωνι κεῖται ἐσχάτη καὶ δεκάτη) he subjoins a confused notice of
a reading of Marcion (Eph. iv. 5) "from the so-called Ep. to the Laodicenes,
in harmony with the Ep. to the Ephesians"; so that the unknown source from
which he borrowed his information about Marcion's text seems to have contained a misunderstood reference to the title used by Marcion.   It is hardly
credible that the Epistle should have received this title, either in a text
followed by Marcion or at his own hands, if the words ἐν Ἐφέσῳ had been
present.   It does not follow that ἐν Λαοδικίᾳ replaced it : a change of the
address in the body of the Epistle itself would hardly have been passed
over in silence ; and it seems more likely that the title was supplied from a
misapplication of Col. iv. 16 in the absence of any indication of address in
the text of the Epistle.   Text ℵ^{c}AD₂G₃K₂L₂P₂ later MSS consulted by Bas.
(see above) cu^{pl} vv^{omn} Cyr. al. *Thes.* 280 pp^{ser} pp^{lat}.

Transcriptional evidence strongly supports the testimony of documents
against ἐν Ἐφέσῳ.   The early and, except as regards Marcion, universal
tradition that the Epistle was addressed to the Ephesians, embodied in the
title found in all extant documents, would naturally lead to the insertion of
the words in the place that corresponding words hold in other epistles; and
on the other hand it is not easy to see how they could come to be omitted,
if genuine.   Nor again, when St Paul's use of the term οἱ ἅγιοι (*e.g.* 1 Cor. xvi.
1) and his view of πίστις in relation to the new Israel are taken into account,
is it in itself improbable that he should write "to the saints who are also
faithful (believing) in Christ Jesus."   The only real intrinsic difficulty here
lies in the resemblance to the phrases used in other epistles to introduce
local addresses.

The variation need not however be considered as a simple case of omission or insertion. There is much probability in the suggestion of Beza and Ussher, adopted by many commentators, that this Epistle was addressed to more than one church. It is certainly marked by an exceptional generality of language, and its freedom from local and personal allusions places it in strong contrast to the twin Ep. to the Colossians, conveyed by the same messenger. St Paul might naturally take advantage of the mission of Tychicus to write a letter to be read by the various churches which he had founded or strengthened in the region surrounding Ephesus during his long stay, though he might have special reasons for writing separate letters to Colossæ and Laodicea. Apart from any question of the reading in i. 1, this is the simplest explanation of the characteristics of the Epistle ; but, if it represents the facts truly, it must have a bearing on the reading. An epistle addressed to a plurality of churches might either be written so as to dispense with any local address, or it might have a blank space, to be filled up in each case with a different local address. The former supposition, according to which καὶ πιστοῖς would be continuous with τοῖς ἁγίοις, has been noticed above. In this case ἐν Ἐφέσῳ would be simply an interpolation. On the other view, which is on the whole the more probable of the two, ἐν Ἐφέσῳ would be a legitimate but unavoidably partial supplement to the true text, filling up a chasm which might be perplexing to a reader in later times. Since it is highly probable that the epistle would be communicated to the great mother church first, and then sent on to the lesser churches around, there is sufficient justification both for the title ΠΡΟΣ ΕΦΕΣΙΟΥΣ and for the retention of ἐν Ἐφέσῳ in peculiar type in the text itself. Whether Marcion's title was derived from a copy actually sent to Laodicea, or, as seems more likely, was a conjectural alteration of ΠΡΟΣ ΕΦΕΣΙΟΥΣ, Ephesus must have had a better right than any other single city to account itself the recipient of the Epistle.

¹⁵Διὰ τοῦτο κἀγώ, ἀκούσας τὴν καθ᾿ ὑμᾶς πίστιν
ἐν τῷ κυρίῳ ᾿Ιησοῦ καὶ τὴν εἰς πάντας τοὺς ἁγίους,
¹⁶οὐ παύομαι εὐχαριστῶν ὑπὲρ ὑμῶν, μνείαν ποιού-

15 καὶ + τὴν ἀγάπην א^cD₂G₃KL₂ vg syrr bo.

II. THANKSGIVING FOR FAITH RE-
ALISED : PRAYER FOR DEEPER KNOW-
LEDGE : GENERAL EXPOSITION OF THE
WORK OF CHRIST FOR MEN (i. 15—
ii. 22).
(1) Thanksgiving for the faith of
the Ephesians (i. 15, 16 a).
(2) Prayer for their fuller enlightenment (i. 16 b—21).
(3) The work of GOD for men in
Christ: personal disqualifications overcome (i. 22—ii. 10).
(4) The union of Jews and Gentiles
in one Divine Body : national differences set aside (ii. 11—22).

i. 15—ii. 22. The opening hymn of
praise is followed by a thanksgiving
for the faith of the readers (v. 15, 16a),
and a prayer for their fuller knowledge
of the privileges of the Christian faith
(16b—21), which leads to a description
of the work of GOD for men through
Christ (i. 22—ii. 10), and specially of
the union of Jews and Gentiles in one
body (ii. 11—22).
(1) Thanksgiving for the faith of
the Ephesians (15, 16a).
¹⁵ For this cause I also having
heard of the faith which is among
you in the Lord Jesus and which
ye shew toward all the saints ¹⁶cease
not to give thanks for you.
15. διὰ τοῦτο...] For this cause...
even that the Gentiles have now been
included within the Church, so that
the fulness of salvation has been
brought within sight.
κἀγώ] I also, though as a Jew I
might have been inclined to cherish
jealously the peculiar privileges of my
people.
ἀκούσας...τοὺς ἁγίους] having heard
of the faith which is among you
resting in the Lord Jesus and
which ye shew unto all the saints.
The phrase πίστις ἐν τῷ κυρίῳ ᾿Ιησοῦ,

which forms as it were a compound
word (comp. Col. i. 4 πίστις ὑμῶν ἐν X. ᾿I.),
represents faith not only as ' directed
to' (πρός, 1 Thess. i. 8 ἡ πίστις ὑμῶν ἡ
πρὸς θεόν) or 'reaching to (into)' (εἰς,
Acts xxvi. 18 πίστει τῇ εἰς ἐμέ), but
as ' grounded and resting in' the
Lord Jesus. Thus we find πίστις ἡ ἐν
X. ᾿I. 1 Tim. iii. 13 ; 2 Tim. iii. 15
(in Gal. iii. 26 ἐν X. ᾿I. is probably to
be taken with υἱοί ἐστε and not
with πίστεως). The use of ὁ κύριος
᾿Ιησοῦς is significant. The confession
' κύριος ᾿Ιησοῦς' was the earliest Christian creed : 1 Cor. xii. 3 ; Rom. x. 9
(ἐὰν ὁμολογήσῃς τὸ ῥῆμα...ὅτι Κύριος
᾿Ιησοῦς).
καὶ τὴν εἰς π. τ. ἁγ.] The insertion
of τὴν ἀγάπην after καί in the later
text is borrowed from Col. i. 4. 'The
faith shewn to all the saints' was the
practical expression of the faith which
rested on union with Christ. Comp.
Philem. 5 τὴν πίστιν ἣν ἔχεις...εἰς
πάντας τοὺς ἁγίους.
16. οὐ παύομαι...προσευχῶν μου]
This combination of prayer with
thanksgiving is characteristic: 1 Thess.
i. 2 ; Rom. i. 8 ff. ; Phil. i. 3 f. ; Col. i.
3 (2 Tim. i. 3). With οὐ παύομαι
compare πάντοτε, c. v. 20 ; 1 Thess. i.
2 ; 2 Thess. i. 3, 11 ; ii. 13 ; 1 Cor. i. 4 ;
Rom. i. 10 ; Col. i. 3 ; Phil. i. 4 ; ἀδιαλείπτως 1 Thess. ii. 13 ; v. 17 (1 Thess.
i. 2 ; Rom. i. 9) ; ἐν παντί 1 Thess. v.
18.
In orationibus, non ut quidam [in]
jucunditate convivii: mihi autem nihil
oratione jucundius (Primas.).
(2) Thanksgiving is combined with
prayer for their fuller enlightenment
(16 b—21).
¹⁶ Making mention of you in my
prayers, ¹⁷ that the GOD of our Lord
Jesus Christ, the Father of glory,
may give unto you a spirit of wisdom

μένος ἐπὶ τῶν προσευχῶν μου, ¹⁷ἵνα ὁ θεὸς τοῦ κυρίου
ἡμῶν Ἰησοῦ Χριστοῦ, ὁ πατὴρ τῆς δόξης, ⌈δῴη⌉ ὑμῖν
πνεῦμα σοφίας καὶ ἀποκαλύψεως ἐν ἐπιγνώσει αὐτοῦ,

17 δώῃ v. δῷ

and revelation in the knowledge of
Him; ¹⁸ to the end that having the
eyes of your heart enlightened ye
may know what is the hope of His
calling, what the riches of the glory
of His inheritance in the saints
¹⁹ and what the exceeding greatness
of His power to us-ward who believe,
according to the working of the
might of His strength ²⁰ which He
wrought in the Christ when He
raised Him from the dead and made
Him to sit at His right hand in the
heavenly order, ²¹ far above all rule,
and authority and power and dominion, and every name that is
named not only in this age but also
in that which is to come.

μνείαν ποιούμενος] The object ʻof
you and your faithʼ is naturally supplied from the preceding clause (Rom.
i. 9 ; Philm. 4).

17. ἵνα...] that, in order that....
The two titles which the Apostle
applies to God bring out his confidence and the full scope of his prayer.

ὁ θεός...ʼΙ. Χ.] the God of our Lord
Jesus Christ, the God whom He
acknowledges and at the same time
reveals. Comp. v. 3 note ; and see
also 1 Cor. xi. 3 ; xv. 27 f.

ὁ πατὴρ τῆς δόξης] the Father of
glory, from Whom all Divine splendour
and perfection proceed and to Whom
they belong ; the source and the object of all revelation.
For τῆς δόξης compare Acts vii. 2 ὁ
θεὸς τῆς δόξης (Ps. xxix. (xxviii.) 3).
James ii. 1 τὸν κύριον ἡμῶν ʼΙ. Χ. τῆς
δόξης. 1 Cor. ii. 8 τὸν κύριον τῆς δόξης.
Hebr. ix. 5 Χερουβεὶν δόξης.
For ὁ πατήρ compare James i. 17
ὁ π. τῶν φώτων. 2 Cor. i. 3 ὁ π. τῶν
οἰκτιρμῶν. Hebr. xii. 9 ὁ π. τῶν πνευμάτων.
On ἡ δόξα see Additional Note.

δώῃ ὑμῖν πν. σοφ. κ. ἀποκαλύψ.] On
Wisdom and Revelation see Dr Dale,
Ephesians, p. 133 [v. App. p. 158].
πν. σοφίας καὶ ἀποκ. ἐν ἐπιγν. αὐτοῦ]
a spirit of wisdom and revelation.
In all corresponding phrases ʻthe
spiritʼ is that through which the principle or power or feeling or characteristic, to which it is referred, becomes
effective in the man. So we read of
πνεῦμα πραότητος (1 Cor. iv. 21 ; Gal.
vi. 1); πνεῦμα ἁγιωσύνης (Rom. i. 4);
πνεῦμα δουλείας, πνεῦμα υἱοθεσίας (Rom.
viii. 15); πνεῦμα κατανύξεως (Rom. xi.
8); πνεῦμα δειλίας (2 Tim. i. 7); πνεῦμα
ζωῆς (Apoc. xi. 11); and in a definite
form τὸ πνεῦμα τοῦ κόσμου (1 Cor. ii. 12);
τὸ πνεῦμα τῆς πλάνης (1 John iv. 6);
τὸ πνεῦμα τῆς ἀληθείας (John xiv. 17 ;
xv. 26 ; 1 John iv. 6); τὸ πνεῦμα τῆς
πίστεως (2 Cor. iv. 13); τὸ πνεῦμα τῆς
χάριτος (Hebr. x. 29); τὸ πνεῦμα τῆς
προφητείας (Apoc. xix. 10); τὸ πνεῦμα
τοῦ νοός (c. iv. 23).

In accordance with this usage ʻthe
spirit of wisdom and revelationʼ will
be that spirit, that influence and
temper, through which ʻwisdom and
revelation,ʼ wisdom and the materials
for growth in wisdom, enter into
human life. Such a spirit is a gift of
the Paraclete ʻWho takes of that
which is Christʼs and declares itʼ to
believers (John xvi. 12 ff.). Through
it the Christian is at once able to test
and to receive and to communicate
Divine truths (1 Cor. ii. 6 ff.).

The characteristic work of the
Spirit is indeed the revelation of the
Son, through Whom the Father is
known. He comes ʻin the Sonʼs
nameʼ (John xiv. 26), even as the Son
came ʻin the Fatherʼs nameʼ (John v.
43). So it is that till the Mission of
the Paraclete the Son could not be
known by men. This fact explains

¹⁸πεφωτισμένους τοὺς ὀφθαλμοὺς τῆς καρδίας [ὑμῶν] εἰς

the remarkable form of the Lord's words in Matt. xi. 27, οὐδεὶς ἐπιγινώσκει τὸν υἱὸν εἰ μὴ ὁ πατήρ, οὐδὲ τὸν πατέρα τις ἐπιγινώσκει εἰ μὴ ὁ υἱός, καὶ ᾧ ἐὰν βούληται ὁ υἱὸς ἀποκαλύψαι. The absence of a second clause after ὁ πατήρ shews that the sentence took shape before the Revealer of the Son had been sent.

This work is not for one age but for all ages. It finds its application ἐν ἐπιγνώσει [τοῦ θεοῦ] and this knowledge can never be final. All that can be learnt of the course of Nature and History becomes under the action of the 'spirit of wisdom and revelation' a disclosure of fresh truth as to the character and purpose and working of God. The eternal life itself consists in this (John xvii. 3 ἵνα γινώσκωσι). He *that loveth is begotten of God and knoweth* (γινώσκει) *God* (1 John iv. 7). *We know that the Son of God is come* (ἥκει) *and hath given us an understanding that we may know Him that is true* (διάνοιαν ἵνα γινώσκομεν [-κωμεν] 1 John v. 20, see notes). In this lies the real glory and hope of experience and labour.

ἐν ἐπιγνώσει αὐτοῦ] *in the knowledge of Him,* i.e. of God, as in τῆς κλήσεως αὐτοῦ, τῆς κληρονομίας αὐτοῦ, τῆς δυνάμεως αὐτοῦ, τῆς ἰσχύος αὐτοῦ (vv. 18, 19). Ἐπίγνωσις has always a moral value and is used in the N.T. exclusively in reference to facts of the religious order and specially in reference to the knowledge which we are enabled to gain of God and of His purpose for man's salvation. It is peculiar to the Epistles. It occurs first in the Epistle to the Romans, and is found in all the later Epistles of St Paul, in Hebrews and 2 Peter. The passages will repay careful study, and furnish a commentary on the thought here.

(*a*) Rom. i. 28 οὐκ ἐδοκίμασαν τὸν θεὸν ἔχειν ἐν ἐπιγνώσει.

Rom. x. 2 ζῆλον θεοῦ ἔχουσιν ἀλλ' οὐ κατ' ἐπίγνωσιν.

Eph. iv. 13 μέχρι καταντήσωμεν οἱ πάντες εἰς τὴν ἑνότητα...τῆς ἐπιγνώσεως τοῦ υἱοῦ τοῦ θεοῦ.

Col. i. 10 αὐξανόμενοι τῇ ἐπιγνώσει τοῦ θεοῦ.

2 Pet. i. 2 χάρις ὑμῖν καὶ εἰρήνη πληθυνθείη ἐν ἐπιγνώσει τοῦ θεοῦ καὶ Ἰησοῦ τοῦ κυρίου ἡμῶν.

id. i. 3 πάντα ... τὰ πρὸς ζωήν... δεδωρημένης διὰ τῆς ἐπιγνώσεως τοῦ καλέσαντος ἡμᾶς.

id. i. 8 οὐκ ἀργοὺς...καθίστησιν εἰς τὴν τοῦ κυρίου ἡμῶν Ἰησοῦ Χριστοῦ ἐπίγνωσιν.

id. ii. 20 ἀποφυγόντες τὰ μιάσματα τοῦ κόσμου ἐν ἐπιγνώσει τοῦ κυρίου καὶ σωτῆρος Ἰησοῦ Χριστοῦ.

(*b*) Col. i. 9 ἵνα πληρωθῆτε τὴν ἐπίγνωσιν τοῦ θελήματος αὐτοῦ.

id. ii. 2 εἰς ἐπίγνωσιν τοῦ μυστηρίου τοῦ θεοῦ, Χριστοῦ.

1 Tim. ii. 4, 2 Tim. ii. 25, iii. 7, Tit. i. 1 ἐπίγνωσις ἀληθείας.

Hebr. x. 26 ἡ ἐπίγνωσις τῆς ἀληθείας.

(*c*) Rom. iii. 20 διὰ νόμου ἐπίγνωσις ἁμαρτίας.

Phil. i. 10 ἵνα ἡ ἀγάπη...περισσεύῃ ἐν ἐπιγνώσει κ. πάσῃ αἰσθήσει εἰς τὸ δοκιμάζειν ὑμᾶς τὰ διαφέροντα.

This ἐπίγνωσις is at once the condition and the result of growing conformity to the Divine likeness:

Col. iii. 10 ἐνδυσάμενοι τὸν νέον [ἄνθρωπον] τὸν ἀνακαινούμενον εἰς ἐπίγνωσιν κατ' εἰκόνα τοῦ κτίσαντος αὐτόν.

For the verb ἐπιγινώσκειν see Matt. xi. 27; Luke i. 4; 2 Pet. ii. 21; 1 Cor. xiii. 12; 2 Cor. i. 13 f.; Rom. i. 32; 1 Tim. iv. 3.

The subject, with which this 'spirit of wisdom and revelation' is to deal, is of all the most overwhelming,—that men are destined to share in the glory of the exaltation of 'the Lord Jesus Christ.'

18. πεφωτ. ... εἰδέναι] *to the end that having the eyes of your heart enlightened ye may know....* The construction is obscure and perhaps confused. It is possible that πεφωτ.

τὸ εἰδέναι ὑμᾶς τίς ἐστιν ἡ ἐλπὶς τῆς κλήσεως αὐτοῦ,

τοὺς ὀφθ. may be paralleled with πν. σοφ. καὶ ἀποκ. and depend directly on δώῃ (give you the eyes of your heart enlightened, i.e. enlighten them). But this is an unnatural construction, and the enlightening of the eyes of the heart is not so much a new element in the Divine teaching as a special result involved in the gift of the spirit of revelation. It is therefore best to connect the words with ὑμῖν, the case being determined by the following infinitive (εἰς τὸ εἰδέναι ὑμᾶς) with which it goes closely. There are somewhat similar irregularities of order : c. iii. 18 ; Luke xxiv. 47 (ἀρξάμ. ἀπὸ Ἰ. ὑμεῖς μάρτυρες).

τοὺς ὀφθ. τῆς καρδίας] The 'heart' expresses the whole personality of man. Comp. c. iv. 17, 18 (νοῦς, διάνοια, καρδία) note. Spiritual sight includes the action of feeling as well as of intellect.

For the image πεφωτισμένους see John i. 9 ; 1 John i. 7 ; ii. 8 ff.; Apoc. xxii. 5 (xxi. 23) ; Hebr. vi. 4 ; x. 32 (notes): 2 Cor. iv. 6; cc. iii. 9; v. 8, 13 notes ; 2 Tim. i. 10. Compare 2 Cor. iv. 4, 6. The corresponding 'darkening' is described Rom. i. 21.

18, 19. τίς ἐστιν ἡ ἐλπίς...τίς ὁ πλοῦτος...τί τὸ ὑπερβ. μέγ....] Three distinct objects of spiritual knowledge are set before us. Two concern the nature of our destiny—the hope of our calling, and the wealth of the glory of GOD's inheritance; and the third, the power of GOD by which it is fulfilled. As we pass from thought to thought, we pass more and more from man to GOD, from our feeling to His works, though all is of Him and referred to Him : it is His calling ; His inheritance ; His might ; the calling which He has given, the inheritance which He has prepared, the power which He has shewn ; there is at the same time an increasing fulness of development in the successive stages :

(1) τίς ἡ ἐλπὶς τῆς κλήσεως αὐτοῦ.
(2) τίς ὁ πλοῦτος τῆς δόξης τῆς κληρ. αὐτοῦ ἐν τοῖς ἁγίοις.
(3) τί τὸ ὑπερβάλλον μέγεθος τῆς δυνάμεως αὐτοῦ εἰς ἡμᾶς τοὺς πιστεύοντας κατὰ τὴν ἐνέργειαν τοῦ κράτους τῆς ἰσχύος αὐτοῦ ἣν ἐνήργηκεν ἐν τῷ χριστῷ.

The three great moments correspond with the experience of life, which brings out into evidence evils, capacities, failures, which a growing intelligence of the nature and will and working of GOD alone can meet. We can face the sorrows and sadnesses of personal and social history 'in the hope of GOD's calling.' We can rejoice in the possession of capacities and needs to which our present circumstances bring no satisfaction when we look to 'the wealth of the glory of GOD's inheritance in the saints.' We can overcome the discouragements of constant failures and weaknesses by the remembrance of the power of GOD shewn in the Raising of Christ.

τίς ἐστιν ἡ ἐλπίς...] The question in each case (τίς...τίς...τί...) is of the essence and not of the quality (ποία). What is the hope of His calling, the hope, the 'one hope of their calling' for all Christians (c. iv. 4), kindled and sustained in us by the fact that GOD has called us to His presence. Such a Divine call is a revelation of human destiny. Man can in Christ behold GOD and live (comp. 1 John iii. 2 f.; 2 Cor. iii. 12). His hope enters within the veil where Christ has entered in (Hebr. vi. 19 f.). Compare 1 Pet. i. 3, 5. His hope is a hope of righteousness (Gal. v. 5). Without GOD man has no hope (c. ii. 12).

Κλῆσις is used in regard to the circumstances of the call to the outward society of Christians (1 Cor. i. 26 ; vii. 20), but more especially of the call as a divine invitation (as here and c. iv. 4 ; Rom. xi. 29 ἀμεταμέλητος ἡ

τίς ὁ πλοῦτος τῆς δόξης τῆς κληρονομίας αὐτοῦ ἐν τοῖς
ἁγίοις, ¹⁹καὶ τί τὸ ὑπερβάλλον μέγεθος τῆς δυνάμεως
αὐτοῦ εἰς ἡμᾶς τοὺς πιστεύοντας κατὰ τὴν ἐνέργειαν

κλῆσις τοῦ θεοῦ ; Phil. iii. 14 ἡ ἄνω
κλῆσις τοῦ θεοῦ), a holy calling (2 Tim.
i. 9), a heavenly calling (Hebr. iii. 1
κλήσεως ἐπουρανίου μέτοχοι note), which
carries with it great obligations (c. iv. 1
ἀξίως περιπατῆσαι τῆς κλήσεως) calling
for responsible effort on the part of
those who had received it (2 Pet. i. 10
σπουδάσατε βεβαίαν ὑμῶν τὴν κλῆσιν...
ποιεῖσθαι), and corresponding with a
unity of corporate life (c. iv. 4).

Comp. 2 Thess. i. 11 προσευχόμεθα
...ἵνα ὑμᾶς ἀξιώσῃ τῆς κλήσεως ὁ θεὸς
ἡμῶν....
The verb καλεῖν is used characteristically of GOD (yet see Gal. i. 6 ; v. 8)
and the call, as His act, is treated as
effectual (1 Cor. i. 9 ; Rom. viii. 30 ;
1 Pet. ii. 9 ; v. 10). At the same time
the call is continuous (1 Thess. ii. 12
τοῦ καλοῦντος ; v. 24 ὁ καλῶν). Under
the human aspect it needs effort (1 Pet.
i. 15 ; 1 Thess. iv. 7 ; 1 Tim. vi. 12 ;
2 Thess. ii. 14). In 1 Cor. vii. 17 ff.
the call appears to be to the outward
society only.

ὁ πλοῦτος τ. δόξης...] Men are not
only called by GOD and so assured that
it is His will that they should come
to His Presence (Ps. xvi. 11 ; xvii. 15),
but the nature of their inheritance is
already known to them ' in the saints.'
Every unfulfilled aspiration is a prophecy of that which shall be. Already
in the Christian fellowship there is a
beginning and a promise. The future
consummation grows out of that which
is. ' Christ in us ' expresses shortly
what is ' the wealth of the glory '
prepared for men (Col. i. 27), the
fulness of their 'inheritance' (Acts xx
32). On the idea of ' inheritance ' see
Hebr. ix. 15 ; xi. 7 ff.

The phrase ὁ πλοῦτος τῆς δόξης
occurs in three other places : Rom. ix.
23 ἵνα γνωρίσῃ τὸν πλοῦτον τῆς δόξης
αὐτοῦ ἐπὶ σκεύη ἐλέους ἃ προητοίμασεν

εἰς δόξαν ; Eph. iii. 16 ἵνα δῷ ὑ. κατὰ
τὸ πλοῦτος τῆς δόξης αὐτοῦ...κραταιω-
θῆναι...εἰς τὸν ἔσω ἄνθρωπον, κατοικῆσαι
τὸν χριστὸν...ἐν ταῖς καρδίαις...; Col.
i. 27 ἠθέλησεν ὁ θεὸς γνωρίσαι τί τὸ
πλοῦτος τῆς δόξης τοῦ μυστηρίου τούτου
...ὅ ἐστιν Χριστὸς ἐν ὑμῖν, ἡ ἐλπὶς τῆς
δόξης.
In each case union with the Incarnate Word is the spring and the
measure of the glory. All is summed
up in 1 Cor. iii. 23 πάντα ὑμῶν, ὑμεῖς
δὲ Χριστοῦ, Χριστὸς δὲ θεοῦ.

19. τί τὸ ὑπερβάλλον...] The attainment of this transcendent glory is
seen to be possible when we consider
what GOD has done in the Christ.
The Resurrection and the Ascension
furnish the type of his working on
behalf of believers, who are members
of His body.

Μέγεθος occurs here only in N.T.
For ὑπερβάλλον comp. c. ii. 7 ; 2 Cor.
iii. 10 ; ix. 14 ; and 2 Cor. iv. 7.

κατὰ τὴν ἐνέργειαν...τῆς ἰσχ. αὐτοῦ]
Compare for κατ' ἐνέργειαν c. iii. 7 κατὰ
τὴν ἐνέργειαν τῆς δυνάμεως αὐτοῦ, c. iv. 16
κατ' ἐνέργειαν ἐν μέτρῳ ἑνὸς ἑκάστου
μέρους. Col. i. 29 κοπιῶ ἀγωνιζόμενος
κατὰ τὴν ἐνέργειαν αὐτοῦ. Phil. iii. 21
μετασχηματίσει...κατὰ τὴν ἐνέργειαν τοῦ
δύνασθαι αὐτὸν καὶ ὑποτάξαι αὐτῷ τὰ
πάντα. 2 Thess. ii. 9 οὗ ἐστιν ἡ παρουσία κατ' ἐνέργειαν τοῦ Σατανᾶ. The
active exercise of the power of GOD in
the case of the Messiah, the Son of
man, supplied a standard of the help
which He would bring to His people.

The combination κράτος τῆς ἰσχύος
occurs again c. vi. 10. A corresponding
phrase is found in Col. i. 11 τὸ κράτος
τῆς δόξης. Κράτος is might, strength
regarded as abundantly effective in
relation to an end to be gained or
dominion to be exercised : ἰσχύς is
strength absolutely. For κράτος see
Hebr. ii. 14 ; and (in doxologies) 1 Tim.

τοῦ κράτους τῆς ἰσχύος αὐτοῦ ²⁰ ἦν ʿἐνήργηκεν᾽ ἐν τῷ
χριστῷ ἐγείρας αὐτὸν ἐκ νεκρῶν, καὶ κΑθίςΑς ἐΝ Δεξιᾷ
Αῦτοῦ ἐν τοῖς ἐπουρανίοις ²¹ ὑπεράνω πάσης ἀρχῆς καὶ
ἐξουσίας καὶ δυνάμεως καὶ κυριότητος καὶ παντὸς ὀνόματος ὀνομαζομένου οὐ μόνον ἐν τῷ αἰῶνι τούτῳ ἀλλὰ

20 ἐνήργησεν

vi. 16; 1 Pet. iv. 11; v. 11; Jude 25;
Apoc. i. 6; v. 13; and for ἰσχύς
2 Thess. i. 9; 1 Pet. iv. 11; 2 Pet.
ii. 11.

20 f. As St Paul touches on 'the
working of the might of GOD's strength'
in the exaltation of Christ as the sure
ground of Christian confidence, he
seems himself to be overpowered by
the wonders which it involves, and
follows its consequences through the
orders of the heavenly hierarchy and
successive stages in the accomplishment of GOD's counsel, that he may
indicate the unimaginable dignity of
which humanity is found capable in
its Head.

20. ἦν ἐνήργ. ἐν τῷ χριστῷ] *which
He hath wrought* (or *wrought*) *in
the Christ.* The title—the Christ—
emphasises the relation in which the
Lord stood to His people in the age-
long counsel of GOD.

The Divine work for the Messiah
is summed up in the two facts that
GOD (1) raised Him from the dead,
and (2) set Him at His right hand in
sovereign power. This was the first
apostolic message : Acts ii. 32 ff.; v.
30 ff.

The exaltation of Christ was the
sign and pledge of the triumph of
the Christian. Comp. 1 Pet. i. 21;
2 Cor. iv. 14; Rom. viii. 11.

ἐγείρας] This is the uniform teaching of the apostles : Acts iii. 15; iv.
10; v. 30; x. 40; xiii. 37; 1 Thess. i.
10; 1 Cor. vi. 14; xv. 15; 2 Cor. iv. 14;
Gal. i. 1; Rom. iv. 24; viii. 11; x. 9;
Col. ii. 12; 1 Pet. i. 21. The words
of the Lord in John x. 18 indicate the
complementary aspect of the truth
which is not further developed. 'To

take life again' is different from 'to
rise.' Comp. *c.* ii. 5. See Additional
Note [p. 189 ff.].
    καθίσας] Ps. cx. 1. Comp. Hebr.
i. 13 note.

21. ὑπεράνω πάσης ἀρχ....] Comp.
iii. 10 and Additional Note.

For ὑπεράνω comp. *c.* iv. 10; Hebr.
ix. 5. V.L. gives *super omne initium.*

παντὸς ὀνόματος] A name describes
a dignity more personal and essential
than an office. The name is designed
to express what he who bears it is and
not simply what he holds. Comp. Phil.
ii. 9.

οὐ μόνον...] For the implied contrast between 'this age' and 'the age
to come,' see *cc.* ii. 2; vi. 12. The
apostle looks forward to 'coming ages,'
springing one out of the other εἰς
πάσας τὰς γενεὰς τοῦ αἰῶνος τῶν αἰώνων
c. iii. 21 note.

For 'the coming age' see Hebr.
vi. 5 (ii. 5 οἰκουμένην τὴν μέλλουσαν).
It occupies a far less prominent
place in the apostolic teaching than
might have been expected. All is
summed up in the παρουσία, which
however is not mentioned in this
Epistle. Primasius dimly feels that
the contrast between the two ages
is not in succession of time but in
character : *in futuro* hoc est in caelesti
quod nobis futurum est, non Deo nec
sibi.

(3) A summary account of the work
of GOD for men through Christ (i. 22—
ii. 10).

²² *And He put all things in subjection under His feet; and He
gave Him to be Head over all things
to the Church* ²³ *which is His body,
the fulness of Him Who reaches*

καὶ ἐν τῷ μέλλοντι· ²²καὶ πάντα ὑπέταξεν ὑπὸ τοὺς πόδας
αὐτοῦ, καὶ αὐτὸν ἔδωκεν κεφαλὴν ὑπὲρ πάντα τῇ ἐκκλη-

His fulness through all things in all; ii. ¹ *and you* He quickened *when ye were dead through your trespasses and sins* ² *wherein aforetime ye walked according to the course of this world, according to the prince of the power of the air, of the spirit that now worketh in the sons of disobedience;* ³ *among whom we also all once lived in the lusts of our flesh, doing the will* (lit. *wills*) *of the flesh and of the mind* (lit. *thoughts*), *and were children by nature of wrath, even as the rest* of men:—⁴ *but* GOD *being rich in mercy, for His great love wherewith He loved us,* ⁵ *even when we were dead through our trespasses quickened us together with the Christ (by grace have ye been saved),* ⁶ *and raised us up with Him and made us to sit with Him in the heavenly* order *in Christ Jesus;* ⁷ *that in the ages to come He might shew the exceeding riches of His grace in kindness towards us in Christ Jesus:* —⁸ *for by grace have ye been saved through faith; and that not of yourselves:* ⁹ *it is the gift of* GOD, *not of works that no man should glory—* ¹⁰ *For it is His workmanship we are, created in Christ Jesus for good works, which* GOD *afore prepared that in them we should walk.*

22. St Paul suddenly changes the form of his writing. In the preceding verses he has set out the truths which the Ephesians were to master for themselves through the teaching of 'the spirit of wisdom and revelation': He now declares directly what GOD has done. The transition is prepared naturally by the reference to the Resurrection and Ascension of Christ. These facts were not only events fitted to confirm the greatest hopes of Christians: they were the beginnings of a new order. Not only was Christ Himself exalted to the heavens: He is invested with universal sovereignty

(comp. Matt. xxviii. 18). He is even now Head of His Church on earth; and He has already exercised His sovereignty by the gift of His quickening grace.

The three points are distinctly marked and just as in the former section they are described with increasing fulness :

(1) πάντα ὑπέταξεν ὑπὸ τοὺς πόδας αὐτοῦ.
(2) αὐτὸν ἔδωκεν κεφαλὴν ὑπὲρ πάντα
τῇ ἐκκλησίᾳ,
ἥτις ἐστιν τὸ σῶμα αὐτοῦ,
τὸ πλήρωμα τοῦ τὰ πάντα ἐν πᾶσιν πληρουμένου.
(3) ὑμᾶς ὄντας νεκροὺς τοῖς παραπτώμασιν καὶ ταῖς ἁμαρτίαις ὑμῶν...
ἐν οἷς [τοῖς υἱοῖς τῆς ἀπειθίας] καὶ ἡμεῖς πάντες ἀνεστράφημέν ποτε...
καὶ ὄντας ἡμᾶς νεκροὺς τοῖς παραπτώμασιν
συνεζωοποίησεν [ἐν] τῷ χριστῷ...
ἵνα ἐνδείξηται...
αὐτοῦ γάρ ἐσμεν ποίημα....

In the last section the construction is sacrificed to the crowding fulness of the thoughts.

22. καὶ πάντα...αὐτοῦ] Ps. viii. 6. The treatment of this passage in Hebr. ii. 5 ff. furnishes a commentary on the words here. Compare also 1 Cor. xv. 27 ff.

καὶ αὐτὸν ἔδωκεν...] The unusual order gives emphasis. 'And He it was—none other—Whom GOD gave to be....'

κεφαλήν] The image occurs in a different yet cognate application in 1 Cor. xi. 3 παντὸς ἀνδρὸς ἡ κεφαλὴ ὁ χριστός ἐστιν, κεφαλὴ δὲ γυναικὸς ὁ ἀνήρ, κεφαλὴ δὲ τοῦ χριστοῦ ὁ θεός. Comp. c. v. 23. The thought of sovereignty, already given, is now connected with that of vital union with a glorious organism which draws its life from Him (c. iv. 15; Col. ii. 19).

ὑπὲρ πάντα] Sovereign over all the other elements included in it.

τῇ ἐκκλησίᾳ] See App. [p. 172 ff.].

σία, ²³ἥτις ἐστὶν τὸ σῶμα αὐτοῦ, τὸ πλήρωμα τοῦ τὰ

23. ἥτις ἐστὶν τὸ σ. αὐ.] which is — seeing it is — His body. The qualitative relation has its full force. For the development of the idea of the Church as the Body of Christ see Additional Note (in App.).

τὸ πλήρωμα...] the fulness of Him Who reaches His fulness through all things in all. Latt. qui omnia in omnibus adimpletur (impletur): some adimplet.

The active sense which is generally given to πληρουμένου (who filleth) finds no support in the use of the word in the N.T. Both voices occur in this Epistle : cc. iii. 19 ἵνα πληρωθῆτε εἰς (or ἵνα πληρωθῇ) πᾶν τὸ πλήρωμα τοῦ θεοῦ. v. 18 πληροῦσθε ἐν πνεύματι and again iv. 10 ἵνα πληρώσῃ τὰ πάντα.

Again even if the active sense were possible it does not appear to fall in with the context. It is indeed true that Christ does 'fill all things' (c. iv. 10). That is the relation in which He stands to them. But here the thought is of the converse relation of created things to Christ. For while, on the one side, Christ gives their true being to all things by His presence (Col. i. 17 ; cf. Ac.s xvii. 28) and Christians in a special sense reach their 'fulness,' their complete development, in Him (c. iv. 15 ; Col. ii. 10); on the other side, all things are contributory to Him, and He himself finds His fulness in the sum of all that He brings into a living union with Himself. Thus the Church is His Body, in which, gathering to itself the first-fruits of creation, He is Himself presented to the eye of faith. The fulness, if we may so speak, is at present representative only. The end is not yet, but it is prepared and prefigured. It will be reached through the summing up of all things in Christ through the Church, that GOD may be all in all (Col. iii. 11 πάντα καὶ ἐν πᾶσιν Χριστός, 1 Cor. xv. 28 τότε καὶ αὐτὸς ὁ υἱὸς

ὑποταγήσεται τῷ ὑποτάξαντι αὐτῷ τὰ πάντα, ἵνα ᾖ ὁ θεὸς πάντα ἐν πᾶσιν).

The present πληρουμένου shews that the process is continuous till all things are brought into subjection to Christ.

The construction of τὰ πάντα with πληρουμένου is illustrated by the remarkable phrase in Col. i. 9 ἵνα πληρωθῆτε τὴν ἐπίγνωσιν τοῦ θελήματος αὐτοῦ. The knowledge itself constituted the fulness for which the Apostle looked. Comp. c. iii. 19.

For πλήρωμα see Lightfoot, Col. i. 19.

Primasius gives the main sense : Qui [Christus] totus in membris omnibus adimpletur non in singulis, ne ulla diversitas meritorum sit ; quando omnes crediderint et perfecti fuerint, tunc erit corpus perfectum in omnibus membris.

ii. 1—10. In describing the third element in the Lord's present work, St Paul enlarges the scope of his original statement, and shews how the mercy and love of GOD was extended not only to Gentiles (1, 2) but to all Christians alike, whether Jews or Gentiles (3—6), who are a new creation designed for the fulfilment of His will (10).

The development of the truth, though the construction is irregular and broken by parentheses, is perfectly natural. After characterising the former life of the Ephesians as answering to the influence of 'the spirit that now worketh in the sons of disobedience' (1, 2), he adds that he and all with him shared their life, and following the impulses of nature were 'children of wrath' as all other men ; and then, having thus exhibited the wider need of GOD's quickening love, he contemplates the whole Christian society, and no longer the Ephesians only or specially, as the objects of salvation in Christ (4—6) and a proof of GOD's exceeding goodness to all future ages (7). For a moment he returns again, as in a brief parenthesis before (v. 5

πάντα ἐν πᾶσιν πληρουμένου. II. ¹Καὶ ὑμᾶς ὄντας
νεκροὺς τοῖς παραπτώμασιν καὶ ταῖς ἁμαρτίαις ὑμῶν,
²ἐν αἷς ποτὲ περιεπατήσατε κατὰ τὸν αἰῶνα τοῦ κόσμου
τούτου, κατὰ τὸν ἄρχοντα τῆς ἐξουσίας τοῦ ἀέρος, τοῦ

χάριτί ἐστε σεσωσμένοι), to the Ephesians (8, 9); and then shews how the
testimony of the Church will be
delivered by the performance of the
works which are prepared for believers
(10).

1. καὶ ὑμᾶς...] And you He quickened when ye were dead through your
trespasses and sins. The clause is
strictly parallel to the two which go
before : And he put all things in
subjection...And he gave Him to be...
And you he quickened....

νεκροὺς τοῖς παρ. καὶ ἁμ.] For νεκρούς
see c. v. 14; Matt. viii. 22 ‖ Lk. ix. 60;
Lk. xv. 24, 32; John v. 25 (21); Rom.
vi. 13 (xi. 15); Apoc. iii. 1. For νεκρ.
τοῖς παραπτ. dead through offences....
compare Col. ii. 13 νεκροὺς ὄντας τοῖς
παραπτώμασιν καὶ τῇ ἀκροβυστίᾳ τῆς
σαρκὸς ὑμῶν, cp. 1 Pet. i. 18. Contrast
Rom. viii. 10 τὸ μὲν σῶμα νεκρὸν δι'
ἁμαρτίαν.

Νεκρός describes generally the
complete absence of the characteristic
power of that to which it is referred.
Sin is dead (Rom. vii. 8) when it is
unable to work its effects. On the
other hand men are regarded as 'dead
to sin' (Rom. vi. 11 νεκροὺς τῇ ἁμαρτίᾳ)
when they are held to be incapable of
sinning. Faith is dead (James ii. 17,
26) when it fails to produce its corresponding works. Works are dead
(Hebr. vi. 1, note; ix. 14) when they
are destitute of that divine element
which alone gives them reality. Men
are dead in respect to that which is
the true characteristic of man when
they are without that power through
which they grow to the Divine likeness for which men were made. This
comes from the indwelling of Christ
(Gal. ii. 20; John xiv. 6; xi. 25 f.).
Sin excludes Him.

The variations in order, v. 1 καὶ ὑμᾶς
ὄντας νεκρούς, v. 5 καὶ ὄντας ἡμᾶς
νεκρούς, Col. ii. 13 καὶ ὑμᾶς νεκροὺς
ὄντας are to be noticed as indicating
subtle differences of emphasis. The
position of ὄντας is unusual, yet it
occurs again v. 20; Rom. v. 6 (contrast
v. 8); xvi. 1. Comp. Acts xix. 31 ;
xxvii. 2, 9.

2. ἐν αἷς ποτὲ περιεπ.] Sins were
more than occasional acts; they were
the medium, the atmosphere, of their
ordinary life.

Περιπατεῖν is used of personal action,
in regard to the man himself : ἀναστρέφεσθαι of social action, converse
among other men (v. 3 ἐν οἷς ἀνεστρά-
φημεν [contrast Col. iii. 6 ἐν οἷς (neut.)
καὶ ὑμεῖς περιεπατήσατε]; 2 Cor. i. 12;
1 Tim. iii. 15; even when this is not
expressly defined, Hebr. x. 33; xiii. 18;
1 Pet. i. 17; 2 Pet. ii. 18); στοιχεῖν
of action directed on particular lines
(Gal. vi. 16; Rom. iv. 12; Phil. iii. 16).
For περιπατεῖν ἐν see 1 John i. 6
note.

κατὰ τὸν αἰῶνα τ. κ. τ.] Latt. secundum seculum mundi hujus, according
to the course of this world. The use of
αἰών recals the familiar phrase 'cor-
rumpere et corrumpi seculum vocatur'
(Tac. Germ. 19). Αἰών describes an
age marked by a particular character:
κόσμος the whole constitution of things.

κατὰ τὸν ἄρχ...] According to the
prince of the power of the air, of the
spirit that now worketh in the children of disobedience. 'The course of
the world' corresponds with the being
who is its god (2 Cor. iv. 4 ὁ θεὸς τοῦ
αἰῶνος τούτου). This temporary and
contingent power (Lk. iv. 6 παραδέδοται, John xii. 31) is contrasted with
the universal sovereignty of God,
1 Tim. i. 17 ὁ βασιλεὺς τῶν αἰώνων.

πνεύματος τοῦ νῦν ἐνεργοῦντος ἐν τοῖς υἱοῖς τῆς ἀπει-
θίας· ³ἐν οἷς καὶ ἡμεῖς πάντες ἀνεστράφημέν ποτε ἐν
ταῖς ἐπιθυμίαις τῆς σαρκὸς ἡμῶν, ποιοῦντες τὰ θελήματα
τῆς σαρκὸς καὶ τῶν διανοιῶν, καὶ ἤμεθα τέκνα φύσει

Comp. John xii. 31; xvi. 11 ὁ ἄρχων
τοῦ κόσμου τούτου; xiv. 30 ὁ τοῦ κόσμου
ἄρχων.
  1 Cor. ii. 6 τῶν ἀρχόντων τοῦ αἰῶνος
τούτου τῶν καταργουμένων.
For the use of κατά compare κατὰ
θεόν c. iv. 24; 2 Cor. vii. 10, 11; Rom.
viii. 27; 1 Pet. v. 2; κατὰ τὸν καλέσαντα
1 Pet. i. 15; κατὰ Χρ. Ἰ. Rom. xv. 5;
κατὰ Χρ. Col. ii. 8; κατὰ κύριον 2 Cor.
xi. 17; κατὰ ἄνθρωπον 1 Cor. iii. 3;
ix. 8; xv. 32; Gal. i. 11; iii. 15;
Rom. iii. 5; (vii. 22); 1 Pet. iv. 6
(κατὰ ἀνθρώπους, κατὰ θεόν).
See Additional Note [App. p. 195].
'The power of the air' is the 'spirit'
which is active in 'the sons of disobedience,' and is subordinate to a
higher, 'personal,' power (ὁ ἄρχων τῆς
ἐξ. τοῦ ἀέρος).
The phrase ἡ ἐξουσία τοῦ ἀέρος
(compare Col. i. 13 ἐρύσατο ἡμᾶς ἐκ
τῆς ἐξουσίας τοῦ σκότους) is borrowed
from the language of current thought
which regarded the lower regions of
the sky (ἀήρ, compare 1 Thess. iv. 17)
as tenanted by evil spirits; and the
adoption of the idea by St Paul justifies us in believing that we can so
most truly represent to ourselves our
relation to the unseen adversaries by
which we are surrounded. They are,
so to speak, within reach of us; and
no fact of experience is more clear
than that we are exposed to assaults
of evil from without.
  ἐν τοῖς υἱοῖς τῆς ἀπ.] Latt. in filiis
diffidentiæ (al. incredulitatis, inobe-
dientiæ, infidelitatis). So in c. v. 6
(inserted by transcribers in Col. iii. 6).
Compare Matt. viii. 12; xiii. 38 οἱ υἱοὶ
τῆς βασιλείας; Matt. ix. 15; Mk ii. 19;
Lk. v. 34 οἱ υἱοὶ τοῦ νυμφῶνος, xx. 36
τῆς ἀναστάσεως υἱοὶ ὄντες, John xii. 36;
1 Thess. v. 5 υἱοὶ φωτός; 1 Thess. v. 5

υἱοὶ ἡμέρας. And note the special title
ὁ υἱὸς τῆς ἀπωλείας John xvii. 12
(Judas); 2 Thess. ii. 3 ὁ ἄνθρωπος τῆς
ἀνομίας (or ἁμαρτίας).
  Similar phrases are formed with
τέκνον; see v. 3 τέκνα φύσει ὀργῆς
and note.
  'Disobedience,' conscious resistance
to the will of GOD, lays men open to
the working of Satan and his hosts
(John iii. 36).
  3. At this point St Paul is constrained to recognise that the description which he has given of the moral
condition of the Ephesians applied
also to himself, a Jew by birth, and his
fellow-believers. Before their con-
version they were not separated from
the 'sons of disobedience,' among
whom, he adds, we all also once
lived...doing the will (lit. wills) of
the flesh and of the mind. The
plurals τὰ θελήματα and τῶν διανοιῶν
(v.l. consiliorum, V. cogitationum,
Hieron. Comm. mentium) do not
admit of a simple translation. The
thought is of the multiplicity of
purposes suggested by 'the flesh' and
by the many thoughts of a discursive
intelligence.
  For τὰ θελήματα comp. Acts xiii. 22
and var. lect. Mk iii. 35; and for
τῶν διαν. Hebr. x. 16 var. lect. (LXX.).
  For the general description compare
1 Cor. vi. 9 ff.; Tit. iii. 3; 1 Pet.
iv. 3.
  καὶ ἤμεθα τέκνα φύσει ὀργῆς...] Latt.
et eramus (fuimus) natura (al. na-
turaliter, al. naturales) filii iræ (ira-
cundiæ filii)[1], and were children by
nature—as we followed our natural
impulses—of wrath even as the rest

---

[1] Hier. ad loc. Quidam pro eo quod nunc ex-
posuimus et eramus natura filii iræ pro natura,
prorsus sive omnino, quia verbum φύσει ambigu-
um est, transtulerunt.

ὀργῆς ὡς καὶ οἱ λοιποί·—⁴ὁ δὲ θεὸς πλούσιος ὢν ἐν ἐλέει,
διὰ τὴν πολλὴν ἀγάπην αὐτοῦ ἣν ἠγάπησεν ἡμᾶς, ⁵καὶ
ὄντας ἡμᾶς νεκροὺς τοῖς παραπτώμασιν συνεζωοποίησεν
ͭτῷ χριστῷ,—χάριτί ἐστε σεσωσμένοι,—⁶καὶ συνήγειρεν

5 ἐν
5 τῷ] praem ἐν B 17 73 118 vg (codd al) bo arm

of men. The word φύσει is in itself
ambiguous. In other passages in the
N.T. where it occurs it means 'by
birth' (Gal. ii. 15 ἡμεῖς φύσει 'Ιουδαῖοι);
'by constitution' (Gal. iv. 8 τοῖς φύσει
μὴ οὖσι θεοῖς) and 'by the exercise of
natural powers' (Rom. ii. 14 ὅταν...
φύσει τὰ τοῦ νόμου ποιῶσιν). In this
place it describes the result of man's
action so far as he is unaided by the
Spirit of GOD. There is in his nature,
as the Jew found in spite of GOD's
covenant with him, that which issues
in sin. Actual Sin is in fact universal
and this deserves GOD's wrath till an
atonement is found (John iii. 36; comp.
Deut. xxv. 2 *a son of beating*). And more
than this: mortality itself, as it is, is,
according to the teaching of the Bible,
the sign of sin, of man's fall from the
divine ideal (Gen. ii. 17; iii. 19;
James i. 15; comp. Hebr. ii. 14 f.).
In this sense also, as sharers in a
mortal nature, Jew and Gentile alike
can be spoken of as objects of GOD's
displeasure. Origen, translated by
Jerome, combines the two thoughts :
ἡμεῖς οἰόμεθα διὰ τὸ σῶμα τῆς ταπεινώ-
σεως γεγονέναι τέκνα φύσει ὀργῆς, ὅτε
(l. ὅτι) ἐνέκειτο ἡμῶν ἡ διάνοια ἐπὶ
τὰ πονηρὰ ἐκ νεότητος.
The record of Bp Butler's death
offers an impressive commentary on
the phrase : Bartlett's *Life*, pp. 221 f.
τέκνα...ὀργῆς] Compare *c.* v. 8,
τέκνα φωτός, 1 Pet. i. 14 τέκνα ὑπακοῆς,
2 Pet. ii. 14 κατάρας τέκνα (Gal. iv. 28;
Rom. ix. 8 τέκνα ἐπαγγελίας). The
general difference which holds between
υἱοὶ θεοῦ and τέκνα θεοῦ (see on 1 Jo.
iii. 1, with Additional Note) appears to
underlie these wider uses of τέκνον and
υἱός (see v. 2 note).

Having shown the universality of
spiritual need, St Paul cannot complete the sentence which he has
begun. To say '(and you...) He quickened' would be to neglect the real
scope of Christian work. So he merges
the less in the greater and continues :
'*but* GOD *being rich in mercy, for
His great love wherewith he loved
us even when we were dead through
our trespasses, quickened us*—us no
less than you—*with the Christ.*'
4. πλούσιος ἐν ἐλέει] Compare
James ii. 5 πλουσίους ἐν πίστει, 1 Tim.
vi. 18 πλουτεῖν ἐν ἔργοις καλοῖς.
The image is characteristic of the
tone of thought in the Epistle. See
i. 18 note.
With ἐν ἐλέει διὰ τὴν πολλὴν (v.l.
multam, V. *nimiam*) ἀγάπην compare
1 Pet. i. 3 ὁ κατὰ τὸ πολὺ αὐτοῦ ἔλεος
ἀναγεννήσας ἡμᾶς, Tit. iii. 5. The
motive of GOD in the redemption of
the world is simply mercy and love.
This truth is affirmed alike by St Peter,
St Paul and St John (iii. 16).
5. καὶ ὄντας ἡμᾶς] *even when we
were*...His love survived our spiritual
death (John iii. 16; 1 John iv. 10).
συνεζ. συνήγ. συνεκάθ.] The three
words express a climax in the manifestation of the love of GOD. He
quickened the dead with life: He
restored them to the full use of the
powers of their former life: He raised
them, without the loss of the perfection of their humanity, to a life in the
heavenly order.
The Latin forms *convivificavit*, conresuscitavit (v.l. coexcitavit) are characteristic.
συνεζωοποίησεν] Col. ii. 13.
χάριτί ἐστε σεσωσμ.] *by grace ye*

καὶ συνεκάθισεν ἐν τοῖς ἐπουρανίοις ἐν Χριστῷ Ἰησοῦ,
⁷ἵνα ἐνδείξηται ἐν τοῖς αἰῶσιν τοῖς ἐπερχομένοις τὸ
ὑπερβάλλον πλοῦτος τῆς χάριτος αὐτοῦ ἐν χρηστότητι
ἐφ᾽ ἡμᾶς ἐν Χριστῷ Ἰησοῦ. ⁸τῇ γὰρ χάριτί ἐστε σεσωσμένοι διὰ πίστεως· καὶ τοῦτο οὐκ ἐξ ὑμῶν, θεοῦ τὸ
δῶρον· ⁹οὐκ ἐξ ἔργων, ἵνα μή τις καυχήσηται. ¹⁰αὐτοῦ

have been saved. The abrupt return
to the second person (so *v.* 8) is
natural and full of force. The tense
must be noticed. It can be said of
the believer, σώζεται, σωθήσεται, ἐσώθη,
σέσωσται. 1 Cor. i. 18 ; . 2 Cor. ii. 15
(οἱ σωζόμενοι) ; Rom. v. 9 f. (σωθησό-
μεθα); Rom. viii. 24 (ἐσώθημεν); 2 Tim.
i. 9 (τοῦ σώσαντος ἡμᾶς).

6. συνήγειρεν] Col. ii. 12; iii. 1. The
Resurrection of Christ was ideally the
quickening of all believers, the first-
fruits of humanity.

συνεκάθισεν] Compare Phil. iii. 20.
These acts which are complete on
the Divine side have to be realised on
the side of man: Rom. viii. 11; 2 Cor.
iv. 14; Apoc. iii. 21. Cf. Rom. vi.
3 ff.
For man, as for the Son of man, the
victory is completed in the triumph.

7. Thought cannot give distinctness to the vision of the counsel of
God wrought out in the succession of
ages. Through all redeemed man
seen in Christ Jesus is seen as a
glorious witness to the amazing
wealth of God's grace, moving, it may
be, other races to faith and hope
and love, to thanksgiving and praise,
through which their destiny will be
reached.

Comp. 1 Pet. i. 12; 1 Cor. iv. 9.

τὸ ὑπερβ. πλ. τ. χ.] His grace
corresponds with His power: *c.* i. 19
τὸ ὑπερβ. μεγ. τῆς δυν. αὐτοῦ.

ἐν χρηστότητι] That kindness which
is tender and considerate. Among
human graces it stands in Gal. v. 22
between long-suffering and goodness,
in 2 Cor. vi. 6 between long-suffering
and holy spirit, and in Col. iii. 12

between tender compassion and
humility. As a Divine attribute
it is joined with forbearance and
long-suffering in Rom. ii. 4, with
φιλανθρωπία in Tit. iii. 4, and contrasted with ἀποτομία in Rom. xi. 22.
Compare Matt. xi. 30; Lk. vi. 35;
1 Pet. ii. 3 [cit. from Ps. xxxiv. 8].

8, 9. These verses are parenthetical,
repeating and developing the brief
parenthesis in *v.* 5.

τῇ γὰρ χ.] It is as if the Apostle said:
I dwell on these facts of the grace and
the kindness of GOD, familiar to us
from past experience, lest any thought
of deserving should arise in your
minds, 'for it is by grace ye have
been saved through faith.'

8. καὶ τοῦτο...] *And this* saving
energy of faith is *not of yourselves :
it is* a gift, and *the gift is GOD'S.* The
variation in construction occurs not
unfrequently: ἐξ ὑ. evolved as it were
from the action of personal powers.
There is an underlying reference to
the Law: cf. Rom. iii. 20, 24.
For καὶ τοῦτο introducing a new
element see 1 Cor. vi. 6, 8 ; Phil.
i. 28.

θεοῦ τὸ δ.] Comp. John vi. 44.

9. οὐκ ἐξ ἔργων] It is not the
result of a natural evolution of
character, and yet more, it is not the
result of self-originated and self-
supported effort: it is *not of works,
that no man may boast.*

ἵνα μή τις καυχ.] Latt. *ut nequis
glorietur* (al. *extollatur*). Self-assertion is fatal to spiritual life.
Comp. 1 Cor. i. 29; Rom. iii. 27.
There is indeed a right boasting:
1 Cor. i. 31; 2 Cor. x. 17; Gal. vi. 14.

γάρ ἐσμεν ποίημα, κτισθέντες ἐν Χριστῷ Ἰησοῦ ἐπὶ
ἔργοις ἀγαθοῖς οἷς προητοίμασεν ὁ θεὸς ἵνα ἐν αὐτοῖς
περιπατήσωμεν.

The group of words καυχᾶσθαι,
καύχημα, καύχησις, is characteristic of
St Paul. They occur in all groups of
his Epistles excepting the Pastoral;
elsewhere only in St James (i. 9; iv. 16)
and Hebr. iii. 6.

10. αὐτοῦ γάρ ἐσμεν π.] V. *Ipsius
enim sumus factura* (v. l. *figmentum*).
*For it is His workmanship—of His
making—we are...* The position of the
pronoun is emphatic. Cp. *vv.* 14, 18.

ποίημα] Rom. i. 20; Is. xxix. 16.
Very frequent in Eccles. e.g. viii. 9.

Diligenter observa quia non dixerit
*Ipsius figuratio sumus atque plas-
matio*, sed *ipsius factura sumus...*
Factura primum locum tenet, deinde
plasmatio (Hier. *ad loc.*).

κτισθέντες... περιπατήσωμεν] *created in Christ Jesus for good works
which God afore prepared that in
them we should walk.* The words
give the whole history of the
Christian life from the divine and
from the human side. The Christian
is a new creation (2 Cor. v. 17), not
alone and independent, but in Christ:
he is not left to self-chosen activity,
but set for the accomplishment of
definite works which God has made
ready for his doing: his works are
prepared, and so the fulfilment of his
particular duty is made possible; and
still it is necessary that he should
accept it with that glad obedience
which is perfect freedom.

κτισθέντες] That which is realised
in time through faith is referred to its
origin in the primal Divine action.
Comp. *c.* i. 4; Col. i. 16f.

Κτίζω emphasises a new beginning,
a creation. It is used characteristically
of the creation of the natural order:
Mc. xiii. 19; Rom. i. 25; Eph. iii. 9;
Col. i. 16; Apoc. iv. 11; and of
particular parts of it: 1 Cor. xi. 9;
1 Tim. iv. 3; Apoc. x. 6. It is used

also of spiritual acts of creation both
social: *c.* ii. 15, archetypal: *c.* iv. 24
(Col. iii. 10), and personal as here.

However definitely the action of
the Christian may be limited by his
inheritance and his environment, by
his powers and his circumstances, he
is still responsibly free; and by true
service he can realise his freedom.
No necessity constrains him, but 'in
Christ' he can fulfil his own part.

ἐπὶ ἔργοις ἀγαθοῖς] Latt. *in operibus
bonis*: some more adequately *in opera
bona, on the condition of...for...*
Comp. 1 Thess. iv. 7 ἐπὶ ἀκαθαρσίᾳ,
Gal. v. 13.

προητοίμασεν] Rom. ix. 23. We
ourselves and our works, so far as they
are our true works, are alike of God's
making.

(4) The special significance of the
call of the Gentiles (ii. 11—22). After
indicating the great mysteries of the
Christian Faith, which he prays that
the Ephesians may be enabled to
understand more thoroughly (i. 15—21),
and the present action of Christ,
exalted to be Saviour and King
towards and through His people
(ii. 1—10), St Paul returns to mark
more clearly their peculiar blessings
as Gentiles. He points out the broad
contrast between their past and
present condition (11—13); and then,
after describing the atoning work of
Christ (14—18), shews in detail its
result for them now that they are
incorporated in the one Church of
God (19—22).

11 *Wherefore, remember that once
ye, the Gentiles in the flesh, those
called 'the Uncircumcision' by that
which is called 'the Circumcision'
in the flesh made by hands,—*12 *that
ye were at that time apart from
Christ, alienated from the commonwealth of Israel, and strangers to the*

¹¹Διὸ μνημονεύετε ὅτι ποτὲ ὑμεῖς τὰ ἔθνη ἐν σαρκί,
οἱ λεγόμενοι ἀκροβυστία ὑπὸ τῆς λεγομένης περιτομῆς

*covenants of the promise, having no
hope and without God in the world.*
¹³*But now in Christ Jesus ye that
once were 'afar' are made 'near'
in the blood of the Christ.* ¹⁴*For He
is our peace, He who made both one,
and broke down the middle wall of
partition, having abolished in His
flesh the enmity, even the law of
commandments* expressed *in ordinances; that He might create* (form
afresh) *the twain in Himself into one
new man, so making peace;* ¹⁶*and
might reconcile them both in one
body unto God through the cross,
having slain the enmity thereby;*
¹⁷*and He came and preached the
glad tidings of peace to you that
were far off and peace to them that
were near;* ¹⁸*because it is through
Him we both have our access in one
Spirit to the Father.* ¹⁹*So then ye
are no more strangers and sojourners,
but fellow-citizens with the saints and
of the household of God,* ²⁰*built upon
the foundation of the apostles and
prophets, the head corner-stone being
Christ Jesus Himself;* ²¹*in Whom
each several building, fitly framed
together, groweth unto a holy sanctuary in the Lord;* ²²*in Whom ye
also are builded together for a
habitation of God in the Spirit.*

11—13. Gentiles must remember
that they were once apart from
Christ, alienated from the divine
commonwealth, strangers to the
covenants, hopeless and godless, but
that now they were brought into the
same position as the chosen people in
the blood of the Christ.

11. διό...] *Wherefore remember
that once ye, the Gentiles in the flesh,
those called 'the Uncircumcision' by
that which is called 'the Circumcision' in the flesh made by hand...
Wherefore,* in view of the glorious
privileges brought to believers by the

victory and triumph of Christ, and
the revelation which they bring of
the purpose and obligations and
capacities of life, *remember*...

μνημονεύετε] Remembrance is enjoined also in the Apocalypse on the
Angels of the Churches of Ephesus
and Sardis (Apoc. ii. 5; iii. 3).

τὰ ἔθνη ἐν σαρκί] The *Gentiles*,
regarded as a class in their outward,
natural, human character and position,
in contrast with ἡ λεγ. περιτομὴ ἐν
σαρκί.

With ἐν σαρκί, where 'flesh' is
regarded as an element of life, must
be compared κατὰ σάρκα, where 'flesh'
is regarded as the standard and rule
of life. The two phrases are used
together in 2 Cor. x. 3. Compare
Rom. viii. 4, 5, 8 ff., 13.

The characterisation of Gentiles
and Jews by the addition 'in the
flesh' serves a double purpose. It
marks the definite exclusion of the
Gentiles from the only Covenant
which GOD had then made with men,
and at the same time the inadequacy
of that Covenant, received only outwardly, to meet human needs even
provisionally. The Gentiles were outside the Society, to which GOD had
been pleased to make His promises,
and therefore necessarily disqualified
for its blessings: the Jews, on the
other hand, keenly alive to the
inferior position of all other men, too
often rested in the outward mark of a
divine relationship, by which they
were distinguished, and so in their
pride missed the spiritual teaching, of
which circumcision was the symbol
and the preparation (Rom. ii. 25 ff.).

οἱ λεγ. ἀ.—τ. λεγ. π.] The masc. is
determined by ὑμεῖς. Ἡ ἀκροβυστία
is used of the uncircumcised: Gal. ii.
7; Rom. ii. 26.

χειροποιήτου] Elsewhere of the
Tabernacle and the Temple: Hebr.

ἐν σαρκὶ χειροποιήτου,— ¹²ὅτι ἦτε τῷ καιρῷ ἐκείνῳ
χωρὶς Χριστοῦ, ἀπηλλοτριωμένοι τῆς πολιτείας τοῦ
Ἰσραὴλ καὶ ξένοι τῶν διαθηκῶν τῆς ἐπαγγελίας, ἐλπίδα

ix. 11 ; Mk. xiv. 58; Acts vii. 48;
xvii. 24 ; Hebr. ix. 24.

12. ὅτι ἦτε...] *Remember that
once ye...that ye were at that time
apart from Christ, alienated from
the commonwealth of Israel, and
strangers to the covenants of the
promise, having no hope and without God in the world.* Καιρός retains
its qualitative sense: 'under those
circumstances,' 'at that season,' and
not simply 'at that point of time.'
Ἐκεῖνος has the same force as in
John xi. 49.
For the simple dat. compare c. iii. 5
ἑτέραις γενεαῖς.

χωρὶς Χριστοῦ—κόσμῳ] These five
points summarise the wants of the Gentiles in their personal, social, spiritual
relations. They were separate from
Christ; they were alienated from the
divine society which existed, and
ignorant of the provisions for one
more comprehensive; they were without hope, and without God in a world
unintelligible except through the sense
of His Presence.

χωρὶς Χριστοῦ] *Apart from, without
Christ,* not as *v.* 13 τοῦ χριστοῦ. The
thought is of the personal relationship now recognised and not of the
national hope. Comp. John xv. 5.

ἀπηλλ....ἐπαγγελίας] *alienated from*
(and not simply 'outside') *the commonwealth of Israel, and strangers to*
(not only unacquainted with but unqualified to enjoy) *the covenants of
the promise.* These words indicate
the two most impressive characteristics of Judaism, its inclusiveness
(not exclusiveness) and its larger hope.
All who accepted its conditions were
admitted to its privileges. It claimed
no finality, but pointed to a universal
Church. But the Gentiles were
alienated from (not alien to) the
institutions of the people of GOD.

By Creation they were fitted for the
Divine fellowship; but, though the
fundamental promise to Abraham
included blessing for them, they had
no place in the Covenants by which
the blessing was brought closer to the
life of the chosen race.

ἀπηλλοτριωμένοι] *c.* iv. 18 ἀπηλλ.
τῆς ζωῆς τοῦ θεοῦ ; Col. i. 21 ἀπηλλοτριωμένους sc. τοῦ θεοῦ. Alienated
from the commonwealth and so ex-
cluded from the citizenship.

πολιτείας] Latt. *a conversatione*
(*societate*). For πολιτεία see Acts
xxii. 28 (citizenship). Here the word
expresses the 'commonwealth' of
Israel as including the spiritual
privileges which were conveyed by
its divine ordering.

ξένοι τ. δ.] Latt. *hospites* (al. *pere-
grini*) *testamentorum.* The word
ξένος had a technical sense in the
city-states of Greece, and carries on
the image of the former clause (comp.
v. 19). It is used in the same construction in classical Greek (Soph.
Œd. R. 219).

τῶν διαθηκῶν τῆς ἐπαγγ.] The one
promise was brought nearer to realisation by successive Covenants. The
many promises (Rom. ix. 4) were
summed up in one: Gal. iii. 16f.; 21f.
Comp. Hebr. x. 36, xi. 9 note, xi. 13
notes.

ἐλπίδα μὴ ἔχ.] 'We need,' it has
been truly said, 'an infinite hope';
and faith in GOD alone can give it.
Faith in GOD, if we consider what are
the grounds of our confidence, alone
justifies our belief in the permanence
of natural 'laws.' By faith alone we
enter on the future and the unseen
(Hebr. xi. 1 note) and so find hope.
The phrase occurs again in view of
death (1 Thess. iv. 13).

ἐλπ. μὴ ἔχ. και ἄθεοι ἐν τῷ κόσμῳ]
There is a strange pathos in the com-

μὴ ἔχοντες καὶ ἄθεοι ἐν τῷ κόσμῳ. ¹³νυνὶ δὲ ἐν Χριστῷ
Ἰησοῦ ὑμεῖς οἵ ποτε ὄντες ΜΑΚΡΑΝ ἐγενήθητε ἐΓΓΥϹ ἐν
τῷ αἵματι τοῦ χριστοῦ. ¹⁴Αὐτὸς γάρ ἐστιν ἡ ΕἰΡΗΝΗ

bination. They were of necessity face to face with all the problems of nature and life, but without Him in Whose wisdom and righteousness and love they could find rest and hope. The vast, yet transitory, order of the physical universe was for them without its Interpreter, an unsolved enigma.

The Gentiles had, indeed, 'gods many and lords many,' and one God as 'a first Cause' in philosophic theories, but no GOD loving men and Whom men could love.

13. The contrast of the present position of the Ephesians with their past desolation and hopelessness is given by a reference to a prophetic word (Is. lvii. 19) which spoke of 'Peace' to those afar and to those near: this Peace had been given to all in Christ. *But now in Christ Jesus ye that once were 'afar' are made 'near' in the blood of the Christ.*

There appears to be a fulness of meaning in the choice of the two titles 'in Christ Jesus,' 'in the blood of the Christ.' 'The Gentiles were now united in Him Who was Son of man, 'Jesus,' no less than Christ: their redemption was wrought by the offered life of Him Who was the hope of Israel, 'the Christ.' The combination recals John xx. 31, and shows how the fulness of the Gospel is expressed by that summary of the scope of the Evangelic narrative. Compare *vv.* 5, 6.

ἐν X. Ἰ.] *in Christ Jesus,* united in Him by a fellowship of life, as members of His body.

ἐγενήθητε] not γεγόνατε, or ἐστέ—'were made' by one decisive act. The reference is primarily to the ideal redemption of the Gentiles

once for all accomplished by Christ's victorious Passion.

From the first proclamation of the Gospel on the day of Pentecost it was recognised that the promise was 'for all those that were afar' (Acts ii. 39).

ἐν τῷ αἵματι τοῦ χριστοῦ] Compare Hebr. x. 19 εἰς τὴν εἴσοδον τῶν ἁγίων ἐν τῷ αἵματι Ἰησοῦ. The offered life was not only the means of reconciliation (διά), but the atmosphere, as it were, in which the reconciled soul lived. The blood of Christ is 'the blood of the New Covenant': Matt. xxvi. 28.

14—18. Having used the language of Isaiah to describe the change in the position of the Gentiles, St Paul goes on to show how the prophet's central thought was fulfilled in Christ. For He is our Peace. He broke down the outward barriers which separated Jew and Gentile, uniting both and reconciling both in one body to GOD; and coming—after His victory—proclaimed Peace to all far and near, because it is through Him that both Jew and Gentile have their access to the Father, as alike children.

14. αὐτὸς γάρ...] *For He is our Peace, He who made both one and broke down the middle wall of partition, having abolished the enmity,* represented by that separation, *in His flesh,* even *the law of commandments* expressed *in ordinances...* St Paul speaks first of the two organisations, systems (τὰ ἀμφότερα), under which Jews and Gentiles were gathered as hostile bodies, separated by a dividing fence, and then afterwards of the two bodies themselves (τοὺς δύο [ἀνθρώπους]) included in them. Christ broke down the barrier by which the two organisations were kept apart and made them one, abolishing the enmity

ἡμῶν, ὁ ποιήσας τὰ ἀμφότερα ἓν καὶ τὸ μεσότοιχον τοῦ
φραγμοῦ λύσας, ¹⁵τὴν ἔχθραν ἐν τῇ σαρκὶ αὐτοῦ, τὸν
νόμον τῶν ἐντολῶν ἐν δόγμασιν, καταργήσας, ἵνα τοὺς

which was shewn openly in the Law
(comp. Rom. v. 13 f.), by His life of
perfect obedience, the virtue of which
He offered to Jew and Gentile alike.
Thus all men were made capable of a
living unity.

αὐτὸς γάρ...] For He—He Himself
and no other (compare Matt. i. 21
αὐτὸς γὰρ σώσει, and v. 10 note)—is
our peace both in our relations one to
another, and in our relation to God.
He is our peace, as He is the Way
and the Truth and the Life. He does
not bring it only, or shew it. So it is
that St Paul speaks of the Gospel—
the Gospel of our Salvation (c. i. 13)
—as 'the Gospel of peace' (c. vi. 15).

ὁ ποιήσας τὰ ἀμφ. ἓν] The two
providential systems under which 'the
nations' and 'the people' lived up to
the Coming of Christ, the orders of
Nature (comp. Rom. ii. 14 ff.) and of
the Law, are first noticed, and then
the corresponding 'men' (v. 15).
Christ removed the partition between
the systems, which became enmity
between the peoples, and united both
'men' in Himself.

τὸ μεσότοιχον τοῦ φραγμοῦ] Latt.
medium parietem maceriae (sepis).
For φραγμός see Matt. xxi. 33 and
parallels. The word μεσότοιχον is probably suggested by the Chel (חֵיל) or
"partition which separated the Court
of the Gentiles from the Temple
proper." The φραγμός was the μεσότοιχον: for this use of the genitive see
c. vi. 14 note.

λύσας] Comp. John ii. 19 λύσατε
τὸν ναὸν τοῦτον. Acts xxvii. 41 ;
2 Pet. iii. 10 ff. ; 1 John iii. 8 ἵνα
λύσῃ τὰ ἔργα τοῦ διαβόλου.

15. τὴν ἔχθραν] The Fall brought
to men a twofold enmity, an enmity
between themselves and an enmity
towards God (v. 16). The Law

brought both into clear light. It
revealed Sin in those who received it
(Rom. vii. 7 ff.), and fixed a gulf
between them and other men. Christ
in His flesh, as has been well said,
'went behind' the Law, and by
fulfilling the will of God (Hebr. x. 5 ff.),
of which the Law was an imperfect
symbol, abolished it, offering to men
the pattern and the power of the
freedom of perfect obedience. That
which was a barrier between heathenism and Judaism became necessarily a cause of active enmity
between Gentile and Jew.

ἐν τῇ σαρκί] Under the conditions
of our mortal life. Comp. Col. i. 22
τὸ σῶμα τῆς σαρκὸς αὐτοῦ, the body
which answered to these conditions.

τὸν νόμον τῶν ἐντ. ἐν δόγμ.] Comp.
Hebr. vii. 16 κατὰ νόμον ἐντολῆς
σαρκίνης.

The addition ἐν δόγμασιν defines
the commandments as specific, rigid,
and outward, fulfilled in external
obedience (Lk. ii. 1 ; Acts xvi. 4 ;
xvii. 7 ; Col. ii. 14 (20)).

καταργήσας] Latt. evacuans (de-
stituens). The Law was abolished,
annulled, because it was fulfilled,
and taken up into something wider
and deeper (Matt. v. 17 f. ; compare
2 Cor. iii. 14. In this sense St Paul
can say (Rom. iii. 31) νόμον οὖν καταρ-
γοῦμεν διὰ τῆς πίστεως ; μὴ γένοιτο,
ἀλλὰ νόμον ἱστάνομεν. The phrase
used by him in 1 Cor. xiii. 11 κατήρ-
γηκα τὰ τοῦ νηπίου presents the
thought very vividly. The words,
the conceptions, the reasoning of
the child are valid for the child.
But by a normal development they
pass away and are lost in the ripe
judgments of the man.

That which is complete in the
Divine act may be yet future in
historic realisation. 'Our Saviour

δύο κτίσῃ ἐν αὐτῷ εἰς ἕνα καινὸν ἄνθρωπον ποιῶν εἰρήνην, ¹⁶καὶ ἀποκαταλλάξῃ τοὺς ἀμφοτέρους ἐν ἑνὶ σώματι

Jesus Christ abolished death' (2 Tim.
i. 10 καταργήσαντος μὲν τὸν θάνατον...),
and yet 'we see not yet all things put
under Him' (Hebr. ii. 8): we wait till
the Father hath put all His enemies
under His feet. The last enemy that
is abolished is death (1 Cor. xv. 26
ἔσχατος ἐχθρὸς καταργεῖται ὁ θάνατος).
So we look in patience for the fulfilment of the Divine will in other
things, sure of the final issue (1 Cor. i.
28 ἵνα τὰ ὄντα καταργήσῃ. Rom. vi. 6
ἵνα καταργηθῇ τὸ σῶμα τῆς ἁμαρτίας.
Hebr. ii. 14 ἵνα διὰ τοῦ θανάτου
καταργήσῃ τὸν τὸ κράτος ἔχοντα τοῦ
θανάτου, τοῦτ' ἔστι τὸν διάβολον).

ἵνα τοὺς δύο] The object of Christ
in abolishing that which divided men
was twofold: (1) that He might unite
the two bodies, the two 'men' in 'one
new man,' and (2) that He might
reconcile both to God (v. 16). This
object He gained, though the result
is not open to our vision. Humanity
is in Him 'one new man.' The
'enmity' is slain, though we live
among the fruits of its earlier vitality.
The abrupt, unprepared, transition
from τὰ ἀμφότερα to τοὺς δύο, from
the systems to the men who lived
under them, and the gathering up of
those two bodies of men into two
representative men is a most instructive illustration of the thought of a personal unity, which Christ has brought
to creation by 'becoming flesh.' This
thought fills the apostle. The institutions of society, as he regards them,
pass over, as it were, into the men
whom they have moulded; and the
men into the one man, in whom they
find their full corporate expression.

κτίσῃ ἐν αὐτῷ εἰς ἓ. κ. ἄ.] That He
might create the twain in Himself,
taking humanity to Him, and form
them into one new man. St Paul
speaks here of 'the two' and not
of 'both,' in order to mark their

separateness. By the assumption of
human nature He gave ideally new
life to all who share it (2 Cor. v. 17).
In Him humanity, if we may so speak,
gained its personality. This truth,
so far as it is realised in the Church,
finds expression in the words to the
Galatians πάντες ὑμεῖς εἷς ('one man'
not ἕν) ἐστὲ ἐν Χριστῷ (Gal. iii. 28).
For κτίσῃ εἰς see v. 21 αὔξει εἰς,
v. 22 συνοικοδομεῖσθε εἰς.
The 'new man' must be 'put on' by
those who are ideally included in him:
c. iv. 24 note. Every man can find
his place in the divine whole.
ποιῶν εἰρήνην] Comp. James iii. 18.

16. καὶ ἀποκαταλλάξῃ...] and reconcile them both in one body to GOD
through the cross, having slain the
enmity thereby. 'Through the cross,'
using it as an altar (comp. Hebr. xiii.
10 note), Christ offered Himself without spot to GOD (Hebr. ix. 14) and
having taken humanity to Himself
'reconciled' Jews and Gentiles united
in one body to GOD.' By His death
he slew the enmity. In Him humanity
bore the doom of sin, and the power
of sin was abolished. The unity of
humanity was gained by the Incarnation, the reconciliation of humanity
to GOD by the Cross.
Jerome notices the error of the
Latin Versions, which give in semet
ipso reading ἐν αὐτῷ for ἐν αὐτῷ.
Comp. Col. ii. 15.
ἀποκατ....ἀποκτείνας] The two acts
are coincident.
For ἀποκαταλλάσσειν see Col. i. 20
ἀποκαταλλάξαι τὰ πάντα εἰς αὐτόν, v.
21 f. ὑμᾶς...ἀποκατήλλαξεν ἐν τῷ σώματι
τῆς σαρκὸς αὐτοῦ διὰ τοῦ θανάτου. The
use of the neuter πάντα will recal the
remarkable Western reading in John
xii. 32 πάντα ἑλκύσω πρὸς ἐμαυτόν.
For σταυρός compare 1 Cor. i 17 f.;
Gal. v. 11; vi. 12, 14; Phil. ii. 8;
iii. 18; Col. i. 20 ii. 14; Heb. xii. 2

τῷ θεῷ διὰ τοῦ σταυροῦ ἀποκτείνας τὴν ἔχθραν ἐν
αὐτῷ· ¹⁷καὶ ἐλθὼν εγΗΓΓελίсατο εἰρΗΝΗΝ ὑμῖν τοῖс
μακρὰν καὶ εἰρΗΝΗΝ τοῖс ἐΓΓύс· ¹⁸ὅτι δι' αὐτοῦ ἔχομεν τὴν προσαγωγὴν οἱ ἀμφότεροι ἐν ἑνὶ πνεύματι πρὸς

note. The double construction διὰ τοῦ
σταυροῦ, ἐν αὐτῷ is significant. In the
former the Cross is the instrument
which the Lord uses: in the latter
it is, so to speak, the vehicle of His
activity in which He is present. He
as Crucified slew the enmity.

ἀποκτείνας] That which seemed to
be defeat was victory. To men's eyes
He was slain: in truth He slew.

17. καὶ ἐλθών...] When the work
of reconciliation was accomplished,
and the enmity slain, the fruit of
victory was proclaimed to men: *and
He came and preached the glad
tidings of peace to you that were
far off and peace to them that were
near.*

ἐλθών] According to His promise
(John xvi. 16 ff.; xiv. 18). At His
first appearance among the disciples
He gave a twofold greeting of 'Peace';
and in the outpouring of the Spirit
the Apostles at once recognised the
presence of the Lord: Acts iii. 26.
The record of the Acts—the Gospel
of the Spirit—is the history of the
extension of the message of peace to
the whole world, beginning at Jerusalem and closing in Rome.

εὐηγγελ. εἰρ.] Cf. *c.* vi. 15 note.

18. This message of Peace through
the work of Christ is universally
effective, *because it is through Him
we both have our access (introduction)
in one Spirit to the Father.*

There is an impressive correspondence between the clauses which describe
the atonement and the issue of the
atonement:

(ἵνα) ἀποκαταλλάξῃ τοὺς ἀμφοτέρους
    ἐν ἑνὶ σώματι
        τῷ θεῷ.
ἔχομεν τὴν προσαγωγὴν οἱ ἀμφότεροι
    ἐν ἑνὶ πνεύματι
        πρὸς τὸν πατέρα.

δι' αὐτοῦ] For order compare *v.* 10
note.

ἔχομεν τὴν προσαγ.] Compare *c.* i.
7 ἔχομεν τὴν ἀπολύτρωσιν. For τὴν
προσαγ. see *c.* iii. 12; Rom. v. 2 δι' οὗ
καὶ τὴν προσαγωγὴν ἐσχήκαμεν. The
word emphasises the work of the Lord
in 'bringing us to God' (1 Pet. iii. 18).
Our 'access' is gained only through
Him. Compare John xiv. 6; Hebr.
iv. 14 ff.

ἐν ἑνὶ πν.] Comp. 1 Cor. xii. 13 ἐν ἑνὶ
πνεύματι...ἐβαπτίσθημεν, Phil. i. 27
στήκετε ἐν ἑνὶ πνεύματι. The Spirit is,
as it were, the surrounding, sustaining,
power, as in the corresponding phrase
Hebr. x. 19 ἔχοντες παρρησίαν εἰς τὴν
εἴσοδον τῶν ἁγ. ἐν τῷ αἵματι Ἰησοῦ.
The difference from διὰ τοῦ πν. (*c.* iii.
16) is obvious.

We might have been inclined to
transpose διά and ἐν: '*in Him* (as *c.*
iii. 12)...*through* one Spirit...' But
St Paul here is thinking of the work
of Christ (*v.* 17). The encompassing
energy of the Spirit makes this effective for us. Compare *c.* iii. 5 note.

πρὸς τὸν πατέρα] The use of this
title emphasises the effect of the
atonement, which restores to its true
character the relation of God to men.
The absolute use of ὁ πατήρ is very
rare in the Epistles except in the
Epistles of St John. Comp. *c.* iii. 14;
Col. i. 12.

St Paul, without any definite purpose, bases the doctrine of the Holy
Trinity upon facts of Christian experience. Comp. 1 Cor. xii. 4 ff. See
also 1 Pet. i. 2.

19—22. After the description of
the results of Christ's work bringing
peace to men as men, St Paul returns
to the blessings which it had brought
to the Gentiles, and shews in detail
how completely it removed the spiri-

τὸν πατέρα. ¹⁹"Ἄρα οὖν οὐκέτι ἐστὲ ξένοι καὶ πάροικοι,
ἀλλὰ ἐστὲ συνπολῖται τῶν ἁγίων καὶ οἰκεῖοι τοῦ θεοῦ,
²⁰ἐποικοδομηθέντες ἐπὶ τῷ θεμελίῳ τῶν ἀποστόλων καὶ

tual disadvantages which they had
suffered. No longer aliens and strangers they were 'fellow-citizens of the
saints and of the household of GOD.'
Without hope before, they were now
included in the solid future of the
Church resting on Christ Himself.
No longer without GOD, they were
made, in fellowship with all believers,
a dwelling-place for Him.

The rhythmical structure, which
characterises the Epistle is seen
with remarkable distinctness in this
section :

Ἄρα οὖν οὐκέτι ἐστὲ ξένοι καὶ πάροικοι
ἀλλὰ ἐστὲ συμπολῖται τῶν ἁγίων καὶ
  οἰκεῖοι τοῦ θεοῦ,
ἐποικοδομηθέντες ἐπὶ τῷ θεμελίῳ
  τῶν ἀποστόλων καὶ προφητῶν,
ὄντος ἀκρογωνιαίου
  αὐτοῦ Χριστοῦ Ἰησοῦ,
ἐν ᾧ πᾶσα οἰκοδομὴ συναρμολογουμένη
  αὔξει
εἰς ναὸν ἅγιον ἐν κυρίῳ,
ἐν ᾧ καὶ ὑμεῖς συνοικοδομεῖσθε
  εἰς κατοικητήριον τοῦ θεοῦ ἐν πνεύματι.

19. ἄρα οὖν...τοῦ θεοῦ] *So then
ye are no more strangers and sojourners but fellow-citizens with the
saints and of the household of GOD.*
This conclusion follows directly from
the equal privilege of all sons in
Christ in regard to their heavenly
Father.

ἄρα οὖν] Comp. Rom. v. 18 ; vii. 3,
25 ; viii. 12 ; ix. 16, 18 ; xiv. 12, 19 ;
Gal. vi. 10 ; 1 Th. v. 6 ; 2 Th. ii. 15.
This combination is, in the N.T., if not
absolutely, peculiar to St Paul.

ξένοι καὶ πάροικοι] Destitute of all
privileges in the state or only enjoy-
ing a provisional toleration. For
ξένοι see *v.* 12; and for πάροικος 1 Pet.
ii. 11 πάροικοι καὶ παρεπίδημοι ; Acts
vii. 6 πάροικον ἐν γῇ ἀλλοτρίᾳ ; *id.* 29

πάροικος ἐν γῇ Μαδιάμ: παροικεῖν Lk.
xxiv. 18; Hebr. xi. 9.

συνπ. τῶν ἁγίων] fellow-citizens (v.l.
concives) with the saints of the spiritual Israel. For the image see Hebr.
xi. 16, 19; xii. 22 ff.; xiii. 14.

οἰκεῖοι τοῦ θεοῦ] Gal. vi. 10 πρὸς
τοὺς οἰκείους τῆς πίστεως, 1 Tim. v. 8.
The singularly happy translation—' of
the household of God '—is due to
Tyndale.

20. ἐποικ....Χριστοῦ Ἰησοῦ] The
new Society was more than a Commonwealth ; it was a fabric in which the
several parts were joined together on
one divine plan.   In this the Gentiles
were *built upon the foundation of
the apostles and prophets, the head
corner-stone being Christ Jesus Himself.*

ἐποικ. ἐπὶ τῷ θεμ.] The image is
worked out in detail in 1 Cor. iii. 10 ff.
Comp. Col. ii. 7 ; Acts xx. 32.

τῶν ἀποστ. καὶ προφητῶν] The order
of the titles seems to shew beyond
doubt that the reference is to the
apostles and prophets of the New
Covenant : those who had divine
authority to found and to instruct
the Church.   Under this aspect they
form one body (τῶν ἀπ. καὶ πρ.).   Elsewhere they are considered separately.
Comp. *cc.* iii. 5 τοῖς ἁγίοις ἀποστόλοις
αὐτοῦ καὶ προφήταις, iv. 11 ἔδωκεν
τοὺς μὲν ἀποστόλους τοὺς δὲ προφήτας....
1 Cor. xii. 28 f. ἔθετο ἐν τῇ ἐκκλησίᾳ
πρῶτον ἀποστόλους δεύτερον προφήτας...
1 Cor. xiv. 29, 32, 37 ; Apoc. xviii. 20;
xxii. 9. So we read of prophets in the
early history of the Church: Acts xi.
27; xiii. 1 ; xv. 32 ; xxi. 10.

θεμελίῳ τῶν ἀποστ.] Comp. Apoc.
xxi. 14.

ἀκρογωνιαίου] Is. xxviii. 16 LXX. εἰς
τὰ θεμέλια Σειὼν λίθον πολυτελῆ ἐκλεκτὸν ἀκρογωνίαιον: 1 Pet. ii. 6.

προφητῶν, ὄντος ἀκρογωνιαίου αὐτοῦ Χριστοῦ Ἰησοῦ,
²¹ἐν ᾧ πᾶσα οἰκοδομὴ συναρμολογουμένη αὔξει εἰς ναὸν
ἅγιον ἐν κυρίῳ, ²²ἐν ᾧ καὶ ὑμεῖς συνοικοδομεῖσθε εἰς
κατοικητήριον τοῦ θεοῦ ἐν πνεύματι.

21 πᾶσα οἰκοδομή ℵ*BD₂G₃KL 17 37 47 etc; Cl-Al Chrys; πᾶσα ἡ οἰκοδομή ℵᵃA
CP al pl; Syrr (ut videtur)

Cf. Mk. xii. 10; Lk. xx. 17; Acts iv.
11 κεφαλὴ γωνίας: Ps. cxviii. (cxvii.) 22.

21.   ἐν ᾧ...ἐν κυρίῳ] in whom each
several building fitly framed together
groweth unto an holy sanctuary in
the Lord. The fabric in which the
Ephesians were built was destined to
become a sanctuary. It was not merely
put together by the workman's skill:
it had in it a principle of life. The
foundation was unchangeable, but,
while this underlay all, there was
room for a harmonious development.
The structure, like the Jewish Temple,
included many 'buildings' (Mk. xiii.
1 f.), but all these were to be equally
parts of the Sanctuary in the new
Temple. The image appears to mark
the consecration of all the ministries
of life in the New Order, in correspondence with the equal inclusion
in it of all the races of men.

ἐν ᾧ] The fabric has its foundation
and its harmonious development in
Christ Jesus. In Him too as 'the
Lord' it finds its consummation.

πᾶσα οἰκοδομή] every building, each
several building: council chambers,
treasuries, chambers for priests, clois-
ters, all become part of the sanctuary
(ναός not ἱερόν), the parts contributing
to the one whole, as the limbs to the
one body. And this whole is divine,
so that in the end the whole city—
the New Jerusalem—becomes a Holy
of Holies: Apoc. xxi. 16.

For πᾶσα see c. i. 3 note. In Acts ii.
36 πᾶς οἶκος Ἰσραήλ is probably to be
rendered 'every house of Israel,' each
in its peculiar place and with its
peculiar character.

συναρμολογουμένη] Compare c. iv.
16.

This harmonious fitting together of
the parts and the building up of the
whole (v. 22) are present and continuous processes. Contrast c. iii. 17
ἐρριζωμένοι καὶ τεθεμελιωμένοι.

αὔξει] Matt. vi. 28; xiii. 32; Lk. i.
80; ii. 40; Col. ii. 19. Each several
building is incorporated in the whole
and grows not by itself but with the
whole.

The phrases αὔξει εἰς...συνοικοδο-
μεῖσθε εἰς...shew that the end is not
yet reached.

εἰς ναὸν ἅγ. ἐν κυρίῳ] The presence
and influence of the Lord with His
sovereign power secures the hallowing of every part. Ἐν Κυρίῳ is to be
taken with αὔξει. Comp. cc. iii. 11; vi.
1, 10.

22. In the structure of this Sanctuary, which is not a shrine of the
Divine glory only, but a dwelling-place
of GOD, the Ephesians have a place,
as incorporated in Christ.

ἐν ᾧ...ἐν πνεύματι] In whom ye
also are builded together for a dwelling-place of GOD in the Spirit.

ἐν ᾧ] taking up the ἐν ᾧ in the
former verse (comp. c. i. 13).

καὶ ὑμεῖς συνοικ.] ye also are joined
with the earlier people of GOD. Even
now the process of incorporation is
going forward.

κατοικητήριον] Compare and contrast
Apoc. xviii. 2.

τοῦ θεοῦ] of the Triune GOD, the
Father (John xiv. 23), the Son (Matt.
xxviii. 20), and the Holy Spirit (John
xiv. 17).

ἐν πνεύματι] Compare c. iii. 5 note.
Opposed to ἐν σαρκί, Rom. viii. 9. The
indwelling is realised in the highest
part of our nature.

III.   ¹ Τούτου χάριν ἐγὼ Παῦλος ὁ δέσμιος τοῦ

III. THE GRANDEUR OF THE REVE-
LATION MADE TO ST PAUL. PRAYER
FOR FURTHER UNDERSTANDING IN
THOSE WHO RECEIVE IT (c. iii.).
1. The revelation to St Paul of a
universal gospel (iii. 1—13).
2. Prayer that those who receive
it may be enabled to apprehend its
lessons (iii. 14—19).
Doxology (20, 21).

The Apostle has declared summarily his great Gospel of the unity
of Jew and Gentile in the Christian
Church, both alike coming to One
Father in One Spirit through One
Mediator, and he prepares to draw
the practical consequences which follow from this divine calling. But he
is twice interrupted in his purpose
by the thought of the marvellous
privileges which are involved in his
mission, for himself, and for his
readers.

First (v. 2) when he recalls his
peculiar charge he shews that his
misery and shame, as they might
seem to others, were to those who
knew the cause for which he suffered
a ground of highest praise for the
light which they brought to the counsel of GOD (iii. 1—13).

And then again when (v. 14) he
resumes the broken sentence, it is
for the loftiest prayer and thanksgiving, before he can at last (c. iv. 1)
enter on direct instruction (iii. 14—21).

iii. ¹*For this cause I Paul, the
prisoner of Christ Jesus (or of the
Christ, even Jesus) on behalf of you,
the Gentiles, ²if at least ye heard
of the dispensation (administration)
of the grace of GOD which was given
me to you-ward: ³how that by revelation was made known unto me the
mystery—as I wrote afore in a few
words, ⁴whereby ye can, as ye read,
perceive my understanding in the
mystery of the Christ, ⁵which in
other generations was not made*

*known unto the sons of men, as
now it was revealed unto His holy
apostles and prophets in the Spirit—
⁶to wit, that the Gentiles are fellow-
heirs with Israel and fellow-members of the one body and fellow-
partakers of the promise in Christ
Jesus through the Gospel, ⁷whereof
I became a minister, according to
the gift of the grace of GOD that was
given to me, according to the working
of His power—⁸to me who am less
than the least of all saints was this
grace given—even to preach to the
Gentiles the unsearchable riches of
Christ; ⁹and to bring to light what
is the dispensation of the mystery
which from all ages hath been hid
in GOD Who created all things, ¹⁰hid,
I say, to the intent that now to the
principalities and the powers in the
heavenly order may be made known
through the Church the manifold
wisdom of GOD, ¹¹according to an
eternal purpose (a purpose of the
ages) which He accomplished in the
Christ, even Jesus our Lord: ¹²in
Whom we have freedom of address
and access (to GOD) in confidence
through our faith in Him. ¹³Where-
fore I beg you not to faint at my
tribulations for you, seeing they are
your glory.*

1. τούτου χάριν] 'Considering that
so great a blessing has been bestowed
on you.' As contrasted with διό (v. 13 ;
cc. ii. 11 ; iv. 8, 25 ; v. 14) this phrase
seems to suggest an idea of personal
feeling and obligation. The reference
is generally to that which is the
ground (because this is so) and not
the object (for the sake of obtaining
this) : v. 14 ; Tit. i. 5, 11 ; Lk. vii. 47.
The sentence, which is broken, is
resumed v. 14 τούτου χάριν κάμπτω....

ἐγὼ Παῦλος...] The abrupt introduction of the name emphasises the
strength of personal feeling. The
truth which has been announced is
no abstract speculation, but one which

χριστοῦ 'Ιησοῦ ὑπὲρ ὑμῶν τῶν ἐθνῶν,— ²εἴ γε ἠκούσατε

has been proved in life by the man who declares it. The name calls up all his history. It is as if the Apostle said : I the Pharisee of old time, I whom you know, of whose labours you have heard, I to whom this great truth has been revealed and who have suffered for it, I to whom you owe your knowledge of the Faith, I who can no longer serve you by my presence pray for you.

Comp. i Thess. ii. 18 ; Gal. v. 2 ; 2 Cor. x. 1 ; Col. i. 23 (v. Lightfoot's note) ; Philm. 19. Cf. 2 Thess. iii. 17 ; 1 Cor. xvi. 21 ; Col. iv. 18.

ὁ δέσμιος τοῦ χ.'Ι.] St Paul was not simply the 'bond-servant' of Christ, he was His prisoner, the one to whom this privilege of suffering was specially given by his Lord (contrast Philm. 1 δέσμιος X. 'Ι.). He was a prisoner, but not for crime or through man's design : he was the Lord's prisoner, prisoner by His will and at the same time prisoner for His work ; Christ's cause kept him in bonds (comp. Philm. 13 ἐν τοῖς δεσμοῖς τοῦ εὐαγγελίου).

Compare Philm. 9 δέσμιος X. 'Ι. ; 2 Tim. i. 8 τὸν δέσμιον αὐτοῦ [τοῦ κυρίου ἡμῶν]. These examples seem to shew that the words in c. iv. 1 ὁ δέσμιος ἐν κυρίῳ are to be taken together. Contrast Acts xxiii. 18 ὁ δέσμιος Π.

The combination ὁ χριστὸς 'Ιησοῦς without addition does not (as far as I have observed) occur again in St Paul. 'Ο χριστός is common, and ὁ 'Ιησοῦς occurs 1 Thess. iv. 14 ; 2 Cor. iv. 10 f. ; Eph. iv. 21. In Rom. xvi. 25 we read τὸ κήρυγμα 'Ιησοῦ Χριστοῦ. The construction of Col. ii. 6 ὡς παρελάβετε τὸν χριστὸν 'Ιησοῦν τὸν κύριον appears to be, 'received the Christ, even Jesus the Lord' (see Lightfoot ad loc.). It is therefore probable that the construction here also is 'the prisoner of the Christ—the hope of Israel—even Jesus, the Son of man, the Saviour of the world.' This at

least is the thought of the names. Comp. v. 11 note ; c. iv. 20 f.

ὑπὲρ ὑμῶν τ. ἐθνῶν] 'I the prisoner' for 'you the Gentiles.' Both are representative. Comp. c. ii. 11 : contrast Gal. ii. 15 ; Rom. xi. 13.

2—13. The thought of his helpless position leads St Paul to unfold its true meaning. His zeal to bring the Gospel to the Gentiles had brought him into bonds. These very bonds, therefore, which might at first sight seem to be a cause of discouragement, eally witnessed to the greatness of the work which he had done (v. 13).

'Yes,' he says, 'for your sakes, as indeed ye know, if—and it cannot be otherwise—ye heard, when the message of the Gospel came to you, what was my special commission, based on the revelation made to the apostles and prophets of Christ, that the Gentiles are fellow-heirs with Jews of the Divine promise of redemption, a truth which it was specially given to me to proclaim, a truth which now at last discloses to the hosts of heaven through the Church GOD's counsel of wisdom and love. Thus the sufferings which are due to the faithful fulfilment of my office are in fact your glory. My chains are the signs of my victory.'

Each part of the statement is developed under the influence of the Apostle's gratitude for the charge which he had received. His Gospel—that 'the nations' share equally with 'the people' in all Divine blessings,—was not gained by the experience of earlier generations, but given in due time by special revelation to appointed ministers. And he was enabled so to declare it as to set in full light before men the eternal counsel of GOD, that at last through the Church the powers of heaven might recognise GOD's wisdom seen in the Incarnation of the Son in Whom believers can draw near to His presence.

τὴν οἰκονομίαν τῆς χάριτος τοῦ θεοῦ τῆς δοθείσης μοι
εἰς ὑμᾶς, ³[ὅτι] κατὰ ἀποκάλυψιν ἐγνωρίσθη μοι τὸ

3 ὅτι om B

In structure the passage may be compared with i. 3—14.

The key words 'mystery,' 'minister [of the Gospel],' 'the wisdom of God,' suggest in succession fresh parentheses which are in essence overflowings of adoring thankfulness.

2. εἴ γε...] *if at least ye heard*, and this is assumed : *c*. iv. 21; Gal. iii. 4; Col. i. 23 (2 Cor. v. 3). In such language I can see nothing inconsistent with St Paul having been the teacher of those to whom he is writing.

ἠκούσατε] *c*. iv. 21; Gal. i. 13 f.: *ye heard* at the crisis when I declared to you the Divine message and you accepted it.

τὴν οἰκ. τ. χ.] St Paul does not say simply 'of the grace of God which was given to me,' but 'of the noble responsibility which was laid upon me of administering the grace which was given to me in a new and unexpected way.' It was exactly this characteristic of his preaching to which he wishes to call attention.

τὴν οἰκονομίαν] V. *dispensationem*, V.L. *dispositionem* (as *v*. 9; *c*. i. 10). The image is natural and frequent. St Paul describes himself as 'entrusted with a stewardship' (1 Cor. ix. 17), which he was bound to fulfil. Apostles were 'ministers of Christ and stewards of God's mysteries (revealed truths),' which it was their duty to dispense faithfully (1 Cor. iv. 1 f.). Comp. Tit. i. 7. This stewardship involved a wise and just dealing with the varied wealth of the Divine treasury (Matt. xiii. 52). All believers share in it, having severally gifts which they must minister to the body (εἰς ἑαυτούς) as 'good—generous (καλοί)— stewards of the manifold grace of God' (1 Pet. iv. 10).

Comp. *c*. i. 10 (note); Col. i. 25; 1 Tim. i. 4.

τῆς χ. τ. θ.] The ministry itself with all its glorious and awful issues was a favour—a grace—of God. The word χάρις is characteristically used of apostleship : *vv*. 7, 8; 1 Cor. iii. 10; Gal. ii. 7 ff.; Rom. i. 5; xii. 3; xv. 15. It is perhaps worthy of notice that χάρισμα (1, 2 Cor.; Rom.; 1, 2 Tim.; 1 Pet.) is not found in the Epistle.

εἰς ὑμᾶς] to bring unto you, to reach unto you. Comp. *c*. i. 19; Rom. xv. 26.

3. ὅτι...] *how that by revelation was made known unto me the mystery*.... This was the ground of St Paul's mission, that to him was communicated the central truth of the universality of the Gospel.

The words καθὼς προέγραψα...*v*. 5 ἐν πνεύματι are parenthetic, unfolding St Paul's peculiar endowments as compared with men of old time.

κατὰ ἀποκάλυψιν] not only in direct communications at the crises of his life (Acts ix. 4 ff.; xxii. 7 ff., 18 ff.; xxvi. 17 ff.; Gal. i. 12; ii. 2) but through widening experience laid in the light of the Gospel (*v*. 4 τὴν σύνεσίν μου ἐν τ. μυστ. τοῦ χρ.).

There is a difference between κατὰ ἀποκάλυψιν (Rom. xvi. 25; Gal. ii. 2) and δι' ἀποκαλύψεως (Gal. i. 12). The former describes the general mode of communication: the latter the specific fact.

τὸ μυστήριον] Comp. *c*. i. 9 note. Truths which are the characteristic possessions of Christians are 'mysteries.' Among these the universality of the Gospel—*v*. 6 εἶναι τὰ ἔθνη... ἐν Χριστῷ—is preeminently 'the mystery.' The single occasion on which the word is used in the Gospels emphasises this thought (Matt. xiii. 11; Mk. iv. 11; Lk. viii. 10) The parable of the Sower implies that the Word is for all. This suggestion natur-

μυστήριον, καθὼς προέγραψα ἐν ὀλίγῳ, ⁴πρὸς ὃ δύνασθε
ἀναγινώσκοντες νοῆσαι τὴν σύνεσίν μου ἐν τῷ μυστηρίῳ
τοῦ χριστοῦ, ⁵ὃ ἑτέραις γενεαῖς οὐκ ἐγνωρίσθη τοῖς
υἱοῖς τῶν ἀνθρώπων ὡς νῦν ἀπεκαλύφθη τοῖς ἁγίοις

ally caused that perplexity to the disciples which appears strange to us. In addition to those parallel texts the word is found in the N.T. only in St Paul and in the Apocalypse. It is used both (1) in the full comprehensive meaning of the Christian revelation, and (2) in regard to special details in it. All the passages deserve to be studied: (1) 1 Cor. ii. 7; Rom. xvi. 25; Eph. i. 9; iii. 4, 9; vi. 19; Col. i. 26 f.; ii. 2; iv. 3; 1 Tim. iii. 9, 16; Apoc. x. 7; (2) 2 Thess. ii. 7; 1 Cor. iv. 1; xiii. 2; xiv. 2; xv. 51; Rom. xi. 25; Eph. v. 32; Apoc. i. 20; xvii. 5, 7.

προέγραψα] in an earlier part of the Epistle: c. ii. 10 ff.

ἐν ὀλίγῳ] V. in brevi, V.L. in modico: briefly, in a few words. Comp. Acts xxvi. 28.

4. πρὸς ὅ...] whereby, looking to which summary statement of the truth, ye can, as ye read, perceive my understanding.... The Apostle is careful to shew that his teaching is not the repetition of a form of words once given to him and to be simply received by his disciples. It had cost him thought and it claimed thought. His readers could see for themselves how it was contained in the right apprehension of the historic Gospel; and he assumes that they will use their power.

ἀναγινώσκοντες] The word implies that the letter was circulated and copied and studied by individual Christians. Comp. Apoc. i. 3; Matt. xxiv. 15 ‖ Mk. xiii. 14; Acts viii. 28. The variant in Gal. iv. 21 (ἀναγινώσκετε) is interesting.

τὴν σύν. μ. ἐν τῷ μυστ.] St Paul had, in the common phrase, entered into the revelation of Christ. His natural

faculties had found scope in shaping the message which he delivered

For νοεῖν comp. Matt. xxiv. 15 ‖ Mk. xiii. 14; 1 Tim. i. 7 &c.; and for σύνεσις comp. Lk. ii. 47; Col. i. 9; ii. 2. The two words occur together 2 Tim. ii. 7. For the omission of the article before ἐν τῷ μ. see Winer iii. 20, 26.

τῷ μυστ. τοῦ χρ.] Col. iv. 3 λαλῆσαι τὸ μυστήριον τοῦ χριστοῦ.

5. The truth which was made known to St Paul by revelation *was not made known in other generations* to the sons of men as now in our own time *it was revealed to* Christ's holy apostles and prophets in the Spirit. The ὡς suggests that some partial knowledge was conveyed in earlier times to those who sought for it through 'the light that lighteth every man.' The prophets looked for the incorporation of 'the nations' in Israel, but not for their equality with 'the people' in the new Church, though this was in fact included in the promise to Abraham: John viii. 56; Gal. iii. 8.

ἑτέραις γενεαῖς] dative of time as in Lk. viii. 29 (πολλοῖς χρόνοις). The use of ἑτέραις suggests the thought of two series of generations, one before and one after the Incarnation.

τοῖς υἱοῖς τ. ἀ.] The phrase occurs again Mk. iii. 28, and in the LXX. As contrasted with τοῖς ἁγ. ἀποστ. αὐ. καὶ πρ. it describes those who represented the natural development of the race.

νῦν] now, in our age. Even to the Twelve the universality of the Gospel was a revelation (Acts x. 47), and St Paul looks back to the crisis when it was acknowledged (ἀπεκαλύφθη). There were indeed abundant traces in the teaching of Christ of this

ἀποστόλοις αὐτοῦ καὶ προφήταις ἐν πνεύματι, ⁶εἶναι
τὰ ἔθνη συνκληρονόμα καὶ σύνσωμα καὶ συνμέτοχα τῆς

truth—it lies in the fundamental parable of the Sower, which naturally perplexed the hearers—but like His teaching on His own Death and Resurrection they were unintelligible at the time. Through the experience which is recorded in the early chapters of the Acts their meaning was made plain by the Spirit. Compare Rom. xvi. 25 ff.; I Pet. i. 10 ff.

τοῖς ἁγ. ἀποστ. αὐ. καὶ προφ.] to those whom He charged with an authoritative office and endowed with spiritual insight. Comp. c. ii. 20 note. Ἁγίοις does not express personal character, but consecration. Comp. Lk. i. 70; Acts iii. 21. The αὐτοῦ naturally goes back to Χριστοῦ. In Col. i. 26 the thought is differently expressed.

ἐν πνεύματι] The phrase appears to correspond to ἐν Χριστῷ. It is of rare occurrence: Apoc. i. 10 ἐγενόμην ἐν πν.; iv. 2; xvii. 3 ‖ xxi. 10 ἀπήνεγκε ἐν πν.; Matt. xxii. 43 ἐν πν....καλεῖ (‖ Mk. xii. 36 ἐν τῷ πν. τ. ἁγ.); Jo. iv. 23 ἐν πν. κ. ἀλ.; Rom. viii. 9 ἐστέ...ἐν πν.; Eph. v. 18 πληροῦσθε ἐν πν.; vi. 18 προσευχόμενοι ἐν πν. (‖ Jude 20 ἐν πν. ἁγ.); Col. i. 8 δηλώσας τὴν ἀγάπην ἐν πν.; I Tim. iii. 16 ἐδικαιώθη ἐν πν. Ἐν τῷ πνεύματι occurs also: Lk. ii. 27 ἦλθεν ἐν τ. πν.; iv. I ἤγετο ἐν τῷ πν.; and ἐν πν. ἁγίῳ: Rom. ix. I συμμαρτυρούσης... ἐν πν. ἁ.; xiv. 17 χαρὰ ἐν πν. ἁ.; xv. 16 ἡγιασμένη ἐν πν. ἁ.; I Cor. xii. 3 εἰπεῖν... ἐν πν. ἁ.; I Pet. i. 12 εὐαγγελισαμένων... ἐν πν. ἁ. Compare βαπτίζειν ἐν πν. ἁγ. Matt. iii. 11 and parallels. The general idea of the phrase is that it presents the concentration of man's powers in the highest part of his nature by which he holds fellowship with GOD, so that, when this fellowship is realised, he is himself in the Holy Spirit and the Holy Spirit is in him.

6. This then is the revelation that the Gentiles are (not shall be) fellow-heirs with the natural Israel of the great hopes of the spiritual Israel,

and fellow-members with them of the one Divine body, and fellow-partakers in the promise which was fulfilled in the mission of the Holy Ghost (Acts x. 45), in virtue of their union in Christ Jesus through the Gospel.

The threefold fellowship of the nations with the people of GOD is established by their incorporation in Christ, which is wrought through the Gospel. In the announcement that the Word became flesh all partial and transitory privileges are lost in one supreme and universal blessing. Jerome (ad loc.) says truly 'hereditas nostra Deus' and 'ubi una comparticipatio est, universa communia sunt.' On the translation he remarks: Scio appositionem conjunctionis ejus per quam dicitur cohaeredes, et concorporales et comparticipes indecoram facere in Latino sermone sententiam. Sed quia ita habetur in Graeco, et singuli sermones, syllabae, apices, puncta, in Divinis Scripturis plena sunt sensibus, propterea magis volumus in compositione structuraque verborum quam intelligentia periclitari.

εἶναι] The position of the verb gives singular emphasis to the statement: that in spite of all difficulties and all opposition 'the Gentiles are....' Compare Hebr. xi. I ἐστί note.

συνκληρονόμα] Rom. viii. 17 συγκλ. Χριστοῦ. Hebr. xi. 9 συγκλ. τῆς ἐπαγγελίας. I Pet. iii. 7 συγκλ. χάριτος ζωῆς.

σύνσωμα] Not elsewhere in the N.T. or in the LXX. Nor is the word found in classical writers.

συνμέτοχα] Cf. c. v. 7 note.

τῆς ἐπαγγελίας] Acts ii. 33. The Gentiles were admitted to the Church because they had been made partakers of the gift of the Holy Ghost: Acts x. 47. Comp. c. i. 13. This specific reference is at once more forcible and, under the circumstances, more natural than the general refer-

ἐπαγγελίας ἐν Χριστῷ 'Ιησοῦ διὰ τοῦ εὐαγγελίου, ᾽οῦ
ἐγενήθην διάκονος κατὰ τὴν δωρεὰν τῆς χάριτος τοῦ
θεοῦ τῆς δοθείσης μοι κατὰ τὴν ἐνέργειαν τῆς δυνάμεως
αὐτοῦ — ⁸ἐμοὶ τῷ ἐλαχιστοτέρῳ πάντων ἁγίων ἐδόθη
ἡ χάρις αὕτη — τοῖς ἔθνεσιν εὐαγγελίσασθαι τὸ ἀνεξ-
ιχνίαστον πλοῦτος τοῦ χριστοῦ, ⁹καὶ φωτίσαι ᵀ τίς ἡ

9 πάντας

9 +πάντας BℵᶜCD₂ etc vv Tert Victor ; om ℵ*A Hil

ence to the promised salvation which
is included in συγκληρονόμα. There
is an expressive sequence in three
elements of the full endowment of the
Gentiles as coequal with the Jews.
They had a right to all for which
Israel looked. They belonged to the
same Divine society. They enjoyed
the gift by which the new society
was distinguished from the old. And
when regarded from the point of
sight of the Apostolic age, the gift of
the Holy Spirit, 'the promise of the
Father' (Lk. xxiv. 49; Acts i. 4; ii. 33;
38 f.), is preeminently 'the promise,'
to which also συμμέτοχα perfectly
corresponds.

διὰ τοῦ εὐαγγ.] Comp. 1 Cor. iv. 15.

7. St Paul's service as *a minister
of the Gospel* was determined by two
conditions: *the* original *gift of the
grace of* God *that was given to*
him, and *the* continuous *working of*
God's *power* in him. The two clauses
κατὰ τὴν δωρεάν..., κατὰ τὴν ἐνέργειαν
...are parallel (comp. *c.* ii. 2) and the
latter clause is not to be connected
with δοθείσης. The whole phrase τῆς
χαρ. τ. θ. τῆς δοθ. μ. is repeated from
v. 2 and is complete in itself. With
τοῦ εὐαγγ. διάκ. compare 2 Cor. iii. 6
καινῆς διαθ. δ. For κατὰ τὴν ἐνέργ.
compare *c.* i. 19; Col. i. 29.

In the N.T ἐνέργεια and ἐνεργεῖν
are characteristically used of moral
and spiritual working whether Divine
(e.g. Col. i. 29; ii. 12; Phil. iii. 21)
or Satanic (2 Thess. ii. 9, 11).

For δωρεά see *c.* iv. 7 note.

8. The construction of the first

clause ἐμοὶ...αὕτη is doubtful. It may
be taken to begin a new sentence, so
that εὐαγγελ. will be the explanation of
ἡ χάρις αὕτη, or it may be a parenthetical reflection of the Apostle. On
the whole the second arrangement
seems to be most consonant with St
Paul's style. In this case εὐαγγελ. will
be connected with διάκονος.

τῷ ἐλαχιστοτέρῳ] Latt. *minimo (in-
fimo, novissimo)*. For the form of the
word see Winer ii. 11, 2 *b.* For the
thought compare 1 Cor. xv. 9; 1 Tim.
i. 15. There is nothing in this confession at variance with the claims
which St Paul asserts for that which
God had given him: 2 Cor. xi. 5.

εὐαγγελίσασθαι...] The scope of the
Apostle's ministry was twofold: (1) to
proclaim the Gospel to the Gentiles,
and (2) to shew to (all) men its fulness
to solve the manifold problems of life
(*v.* 9).

τὸ ἀνεξιχν. πλ. τοῦ χ.] Vulg. al. *in-
investigabiles divitias Christi.* (Compare Prov. v. 6; Rom. xi. 33 f.) The
fulfilment of his work disclosed to St
Paul, as we can see from his Epistles,
ever-widening views of the scope and
power of the Gospel. His own experience assured him that no one
could exhaust its depths. And all lies
in the Person and work of Christ (Col.
i. 27; ii. 2 τοῦ μυστηρίου τοῦ θεοῦ,
Χριστοῦ).

9. καὶ φωτίσαι...] *to bring to light
what is....* In addition to his special
office of evangelising the Gentiles, and
indeed through the accomplishment
of it, St Paul was called to shew how

οἰκονομία τοῦ μυστηρίου τοῦ ἀποκεκρυμμένου ἀπὸ τῶν
αἰώνων ἐν τῷ θεῷ τῷ τὰ πάντα κτίσαντι, ¹⁰ἵνα γνωρισθῇ νῦν ταῖς ἀρχαῖς καὶ ταῖς ἐξουσίαις ἐν τοῖς ἐπουρανίοις διὰ τῆς ἐκκλησίας ἡ πολυποίκιλος σοφία τοῦ

9 οἰκονομία אBAD₂G₃K₂L₂P₂ 17 37 47 vv omn Tert Hil; κοινωνία rec c 37 mg al pauc

the truth made known to him met
the various needs of men. The universality of the Gospel—the 'mystery'
opened to him—rested upon the fact
of the Incarnation. This, as a wise
steward, he shewed to furnish a harmony of GOD's dealings with men,
bringing it into true relation with the
course of human life. 'The dispensation of the mystery' is, in other words,
the apostolic application of the Gospel
to the facts of experience.
Elsewhere in the N. T. φωτίζειν has
a direct object.

τοῦ ἀποκεκρ....ἵνα γνωρ.] The truth
had been hidden in order that it
might be made known at the right
moment, in 'the fulness of time,'
c. i. 10. Comp. Rom. xvi. 25 f. See
also Mk. iv. 22 (ἵνα).

ἀπὸ τῶν αἰ.] from the beginning of
time. Col. i. 26. Comp. Lk. i. 70;
Acts iii. 21; xv. 18 ἀπ' αἰῶνος. John
ix. 32 ἐκ τοῦ αἰῶνος. Contrast πρὸ τῶν
αἰώνων (1 Cor. ii. 7).

ἐν τῷ θεῷ] GOD, as the Creator of
all things, includes in the one creative
thought all the issues of finite things.
Compare Apoc. iv. 11 διὰ τὸ θέλημά
σου ἦσαν καὶ ἐκτίσθησαν, John i. 3 f.
ὃ γέγονεν ἐν αὐτῷ ζωὴ ἦν. See also
Col. iii. 3.

10. The personal ministration of
the Apostle had a wider scope than
the gaining individual converts. It
subserved to the display of GOD's
wisdom before the intelligences of the
heavenly order. This was the work
of the Church gathered by apostolic
teachings. In various ways the results of age-long discipline of 'the
people' and of 'the nations' were
made contributory to the universal
society, and thus the Divine purpose

was seen to be justified by its fruits.
There can be no doubt that St Paul
was conscious of the debt which he
owed to the spectacle of the organisation of the Roman Empire in his later
conception of the Catholic Church.
And if he could not clearly anticipate
how the tribute of other peoples would
enrich Christendom, yet he recognises
the principle of national service to
the City of GOD (Apoc. xxi. 24). He
foresaw that, as in the past, so in
the future the history of the several
families of mankind would vindicate
πολυμερῶς καὶ πολυτρόπως GOD's education of the world for Himself.

νῦν] in the fulness of time : c. i. 10;
Gal. iv. 4.

ταῖς ἀρχ. καὶ τ. ἐξ.] The effect of
the Gospel reaches through all being
(Eph. i. 10; Col. i. 20), and we are
allowed to see—though we are necessarily unable to give distinctness to the
vision—how other rational creatures
follow the course of its fulfilment.
Compare 1 Pet. i. 12; Lk. xv. 7, 10;
Apoc. v. 13.

The allusions to different classes
in the heavenly hierarchy—'Thrones,
dominations, virtues, princedoms,
powers'—give a vivid conception of
fulness and ordered intercourse in the
unseen life which we have no faculties
to realise; but such indications, however indefinite, correct our natural
tendency to narrow the range of
rational existence. In this sense the
Gospel anticipates and deals with the
thoughts suggested by our present
knowledge of the immensity of the
universe. Comp. c. i. 21; Col. i. 16
(with Lightfoot's note).

διὰ τῆς ἐκκλησ.] In the Church
humanity advances towards its true

θεοῦ, ¹¹κατὰ πρόθεσιν τῶν αἰώνων ἣν ἐποίησεν ἐν τῷ
χριστῷ Ἰησοῦ τῷ κυρίῳ ἡμῶν, ¹²ἐν ᾧ ἔχομεν τὴν παρρησίαν καὶ προσαγωγὴν ἐν πεποιθήσει διὰ τῆς πίστεως
αὐτοῦ. ¹³Διὸ αἰτοῦμαι μὴ ἐνκακεῖν ἐν ταῖς θλίψεσίν μου
ὑπὲρ ὑμῶν, ἥτις ἐστὶν δόξα ὑμῶν.

unity, and at the same time the whole
creation in man, who is its head.
Comp. Rom. viii. 18 ff.; James i. 18.

ἡ πολυποίκ. σοφ.] Latt. *multiformis
sapientia*. This wisdom is seen in the
adaptation of the manifold capacities
of man and the complicated vicissitudes of human life to minister to
the one end to which 'all creation
moves.'

11 f. This marvellous harmony of
all the parts of creation and life, as
tending to one end, now at last made
manifest by the coming of the Son of
God, answered to an eternal purpose
which was thus fulfilled. The same
Lord Who is the stay of our faith and
hope is also the crown of the whole
development of the world.

11. κατὰ πρόθ. τ. αἰ.] V. *secundum
praefinitionem* (V. L. *propositum*)
*saeculorum, according to an eternal
purpose*, a purpose to the accomplishment of which each age contributed
in turn, and which bound all the ages
together as ministrant to the one
supreme issue. If this purpose has
only lately been disclosed, it was
eternally designed. Through all the
changes of time God prepared the
way to the fulfilment of His counsel
unceasingly, and now at length the
steps towards it can be seen.

For πρόθεσις see c. i. 11; Rom.
viii. 28; ix. 11; 2 Tim. i. 9.

ἣν ἐποίησεν ἐν...] *which He accomplished*, brought to fulfilment, *in...*
(not formed or purposed). Comp.
Apoc. xvii. 17. For ποιεῖν see Winer,
iii. 38, 5.

The rendering 'which he purposed'
gives finally the same general meaning, but it is less forcible, less suitable
to the context, and it would have

naturally required 'in the Christ'
without the Lord's historic name.

ἐν τῷ χ. Ἰ. τῷ κ. ἡ.] *in the Christ*,
the hope of Israel, *even Jesus*, the
Son of man, *our Lord*. Compare
v. 1 (note). In the two parts of this
title we have a summary of the first
characteristic confessions of Jew and
Gentile: 'Jesus is the Christ' (Acts
v. 42; xvii. 3; comp. ix. 34), and
'Jesus is the Lord' (1 Cor. xii. 3;
Rom. x. 9).

12. ἐν ᾧ...] *in Whom*, in vital
fellowship with Him, *we have freedom
of address and freedom of access* to
God. The right of address and the
right of access are coupled together
(τὴν παρρ. καὶ προσ., not τὴν παρρ. καὶ
τὴν προσ.) as parts of the right of
personal communion with God.

For παρρησία see Hebr. iii. 6; iv. 16;
x. 19; 1 John iii. 21; v. 14. For
προσαγωγή see c. ii. 18 (note).

ἐν πεποιθ.] The privilege of communion is realised *in* personal *confidence through our faith in* Christ.
For πεποίθησις see 2 Cor. iii. 4.

τῆς πίστ. αὐτοῦ] *our faith in Him*.
Comp. Mk. xi. 22; Gal. ii. 16, 20;
iii. 22; Rom. iii. 22; Phil. i. 27; iii. 9;
James ii. 1; Apoc. xiv. 12.

13. St Paul goes back to the
thought of his imprisonment (*v.* 1
ὁ δέσμιος) and points out that his
readers should not be disheartened
at the afflictions which his teaching
had brought to him (comp. *c.* vi. 22).
These were as nothing in comparison
to the privilege of preaching the
Gospel, so that they were their 'glory,'
inasmuch as they shewed the grandeur
of the truth which they had received.

διό...] *therefore*, since the message
of a universal Gospel is immeasurable

¹⁴ Τούτου χάριν κάμπτω τὰ γόνατά μου πρὸς τὸν
πατέρα, ¹⁵ἐξ οὗ πᾶσα πατριὰ ἐν οὐρανοῖς καὶ ἐπὶ γῆς

14 τὸν πατέρα + τοῦ Κυρίου ἡμῶν Ἰησοῦ Χριστοῦ ℵᶜDEG₃K₂L₂ Vulg codd latt ap
Hier, Theod Mo-lat : syrr vg-hr ⅓ Victn Text ℵ*BACP₂ 17 67ᶜ bo Cl al Or ⅔ Hier ad
loc "non ut in Latinis codicibus additum est *ad Patrem Domini nostri Jesu Christi*,
sed simpliciter *ad Patrem* legendum" Cyr-Hier, Cyr-Al

in its range and the spring of personal
assurance.

αἰτοῦμαι] *I beg you.* The rendering
'I pray that I may not lose heart'
appears to be equally inconsistent
with the whole tenor of the passage
and with the language.

ἥτις] *seeing they are.* For the
attraction compare *c.* vi. 17 ; 1 Cor.
iii. 17 ; 1 Tim. iii. 15.

14—19. St Paul resumes his broken
sentence (*v.* 1), but again only to contemplate in prayer the view of GOD's
providence opened by the coming of
Christ. Just as (in *vv.* 2—13) he had
dwelt on the grandeur of his own
mission, he now is filled with the
thought of the opportunities offered
to his readers. Their own experience
would, if rightly interpreted, throw
fresh light on the Divine wisdom; and
therefore he prays that they, through
the presence of Christ within them,
might, with fuller knowledge of the
sphere and power of Christ's love, be
enabled to discharge their office for
the whole body.

¹⁴ *For this cause I bow my knees
unto the Father, ¹⁵ from Whom every
family in heaven and on earth derives its name, ¹⁶ that He may grant
you, according to the riches of His
glory, that ye may be strengthened
with power through His Spirit in
the inward man : ¹⁷ that Christ may
dwell in your hearts through faith ;
to the end that having been rooted
and grounded in love ¹⁸ ye may be
strong enough to apprehend with all
the saints what is the breadth and
length and height and depth, ¹⁹ and
to know the love of Christ which
passeth knowledge, that ye may be
filled unto all the fulness of GOD.*

14 f. τούτου χάριν] as in *v.* 1 having
regard to the new view of life laid
open by the universal Gospel.

κάμπτω τὰ γ.] The phrase is found
in LXX. 1 Chron. xxix. 20, and in Phil.
ii. 10 ; Rom. xi. 4 (a quotation from
1 K. xix. 18 not LXX.) ; xiv. 11 (from Is.
xlv. 23 LXX.). More commonly we find
θεῖναι τὰ γ. (Lk. xxii. 41 ; Acts vii.
60, &c.). Clement (i. 57) speaks of τὰ
γόνατα τῆς καρδίας. On the attitude in
prayer see D.C.A. s.v. *Genuflexion.*

πρὸς τὸν πατέρα] The absolute title
expresses an important truth. In
prae-Christian times GOD had revealed
Himself as Father to one race : now
it is made known that all the races of
men are bound to Him in Christ by a
like connexion ; and far more than
this (*v.* 15). He Who is the Father of
men is also the source of fellowship
and unity in all the orders of finite
being. The social connexions of earth
and heaven derive their strength from
Him ; and represent under limited
conditions the power of His Fatherhood.

The preposition πρός implies ' coming before Him,' 'addressing Him in
prayer,' a fuller thought than the
simple dative (Rom. xi. 4).

15. ἐξ οὗ ... ὀνομάζεται] Every
'family,' every society which is held
together by the tie of a common head
and author of its being, derives that
which gives it a right to the title
from the one Father. From Him
comes the spirit by which the members have fellowship one with another
and are all brought together into a
supreme unity.

πᾶσα πατριά] Latt. *omnis paternitas, every family,* every group of
beings united by a common descent

ὀνομάζεται, ¹⁶ἵνα δῷ ὑμῖν κατὰ τὸ πλοῦτος τῆς δόξης
αὐτοῦ δυνάμει κραταιωθῆναι διὰ τοῦ πνεύματος αὐτοῦ
εἰς τὸν ἔσω ἄνθρωπον, ¹⁷κατοικῆσαι τὸν χριστὸν διὰ
τῆς πίστεως ἐν ταῖς καρδίαις ὑμῶν· ἐν ἀγάπῃ ἐρριζω-

or origin. Comp. Lk. ii. 4; Acts iii. 25; Gen. xii. 3, xxviii. 14. *Familia* was naturalised by Rabbinic writers.

ἐν οὐρ. καὶ ἐπὶ γ.] It is characteristic of St Paul to recognise the variety and unity of the manifold life in earth and heaven. Origen endeavoured to give precision to the thought by supposing that there were races in heaven corresponding to the races on earth.

The phrase ἐν οὐρανοῖς καὶ ἐπὶ γῆς is apparently unique and to be noticed (comp. *c*. i. 10; Col. i. 16, 20; 2 Pet. iii. 13). Generally οὐρανός and γῆ are combined.

ὀνομάζεται] *derives its name*, and further, since the name is designed to express the essence of that to which it belongs, 'derives that which truly makes it what it is.'

16—19. The prayer corresponds with that in *c*. i. 16 ff. In both cases the Apostle enforces the need of spiritual illumination for the full understanding of the Gospel. In the former prayer he begins with the thought of personal enlightenment which leads to a living sense of the greatness of the Divine power: in this he begins with the thought of personal strengthening which issues in higher knowledge and completer work.

16. ἵνα...] depending on the idea of prayer involved in κάμπτω τὰ γ. *v*. 15. See Mk. xiii. 18; xiv. 35; 1 Cor. xiv. 13, &c.

κατὰ τὸ πλ. τ. δ.] The glory of GOD is the sum of His perfections as manifested to us. This, in its inexhaustible wealth, is the only limit of our prayers. Comp. Rom. ix. 23.

δυν. κρατ....εἰς τ. ἐ. ἄνθρ.] *that ye may be strengthened* (V. *corroborari*,

V.L. *confortari*) *with power* answering to your need *through His Spirit*, so that each access of vigour shall penetrate to and find scope *in the inward man*.

'The inward man' is the true self, which answers to the Divine pattern; and is contrasted with 'the outer man' (2 Cor. iv. 16), the material frame, through which for a time the 'self' finds expression in terms of earth. Comp. 2 Cor. iv. 16 ὁ ἔσω ἡμῶν ἄνθρωπος; Rom. vii. 22. This is according to GOD's will our informing personality, moulding, if it fulfils its part, all that comes within its influence. This idea is suggested by the variant ὁ ἔσωθεν ἄνθρωπος in 2 Cor. *l. c*.

Thus the prayer is that Divine influence may reach to the master spring of the whole life and not simply contribute to the development of any one part of it.

17. The object of the prayer is expressed in another and a final form, even the continual indwelling of Christ according to His promise (John xiv. 23) which is the most perfect strengthening. Κατοικῆσαι is parallel with κραταιωθῆναι, and in both cases the aorist marks the decisive act by which the blessing is conveyed.

For κατοικεῖν the permanent dwelling, as opposed to παροικεῖν the temporary sojourning (Lk. xxiv. 18; Hebr. xi. 9), see Col. i. 19; ii. 9; and compare κατοικητήριον *c*. ii. 22; Apoc. xviii. 2.

ἐν ταῖς καρδίαις] the seat of character.

διὰ τ. π.] through the constant action of Christian faith, which is at once the expression and the support of personal strength.

ἐν ἀγ. ἐρριζ. καὶ τεθεμ.] The con-

μένοι καὶ τεθεμελιωμένοι, ¹⁸ἵνα ἐξισχύσητε καταλαβέσθαι σὺν πᾶσιν τοῖς ἁγίοις τί τὸ πλάτος καὶ μῆκος καὶ
⌜ὕψος καὶ βάθος⌝, ¹⁹γνῶναί τε τὴν ὑπερβάλλουσαν τῆς

18 βάθος καὶ ὕψος

18 ὕψος κ. βάθος BCD₂G₃ 17 37 Vulg syr-vg bo ; βάθος κ. ὕψος ℵAK₂L₂ 47 Or

struction of these words is most
difficult. It is possible to connect ἐν
ἀγάπῃ alone or the whole clause with
the preceding sentence. In favour of
connecting ἐν ἀγ. with what precedes
the parallels of i. 4, iv. 2 may be
urged ; but the usage in the Epistle
is not uniform (vi. 7 μετ᾽ εὐν. δουλ.),
and the words give a peculiar force to
ἐρριζ. καὶ τεθεμ. which seem to require
some such definition. On the other
hand the examples which are quoted
to justify the connexion of the whole
clause with the foregoing sentence as
an irregular nominative are not really
adequate. In Col. ii. 2 συμβιβασ-
θέντες is equivalent to αἱ καρδίαι, and
in other cases c. iv. 2 ; Col. iii. 16,
&c., the transition is part of a complete change of construction. It
seems best therefore to connect the
clause with what follows : *that having
been rooted and grounded in love—*
this would be the characteristic fruit
of Christ's presence—*ye may be strong
enough...to know the love of Christ....*
The peculiar emphasis on ἐν ἀγάπῃ
explains the irregular position of ἵνα
as in similar cases, Acts xix. 4; 2 Cor.
ii. 4, &c. A like reason explains the
order in Lk. xxiv. 48 f. ἀρξάμενοι ἀπὸ
Ἰερουσ. ὑμεῖς μαρτ. τ. ; and in c. i. 18
πεφωτ. τ. ὀφθ. τ. κ. εἰς τὸ εἰδέναι and
c. vi. 18 διὰ πάσης προσευχῆς καὶ
δεήσεως προσευχόμενοι.
   The words ἐρριζ. καὶ τεθ. combine
without confusing the images of the
vine and the temple, the ideas of life
and stability (comp. 1 Cor. iii. 9). Love,
which Christ's presence brings (John
xvii. 26), is the source of growth and
the stay of endurance. The perfects,
which express the abiding result of
Christ's dwelling, do not exclude the

idea of progress which is marked in
the parallel phrase in Col. ii. 7 ἐρριζωμένοι καὶ ἐποικοδομούμενοι. Ἐρριζωμένοι (Latt. *radicati*) occurs in the
N. T. only in these two passages. For
τεθεμελιωμένοι see Col. i. 23.
   18. ἐξισχύσητε] *may be fully
strong enough.* Ἰσχύς describes
strength absolutely, δύναμις power re-
latively, κράτος might as overpowering.
   καταλαβέσθαι] *to apprehend.* See
Acts iv. 13 ; x. 34 ; xxv. 25.
   σὺν πᾶσιν τοῖς ἁγ.] Such knowledge
is not an individual privilege, but a
common endowment. The co-operation of all is required for the attainment of the full conception. Saint-
ship—consecration—is the condition
of spiritual knowledge.
   τί τὸ πλ. καὶ μῆκ....καὶ βάθος] The
form of the clause shews that the
four words express one thought, the
whole range of the sphere in which
the Divine wisdom and love find
exercise. Though space has only three
dimensions, we naturally in common
language distinguish height and depth
as well as length and breadth. The
words are not to be interpreted separately : this would require τί τὸ πλάτος,
τί τὸ μῆκος, &c.
   19. γνῶναί τε...] First we come
to apprehend the dimensions (so to
speak) of the sphere in which the
Divine counsel finds its fulfilment and
then we come to know the love which
occupies it.
   τὴν ἀγ. τ. χ.] *the love of Christ*
simply as His, answering to His very
nature, without any distinct definition
of the object to which it is directed,
including both His love for the Church
and for the believer (comp. John xv.
9 f.).

γνώσεως ἀγάπην τοῦ χριστοῦ, ἵνα ⌈πληρωθῆτε εἰς⌉ πᾶν
τὸ πλήρωμα τοῦ θεοῦ.

²⁰ Τῷ δὲ δυναμένῳ ὑπὲρ πάντα ποιῆσαι ὑπερεκπερισσοῦ ὧν αἰτούμεθα ἢ νοοῦμεν κατὰ τὴν δύναμιν τὴν
ἐνεργουμένην ἐν ἡμῖν, ²¹ αὐτῷ ἡ δόξα ἐν τῇ ἐκκλησίᾳ καὶ

19 πληρωθῇ

19 πληρωθῆτε εἰς ℵACD₂G₃K₂L₂P₂ cu^{plur} vv^{omn} ; πληρωθῇ B 17 73 116

γνῶναι...γνώσεως] Latt. *scire (cognoscere) supereminentem scientiae caritatem.* A natural paradox : to know that which never can be known. The thought in Phil. iv. 7 ἡ εἰρήνη τ. θ. ἡ ὑπερέχουσα πάντα νοῦν is different.

ἵνα πληρ....τοῦ θεοῦ] Latt. *ut impleamini in omnem plenitudinem Dei :* that ye may severally *be filled* with the gifts of GOD's grace, and so be made contributory *unto all the fulness of* GOD. 'The fulness of GOD' is that perfect consummation of finite being which answers to the Divine idea. This is reached representatively when every member of Christ brings his full share to the perfecting of that glorious humanity which is the Body of Christ ; and finally when the corresponding work of the Church for creation is accomplished (James i. 18). Comp. *c.* i. 23 note. The reading of B ἵνα πληρωθῇ π. τ. πλ. τ. θ. gives substantially the same sense more simply and directly : 'that through your individual completeness the whole fulness of GOD may be realised.'

20, 21. The contemplation of the glorious fulness of Divine blessing in the Gospel, both in relation to the mission of the Apostle and in relation to the opportunities of believers, naturally closes with a Doxology of singular simplicity and depth, in which GOD's work in man is regarded as issuing in His glory 'in the Church and in Christ Jesus' to the last development of life in time.

Similar Doxologies are found : Gal.

i. 5 ; Rom. ix. 5 ; xi. 33 ff. ; 1 Tim. i. 17 ; 1 Pet. iv. 11.

²⁰ *Now to Him that is able to do exceeding abundantly beyond all that we ask or think, according to the power that worketh in us,* ²¹ *to Him be the glory in the Church and in Christ Jesus unto all the generations of the age of the ages.*

20 f. τῷ δὲ δυν....αὐτῷ ἡ δόξα] We may supply either εἴη or ἐστί, 'be the glory' or 'is the glory.' The one thought passes into the other. Man does not offer of his own to GOD, but recognises and ascribes to Him what is His. In this sense angels and men can 'give glory to GOD' by acknowledging in that which stirs their wonder and gratitude a revelation of His power and love : Lk. xvii. 18 ; John ix. 24 ; Acts xii. 23 ; Rom. iv. 20 ; Apoc. iv. 9 ; xi. 13 ; xiv. 7 ; xvi. 9 ; xix. 7.

ὑπὲρ π....ὑπερεκπερ. ὧν...] Latt. *omnia facere resuperabundanter (superabundantius) quam...* all. *super omnia ...abundantius quam...*&c. : *beyond all, abundantly beyond all that...* Ὧν depends upon ὑπερεκπερισσοῦ which emphasises ὑπὲρ (πάντα). Ὑπερεκπερισσοῦ occurs again 1 Thess. iii. 10 ; v. 13. Comp. Mk. vi. 51 ; xiv. 31.

αἰτ. ἢ νοοῦμεν...] Some thoughts occur to us which we do not shape into petitions ; GOD's gifts go beyond petitions and thoughts alike. 'His power working in us' is the measure of that which He does. Comp. Col. i. 29.

21. ἡ δόξα] This characteristic

ἐν Χριστῷ Ἰησοῦ εἰς πάσας τὰς γενεὰς τοῦ αἰῶνος τῶν
αἰώνων· ἀμήν.

use of the article in the doxologies
implies that all perfection which is
disclosed to us flows finally from GOD.
'The glory,' through which whatever
is glorious gains its splendour, belongs
to Him only. Comp. [Matt. vi. 13];
Gal. i. 5 ; Rom. xi. 36 ; xvi. 27 ; Phil.
iv. 20; 2 Tim. iv. 18; Hebr. xiii. 21 ;
1 Pet. iv. 11 ; v. 11 ; 2 Pet. iii. 18 ;
Apoc. i. 6 ; v. 13 ; vii. 12 ; xix. 1.
Yet see 1 Tim. i. 17 ; Jude 25 (Lk.
ii. 14 ; xix. 38).

ἐν τῇ ἐκκλ. καὶ ἐν Χ. Ἰ.] *in the Church
and in Christ Jesus.* The combination presents different aspects of the
same truth, and perhaps points to
different orders of the Divine working. The Church is the Body of Christ
and the Bride of Christ (*c.* v. 32). As
the Church approaches to its ideal,
humanity embodies more and more
perfectly the idea of GOD in creation,

and Christ is revealed in further perfection as the spring of man's growth.
So the glory of GOD is shewn, as the
universe moves forward to its end, by
the fulfilment of GOD's will in man
and by the offering of man's service
in Christ to GOD. Yet it may be that
Christ's work through the Church does
not exhaust His action (i. 10).

εἰς πάσας τ. γ. τοῦ αἰ. τ. αἰ.] V. *in
omnes (universas) generationes saeculi
saeculorum.* V.L. *in omnia saecula
saeculorum : unto all the generations
of the age of the ages.* Two main
thoughts underlie this most remarkable phrase : (1) the natural succession
and development of things represented
by successive generations; and (2) the
immeasurable vastness of the Divine
plan expressed in terms of time. The
units of the great age are contributory ages.

B. THE CHRISTIAN LIFE (iv. 1—vi. 20).

    I. THE GROUND, THE GROWTH, THE CHARACTER OF THE CHRISTIAN LIFE (iv. 1—24).

    II. THE OUTWARD MANIFESTATION OF THE CHRISTIAN LIFE, PERSONAL AND SOCIAL (iv. 25—vi. 9).

    III. THE CHRISTIAN CONFLICT (vi. 10—20).

PERSONAL MESSAGE (vi. 21, 22).

BLESSING (23, 24).

IV. ¹ Παρακαλῶ οὖν ὑμᾶς ἐγὼ ὁ δέσμιος ἐν κυρίῳ
ἀξίως περιπατῆσαι τῆς κλήσεως ἧς ἐκλήθητε, ² μετὰ

St Paul at length after the twofold digression in *c.* iii. proceeds to apply to practice throughout the remainder of the Epistle the great truths which he has already unfolded. But the truths themselves are never out of sight. The simplest duties are shewn to be grounded upon them. The Christian life is the natural application of Christian doctrine to our special circumstances : Christian conduct rests upon 'supernatural' sanctions. He first gives a general view of the Christian life (iv. 1—24) ; and then examines it in detail (iv. 25—vi. 9), adding a vivid description of the Christian warfare (vi. 10—20).

I. THE GROUND, THE GROWTH, THE CHARACTER OF THE CHRISTIAN LIFE (iv. 1—24).

St Paul states briefly that the Christian life must correspond with the Christian faith (iv. 1—3). This principle brings into relief the cardinal lessons of unity and harmonious growth (4—16) ; and leads to a general contrast between the Gentile and the Christian life, the old life and the new (17—24).

(1) The correspondence of life and faith (1—3). The wonderful greatness of the heritage of Christians might tempt them to pride, self-confidence, self-assertion. St Paul lays down that they are bound to cultivate the opposite graces of lowliness, meekness, long-suffering. It is through these that the unity of the Church is established and maintained. Our Faith sets before us not our own greatness but the greatness of GOD. We are all, the strongest no less than the weakest, dependent on Him in all things. Therefore in view of His glorious purpose for us, we must strive to attain to a corresponding life, first recognising in deepest humility our true relation towards Him.

¹ *I beseech you therefore, I the prisoner in the Lord* (or, *I beseech you therefore, I, the prisoner, beseech you in the Lord*) *to walk worthily of the calling wherewith ye are called,* ² *with all lowliness and meekness, with long-suffering, forbearing one another in love ;* ³ *giving diligence to keep the unity of the spirit in the bond of peace.*

1. παρακαλῶ οὖν...] *I beseech—entreat—you therefore, I the prisoner in the Lord...* or, *I beseech you therefore, I, the prisoner, beseech you in the Lord.* The connexion of ἐν κυρίῳ is very doubtful. It may be taken with παρακαλῶ, 'I beseech you in the Lord'; or with ὁ δέσμιος, 'the prisoner in the Lord.' The first connexion is supported by *v.* 17 (*I adjure you in the Lord,* see note) where the words are resumed : comp. 1 Thess. iv. 1. But the connexion with ὁ δέσμιος is also correct : *c.* vi. 21 ; Phil. i. 14 ; Rom. xvi. 10—13 ; and ὁ δέσμιος by itself is perhaps abrupt, though the position of ἐγώ relieves the abruptness. In any case St Paul refers to his position in order to shew that his sufferings had not lessened his joy in that faithful service to which he calls his readers. Comp. Philem. 9. Ign. *ad Trall.* 12 παρακαλεῖ ὑμᾶς τὰ δεσμά μου.

For οὖν compare Rom. xii. 1 ; 1 Cor. iv. 16 ; 1 Tim. ii. 1.

ἀξίως] 1 Thess. ii. 12; Rom. xvi. 2; Phil. i. 27; Col. i. 10; 3 John 6.

κλήσεως] Compare *c.* i. 18, and Epict. *Diss.* i. 29, 46 f. (quoted by Lightfoot on Philippians p. 314 note).

ἧς ἐκλήθητε] The tense carries back the thought to the decisive moment when they accepted the Gospel. Comp. ἠκούσατε *c.* iii. 2; *v.* 21. For the attraction ἧς (for ἥν) see *c.* i. 6.

2. μετὰ π. ταπ....] The test of our true apprehension of the Gospel is our sense of the majesty of GOD.

πάσης ταπεινοφροσύνης καὶ πραΰτητος, μετὰ μακροθυμίας, ἀνεχόμενοι ἀλλήλων ἐν ἀγάπῃ, ³σπουδάζοντες
τηρεῖν τὴν ἑνότητα τοῦ πνεύματος ἐν τῷ συνδέσμῳ τῆς

Humility, which answers to reverence, is the sign of a noble character. The proud man only looks at that which is (or which he thinks to be) below him; and so he loses the elevating influence of that which is higher.

ταπεινοφροσύνη and πραΰτης are closely related. 'Humility' is a thankful sense of dependence upon GOD, as opposed to pride and self-confidence. Meekness is a consideration for others even under provocation, as opposed to self-assertion. 'Long-suffering' has regard to a different kind of trial which comes from the mysteriousness of the ways of Providence and the unreasonableness of men. 'Long-suffering' supports us when we are disappointed in not finding the results for which we naturally looked.

'Meekness' and 'humility' are claimed by the Lord for Himself: Matt. xi. 29; and the perversity of man brings out the 'long-suffering' of GOD: 2 Pet. iii. 9, 15; 1 Pet. iii. 20. The three graces occur together with others Col. iii. 12.

πάσης] in all its forms: Acts xx. 19; c. i. 8; iv. 19, 31; v. 3, 9; vi. 18, &c. It is to be taken with both nouns. The use of μετά in place of the simple dat. gives greater distinctness to the qualities: 2 Cor vii. 15.

ἀνεχ. ἀλλ.] Latt. supportantes (sustinentes, sufferentes), forbearing one another in the case of real grievances: Col. iii. 13. The motto of Epictetus was ἀνέχου καὶ ἀπέχου (Aul. Gell. xvii. 19). The nom. is used for the accus. as the entreaty passes into a command (comp. Col. i. 10). Such exhortations point to the fact that even in the Apostolic Church faults of self-assertion and occasions of offence existed.

3. But, while there is need of forbearance in the Christian, there is need of effort also. We must give

diligence 'to keep the unity of the spirit.' As yet there was no outward organisation binding together local Churches. Their unity lay in their common vital relation to Christ, maintained by the spiritual sympathy which held together the members of each Church. External peace tends to guard this inner fellowship.

σπουδάζοντες] 2 Tim. ii. 15; Hebr. iv. 11; 2 Pet. i. 10; iii. 14.

τὴν ἑν. τ. πν.] the unity of the spirit. The phrase is ambiguous. It may mean either 'the unity which finds expression in the human spirit,' or 'the unity which is inspired by the Holy Spirit.' In the end the two thoughts are coincident; for the unity which rules man's spirit cannot but be a gift of the Spirit of GOD. Yet the parallel of v. 13 τὴν ἑν. τῆς πίστεως, the only other place where ἑνότης occurs in the N.T., is in favour of the first interpretation. Unity in the faith which we hold corresponds with unity in the spirit by which we are animated. Oneness in the faith and the knowledge of Christ must issue in oneness of spirit.

In Col. iii. 14 love is spoken of as 'the bond of perfectness,' but it is not possible to suppose that St Paul used such a periphrasis as 'the bond of peace' for love itself. Peace itself is the bond; for this use of the gen. see c. vi. 14. The destruction of peace is self-seeking (πλεονεξία).

(2) The unity and harmonious growth of the Christian Body (4—16).

Having spoken of 'the unity of the spirit,' the keeping of which is the aim of Christian effort, St Paul seems to pause for a while, and then, moved by the greatness of the thought, he thinks, as it were, aloud and lays open

εἰρήνης· ⁴ἐν σῶμα καὶ ἓν πνεῦμα, καθὼς [καὶ] ἐκλήθητε ἐν

a view of the unity of the whole Christian society, first in its objective foundation (4—6) and then in the provision for its vital realisation (7—16).

The whole paragraph is essentially parenthetical, and the line of thought in *vv.* 1—3 is resumed in *v.* 17.

⁴ There is *one body and one spirit, even as also ye were called in one hope of your calling;* ⁵ *one Lord, one Faith, one Baptism;* ⁶ *one GOD and Father of all, Who is over all and through all and in all.*

⁷ *But to each one of us was the grace given according to the measure of the gift of the Christ.* ⁸ *Wherefore* the Psalmist *saith*

When He ascended on high He led a host of captives in His train, And gave gifts unto men.

⁹ *Now the* statement *He ascended, what is it but that He descended* [first] *into the lower parts of the earth?* ¹⁰ *He that descended, He Himself is also He that ascended far above all the heavens, that He might bring all things to their completeness.* ¹¹ *And He gave some as apostles, and some as prophets, and some as evangelists, and some as pastors and teachers,* ¹² *with a view to the perfecting of the saints for a work of ministering, for building up the Body of Christ,* ¹³ *till we all attain unto the unity of the faith and of the knowledge of the Son of GOD, unto a full-grown man, unto the measure of the stature of the fulness of Christ,* ¹⁴ *that we be no longer children, storm-tossed and carried about with every wind of doctrine, victims of (in) fraud, of (in) craftiness, directed to further the wiles of error;* ¹⁵ *but, living the truth in love, may grow up into Him in all things, Who is the Head, even Christ;* ¹⁶ *from Whom all the Body fitly framed and knit together, through every contact, according to the effec-*

tive working of that which is supplied in due measure by each several part, maketh for itself the growth of the Body, unto the building up of itself in love.

4—6. The unity of the Christian Society is witnessed by its unity in itself, which answers to the Christian call (*v.* 4); by its historical foundation (*v.* 5); by the unity of GOD Whose will it expresses (*v.* 6).

4. ἐν σ. καὶ ἐν πν.] The Christian Society is one in its visible constitution and one in its informing spirit. The body and the spirit (as in *v.* 3) refer to the human, earthly organism. Outwardly and inwardly this is one. The spirit is necessarily in fellowship with the Holy Spirit, but a personal reference to the Holy Spirit seems to be foreign to the context, though His work is recognised in the formation of the Church.

καθὼς καὶ ἐκλήθ....ὑμῶν] The unity of the corporate life of Christians corresponds with the unity of hope involved in their 'heavenly calling' (Hebr. iii. 1). The call to fellowship with GOD 'in Christ,' if welcomed, could not but issue in unity. Comp. i. 18 note.

The hope is coincident with the calling (1 Thess. iv. 7; Gal. i. 6; 1 Cor. vii. 15) and not consequent upon it (καλεῖν εἰς) as in 1 Cor. i. 9; Col. iii. 15; 1 Tim. vi. 12.

For καθὼς καί as in fact see *v.* 17 note.

5. The historical foundation of the Christian Society also witnesses to its unity. It is established by the acknowledgment of *one Lord* as sovereign over all life: it confesses *one faith* in proclaiming that 'Jesus is Lord' (1 Cor. xii. 3): it is entered by *one Baptism,* in which the believer is brought into fellowship with Christ Jesus (Gal. iii. 27).

We might naturally have looked for a reference to Holy Communion

μιᾷ ἐλπίδι τῆς κλήσεως ὑμῶν· ⁵εἷς κύριος, μία πίστις, ἓν
βάπτισμα· ⁶εἷς θεὸς καὶ πατὴρ πάντων ὁ ἐπὶ πάντων

in which, as the Apostle shews elsewhere, 'the one bread' is the pledge
that 'the many' are 'one body' (1 Cor.
x. 17 R.V. mg.). But the Apostle is
speaking of the initial conditions of
Christian life. Holy Communion belongs to the support and development
of it.

μία πίστις] For the objective sense
of πίστις see *v.* 13 ; Col. ii. 7 (καθὼς
ἐδιδάχθητε); Gal. i. 23 (see Meyer);
Rom. x. 8 ; xii. 6; 1 Tim. iii. 9 ; iv. 1,
6 &c.; Jude 3 (τῇ ... παραδοθείσῃ ...
πίστει), 20 ; Apoc. ii. 13.

The essential substance of the
Christian Creed is given in the words
already quoted : Κύριος Ἰησοῦς (1 Cor.
xii. 3) opposed to the declaration of
the apostate Ἀνάθεμα Ἰησοῦς (*l.c.*).
Comp. Rom. x. 9 ἐὰν ὁμολογήσῃς τὸ
ῥῆμα...ὅτι Κύριος Ἰησοῦς.

6. Yet more the unity of the
Christian Society is involved in the
very conception of *one* GOD *and
Father of all* made known by the
Incarnate Son. He who sees the
range of the Divine action must find
in it the strongest possible motive
for guarding the unity already realised
in the Church, which is the beginning
and the pledge of a wider unity (James
i. 18).

εἰς θ. καὶ πατὴρ π.] Cf. *c.* v. 20 τῷ
θεῷ καὶ πατρί. [See Appendix.] The
revelation communicated to the Church
is of the universal Fatherhood of GOD.
This is the power of its missionary
activity. We can appeal to men because in a true sense they are GOD'S
children. At the same time the vision
of a universal sovereignty (Apoc. xxi.
24, 26 ; xi. 15) is continually present.
All progress is a foreshadowing of the
end. The addition of ἡμῶν in *v.* 7
emphasises the simple πάντων here.
Perhaps the most dangerous symptom
in popular theology is the neglect of
the doctrine of GOD in His unity.

ὁ ἐπὶ π. καὶ διὰ π. καὶ ἐν π.] Latt.
super omnes et per omnia, al. *super
omnia, per omnes.* The reference is
not to the Person of the Father, but
to the triune GOD, ruling, pervading,
sustaining all. Cf. Rom. xi. 36. [See
App.]

The address of Marcus Aurelius to
Nature (iv. 23) ἐκ σοῦ πάντα, ἐν σοὶ
πάντα, εἰς σὲ πάντα recognises part of
St Paul's thought.

7—16. Unity is stamped on the
Christian Society by the form, the
method and the ruling idea of its
institution. St Paul now goes on to
consider how provision is made for
the practical realisation of that idea
in the Body of Christ. In this he
marks first the types of ministry with
which the Church is endowed (7—11);
and then he shews how they serve for
the perfecting, the guiding, the har-
monising of every part of the complex
whole (12—16). The one section
passes into the other.

7—11. The unity of the Christian
Society is due to the combination and
ministry of all its members. Some
things are common to all; but each
has a special function, and each receives the grace which is necessary
for the fulfilment of his own office.

This manifold endowment of the
Christian Society is foreshadowed in
the Psalmist's description of the triumph of the great Conqueror.

Even in a work of art the perfection
of details, as contributory to the
design, is necessary to its completeness. It is only when we neglect
to recognise the specific differences
of parts that we miss the truth that
they belong to a whole and suggest a
larger unity.

St Paul first states the fact of the
individual endowment of the several
members of the Christian Society
(*v.* 7); he then points out how the

καὶ διὰ πάντων καὶ ἐν πᾶσιν. ⁷Ἑνὶ δὲ ἑκάστῳ ἡμῶν
ἐδόθη [ἡ] χάρις κατὰ τὸ μέτρον τῆς δωρεᾶς τοῦ χριστοῦ.
⁸διὸ λέγει

Ἀναβὰς εἰς ὕψος ᾐχμαλώτευσεν αἰχμαλωσίαν,
[καὶ] ἔδωκεν δόματα τοῖς ἀνθρώποις.

many gifts taken together form the
Divine endowment of the whole (vv.
8—10); and lastly notes that certain
special gifts have been made for its
due government (v. 11).

7. ἑνὶ δὲ ἑ. ἡ.] But to each....
Passing from the largest vision of the
working of GOD, St Paul shews how
preparation is made in the Church for
giving effect to it. We believers
recognise this crowning truth of the
unity of the Christian body, but, looking at our own position we see that
to each one of us was the grace given
which we severally need and which
we have according to the measure of
the gift of Christ.

ἐδόθη] when each took his place in
the body. Compare Rom. xii. 6 ff.;
I Pet. iv. 10.

κατὰ τὸ μέτρον...] The fulness of
the endowment of the Church according to Christ's boundless love and
wisdom is the rule which determines
each man's special endowment. There
is perfect order and a true relation to
the whole in His several gifts. Comp.
Rom. xii. 6.

The word δωρεά is specially used of
a spiritual and bountiful gift: c. iii. 7;
John iv. 10; Acts ii. 38 &c.; Rom. v.
15; 2 Cor. ix. 15; Hebr. vi. 4.

τοῦ χριστοῦ] The Christ in Whom
all the hopes of Israel were concentrated and all the traits of the
Messianic king fulfilled.

8—10. The Christian Society received its spiritual endowment from
the ascended Lord at Pentecost, and
St Paul finds this outpouring of Divine
gifts prefigured in the triumph-song
of the Messianic king. But in apply-
ing the Psalm he substitutes for the
words 'received gifts among men' the

very different phrase 'gave gifts unto
men.' The same rendering is found
in the Targum, and it probably represents a gloss which was current in
St Paul's time. The origin is obvious.
It seemed more natural that the
Divine Conqueror should bestow gifts
than receive them, or rather, as St
Paul applies the thought, that he
should return to men what he took
from them fitted for nobler uses. So
Rashi distinctly paraphrases the text:
'took that thou mightest give.'

8. διὸ λέγει...] Wherefore the
Psalmist saith... Ps. lxviii. (lxvii.) 18.
There is, that is, a necessary correspondence between the actions of GOD at
all times. What is recorded of the
Divine King of old must find its complete fulfilment in the Christ. The
King's ascent to the sanctuary in
Zion foreshadowed Christ's ascent to
the Father's throne: His royal magni-
ficence, Christ's royal bounty.

The subject of λέγει is either 'Scripture' generally, or, more simply, 'the
sacred writer,' 'the Psalmist.' Comp.
c. v. 14; Gal. iii. 16; 1 Cor. vi. 16. Θεὸς
is not to be supplied unless it is
implied by the context (2 Cor. vi. 2).

ᾐχμαλ. αἰχμ.] he led a host of captives in his train, and these, unlike
earthly conquerors, he numbered a-
mong his own people and enriched
and used them. Their presence implies the conquest of his enemies, and
far more, for he made those whom he
conquered his ministers to men. Compare 2 Cor. ii. 14 τῷ θεῷ χάρις τῷ
πάντοτε θριαμβεύοντι ἡμᾶς, Col. ii. 15.

For αἰχμαλωσία see Judg. v. 12;
1 Esdr. v. 56; Jud. ii. 9 (LXX.).

ἔδ. δόμ. τ. ἀνθρ.] Those whom he
had taken he gave to serve others.

⁹τὸ δέ Ἀνέβη τί ἐστιν εἰ μὴ ὅτι καὶ κατέβη ᵀ εἰς τὰ κατώτερα μέρη τῆς γῆς ; ¹⁰ὁ καταβὰς αὐτός ἐστιν καὶ ὁ ἀναβὰς ὑπεράνω πάντων τῶν οὐρανῶν, ἵνα πληρώσῃ

9 πρῶτον

9 + πρῶτον BK₂L₂P₂ 37 syrr ; om אACD₂G₃ bo

Compare the promise made under a different figure in Lk. v. 10. Similarly the Levites are spoken of as 'a gift to Aaron and his sons' (Num. viii. 19 δόμα LXX. ; xviii. 6). See Just. M. *Dial.* 39 ἔδωκε δόματα τοῖς ἀνθρ.: 87 ἔδωκε δόματα τοῖς υἱοῖς τῶν ἀνθρ.

9 f. τὸ δὲ Ἀνέβη...] *Now* the implied statement '*He ascended*'.... Comp. Gal. iv. 25 and Lightfoot's note. The words that follow are beset by difficulties. To what does κατέβη refer? What is described by τὰ κατώτερα μέρη τῆς γῆς?

Κατέβη has been taken for the descent at the Incarnation, the descent to Hades, the descent through the Holy Spirit at Pentecost.

So τὰ κατώτερα μέρη τ. γ. (V. *inferiores partes terrae*, V. L. *inferiora terrae*) has been held to describe the earth itself, lower in respect of heaven, and again to describe the regions lower than the earth, that is Hades. Why again is stress laid on the identity of him who ascended with him who descended?

The answer to these questions may be given most satisfactorily by considering the scope of the whole passage.

The central thought is the endowment of the Church by the ascended Christ. To understand this we must recognise what the Ascension was in relation to the gifts. Ascension implies a previous descent. The Lord left 'the glory which He had' (John xvii. 5) to enter on a true human life on earth, and more, to share man's death and fate after death. Thus He perfectly learnt all man's needs and by rising again overcame man's last

enemy. In this work He won to Himself some who were alienated from Him. When He ascended to reassume in His glorified humanity His place on the Father's throne, these ascended with Him (c. ii. 5), and these He gave to minister to men. His personality is throughout unchanged. As the Son of man, still truly GOD, he passed through all the scenes of man's life : as the Son of GOD, still truly man, he ascended far above all the heavens, that He might bring all things through man, their appointed representative and head, to the end proposed for them in the counsel of creation (cf. i. 23 note).

The insertion of πρῶτον is a true gloss.

9. καὶ κατέβη] The word 'ascended' used of Christ, Whose pre-existence is assumed, implies a descent also. Comp. John iii. 13.

τὰ κατώτερα μ. τ. γ.] It is most unlikely that such a phrase would be used to describe the earth. Μέρη has no force whatever in such a case. But Hades might, according to the prevalent cosmogony, reasonably be called either τὰ κατώτερα [μέρη] τῆς γῆς or τὰ κατώτατα τῆς γῆς (Ps. lxiii. 10, LXX.). It may be observed that in c. i. 10 and Col. i. 20 there is nothing directly answering to τὰ καταχθόνια in Phil. ii. 10.

10. ὁ καταβὰς αὐτός ἐστιν...] *He that descended, He Himself, is also He that ascended....* The sense is given substantially by the grammatically incorrect rendering 'is the same also that....' Comp. John iii. 13.

ἵνα πληρώσῃ] *That He might by* His presence *bring all things to their completeness,* give reality to all that

τὰ πάντα. ¹¹καὶ αὐτὸς ἔδωκεν τοὺς μὲν ἀποστόλους,
τοὺς δὲ προφήτας, τοὺς δὲ εὐαγγελιστάς, τοὺς δὲ ποιμένας καὶ διδασκάλους, ¹²πρὸς τὸν καταρτισμὸν τῶν

the universe of created things presented in sign and promise. Christ
first 'fulfils' all things and then receives
them to Himself when brought to their
true end. Time is no element in this
work. It is essentially like creation
itself 'one act at once,' though it is
slowly realised under the conditions
of earthly being.

11. καὶ αὐτὸς ἔδωκεν...] And in
fulfilment of His victor's work He
Himself, of His own free love (αὐτός),
gave.... The gift was a double gift.
Christ first endowed the men, and
then He gave them, so endowed, to the
Church.

τοὺς μέν...] Some of those whom
He had taken and fashioned for His
service as apostles, and some, as prophets....

The three groups 'apostles,' 'prophets,' 'evangelists,' represent ministers
who had a charge not confined to any
particular congregation or district.
In contrast with these are those who
form the settled ministry, 'pastors and
teachers,' who are reckoned as one
class not from a necessary combination
of the two functions but from their
connexion with a congregation.

For ἀπόστολος see Lightfoot on Gal.
i. 17.

The προφήτης was an inspired
teacher: Acts xv. 32; 1 Cor. xiv. 3.
The prophets are frequently combined
with the apostles as having peculiar
authority: c. ii. 20; iii. 5; Apoc. xviii.
20. There is a vivid description of
their work at a later period in the
Teaching of the Apostles cc. xi. ff.

The work of the εὐαγγελιστής was
probably that of a missionary to the
unbelieving (Acts xxi. 8). Comp.
2 Tim. iv. 5.

This is the only place in which
ποιμήν is the definite title of an office.
But in addressing the 'elders' at

Miletus, St Paul bids them 'take
heed to the flock in which the Holy
Ghost had made them "bishops" and
feed (ποιμαίνειν) the Church of God'
(Acts xx. 28); comp. 1 Pet. v. 2; John
xxi. 16. Christ Himself is spoken of as
'the shepherd and bishop of our souls'
(1 Pet. ii. 25), and 'the great Shepherd' (Hebr. xiii. 20). For διδάσκαλος
see Acts xiii. 1; 1 Cor. xii. 28 f.

From a consideration of these passages it is evident that there was not
as yet a recognised ecclesiastical hierarchy; while there is a tendency to
the specialisation of functions required
for the permanent well-being of the
Church.

See Additional Note.

12—16. The object of this manifold ministry is the perfecting of every
member after the pattern of Christ
(12, 13), that all realising the truth in
life may grow up to complete fellowship with Him (14, 15), Who provides
through the ministry of every part
for the growth of the whole body in
love (16).

12. πρὸς τὸν καταρτ....εἰς ἔργον...
εἰς οἰκ.] Latt. ad consummationem...
in opus ministerii, in aedificationem
...With a view to the perfecting of
the saints for a work.... The work
of the ministry is directed to the
preparation of the saints—the whole
body of the faithful—for the twofold
work which in due measure belongs
to all Christians, a personal work and a
social work. Every believer is charged
with the duty of personal service to
his fellow-believers and to his fellow-
men (2 Pet. i. 7 φιλαδελφία, ἀγάπη),
and has some part in building up the
fabric of the Christian Society.

A consideration of the scope of the
whole passage in which special stress
is laid upon the ministry of every part
to the welfare of the whole, seems to

ἁγίων εἰς ἔργον διακονίας, εἰς οἰκοδομὴν τοῦ σώματος
τοῦ χριστοῦ, ¹³μέχρι καταντήσωμεν οἱ πάντες εἰς τὴν
ἑνότητα τῆς πίστεως καὶ τῆς ἐπιγνώσεως τοῦ υἱοῦ τοῦ
θεοῦ, εἰς ἄνδρα τέλειον, εἰς μέτρον ἡλικίας τοῦ πληρώματος τοῦ χριστοῦ, ¹⁴ἵνα μηκέτι ὦμεν νήπιοι, κλυδωνι-

be absolutely decisive as to the interpretation of εἰς ἔργον διακ. εἰς οἰκοδ.
τ. σ. τ. χ. The change of the preposition shews clearly that the three
clauses (πρὸς...εἰς...εἰς...) are not co-
ordinate, and however foreign the idea
of the spiritual ministry of all 'the
saints' is to our mode of thinking, it
was the life of the apostolic Church.
The responsible officers of the congregation work through others, and find no
rest till every one fulfils his function.
The personal dealing of Christian with
Christian necessarily contributes to
the extension and consolidation of the
Society.

Καταρτισμός does not occur elsewhere in the N. T. Comp. κατάρτισις
2 Cor. xiii. 9; and καταρτίζω Lk. vi. 40;
1 Thess. iii. 10; 2 Cor. xiii. 11; Gal.
vi. 1; Hebr. xiii. 21; 1 Pet. v. 10; (ἐξαρ-
τίζω 2 Tim. iii. 17). The idea is of
the perfect and harmonious development of every power for active service
in due relation to other powers.

τῶν ἁγίων] See c. i. 1, note.

εἰς ἔργ. διακ.] There is no evidence
that at this time διακονία or διακονεῖν
had an exclusively official sense. Comp.
1 Cor. xii. 5; xvi. 15; Hebr. vi. 10.

εἰς οἰκοδ. τ. σ. τ. χ.] The metaphor
is expressive and accurate. The body
of Christ, like our own frames, is built
up by the addition of each element
which is required for its completion.
Comp. v. 16; 1 Pet. ii. 5 ff.

13. μέχρι καταντ.] Latt. donec
occurramus. The limit, unattainable
under present conditions, is an effective call to unceasing endeavour. For
καταντήσωμεν see Phil. iii. 11; Acts
xxvi. 7. The origin of the image in
Acts xxvii. 12 &c.

οἱ πάντες] we Christians all as a

body, not simply πάντες: 1 Cor. x. 17;
Rom. xi. 32; Phil. ii. 21.

εἰς...εἰς...εἰς...] St Paul distin-
guishes three stages or aspects of
Christian progress. The first is intellectual, where faith and knowledge
combine to create unity in the soul,
the object of both being the Son or
God. The second is personal maturity.
The third is the conformity of each
member to the standard of Christ in
whom all form one new man (Gal. iii.
28 εἰς; c. ii. 15.

τῆς ἐπιγνώσεως] See c. i. 17 note.
τοῦ υἱοῦ τ. θ.] Gal. ii. 20. The
express title is very rare in St Paul's
Epistles, though it is found not unfrequently by implication: Rom. i. 3,
9 &c.; Col. i. 13. The force of the
title is conspicuous in the Epistle to
the Hebrews: iv. 14; vi. 6; vii. 3; x. 29.

εἰς ἄ. τέλειον] 1 Cor. ii. 6; xiv. 20;
Col. i. 28; iv. 12; Phil. iii. 15; Hebr. v.
14. The phrase seems to point on-
ward to that perfectness of ideal
humanity in Christ in which each
believer when perfected finds his place
(Gal. iii. 28 quoted above).

εἰς μέτρον...] Latt. in mensuram
aetatis plenitudinis Christi. The perfection of each Christian is determined
by his true relation to Christ to Whose
fulness he is designed in the counsel
of God to minister. This ideal fulness
is the standard of his personal aim.
For ἡλικία, maturity of development,
see John ix. 21, 23.

14. This verse appears to be co-
ordinate with v. 13 and not dependent
upon it. The ministry of the Church
serves both for growth and for protection.

νήπιοι] opposed to τέλειοι (Hebr.
l.c.).

ζόμενοι καὶ περιφερόμενοι παντὶ ἀνέμῳ τῆς διδασκαλίας
ἐν τῇ κυβείᾳ τῶν ἀνθρώπων ἐν πανουργίᾳ πρὸς τὴν μεθοδίαν τῆς πλάνης, ¹⁵ἀληθεύοντες δὲ ἐν ἀγάπῃ αὐξήσωμεν
εἰς αὐτὸν τὰ πάντα, ὅς ἐστιν ἡ κεφαλή, Χριστός, ¹⁶ἐξ
οὗ πᾶν τὸ σῶμα συναρμολογούμενον καὶ συνβιβαζόμενον διὰ πάσης ἁφῆς τῆς ἐπιχορηγίας κατ᾽ ἐνέργειαν ἐν

κλυδωνιζόμενοι] Latt. *fluctuantes*.
The word does not occur elsewhere
in N. T. Comp. James i. 6.
περιφ.] This word (in the passive)
occurs in the New Testament here
only. In Heb. xiii. 9, as also in Jude
12, it is a false reading. But the
former passage (διδαχαῖς ποικίλαις κ.
ξέναις μὴ παραφέρεσθε) is to be compared, as describing the same dangers
under a slightly different image,—that
of being 'carried away from the straight
course' (see note *ad loc.*). [Here the
Ephesians are warned against being
carried about hither and thither by
various winds of erroneous doctrine,
which are thus characterised in contrast
with the unity of Christian teaching.]
τῆς διδασκ.] The teaching of such as
lead astray.
ἐν τῇ κυβ....] Latt. *in nequitia*
(*fallacia, illusione*) *hominum, in
astutia ad circumventionem (remed-
ium, machinationem) erroris*: encom-
passed, as it were, by the fraud (or the
gambling spirit) of religious adven-
turers, who turn them by their selfish
ability after the scheming of error.
κυβείᾳ] The word κυβεία occurs in
the literal sense of 'dice-playing' in
Pl. *Phaedr.* 274 D; Xen. *Mem.* i. 3, 2
&c. It is used metaphorically in Arr.
Epict. ii. 19; iii. 21. The word was
transliterated in Rabbinic. [See Add.
Note.]
πανουργίᾳ] Luke xx. 23; 1 Cor. iii.
19; 2 Cor. iv. 2; xi. 3. (2 Cor. xii. 16
πανοῦργος.)
For πρὸς τ. μ. see Gal. ii. 14; Lk.
xii. 47; and for μεθοδία c. vi. 11.
15. ἀληθεύοντες...] Latt. *veritatem
facientes, living the truth in love,*

not simply *speaking the truth.* The
appropriation of the truth is not
intellectual only but moral, expressed
through our whole being, in character
and action.
αὐξήσ. εἰς αὐ.] Latt. *crescamus in
illo:* may realise our fellowship with
Him more closely as our growth
advances and be conformed to Him
more perfectly.
16. ἐξ οὗ...] *from Whom,* as the
source of all vital energy, *all the body
...maketh for itself the growth of
the body unto the building up of
itself in love.* While Christ is the
one source of life, the gradual formation of His body, the Church, is
still described under the two complementary figures of 'a growth' and 'a
building up.' Αὔξησις obviously refers
to αὐξήσωμεν in *v.* 15. The increase
of the Church depends in part on the
due development of its members, and
in part on their harmonious combination.
The process of increase is continuous
(συναρμολογούμενον *pres.* as *c.* ii. 21 f.),
and it involves the putting together
of parts (συναρμ. *c.* ii. 21), and the
combination of persons (συμβιβ. Col. ii.
19).
διὰ π. ἁ.] Latt. *per omnem junc-
turam subministrationis, through
every contact.* Wherever one part
comes into close connexion with another, it communicates that which it
has to give. For the sense of ἁφή
see Lightfoot on Col. ii. 19.
The construction of τῆς ἐπιχορηγίας
is uncertain. The only connexion
which gives a satisfactory meaning
appears to be τῆς ἐπιχ. κατ᾽ ἐνέργ.

μέτρῳ ἑνὸς ἑκάστου ⌜μέρους⌝ τὴν αὔξησιν τοῦ σώματος
ποιεῖται εἰς οἰκοδομὴν ἑαυτοῦ ἐν ἀγάπῃ.

¹⁷ Τοῦτο οὖν λέγω καὶ μαρτύρομαι ἐν κυρίῳ, μηκέτι
ὑμᾶς περιπατεῖν καθὼς καὶ τὰ ἔθνη περιπατεῖ ἐν ματαιό-

16 μέλους

16 μέρους BℵD₂G₃K₂L₂P₂ 17 37 Iren ; μέλους AC vg syr-vg bo

The unusual order is intelligible from
the emphasis on τῆς ἐπιχ. (comp. iii. 17
note). The sense will then be : 'according to the effectual working of
the service rendered in due measure
by every part.' If ἐν μέτρῳ cannot be
used absolutely, then ἐν μέτρῳ ἑ. ἑ. μ.
gives the same meaning.

The rendering 'through every contact with the supply' gives no clear
sense. The 'supply' is not a definite
current of force, but varies with every
part. In any case the sense is clear.
Each part as it is brought into contact
with other parts, fulfils its own office
and contributes to the growth of the
whole.

ἐπιχορηγία occurs again Phil. i. 19.

ἐν ἀγάπῃ] The words re-echo the
language of v. 2. The repetition of ἐν
ἀγάπῃ is characteristic of the Epistle :
i. 4; iii. 18; iv. 2, 15; v. 2.

(3) The contrast of the old life and
the new (17—24).
The old life (17—19).
The new life (20—24).

¹⁷ This I say therefore and adjure
you in the Lord that ye no longer
walk as the Gentiles also walk in the
vanity of their mind, ¹⁸being darkened in their understanding, alienated from the life of GOD, because
of the ignorance that is in them
because of the hardening of their
heart ; ¹⁹in that having lost feeling
they gave themselves up to lasciviousness to work all uncleanness in
selfishness. ²⁰But ye did not so learn
the Christ, ²¹if at least it was He
Whom ye heard, and it was in Him
ye were taught, even as there is truth
in Jesus ; that ye put away, ²²having

regard to your former conversation,
the old man, which waxeth corrupt
after the lusts of deceit ; ²³and that
ye be renewed in the spirit of your
mind, ²⁴and put on the new man,
which hath been created after GOD
in righteousness and holiness of the
truth.

17—24. St Paul now returns to the
practical counsels on which he had
entered (vv. 1—3), and contrasts
generally the old life (17—19) and the
new (20—24).

17. τοῦτο οὖν λ. καὶ μαρτ.] This I
say therefore and adjure you in the
Lord.... The words take up παρακαλῶ
οὖν of v. 1. Here there can be no
question of the connexion of ἐν κυρίῳ
with μαρτύρομαι : I adjure you, recognising as I do so my fellowship
with the Lord, speaking as in Him.
Comp. 1 Thess. iv. 1. For similar
combinations see 2 Thess. iii. 4 πεποί-
θαμεν ἐν κ.; Gal. v. 10 ; Phil. ii. 24 ;
Rom. xiv. 14 πέπεισμαι ἐν κ. 'Ι. ; xvi. 2
ἵνα προσδέξησθε...ἐν κ. ; Phil. ii. 29 ;
ii. 10 ἐλπίζω ἐν κ. ; iv. 10 ἐχάρην ἐν κ. ;
Col. iv. 17 παρέλαβες ἐν κ.

μηκέτι ὑμᾶς...καθὼς καὶ τὰ ἔ.] that you
who have embraced the faith walk no
longer as in fact the Gentiles walk.
No longer should it so be that there
is no difference between your life and
theirs.

In καθὼς καί, the καί emphasises the
words which follow : c. iv. 4, 32 ; v. 2,
25, 29, &c.

The description of heathen life is
closely parallel both in thought and
language with Rom. i. 21 ff.

ἐν ματαιότητι τ. ν.] V. in vanitate
sensus sui, V.L. mentis suae, so v. 23.

τητι τοῦ νοὸς αὐτῶν, ¹⁸ ἐσκοτωμένοι τῇ διανοίᾳ ὄντες,
ἀπηλλοτριωμένοι τῆς ζωῆς τοῦ θεοῦ, διὰ τὴν ἄγνοιαν
τὴν οὖσαν ἐν αὐτοῖς, διὰ τὴν πώρωσιν τῆς καρδίας
αὐτῶν, ¹⁹ οἵτινες ἀπηλγηκότες ἑαυτοὺς παρέδωκαν τῇ
ἀσελγείᾳ εἰς ἐργασίαν ἀκαθαρσίας πάσης ἐν πλεονεξίᾳ.

19 ἀπηλγηκότες codd plur : syr hcl bo : Cl-Al Or Chrys Theod-Mops (non vers lat) ; item agnoscit Hieron ; ἀπηλπικότες DEG codd latt ap Hieron ; m Vg syr-vg arm ; aeth ; Victn ; Theod-Mops-lat

Rom. i. 21 ἐματαιώθησαν ἐν τοῖς διαλογισμοῖς αὐτῶν. Their hold on the spiritual and eternal was lost. Comp. Rom. viii. 20 τῇ ματαιότητι ἡ κτίσις ὑπετάγη. 1 Pet. i. 18 ἐκ τῆς ματαίας ὑμῶν ἀναστροφῆς. Idols were essentially μάταια Acts xiv. 15.

18. ἐσκοτωμ. τῇ διαν. ὄντες] Rom. i. 21 ἐσκοτίσθη ἡ ἀσύνετος αὐτῶν καρδία. Comp. c. v. 8, 11 ; 1 John ii. 11. That which should have been light was darkened : Matt. vi. 23. The converse change is noticed c. i. 18 πεφωτισμένους τοὺς ὀφθαλμοὺς τῆς καρδίας.

For διάνοια see Hebr. viii. 10 ; 1 Pet. i. 13 ; 2 Pet. iii. 1 ; 1 John v. 20. It is combined with καρδία Lk. i. 51.

The rhythm of the sentence is decisive for the connexion of ὄντες with ἐσκοτωμένοι, in spite of the parallel Col. i. 21, the only other passage in the N.T. in which the double participle is found.

ἀπηλλοτρ. τ. ζ. τ. θ.] For ἀπηλλοτρ. see c. ii. 12. The life of GOD is that life which answers to the nature of GOD and which He communicates to His children. This had become wholly foreign to their nature. Their spiritual darkness corresponded with a moral alienation from GOD.

See Ruskin Modern Painters ii. Pt. iii, c. 2 § 8, p. 18 small edn.

Ignorance or forgetfulness of GOD is the spring of all error, as 'the fear of GOD is the beginning of wisdom.' Comp. 1 Thess. iv. 5 τὰ ἔθνη τὰ μὴ εἰδότα τὸν θεὸν [a description which goes back to Jer. x. 25 ; Ps. lxxix. 6].

διὰ τὴν ἄγν....διὰ τὴν πώρ....] Latt. per ignorantiam quae est in illis, propter caecitatem.... The style of the Epistle suggests that these two clauses are coordinate. Even if they are so taken, it still remains true that their ignorance was due to hardening of their heart, though the two are noted separately; and it must be admitted that τὴν οὖσαν ἐν αὐτοῖς has more force if it is joined directly with what follows : 'the ignorance that is in them because of....'

For πώρωσις see Rom. xi. 7, 25 ; 2 Cor. iii. 14 (ἐπωρ. τὰ νοήματα) ; and specially in connexion with καρδία : Mk. iii. 5 ; vi. 52 ; viii. 17 ; John xii. 40. The root of the word is πῶρος, callus.

19. The issue of moral insensibility and guilty ignorance was gross corruption of life. This is represented as the result of their own action here (ἑαυτ. παρέδωκαν τῇ ἀσελγ.), and on the other hand is ascribed to GOD in Rom. i. 24 παρέδωκεν αὐτοὺς ὁ θεὸς...εἰς ἀκαθαρσίαν.... GOD does that which follows from the laws that express His will ; yet man does not lose his responsibility.

οἵτινες] being such that they....

ἀπηλγηκότες] Hier. dicamus indolentes sive indolorios, having lost feeling, expresses exactly the result of πώρωσις. The reading ἀπηλπικότες, Latt. desperantes, is inadequately supported and less suitable to the context.

τῇ ἀσελγείᾳ] as a mistress.

εἰς ἐργασίαν ἀκ. π.] They made a business (Acts xix. 24 f.) of impurity,

²⁰ʿΥμεῖς δὲ οὐχ οὕτως ἐμάθετε τὸν χριστόν, ²¹ εἴ γε αὐτὸν
ἠκούσατε καὶ ἐν αὐτῷ ἐδιδάχθητε, ⸢καθὼς ἔστιν ἀλήθεια
ἐν⸣ τῷ Ἰησοῦ, ²²ἀποθέσθαι ὑμᾶς κατὰ τὴν προτέραν

21 καθώς ἐστιν ἀληθείᾳ, ἐν

not simply yielding to passion but seeking out deliberately the means of sensual gratification. For ἐργασία see Plat. *Protag.* 353 D τῆς ἡδονῆς ἐργασίαν. [For the word cf. also Lk. xii. 58 δὸς ἐργασίαν and for the mode of speech the phrase ἐργάται ἀδικίας (Lk. xiii. 27), which itself comes from Ps. vi. 8.] ἐν πλεονεξίᾳ] *in selfishness.* This appears to be the general sense of πλεονεξία, whatever form it may take. The commonest and most typical form is when one sacrifices another to the gratification of his own appetite, as here: *c.* v. 3. This sense of the word is constant in the N.T.: Mk. vii. 22 ; Rom. i. 29 ; 2 Pet. ii. 14: compare 1 Thess. iv. 6. Self takes the place of GOD (Col. iii. 5).

20—24. In contrast with the old life which was summed up in 'selfishness,' St Paul sketches the new life which answers to 'the new man,' an embodiment of Christ Himself in Whom the isolated self is lost.

20. ὑμεῖς δέ...] taking up *v.* 17 μηκέτι ὑμᾶς.... But ye did not so learn the Christ.... This is not the life which answers to faith in Him. Christ is Himself the sum of the Gospel. He is preached, received, known (Phil. i. 15 ; Col. ii. 6 ; Phil. iii. 10). No similar phrase is quoted.

21. εἴ γε αὐτὸν...καὶ ἐν αὐτῷ...] *If at least it was He Whom ye heard* (*c.* i. 13) when He called you, *and it was in fellowship with Him ye were* further *taught*, as ye were then enabled to receive further instruction, *that you* as Christians should *put away....*

καθὼς ἔστιν...Ἰησοῦ] *even as there is* essentially *truth in Jesus.* The humanity of Christ (*Jesus*) gives reality to our limited conceptions. Truth is

no convention. Just as the Lord said 'I am the Truth,' so His disciples may say, perplexed by the many conflicting appearances and representations of things and duties, 'There is Truth— we can find it—in Jesus.' The Son of man helps us to find that there is something substantial under all the fleeting forms of earthly phenomena. Ἐν τῷ Ἰ. refers back to τὸν χ. The Messiah was revealed in Jesus in terms, so to speak, of human experience. As we look to Him we see that Pilate's question (John xviii. 38) Τί ἐστιν ἀλήθεια; is answered. Compare the converse declaration John viii. 44 ἐν τῇ ἀληθείᾳ οὐκ ἔστηκεν, ὅτι οὐκ ἔστιν ἀλήθεια ἐν αὐτῷ. [v. Add. Note, p. 70.]

For the position of ἐστίν see Hebr. xi. 1 note ; and for the anarthrous ἀλήθεια *v.* 25 ; *c.* v. 9 ; 2 Cor. xi. 10 ; Rom. xv. 8 [contrast iii. 7]; Jo. xviii. 38.

The whole structure of the passage seems to shew that the clause is parenthetical. It seems to indicate why Christian conduct must correspond to Christian doctrine.

22 ff. The new life is realised by three processes : the putting off 'the old man,' the renewal of spiritual power, the putting on 'the new man.' The first and third are acts done once for all (ἀποθέσθαι, ἐνδύσασθαι) ; and the second and third are connected together (ἀνανεοῦσθαι δέ...καὶ ἐνδύσ.) so that the decisive change is apprehended little by little by growing spiritual discernment. The infinitives depend on ἐδιδάχθητε in *v.* 21.

22. ἀποθέσθαι ὑ....] *that you should put away.* The word, though it is used of garments (Acts vii. 58), appears to be chosen instead of ἐκδύσασθαι (2 Cor. v. 4), ἀπεκδύσασθαι (Col. iii. 9), the natural correlative to ἐνδύσασθαι (*v.* 24) as expressing a

ἀναστροφὴν τὸν παλαιὸν ἄνθρωπον τὸν φθειρόμενον
κατὰ τὰς ἐπιθυμίας τῆς ἀπάτης, ²³ἀνανεοῦσθαι δὲ τῷ
πνεύματι τοῦ νοὸς ὑμῶν, ²⁴καὶ ἐνδύσασθαι τὸν καινὸν

more complete separation : *v.* 25 ;
Rom. xiii. 12 ; Col. iii. 8 ; Hebr. xii. 1,
&c. The ὑμᾶς is emphatic, 'you as
Christians' (*vv.* 17, 20).

κατὰ τ. πρ. ἀν.] *having regard to....*
Their former conversation was the
measure and rule of their renunciation.

For ἀναστροφή see Hebr. xiii. 7.
[Comp. Gal. i. 13; Ja. iii. 13; 1 Pet. i.
15 ἐν πάσῃ ἀναστροφῇ (where see Hort's
note), 18 ἐκ τῆς ματαίας ὑμῶν ἀναστροφῆς πατροπαραδότου, ii. 12, iii. 1, 2, 16.
The manner of life and intercourse had
to be renounced has already been described by St Paul in *c.* ii. 2, 3 ἐν αἷς
ποτε περιεπατήσατε......· ἐν οἷς καὶ ἡμεῖς
πάντες ἀνεστράφημέν ποτε ἐν ταῖς ἐπιθυμίαις τῆς σαρκὸς ἡμῶν.]

τὸν παλ. ἄν.] the whole character
representing the former self. This
was not only corrupt, but ever growing more and more corrupt (φθειρόμενον. cf. Rom. viii. 21 τῆς δουλείας
τῆς φθορᾶς) under the influence of
lusts, of which deceit was the source
and strength (cf. Hebr. iii. 13). To
follow these was the exact opposite to
'living the truth' (*v.* 15).

Compare Rom. vi. 6 ; Col. iii. 9.
Corresponding phrases are ὁ καινὸς ἄνθ.
v. 24 note ; ὁ ἔσω ἄνθ. *c.* iii. 16 note ;
ὁ κρυπτὸς τῆς καρδίας ἄνθ. 1 Pet. iii. 4 ;
ὁ ἄνθ. τῆς ἁμαρτίας [al. ἀνομίας] 2 Thess.
ii. 3 ; ὁ ἄνθ. τοῦ θεοῦ 1 Tim. vi. 11 ;
2 Tim. iii. 17.
There is much in the general temper
of the world—self-assertion, self-seeking—which answers to 'the old man.'

23 f. Two things are required for
the positive formation of the Christian
character, the continuous and pro-
gressive renewal of our highest faculty,
and the decisive acceptance of 'the
new man.'

ἀνανεοῦσθαι δέ...] *and* on the other

hand *that ye be....* The word ἀνανεοῦσθαι occurs here only in the N.T. ;
ἀνακαινοῦσθαι occurs Col. iii. 10; 2 Cor.
iv. 16 (ἀνακαίνωσις Rom. xii. 2 ; Tit.
iii. 5). The general distinction of νέος
and καινός passes into the two words.
The variations in Col. iii. 9 f. are instructive : ἀπεκδυσάμενοι τὸν παλαιὸν
ἄνθρωπον σὺν ταῖς πράξεσιν αὐτοῦ, καὶ
ἐνδυσάμενοι τὸν νέον τὸν ἀνακαινούμενον
εἰς ἐπίγνωσιν κατ᾽ εἰκόνα τοῦ κτίσαντος
αὐτόν.

τῷ πν. τοῦ ν.] The spirit, by which
man holds communion with GOD, has
a place in his higher reason. The
spirit when quickened furnishes new
principles to the νοῦς (comp. Arist.
Eth. N. vi.) by which it is delivered
from ματαιότης (*v.* 17). This St Paul
speaks of as ἡ ἀνακαίνωσις τοῦ νοός
(Rom. xii. 2). When the spirit is
dormant, man is led astray εἰκῇ φυσιού-
μενος ὑπὸ τοῦ νοὸς τῆς σαρκὸς αὐτοῦ
(Col. ii. 18), a vivid description of
'vanity of the mind.' But the νοῦς
itself must fulfil its true function :
1 Cor. xiv. 14.

24. ἐνδύσ. τ. κ. ἄ.] Comp. Gal. iii. 27
Χριστὸν ἐνεδύσασθε. Rom. xiii. 14
ἐνδύσασθε τὸν κύριον ᾽Ι. Col. iii. 10.
Christ is 'the new man' (1 Cor.
xv. 45 ff.) Who through His Divine
personality makes His human nature
effective in due measure for every
believer.

τὸν κ. θ. κτ.] This ideal humanity
already exists, answering perfectly to
the will of GOD ; but it has to be
personally appropriated.

For κατὰ θεόν see 2 Cor. vii. 9 ff. ;
c. ii. 2 note.

ἐν δικ. καὶ ὁσ. τ. ἀλ.] finding its expression *in righteousness and holiness*
—in the fulfilment of duties to others
and to self—inspired and supported
by the influence *of the truth.*

ἄνθρωπον τὸν κατὰ θεὸν κτισθέντα ἐν δικαιοσύνῃ καὶ
ὁσιότητι τῆς ἀληθείας.

ὁσιότης is found only here and
Lk. i. 75 in the N.T. [In the Song
of Zacharias, *l.c.*, as here, it is con-
joined with δικαιοσύνη. So too Wisd.
ix. 3.] For ὅσιος see Hebr. vii. 26.

[In 1 Thess. ii. 10 ὁσίως καὶ δικαίως κ.
ἀμέμπτως and Tit. i. 8 δίκαιον, ὅσιον
we see how, as here and in the 'Benedictus,' the two qualities are co-ordinated and complementary.]

Additional Note on the reading of Eph. iv. 21.

(*The following discussion of the text of* Eph. iv. 21 *is taken by permission from the private correspondence between Dr Westcott and Dr Hort preparatory to the formation of the text of the Epistle in their edition of the Greek Testament.*)

καθὼς ἔστιν ἀλήθεια ἐν τῷ Ἰησοῦ

Dr Hort writes: 'I have never from a boy been able to attach any meaning to the nominative here.'

He accordingly proposes to read

καθώς ἐστιν ἀληθείᾳ ἐν τῷ Ἰησοῦ

'with or without a comma after ἀληθείᾳ, though the comma seems to give a fuller and truer sense.'

Dr Westcott replies: 'I cannot construe ἀληθείᾳ. And ἐδιδάχθητε requires ἀλήθεια as does v. 24. Surely such a use of the dative with such a pregnant word as ἀλήθεια is inconceivable, to say nothing of authority.'

Dr Hort rejoins: 'Not a word to help me to the *right* meaning! Mine may be wrong; it only seems more likely to me than others to which I can attach no meaning.

'In v. 24 τῆς ἀληθείας simply corresponds to τῆς ἀπάτης of v. 22 according to St Paul's favourite antithesis, and needs no other explanation. Again, even if I took ἀληθείᾳ (cf. Phil. i. 18) as only equivalent to ἀληθῶς, I do not know why every single word is bound to be pregnant. But it seems to me that I give it its full theological sense, as full as in St John's Epistles. What is the alternative? Surely not with Meyer to join it with what follows "*as it is in Jesus for you to put off*..." I could easier believe with Credner (and, apparently, Origen) that it means 'As He is in truth in Jesus': but then that is only my own sense in a clumsy and unnatural form. All the other multitudinous renderings in Meyer convey nothing to my mind. A modification of Meyer's own view has just struck me as imaginable: "were taught that, as is truth in Jesus, ye should put off..." But (1) this renders the Greek horribly obscure, and (2) it requires ἐν τῷ χριστῷ. The right interpretation must be one which justifies the transition to ἐν τῷ Ἰησοῦ. Surely ἐν αὐτῷ ἐδιδάχθητε needs nothing to follow: first the learning *Him*, then the expansion of that by all manner of teaching received, but still *in Him*.'

Dr Westcott replies: 'I thought that I had indicated my meaning clearly enough. My idea is that, just as the Lord said "I am the Truth," so here St Paul reminds the Ephesians that there is Truth in Jesus, i.e. in the true humanity of the Word, whereby all the offices of life are revealed in the right relations. This appears to me obvious and pointed.'

Dr Hort rejoins: 'Your construction fits the Greek (if ἀλήθεια is read) better than any other; but the chasm which divides it from your interpretation is surely wide. I cannot by any process read such a sense into the statement, surely on any view a strange *under*statement, "there is truth in Jesus." The idea seems to me on the other hand to be already given in my interpretation in the words αὐτὸν ἠκούσατε καὶ ἐν αὐτῷ ἐδιδάχθητε, and without some such sense as mine I do not see how you can pass from τὸν χριστὸν (*v.* 20) to τῷ 'Ιησοῦ, all the more as this is the only passage of Ephesians where 'Ιησοῦς occurs not *combined* with Χριστός.

'The whole idea may be thus analysed:

    (a)   Jesus is the truth of the Christ.

    (β)   The Christ is the truth of humanity.

    (γ)   The Christ is the truth of God.

'Now according to my view *v.* 20 expresses (β), the special doctrine of this Epistle, and *v.* 21 expresses (a), shewing that those who had received the Gospel had implicitly received (β). But it seems to me that your view either omits (a) or confuses it with (β), and fails to explain either καθώς or τῷ 'Ιησοῦ. The use of ἀληθείᾳ seems to me *analogous* (at a different level) to the use of ἀληθινός in 1 Jo. v. 20: the God *in* His Son is the true God. I must claim *margin* for ἀληθείᾳ, ἐν.'

Dr Westcott replies: 'I don't in the least degree admit the force of your objections to my interpretation, nor see the possibility of such a dative as ἀληθείᾳ; but I admit your "claim" as a freeborn Englishman—till you give it up!'

Dr Hort writes finally: 'I don't see how margin can be dispensed with, as your interpretation seems to me absolutely impossible; and, as far as I can find, it is as completely without authority as, I fear, mine is. But your *construction* has all authority; so I do not ask for text, as I have failed to persuade you.'

Dr Westcott replies: 'Very well.'

(As a result of this discussion Dr Hort's proposed emendation καθώς ἐστιν ἀληθείᾳ, ἐν was placed in the margin, as an alternative reading to that of the text, in Westcott and Hort's edition.)

II. THE OUTWARD MANIFESTATION
OF THE CHRISTIAN LIFE PERSONAL
AND SOCIAL (iv. 25—vi. 9).

   1. Special features in the Christian character (iv. 25—v. 14).
   2. Cardinal social relationships
(v. 15—vi. 9).

After completing the general view
of the Christian Life, St Paul illustrates it in detail. He first deals
with some personal characteristics of
Christians (iv. 25—v. 14); and then
with the cardinal social relationships
(v. 15—vi. 9).

   (1) Some personal characteristics
of Christians (iv. 25—v. 14).

St Paul notices first special traits
as to truth (iv. 25), self-control (26 f.),
labour (28), language (29 f.), tender-
ness (31 f.). He then marks the
fundamental contrast between self-
sacrifice and selfishness (v. 1—6);
and develops the thought that the
Christian life is the life of a child of
light (7—14).

²⁵ *Wherefore, putting away falsehood, speak ye the truth each one
with his neighbour, because we are
members one of another.* ²⁶ *Be ye
angry, and sin not: let not the sun
go down upon your sense of provocation,* ²⁷ *nor give place to the devil.*
²⁸ *Let him that stealeth steal no more;
but rather let him labour, working
with his hands the thing that is good
that he may have whereof to give to
him that hath need.* ²⁹ *Let no corrupt
speech proceed out of your mouth,
but whatever is good to supply* (build
up) *that which is needed, that it
may give grace to them that hear.*
³⁰ *And grieve not the Holy Spirit of
GOD, in Whom ye were sealed unto
a day of redemption.* ³¹ *Let all bitterness and wrath and anger and
clamour and railing be taken away
from you, with all malice;* ³² *and
shew yourselves kind one to another,
tender-hearted, forgiving each other,
even as God also in Christ forgave
you.* v. ¹ *Shew yourselves therefore
imitators of God, as beloved chil-*

dren; ² *and walk in love, even as
Christ also loved you and gave Himself up for us, an offering and a
sacrifice to God for an odour of
fragrance.* ³ *But fornication and all
uncleanness or selfishness, let it not
even be named among you as becometh
saints;* ⁴ *and so of filthiness and
foolish talking or jesting, which are
not befitting; but rather giving of
thanks.* ⁵ *For this ye know by what
ye observe, that no fornicator nor
unclean person nor selfish man,
which is an idolater, hath any inheritance in the kingdom of Christ
and GOD.* ⁶ *Let no man deceive you
with empty words; for because of
these things cometh the wrath of
GOD upon the sons of disobedience.*
⁷ *Do not therefore shew yourselves
partakers with them;* ⁸ *for ye were
once darkness, but now are light in
the Lord: walk as children of light—*
⁹ *for the fruit of light is in all goodness
and righteousness and truth—* ¹⁰ *prov-
ing what is well-pleasing to the Lord;*
¹¹ *and have no fellowship with the
unfruitful works of darkness, but
rather even shew them in their true
nature* (*convict them*); ¹² *for the
things which are done by them in
secret it is a shame even to speak of.*
¹³ *But all things when they are shewn
in their true nature* (*convicted*) *by
the light are made manifest; for
everything that is made manifest is
light.* ¹⁴ *Wherefore* the poet *saith*
  *Awake thou that sleepest
  and arise from the dead,
  and Christ shall shine upon thee.*

iv. 25—32. At first sight the Apostle
appears, as in *vv.* 1—3, to descend to
humble deductions from great principles; but the point of his teaching
lies not in the precepts themselves,
but in the sanctions by which he
enforces them. Christian action is
shewn to be ruled not by law, but
by love. The obligations of Christian
to Christian, determined by their
personal relation to Christ, reveal and
determine the relations of man to

²⁵ Διὸ ἀποθέμενοι τὸ ψεῦδος λαλεῖτε ἀλήθειαν ἕκαστος μετὰ τοῦ πλησίον αὐτοῦ, ὅτι ἐσμὲν ἀλλήλων μέλη. ²⁶ ὀργίζεςθε καὶ μὴ ἁμαρτάνετε· ὁ ἥλιος μὴ ἐπιδυέτω ἐπὶ παροργισμῷ ὑμῶν, ²⁷ μηδὲ δίδοτε τόπον τῷ διαβόλῳ. ²⁸ ὁ κλέπτων μηκέτι κλεπτέτω, μᾶλλον δὲ κοπιάτω ἐργαζόμενος ταῖς ᵀ χερσὶν τὸ ἀγαθόν, ἵνα ἔχῃ μετα-

28 ἰδίαις

28 ταῖς + ἰδίαις אAD₂G₃K₂ 37 bo :—text BאᶜL₂ vg (am) :—om τ. χερσὶν P₂ 17 m ; Cl-Al

man. Here also the cardinal truth that love rests on the love of the brethren finds its application.

25. διό...] *Wherefore*, seeing that Christ is your life (Gal. ii. 20), *putting away* all *falsehood speak ye truth*.... (Zech. viii. 16). For ἀποθέμενοι see *v.* 22 and note. Τὸ ψεῦδος, 'the lie,' expresses falsehood in all its forms.

Falsehood is unnatural: it is disloyalty to Christ in Whom we all are. In a healthy body the eye cannot deceive the hand.

ἀλλήλων μέλη] Latt. *invicem membra*. Compare Rom. xii. 5; 1 Cor. xii. 12 ff. See also Marcus Aurelius ix. 1.

26. Men claim truth from us; and, if they move our just resentment, they claim the moderation of self-control. Ὀργίζεσθε assumes a just occasion for the feeling.

ὁ ἥλιος...] Perhaps as if he would say 'Let the returning calm of nature restore calm to your soul,' or simply 'Let the feeling of provocation end with the day.' This rule was followed by the Pythagoreans: Plut. *de am. frat.* p. 488 B.

ἐπὶ παροργισμῷ ὑ.] Latt. *super iracundiam vestram*. Παροργισμός, which occurs here only in N.T., is not the feeling of wrath but that which provokes it (cf. *c.* vi. 4 μὴ παροργίζετε, Deut. xxxii. 21, Rom. x. 19). The first keenness of the sense of provocation must not be cherished,

though righteous resentment may remain.

27. μηδέ...] Unchecked passion leaves the way open to the Tempter. Compare and contrast Rom. xii.˙19 μὴ ἑαυτοὺς ἐκδικοῦντες, ἀγαπητοί, ἀλλὰ δότε τόπον τῇ ὀργῇ. τῷ διαβ.] *c.* vi. 11. The word does not occur elsewhere in St Paul except in the Pastoral Epistles (1, 2 Tim., Tit.). It is found in St Matthew, St Luke, St John, Acts, Hebr., Cath. Epp. and Apoc.

28. ὁ κλέπτων...] *Let him that stealeth*.... If sins from the old life still remain, they must be abandoned under the constraining force of a new obligation. Our faith constrains us to serve one another. Stealing is the typical form of using the labour of another to supply our wishes, while it is our duty to make our own labour minister to the needs of others. The inspiration of labour is not personal gain but fulness of service.

Ὁ κλέπτων must mean 'he that stealeth' and not 'he that used to steal' (Vulg. *qui furabatur*).

μεταδιδόναι...] Latt. *unde tribuat* (V.L. *tribuere*) *necessitatem patienti* (*indigenti, cui opus est*). Lk. iii. 11; Rom. xii. 8. In the gift there is the thought of fellowship.

29 f. We wrong by action and we wrong by word. Evil speech corrupts: our duty is to edify. And more than this: evil speech grieves the Holy

διδόναι τῷ χρείαν ἔχοντι. ²⁹πᾶς λόγος σαπρὸς ἐκ τοῦ στόματος ὑμῶν μὴ ἐκπορευέσθω, ἀλλὰ εἴ τις ἀγαθὸς πρὸς οἰκοδομὴν τῆς χρείας, ἵνα δῷ χάριν τοῖς ἀκούουσιν. ³⁰καὶ μὴ λυπεῖτε τὸ πνεῦμα τὸ ἅγιον τοῦ θεοῦ, ἐν ᾧ ἐσφραγίσθητε εἰς ἡμέραν ἀπολυτρώσεως. ³¹πᾶσα πικρία καὶ θυμὸς καὶ ὀργὴ καὶ κραυγὴ καὶ βλασφημία ἀρθήτω ἀφ᾽ ὑμῶν σὺν πάσῃ κακίᾳ. ³²γίνεσθε

29 χρείας אBAK₂L₂P₂ 17 37 vg (am et fu) bo sah syrr Cl-Al Chrys Theod-Mops-lat; πίστεως D₂E₃G₃ 46 vg (codd al) codd lat ap Hier in loc ("Pro eo autem quod nos posuimus ad aedificationem opportunitatis, hoc est quod dicitur Graece τῆς χρείας, in Latinis codicibus propter euphoniam mutavit interpres et posuit ad aedificationem fidei") Greg-Nyss Bas Tert Cypr

Spirit. By using it we offend man and GOD.

29. πᾶς...μὴ ἐκπορ.] A Hebraism which emphasises the negation. 'Let every corrupt speech, if it is suggested in thought, be refused utterance.' It is, so to speak, a positive form of expressing the negation. Comp. 1 John ii. 21 note.

σαπρός] elsewhere used in N.T. only of material things. The word conveys the idea of life corrupted or lost: Matt. vii. 17 f.; xii. 33; xiii. 48.

ἀλλ᾽ εἴ τις...] but whatever is.... Matt. xviii. 28 Ἀπόδος εἴ τι ὀφείλεις : 2 Cor. ii. 10.

πρὸς οἰκοδ. τ. χρ.] Latt. ad aedificationem fidei, Hier. ad aedif. opportunitatis, to supply that which is needed in each case. The need represents a gap in the life which the wise word 'builds up,' fills up solidly and surely. Of the Latin text Jerome says: propter euphoniam mutavit interpres.

δῷ χάριν τ. ἀκ.] That which is elsewhere a Divine prerogative (Acts vii. 10; 1 Cor. i. 4; Rom. xii. 3; xv. 15; Eph. iii. 8; iv. 7; 2 Tim. i. 9; James iv. 6; 1 Pet. v. 5) is here attributed to human speech. Words can, by GOD's appointment, convey spiritual benefit to those who hear them. Their influence reaches beyond those to whom they are addressed.

30. μὴ λυπεῖτε...] cf. Is. lxiii. 10 τὸ πνεῦμα τ. ἅγ....] the indwelling Spirit. ἐν ᾧ ἐσφραγ.] Comp. Matt. iii. 11 αὐτὸς ὑμᾶς βαπτίσει ἐν πν. ἁγίῳ καὶ πυρί. For ἐσφραγίσθητε see c. i. 13. Compare Apoc. vii. 3 ff. ἀπολυτρώσεως] See note on c. i. 14. Comp. Rom. viii. 21.

31 f. From sins in word St Paul passes on to sins in temper which often find expression in word. All these must be taken away from among Christians, who must strive to shew to their fellows the tender love which they had received in Christ.

31. πικρία...] There is a natural progress: bitterness, passion, anger, loud complaint, railing accusation. All these must be utterly removed. In v. 26 St Paul had spoken of anger just in itself but requiring control. Here he speaks of that which is itself wrong. For ἀρθήτω see Col. ii. 14; 1 John iii. 5.

θυμός...ὀργή...] Comp. Rom. ii. 8; Col. iii. 8; Apoc. xix. 15. Θυμός is the special, transient excitement; ὀργή the settled feeling; see Lk. iv. 28; Acts xix. 28; Hebr. xi. 27; Matt. ii. 16.

ἀρθήτω] Comp. Matt. xiii. 12; xxi. 21 &c.; 1 Cor. v. 2. The difference in thought from ἀποθέσθαι, ἀποθέμενοι (vv. 22, 25) will be noticed.

σὺν π. κακίᾳ] 1 Pet. ii. 1. Ill-feeling

[δὲ] εἰς ἀλλήλους χρηστοί, εὔσπλαγχνοι, χαριζόμενοι ἑαυτοῖς καθὼς καὶ ὁ θεὸς ἐν Χριστῷ ἐχαρίσατο ⌜ὑμῖν.⌝ V. ¹γίνεσθε οὖν μιμηταὶ τοῦ θεοῦ, ὡς τέκνα ἀγαπητά, ²καὶ περιπατεῖτε ἐν ἀγάπῃ, καθὼς καὶ ὁ χριστὸς ἠγάπησεν ὑμᾶς καὶ παρέδωκεν ἑαυτὸν ὑπὲρ ⌜ὑμῶν⌝ προσφορὰΝ κὰι θυςίαΝ τῷ θεῷ εἰς ὀcμὴΝ εγωΔίαc.

32 ἡμῖν   2 ἡμῶν

is the spring of the faults which have been enumerated.

32. χρηστοί] a Divine trait: see Lk. vi. 35; 1 Pet. ii. 3.

εὔσπλαγχνοι] 1 Pet. iii. 8.

χαριζόμενοι...ἐχαρ....] V. donantes invicem (V.L. vobis) sicut et Deus in Christo donavit vobis. Perhaps more than 'forgiving,' though this is specially brought out in Col. iii. 13 (comp. Lk. vii. 42 f.; 2 Cor. ii. 7, 10; Col. ii. 13),—'dealing graciously with.' For the thought comp. Lk. vi. 36; Matt. xviii. 33; 1 John iv. 11.

ἑαυτοῖς] V. The pronoun suggests the thought of their corporate union in Christ: Orig. διὰ τὸ συσσώμους ἡμᾶς εἶναι.

Comp. Col. iii. 12 (and Lightfoot's note); 1 Pet. iv. 8—10.

ἐν Χριστῷ] Compare 2 Cor. v. 19 θεὸς ἦν ἐν Χριστῷ κόσμον καταλλάσσων ἑαυτῷ. So in Col. iii. 13 ὁ κύριος ἐχαρίσατο ὑμῖν.

v. 1—6. The thought of the loving-kindness of God in Christ leads St Paul to speak of the self-sacrifice of Christ which is our pattern (1, 2), as contrasted with the life of selfish indulgence (3, 4), which is exposed to the wrath of God (5, 6).

1. γίνεσθε οὖν...] Shew yourselves therefore, touched by the love of God... 1 John iv. 10 f.; iii. 1. Γίνεσθε is emphatic: c. iv. 32; James i. 22; Apoc. ii. 10; iii. 2. Contrast 1 Cor. iv. 16 μιμηταί μου γίνεσθε; xv. 58; Phil. iii. 17; Col. iii. 15; 1 Tim. iv. 12; 1 Pet. i. 16. The attainment of the Divine character is a process of life and growth. It was purposed and

prepared at the Creation, Gen. i. 26 'after our likeness.' This expressed purpose is the true Protevangelium.

μιμηταὶ τοῦ θ.] Elsewhere of human examples : 1 Cor. iv. 16; xi. 1; 1 Thess. ii. 14; Heb. vi. 12; 1 Pet. iii. 13; 2 Thess. iii. 7, 9; Heb. xiii. 7 (μιμεῖσθαι). Compare Matt. v. 45, 48; Luke vi. 36 γίνεσθε οἰκτίρμονες καθὼς ὁ πατὴρ ὑμῶν οἰκτίρμων ἐστίν.

ὡς τέκνα ἀγ.] as sharing His nature and conscious of His love. The child grows up by effort to the Father's likeness. For τέκνον see v. 8 note. Note the sequence ἀγαπητά, ἐν ἀγάπῃ, ἠγάπησεν.

2. περιπ. ἐν ἀ.] in love, which is the essence of God : 1 John iv. 8, 16. For περιπατεῖν see Rom. vi. 4 ἐν καινότητι ζωῆς π.; 2 Cor. x. 3; Col. iv. 5 ἐν σοφίᾳ π. πρὸς τοὺς ἔξω; 1 John i. 6 ἐν τῷ σκότει π.; 2 John 4 π. ἐν ἀληθείᾳ.

καθὼς καί...] c. iv. 17 note. The love of Christians answers to the love of Christ : John xiii. 34; xv. 12 f.; 1 John iii. 16.

ἠγάπ. ... καὶ παρέδ....] Gal. ii. 20 τοῦ ἀγαπήσαντός με καὶ παραδόντος ἑαυτὸν ὑπὲρ ἐμοῦ. Παρέδωκεν is absolute (not to be taken with τῷ θεῷ).

προσφ. καὶ θυσ.] The one word expresses the devotion and the other the sacrifice of life. Comp. Hebr. x. 5.

εἰς ὀσμ. εὐωδ.] Latt. in odorem suavitatis, for an odour of fragrance. The phrase (cf. Ezek. xx. 41 ἐν ὀσμῇ εὐωδίας προσδέξομαι ὑμᾶς) is used in the O.T. only of free-will offerings. In Christ the free-will offering and the sin-offering are combined.

So Christian teachers are 'a fra-

³ Πορνεία δὲ καὶ ἀκαθαρσία πᾶσα ἢ πλεονεξία μηδὲ
ὀνομαζέσθω ἐν ὑμῖν, καθὼς πρέπει ἀγίοις, ⁴καὶ αἰσχρότης καὶ μωρολογία ἢ εὐτραπελία, ἃ οὐκ ἀνῆκεν, ἀλλὰ
μᾶλλον εὐχαριστία. ⁵τοῦτο γὰρ ἴστε γινώσκοντες ὅτι
πᾶς πόρνος ἢ ἀκάθαρτος ἢ πλεονέκτης, ὅ ἐστιν εἰδωλο-

grance of Christ (Χριστοῦ εὐωδία) to
GOD,' 2 Cor. ii. 15.

In Phil. iv. 18 St Paul describes the
gifts received by him, Christ's apostle
and bondservant, from the Philippians
(τὰ παρ' ὑμῶν) as ὀσμὴν εὐωδίας, θυσίαν
δεκτήν, εὐάρεστον τῷ θεῷ [language
which recals not only Ez. xx. 41, but
also Mal. iii. 3, 4 καὶ ἔσονται τῷ κυρίῳ
προσάγοντες θυσίαν ἐν δικαιοσύνῃ, καὶ
ἀρέσει τῷ κυρίῳ θυσία 'Ιούδα καὶ 'Ιερου-
σαλήμ καθὼς αἱ ἡμέραι τοῦ αἰῶνος καὶ
καθὼς τὰ ἔτη τὰ ἔμπροσθεν].

3. Love answers to holiness, and
honours and cherishes the highest in
all. All sins of self-indulgence therefore, in which a man sacrifices another
to himself, or his own higher nature
to the lower, are diametrically opposed
to love.

πορνεία] This is a general term for
all unlawful intercourse, (1) adultery :
Hos. ii. 2, 4 (LXX.) ; Matt. v. 32 ; xix. 9 ;
(2) unlawful marriage, 1 Cor. v. 1 ;
(3) fornication, the common sense as
here.

ἀκαθ. π. ἢ πλεον.] One sin under
two aspects as affecting the man himself and others. For πλεονεξία, which
here evidently means sensual indulgence at the cost of others, see c. iv.
19; and cf. 1 Thess. iv. 6.

μηδὲ ὀνομ.] Such sins are not to be
spoken of. This simple sense is better
than that no occasion should be given
for even a rumour of their existence
among Christians.

πρέπει] Comp. 1 Tim. ii. 10; Tit.
ii. 1 ; Hebr. ii. 10 (with note), vii. 26.

4. καὶ αἰσχρ.] that is, let it not be
named among you. Αἰσχρότης (Latt.
turpitudo) occurs here only in N.T.
It is probably not to be limited to
language (αἰσχρολογία Col. iii. 8).

μωρ. ἢ εὐτραπ.] Latt. stultiloquium
aut scurrilitas, foolish talking, or—
if it is called by its fashionable name—
ready wit. For μωρολογία see Plut.
Moral. p. 504 B. For εὐτραπελία see
Arist. Eth. Nic. ii. 7, 13, Rhet. ii. 12,
16.

ἃ οὐκ ἀνῆκ.] Latt. quae ad rem non
pertinet (-ent). See Lightfoot's note
on Col. iii. 18.

ἀλλὰ μᾶλλον] a sharper opposition
than μᾶλλον δέ (v. 11). It occurs also
Matt. xxvii. 24 ; Mk. v. 26 ; 1 Tim. vi.
2 ; while μᾶλλον δέ is found also in
c. iv. 28 ; Acts v. 14 ; 1 Cor. xiv. 1 ;
Gal. iv. 9.

εὐχαριστία] It is our duty to look
at the noble, the divine, aspect of
things and not at the ludicrous, as
recognising the manifold endowments
of humanity, and the signs of GOD's
love in every good thing. In the
reverent mind not 'the thought of
past years' alone, but the great spectacle of life and nature 'doth breed
perpetual benediction.' Compare 1
Thess. v. 18 ; Col. ii. 7; and v. 20.
The words εὐχαριστεῖν, εὐχαριστία, are
characteristic of St Paul.

5, 6. Such sins as have been enumerated exclude from the kingdom of
GOD and bring down the wrath of GOD
upon those who are guilty of them.

5. τοῦτο γὰρ ἴστε γιν....] Latt. hoc
enim scitote (scire debetis) intelligen-
tes. For this ye know by what you
observe.... Actual experience confirms
the lessons of the teacher. The indi-
cative appears to be more suited to
the context than the imperative.

πᾶς...οὐκ...] Compare c. iv. 29 note.
For πλεονέκτης see c. iv. 19 note.

ὅ ἐστιν...] Latt. quod est idolorum
servitus : which character is.... In

λάτρης, οὐκ ἔχει κληρονομίαν ἐν τῇ βασιλείᾳ τοῦ χριστοῦ καὶ θεοῦ.   ⁶Μηδεὶς ὑμᾶς ἀπατάτω κενοῖς λόγοις,
διὰ ταῦτα γὰρ ἔρχεται ἡ ὀργὴ τοῦ θεοῦ ἐπὶ τοὺς υἱοὺς
τῆς ἀπειθίας.   ⁷μὴ οὖν γίνεσθε συνμέτοχοι αὐτῶν· ⁸ἦτε
γάρ ποτε σκότος, νῦν δὲ φῶς ἐν κυρίῳ· ὡς τέκνα φωτὸς

subservience to selfish desires there is
a form of idolatry to which converts
from heathenism are exposed. Comp.
Phil. iii. 19 ὧν ὁ θεὸς ἡ κοιλία.
ἔχει κληρον.] Cf. Heb. vi. 12 (Add.
Note); ix. 15.
ἐν τῇ βασ. τοῦ χριστοῦ καὶ θεοῦ] The
phrase is without parallel. The kingdom is spoken of as 'the kingdom of
the Son of [GOD's] love' (Col. i. 3).
And again it is said 'The kingdom of
the world is become the kingdom of
our Lord and of His Christ' (Apoc. xi.
15). The names occur substantially
in a different order in 2 Thess. i. 12
κατὰ τὴν χάριν τοῦ θεοῦ ἡμῶν καὶ κυρίου
Ἰ. Χρ.; 1 Tim. v. 21 ἐνώπιον τοῦ θεοῦ
καὶ Χρ. Ἰ.; 1 Tim. vi. 13 ἐνώπιον τοῦ
θεοῦ τοῦ ζωογονοῦντος τὰ πάντα καὶ Χρ.
Ἰ. τοῦ μαρτυρ. ἐπὶ Π. Π....; 2 Tim. iv. 1
ἐνώπιον τοῦ θεοῦ καὶ Χρ. Ἰ. τοῦ μέλλοντος κρίνειν ζῶντας καὶ νεκρούς. Compare
also Tit. ii. 13 τοῦ μεγάλου θεοῦ καὶ σωτῆρος ἡμῶν Χρ. Ἰ.; 2 Pet. i. 1 τοῦ θεοῦ
ἡμῶν καὶ σωτῆρος Ἰ. Χρ. From these
passages it appears that Χριστοῦ and
θεοῦ are to be treated as proper names.
But the combination under a common
article brings them into a connexion
incompatible with a simply human
view of the Lord's Person (comp. Tit.
ii. 13; 2 Pet. i. 1).

6. μηδεὶς ὑ. ἀ.] The ὑμᾶς is emphatic. Let no one deceive you who
have learnt the truth.... The μηδεὶς
probably refers to heathen friends who
thought lightly of the offences.
ἀπατάτω] deceive you by giving a
false appearance to the sins: 1 Tim.
ii. 14; James i. 26; ἐξαπατᾶν 2 Thess.
ii. 3; 1 Cor. iii. 18 (v. l.); 2 Cor. xi. 3;
Rom. vii. 11; xvi. 18.
ἔρχεται] even now.
ἡ ὀργὴ τ. θ.] John iii. 36; Col. iii. 6;

Apoc. xix. 15. Compare Rom. iii. 5;
ix. 22. See also Rom. i. 18 (ὀργὴ θ.);
1 Thess. ii. 16 (ἡ ὀργή); Rom. v. 9;
xii. 19.
The phrase is not to be limited to
any particular manifestation of GOD's
wrath. So He regards such offenders
generally.
ἐπὶ τ. υἱ. τ. ἀπ.] Conscience gave
the law and they disobeyed it. Comp.
ii. 2 note.
7—14. The lessons already enforced
are now gathered together under the
familiar contrast of darkness and
light.
7.   μὴ οὖν γίν....] Do not therefore,
knowing GOD's judgment, shew yourselves partakers with them in such
conduct. The present (γίνεσθε) indicates the imminence of the danger:
v. 17; John xx. 27; Rom. xii. 16;
1 Cor. vii. 23; x. 7; xiv. 20; 2 Cor. vi.
14.
συνμέτοχοι] Latt. participes (comparticipes), partakers with them in
their sins and in their punishment:
c. iii. 6. Contrast συγκοινωνός 1 Cor.
ix. 23; Rom. xi. 17; Phil. i. 7; Apoc.
i. 9. See v. 11.
8.   ἦτε...σκότος] Not simply ἐν
σκότει. The thought is dominantly
not of individual character but of
social influence. No parallel to this
use is quoted.
φῶς ἐν κυρίῳ] Light in fellowship
with Him Who is the light of the
world (John viii. 12), which you are
called to be derivatively (Matt. v. 14).
τέκνα φ.] Compare John xii. 36
υἱοὶ φ.; Lk. xvi. 8 οἱ υἱοὶ τ. φ.; 1 Thess.
v. 5. Τέκνον indicates a community
of nature as υἱὸς marks privilege. See
1 John iii. 1 τέκνα θεοῦ (and note).
In a figurative sense τέκνον is com-

περιπατεῖτε, ⁹ὁ γὰρ καρπὸς τοῦ φωτὸς ἐν πάσῃ ἀγαθωσύνῃ καὶ δικαιοσύνῃ καὶ ἀληθείᾳ, ¹⁰δοκιμάζοντες τί ἐστιν
εὐάρεστον τῷ κυρίῳ· ¹¹καὶ μὴ συνκοινωνεῖτε τοῖς ἔργοις
τοῖς ἀκάρποις τοῦ σκότους, μᾶλλον δὲ καὶ ἐλέγχετε,

9 φωτὸς אBAD₂E₃G₃P₂ 17 al, vg syr-vg bo arm, Lucif Vict-Afr; πνεύματος D°₂K₂L₂
etc, syr-hcl, Chrys Theod-Mops-lat

paratively rare and occurs only in the
plural: τ. (σοφίας) Lk. vii. 35; τ. ὀργῆς
Eph. ii. 3; τ. φωτὸς Eph. v. 8; τ. ὑπακοῆς 1 Pet. i. 14; τ. κατάρας 2 Pet. ii. 14
(τ. ἐπαγγελίας Gal. iv. 28, Rom. ix. 8
is different).

Υἱός is widely used and is found
both in the singular and in the plural:
υἱ. τῆς βασιλείας Matt. viii. 12; xiii. 38;
υἱ. γεέννης Matt. xxiii. 15; υἱ. εἰρήνης
Lk. x. 6; υἱ. (τοῦ) φωτός Lk. xvi. 8;
Joh. xii. 36; 1 Thess. v. 5; υἱ. τοῦ
αἰῶνος τούτου Lk. xx. 34; υἱ. τῆς ἀναστάσεως Lk. xx. 36; υἱ. τῆς ἀπωλείας
Joh. xvii. 12; 2 Thess. ii. 3; υἱ. τῶν
προφητῶν καὶ τῆς διαθήκης Acts iii. 25;
υἱ. τῆς ἀπειθείας Eph. ii. 2; v. 6; Col.
iii. 6; υἱ. ἡμέρας 1 Thess. v. 5. To
these may be added the interpretations of two names; υἱ. βροντῆς Mk. iii.
17; υἱ. παρακλήσεως Acts iv. 36.

9. ὁ γὰρ κ.] Light will reveal itself
in action (περιπατεῖτε) for the fruit of
light is.... There is a definite character
in life which follows naturally from
'the light.' For ὁ καρπὸς τ. φ. comp.
Gal. v. 22; Rom. vi. 21 f.; Phil. i. 11;
and John xv. 2 ff.

ἐν πάσῃ...] The life in light is not
rigid and monotonous. It is shewn in
every form of goodness and righteousness and truth, in all moral duties
reckoned under the familiar classification, the good, the right, the true.
The first includes personal character,
the second social dealings, the third
ruling principles, marking generally
our obligation to self, our neighbours,
God.

For ἀγαθωσύνη see Lightfoot on Gal.
v. 22.

10. δοκιμάζοντες] Each step in
action involves careful thought. We

cannot divest ourselves of the responsibility of judgment. An important
part of the discipline of life lies in the
exercise of that power of discrimination
which God quickens and strengthens.
Comp. Rom. xii. 2. For δοκιμάζειν see
1 Thess. v. 21; Gal. vi. 4; Rom. ii. 18;
xii. 2; 1 John iv. 1.

εὐάρεστον] V. beneplacitum. Εὐά-
ρεστος is used both of things, Rom.
xii. 1, 2; Phil. iv. 18; Col. iii. 20; Hebr.
xiii. 21; and of persons, 2 Cor. v. 9;
Rom. xiv. 18; Tit. ii. 9.

τῷ κυρίῳ] The Lord Jesus. His
judgment is the judgment of God:
Rom. xii. 1; xiv. 18.

11. μὴ συνκοινωνεῖτε] Latt. nolite
communicare. Phil.iv.14; Apoc. xviii.
4. In this word, as in συγκοινωνός
see v. 7 note, the idea of personal
fellowship prevails over that of parti-
cipation in something outward. Comp.
Hebr. ii. 14 (κεκοινώνηκεν, μετέσχεν)
note.

τοῖς ἔργοις τοῖς ἀκ.] The form of
expression, as distinguished from τοῖς
ἀκ. ἔργοις, gives emphasis to the epi-
thet: 'the works, the fruitless works.'
Comp. c. vi. 13, 16; Col. i. 15, 21; iv.
14 &c.

ἀκάρποις] The self-originated sinful
deeds of men have no 'fruits,' divinely
ordered issues of lasting good, though
terrible results follow them. Notice
Gal. v. 19 ff. contrasted with v. 22;
and compare Rom. ii. 7 ζωὴν αἰώνιον,
9 ὀργὴ καὶ θυμός.

μᾶλλον δέ...] The Christian is not
only to have light; but as he is light, he
must spread it, and that in virtue of
its very nature. He must not only
avoid evil: he must expose it.

ἐλέγχετε] Shew it to be what it

¹²τὰ γὰρ κρυφῇ γινόμενα ὑπ᾽ αὐτῶν αἰσχρόν ἐστιν καὶ
λέγειν· ¹³τὰ δὲ πάντα ἐλεγχόμενα ὑπὸ τοῦ φωτὸς φανεροῦται, πᾶν γὰρ τὸ φανερούμενον φῶς ἐστίν. ¹⁴διὸ λέγει
Ἔγειρε, ὁ καθεύδων,
καὶ ἀνάστα ἐκ τῶν νεκρῶν,
καὶ ἐπιφαύσει σοι ὁ χριστός.

14 ἐπιφαύσει σοι ὁ χριστός codd Graec tantum non omnes ; vg, Marcion (ap
Epiph) Naasseni (ap Hipp) Cl-Al Orig Hipp Chrys Theod-Mops-lat Hier ; ἐπιψαύσεις
τοῦ χριστοῦ D₂ codd ap Chrys ap Theodrt et (ut videtur) ap Theod-Mops Vict-Af
Ambst ; continget te Christus quidam ap Hier (? codd ap Theod-Mops) Ambst ed Rom
Aug ed Ben

truly is : Matt. xviii. 15 ; John iii. 20 ;
xvi. 8 ; 1 Cor. xiv. 24.

12. τὰ γάρ...] Their offences require only to be recognised as what
they are in order that they may be
condemned at once ; while we naturally shrink from discussing them.

ὑπ᾽ αὐτῶν] i.e. the source of disobedience v. 6. The verses 8—10 are
substantially parenthetical, and v. 11
takes up v. 7.

13. And yet more follows : the evil
is not only condemned, it is destroyed.
All things, when they are convicted,
tried, tested, shewn to be what they
really are, *by the light, are made
manifest* ; and that only can bear
the light and be made manifest, which
is akin to it. Darkness perishes in
its presence. *For everything that is
made manifest is light* (Latt. *omne
enim quod manifestatur lumen est*),
it is manifest only so far as it partakes
of the light. A man who receives the
light of Christ reflects it. He cannot
receive it except so far as he has
affinity with it, and he cannot receive
it without reflecting it. The light
is itself a purifying force. When it acts
it brings out all that is able to sustain
its presence. All else 'is null, is
nought.'

Compare John iii. 20 f. which serves
as a commentary on this passage.

The course of the argument is certainly obscure, but it is inconceivable

that after φανεροῦται, which is unques-
tionably passive, the φανερούμενον in
the next clause which obviously refers
to it should be 'middle.' Nor indeed
is there any force in the statement
'for everything that makes manifest
is light.' On the other hand if we
suppose that St Paul is filled with
the thought that darkness flies before
the light, the πᾶν γὰρ φανερούμενον
becomes intelligible : 'All things being
tested by the light are made manifest.
And this is what we desire ; the darkness goes from them ; for everything
that is made manifest is light.' This
thought is illustrated by the quotation
which follows. So Primasius : Incipit
lumen esse cum credit et nobis jun-
gitur. There is a similar assumption
of an unexpressed consequence in
v. 29.

14. διὸ λέγει...] *Wherefore*, because the light has this transforming
power, the poet *saith*.... Just as the
subject of λέγει in iv. 8 is the author
of the familiar Psalm, so here the
subject is the author of the Hymn,
of which however no other trace has
been preserved. Comp. Is. lx. 1.

ἔγειρε...ἀνάστα] awake from sleep
...arise to action.

ἀνάστα ἐκ τ. ν.] John v. 25 ἀμὴν ἀμὴν
λέγω ὑμῖν ὅτι ἔρχεται ὥρα καὶ νῦν ἐστιν
ὅτε οἱ νεκροὶ ἀκούσουσιν τῆς φωνῆς τοῦ
υἱοῦ τοῦ θεοῦ καὶ οἱ ἀκούσαντες ζήσουσιν.
For τῶν ν. comp. Col. i. 18 ‖ Apoc. i. 18

¹⁵ Βλέπετε οὖν ἀκριβῶς πῶς περιπατεῖτε, μὴ ὡς
ἄσοφοι ἀλλ᾽ ὡς σοφοί, ¹⁶ἐξαγοραζόμενοι τὸν καιρόν,

(not Col. ii. 12): elsewhere (40 times)
ἐκ νεκρῶν.

ἐπιφαύσει σοι] V. *illuminabit (il-
lucescet) te (tibi), Christ shall shine
upon thee*, and in His light thou too
shalt become light. For ἐπιφ. see
Gen. xliv. 3. The V. L. implies the
reading ἐπιψαύσει σοι ὁ χριστός or
ἐπιψαύσεις τοῦ χριστοῦ and gives
continget te Christus or *continges
Christum*.

In looking back over the sanctions
on which the different precepts (iv.
25—v. 14) are based, it will be seen
that they spring from the relation of
the believer to Christ. The loftiest
Christian doctrine becomes the motive
of the simplest duty. Truthfulness
rests on the position in which we
stand towards one another as members
of one body (iv. 25). Undisciplined
resentment opens a way to Christ's
adversary (27). Honest labour enables us to fulfil our corporate duty
(28). Evil speech grieves the Holy
Spirit, Who works through good
words (29, 30). All bitterness is alien
from Christ's mind and work (31, 32).
Generally all sensual self-indulgence
is opposed to love (v. 1—6). The
light which Christ has given must
have its perfect work (7—14).

At the same time positive duties
are enjoined. 'Thou shalt' is added
to 'Thou shalt not': 'put on' com-
pletes 'put off': iv. 25 speak truth:
28 let him labour: 29 give grace to
them that hear: 32 be kind: v. 1 walk
in love: 4 giving of thanks: 8 walk as
children of light: 11 reprove works
of darkness.

Christian morality cannot be separated from the Christian revelation.
In Christ man is seen in new relations.
His conduct cannot be rightly considered apart from these.

(2) Cardinal social relationships (v.
15—vi. 9).
St Paul now passes on to the con-

sideration of social duties. As 'light'
Christians must affect those among
whom they live. Both in their general
temper (v. 15—21) and in the relations
of the family (v. 22—vi. 9) they will
shew the power of their Faith.

v. 15—21. The general temper of
Christians.

¹⁵ *Look therefore carefully how ye
walk, not as unwise but as wise,
¹⁶ buying up the opportunity, because
the days are evil.* ¹⁷ *For this reason
do not shew yourselves foolish, but
understand what the will of the Lord
is.* ¹⁸ *And be not drunken with wine
wherein is riot, but be filled in spirit,
¹⁹ speaking one to another in psalms
and hymns and spiritual songs, singing and making melody with your
heart to the Lord;* ²⁰ *giving thanks
always for all things in the name of
our Lord Jesus Christ, to our* GOD
and Father; ²¹ *subjecting yourselves
one to another in the fear of Christ.*

15. βλέπετε οὖν...] *Look therefore
carefully how ye walk*, because you
are called to a great service and are
enabled to fulfil it. Conduct is difficult; and it is for action not for
knowledge we were made.

ἀκριβῶς] Comp. *v.* 10. The Divine
light does not make man's carefulness
less needful. For βλέπετε see 1 Cor.
iii. 10.

μὴ ὡς...] The negative is determined by the implied command.

16. ἐξαγορ. τ. κ.] Latt. *redimentes
tempus, buying up the opportunity*,
making your own at all cost the season
for action. For each one there is
but a limited time for service and that
under special conditions. Each one
therefore must make himself master
of his position and use all the helps
and occasions which it brings.

Elsewhere ἐξαγοράζειν (act.) is used
for *to redeem* Gal. iii. 13; iv. 5; and
some have supposed that it has that
sense here: *redeeming the season* from

ὅτι αἱ ἡμέραι πονηραί εἰσιν. ¹⁷διὰ τοῦτο μὴ γίνεσθε
ἄφρονες, ἀλλὰ συνίετε τί τὸ θέλημα τοῦ κυρίου· ¹⁸καὶ
ΜΗ ΜΕΘΎΣΚΕΣΘΕ ΟΪΝῳ, ἐν ᾧ ἐστὶν ἀσωτία, ἀλλὰ πληροῦσθε ἐν πνεύματι, ¹⁹λαλοῦντες ἑαυτοῖς ᵀ ψαλμοῖς καὶ

19 ἐν

19 ψαλμοις] praem. ἐν BP₂ 17 vg Vict-Af

the evil powers who are lords of the
world (c. vi. 12; 1 John v. 19). The
use of the middle in Col. iv. 5 is
parallel to the use in this passage;
and there can be no doubt that in
these two places the word means
'buying up for yourselves.' Ἐξαγοράζειν occurs in Plut. Crass. 2: i. 543 E
and in Polyb. iii. 42, 2 in the sense of
'buying up,' and this sense of ἐκ in
compounds is justified by abundant
examples (e.g. ἐκδαπανάω 2 Cor. xii. 15).
Comp. Dan. ii. 8 καιρὸν ὑμεῖς ἐξαγορά-
ζετε : Polyc. Mart. 2, διὰ μιᾶς ὥρας τὴν
αἰώνιον κόλασιν ἐξαγοραζόμενοι.

ὅτι αἱ ἡμ....] because the days are
evil, and the season for action is brief
and precarious and precious. The
connexion in Col. iv. 5 is different:
walk in wisdom toward them that
are without, buying up the opportunity. Wise conduct in some degree
disarms opposition and makes it easier
to obtain our end.

17. διὰ τοῦτο...] For this reason,
because the danger is great and the
need of walking carefully is urgent,...
do not fall to a lower level, but....

For μὴ γίνεσθε see v. 7 note. Such
degeneracy is noticed Hebr. v. 11
νωθροὶ γεγόνατε ταῖς ἀκοαῖς ; vi. 12 ἵνα
μὴ νωθροὶ γένησθε.

Ἄφρων, as distinguished from ἄσοφος, expresses a want of practical
judgment : 1 Cor. xv. 36; 1 Pet. ii. 15.
Compare i. 8 note.

συνίετε τί τὸ θ. τ. κ.] understand
by careful consideration of the circumstances in each case what the
will of the Lord is, which it is your
purpose to recognise and to fulfil.
Generally we read τὸ θέλ. τοῦ θεοῦ

c. vi. 6; 1 Thess. iv. 3; Hebr. x. 36;
1 Pet. ii. 15, &c. But τὸ θέλ. τοῦ
κυρίου is found Acts xxi. 14.

18. καὶ μὴ μεθ.] The transition to
a particular precept is abrupt. But
the precept affects the whole temper
of the Christian like the teaching of
vv. 15—17. It expresses in the most
striking form the necessity of guarding carefully the completeness of
self-control in the times of highest
exaltation. Men naturally seek for
times of keener life in which feeling,
thought, expression are quickened.
This is good, but do not, St Paul
says, look for your exhilaration from
unlawful sources. Be not drunken
with wine, in which indulgence is
not healthy excitement but riot, but
be filled in spirit : seek a loftier
inspiration : let your highest faculty,
not your lowest, be richly supplied
with that which you crave, so that
its especial powers are called into
play. It is assumed that the Spirit
of GOD can alone satisfy the spirit of
man.

ἀσωτία] Latt. luxuria (lascivia).
The word occurs Tit. i. 6 ; 1 Pet. iv. 4.
Compare Arist. Eth. N. iv. 1, 4 f.

πληροῦσθε] be filled, that is, let your
utmost capacities be rightly satisfied :
find the completest fulfilment of your
nature. For this absolute sense of
πληροῦσθαι compare c. iii. 19 (i. 23) ;
Phil. iv. 18 ; Col. ii. 10.

ἐν πνεύματι is opposed to ἐν σαρκί.

19—21. The intenser quickening of
the higher life shews itself in many
ways, in the joy of intercourse, in
personal feeling, in thanksgiving to
GOD, in mutual consideration.

ὕμνοις καὶ ᾠδαῖς πνευματικαῖς, ᾄδοντες καὶ ψάλλοντες
τῇ καρδίᾳ ὑμῶν τῷ κυρίῳ, ²⁰ εὐχαριστοῦντες πάντοτε
ὑπὲρ πάντων ἐν ὀνόματι τοῦ κυρίου ἡμῶν Ἰησοῦ Χριστοῦ
τῷ θεῷ καὶ πατρί, ²¹ ὑποτασσόμενοι ἀλλήλοις ἐν φόβῳ

19. Men whose spirit is kindled by noble emotion express themselves in the highest forms of speech, and their hearts are in harmony with their words.

λαλοῦντες ἑαυτοῖς] Vulg. *loquentes vobismet ipsis.* The Christian congregation as Christian joins in the various forms of praise; and the same strains which set forth aspects of GOD's glory elevate the feelings of those who join in them.

In the earliest picture of a Christian service which has been preserved (Plin. *epist.* x. 97) Christians in the reign of Trajan (A.D. 98—117) are described as ' soliti stata die ante lucem convenire carmenque Christo, quasi Deo, dicere secum invicem.'

This ' divine music,' however, is not to be confined to religious assemblies alone.

ψ. καὶ ὑ. καὶ ᾠ. πν.] Jerome after Origen says : Quid intersit inter psalmum et hymnum et canticum in Psalterio plenissime discimus. Nunc autem breviter hymnos esse dicendum, qui fortitudinem et majestatem praedicant Dei et ejusdem vel beneficia vel facta mirantur.... Psalmi autem proprie ad ethicum locum pertinent, ut per organum corporis quid faciendum sit et quid vitandum noverimus. Qui vero de superioribus disputat et concentum mundi omniumque creaturarum ordinem atque concordiam subtilis disputator eduxerit, iste spirituale canticum canit.

The *Codex Alex.* A includes a rudimentary collection of Psalms, Canticles and Hymns.

ᾄδ. καὶ ψάλλ. τῇ κ.] The outward music was to be accompanied by the inward music of the heart.

20. εὐχαριστοῦντες...] The chief element in all is thanksgiving to GOD : see *v.* 4. This springs out of the sense of our relation to 'our Lord Jesus Christ.'

ἐν ὀνόμ....] 2 Thess. iii. 6 ; 1 Cor. v. 4 ; vi. 11 ; Col. iii. 17.

τῷ θ. καὶ π.] So James i. 27 ; ὁ θ. καὶ π. ἡμῶν 1 Thess. i. 3 ; Gal. i. 4 ; Phil. iv. 20 ; comp. *c.* iv. 6 θ. καὶ π. πάντων ; ὁ θεὸς πατήρ Col. iii. 17 ; [ὁ] θ. ὁ πατήρ 2 Thess. ii. 16. Comp. ὁ κύριος καὶ πατήρ James iii. 9.

21. Each man feels his own place in the unity of the one body in Christ. In mutual subjection all realise the joy of fellowship. Such harmonious subjection of one to another is the social expression of the personal feeling of thankfulness.

ἐν φόβῳ Χρ.] 2 Cor. v. 11 τὸν φόβον τοῦ κυρίου ; Acts ix. 31.

The special family relationships (v. 22—vi. 9).

After describing the general temper of Christians, St Paul goes on to illustrate their mutual subjection by their fulfilment of the special family relations, (1) wives and husbands (22—33), (2) children and parents (vi. 1—4), (3) servants and masters (5—9). In each case he considers the weaker first ; and the fulfilment of duty by the weaker is met by the answering duty of the stronger : subjection by love ; obedience by tender education ; obedient and sincere service by corresponding service.

It is to be observed that he limits his instructions to the members of families. He says nothing of civic relations. The home, in its fullest sense, is a creation of the Gospel, the immediate application of the Incarnation to common life.

In each case the obligation is based

Χριστοῦ. ²²Αἱ γυναῖκες, τοῖς ἰδίοις ἀνδράσιν ⸆ ὡς τῷ κυρίῳ, ²³ὅτι ⸂ἀνήρ ἐστιν κεφαλὴ⸃ τῆς γυναικὸς ὡς καὶ ὁ

22 ὑποτασσέσθωσαν

22 + ὑποτασσέσθωσαν ℵAP₂ 17 vg me Cl-Al 308 Or; om. B codd ap Hier Cl-Al 592 ὑποτάσσεσθε K₂L₂ syrr item (ante τ. ἰδ. ἀνδρ.) D₂G₃. 'Hoc quod in Latinis exemplaribus additum est, *subditae sint*, in Graecis codicibus non habetur ; siquidem ad superiora refertur et subauditur *Subjecti invicem in timore Christi*, ut ἀπὸ κοινοῦ resonet *subjectae* et *mulieres viris suis sicut Domino*. Sed hoc magis in Graeco intelligitur quam in Latino.' Hier. ad loc.

23 ἀνὴρ κεφαλή ἐστιν

23 ἀνήρ] praem ὁ 47 Cl-Al rec.   Text BℵAD₂G₃K₂L₂P₂ 17 37

on the connexion of the believer with Christ (*v.* 22 ὡς τῷ κυρίῳ. vi. 1 ἐν κυρίῳ. vi. 5 ὡς τῷ χριστῷ). We are to see Christ in those to whom we owe subjection and reverence. Our duty does not depend on their personal character.

It may be added that there is more instruction on the duties of home in the Epistles to the Ephesians and the Colossians than in all the rest of the New Testament.

Wives and husbands (22—33).

The Apostle deals first with the relation which is the foundation of ordered human life. He points out that the wife is to the husband as the Church to Christ. In this we find the type of the wife's subjection (22—24), and of the husband's love (25—30). Marriage issues in a vital unity which points to the ideal consummation of humanity (31, 32).

²² *Wives, be in subjection to your own husbands, as unto the Lord.* ²³ *For a husband is head of the wife, as Christ also is head of the Church, being Himself Saviour of the body.* ²⁴ *But as the Church is subject to Christ, so let the wives be to their husbands in everything.* ²⁵ *Husbands, love your wives even as Christ also loved the Church and gave Himself up for it ;* ²⁶ *that He might sanctify it, having cleansed it by the bath of water accompanied by a confession of faith (a word),* ²⁷ *that He might*

present the Church to Himself a glorious Church, not having spot or wrinkle or any such thing ; but that it should be holy and without blemish. ²⁸ *Even so ought husbands also to love their own wives as being their own bodies. He that loveth his own wife loveth himself ;* ²⁹ *for no one ever hated his own flesh ; but nourisheth and cherisheth it, even as Christ the Church,* ³⁰ *because we are members of His body.* ³¹ *For this cause shall a man leave his father and mother, and shall cleave to his wife, and the twain shall become one flesh.* ³² *This revelation (mystery) is great ; but I speak looking to Christ and to the Church.* ³³ *However, do ye also severally each so love his own wife as himself ; and let the wife see that she fear her husband.*

22. αἱ γυναῖκες...] We must supply ὑποτάσσεσθε from the previous verse.

ἰδίοις ἀνδρ.] etiamsi alibi viderentur meliora habere consilia (Beng.). Comp. 1 Cor. vii. 2 ; xiv. 35 ; Tit. ii. 5 ; 1 Pet. iii. 1.

ὡς τῷ κυρίῳ] All natural authority comes from Him.

23. The relation of husband to wife, like that of Christ to the Church, points to a unity included in the idea of creation (*vv.* 31 f.).

ἀνήρ...κεφ. τ. γ.] *a husband is head of the wife.* Compare 1 Cor. xi. 3, where the relations are differently expressed.

The marriage relation of 'the Lord'

χριστὸς κεφαλὴ τῆς ἐκκλησίας, αὐτὸς σωτὴρ τοῦ σώματος. ²⁴ἀλλὰ ὡς ἡ ἐκκλησία ὑποτάσσεται τῷ χριστῷ,
οὕτως καὶ αἱ γυναῖκες τοῖς ἀνδράσιν ἐν παντί. ²⁵Οἱ
ἄνδρες, ἀγαπᾶτε τὰς γυναῖκας, καθὼς καὶ ὁ χριστὸς
ἠγάπησεν τὴν ἐκκλησίαν καὶ ἑαυτὸν παρέδωκεν ὑπὲρ
αὐτῆς, ²⁶ἵνα αὐτὴν ἁγιάσῃ καθαρίσας τῷ λουτρῷ τοῦ
ὕδατος ἐν ῥήματι, ²⁷ἵνα παραστήσῃ αὐτὸς ἑαυτῷ ἔνδοξον

23 αὐτὸς] praem καὶ אᶜD₂K₂L₂P₂ 17 37 47 syrr.   Text אD₂G₃ vg ba Cl-Al Or
27 αὐτὸς] אADG₃L₂P₂ 17 47 vg syr-hcl Or (ter); αὐτὴν DᶜK₂ 37ᶜ (ἑαυτην 37) syr-vg

to Israel runs through the O.T. The
application of this relation to Christ
and the Church—the spiritual Israel
—implies His Divinity.

The Church offers to Christ the
devotion of subjection, as the wife to
the husband. Christ offers to the
Church the devotion of love, as the
husband to the wife. Both are equal
in self-surrender.

αὐτὸς σ. τοῦ σ.] *being Himself* not
only head but *saviour of the body.*
This cannot be said of the husband
except in a far inferior sense.

24. ἀλλὰ ὡς...] *But,* though the
parallel is not complete, and the
husband does not hold towards the
wife the unapproachable preeminence
which Christ holds towards the Church
as its Saviour, still *as the Church is
subject to Christ, so let....*

ἐν παντί] The connexion is supposed
to fulfil the ideal.

25. As the duty of the wife is
subjection, so the duty of the husband
is love, answering to the love of Christ
crowned by His sacrifice of Himself.

ἠγάπησεν τὴν ἐκκλ.] Comp. Acts
xx. 28. So Christ spoke to the representatives of the Church on the eve of
the Passion : John xiii. 34 ; xv. 9, 12.
Christ loved the Church not because
it was perfectly lovable, but in order
to make it such.

For ἑ. παρέδωκεν see v. 2 ; Gal. ii. 20.
The word is used of the Father in
relation to the Son: Rom. viii. 32 ὑπὲρ
ἡμῶν πάντων παρέδωκεν αὐτόν.

26—7. The purpose of the self-
sacrifice of Christ for the Church is
described as threefold, (1) to hallow
it (ἵνα ἁγιάσῃ), (2) to present it to
Himself a glorious Church (ἵνα παραστήσῃ...ἔνδοξον), (3) that it may continue to be holy and without blemish
(ἵνα ᾖ ἁγ. καὶ ἄμ.). Under the imagery
which is chosen, the bride is first
prepared for her Husband (Apoc. xxi.
2, 9): she is then presented to Him :
and afterwards in fellowship with Him
she fulfils her work.

26. ἵνα...ἁγ. καθαρ....] The initiatory sacrament of Baptism is the hallowing of the bride. In this she is,
as by a bridal bath, at once cleansed
and hallowed. The actions are coincident (ἁγιάσῃ καθαρίσας comp. i. 8, 9).

τῷ λ. τοῦ ὕδ.] *by the bath of water.*
Comp. Tit. iii. 5 διὰ λουτροῦ παλιγγενεσίας, and 1 Cor. vi. 11 ἀλλὰ ἀπελούσασθε, ἀλλὰ ἡγιάσθητε, ἀλλὰ ἐδικαιώ-
θητε ἐν τῷ ὀνόματι τοῦ κυρίου ἡμῶν
Ἰησοῦ Χριστοῦ καὶ ἐν τῷ πνεύματι τοῦ
θεοῦ ἡμῶν. For τοῦ ὕδατος see Acts
x. 47.

ἐν ῥήματι] accompanied by a confession of the Christian Faith. For
ῥῆμα compare Rom. x. 9 ἐὰν ὁμολογήσῃς τὸ ῥῆμα ἐν τῷ στόματί σου ὅτι
κύριος Ἰησοῦς.... There can be little
doubt that this simple creed κύριος
Ἰησοῦς (comp. 1 Cor. xii. 3) was the
Baptismal Confession. This Confession is involved in the baptismal formula εἰς τὸ ὄνομα τοῦ πατρὸς καὶ τοῦ
υἱοῦ καὶ τοῦ ἁγίου πνεύματος (Matt.

τὴν ἐκκλησίαν, μὴ ἔχουσαν σπίλον ἢ ῥυτίδα ἤ τι τῶν
τοιούτων, ἀλλ᾽ ἵνα ᾖ ἁγία καὶ ἄμωμος. ²⁸ οὕτως ὀφείλουσιν [καὶ] οἱ ἄνδρες ἀγαπᾶν τὰς ἑαυτῶν γυναῖκας ὡς
τὰ ἑαυτῶν σώματα· ὁ ἀγαπῶν τὴν ἑαυτοῦ γυναῖκα
ἑαυτὸν ἀγαπᾷ, ²⁹ οὐδεὶς γάρ ποτε τὴν ἑαυτοῦ σάρκα
ἐμίσησεν, ἀλλὰ ἐκτρέφει καὶ θάλπει αὐτήν, καθὼς καὶ ὁ

xxviii. 19). The use of the formula implies the acceptance of it. Both τῷ λ. and ἐν ῥήματι are connected with καθαρίσας, the different relations of the effect to the material act and the spiritual accompaniment being indicated by the change from the instrumental dative to the preposition. The omission of the article is intelligible on the ground that St Paul wishes to insist on the fact of a personal response in the administration of the sacrament and not on the contents of it. For ἐν compare c. vi. 2 ἐν ἐπαγγελίᾳ.

The two phrases τῷ λουτρῷ (or διὰ λουτροῦ) and ἐν ῥήματι mark what was afterwards known technically as the 'matter' and 'form' of the sacrament.

Compare Aug. in Joh. lxxx. 3 (on John xv. 3): Quare non ait, Mundi estis propter Baptismum quo loti estis, sed ait *Propter verbum quod locutus sum vobis*, nisi quia et in aqua verbum mundat? Detrahe verbum et quid est aqua nisi aqua? Accedit verbum ad elementum et fit sacramentum, etiam ipsum tanquam visibile verbum.... Unde ista tanta virtus aquae ut corpus tangat et cor abluat, nisi faciente verbo, non quia dicitur sed quia creditur? Nam et in ipso verbo aliud est sonus transiens, aliud virtus manens.

27. ἵνα παρασ. αὐτὸς ἑ....] In this case it is the work of the Bridegroom to prepare and to present (αὐτὸς ἑαυτῷ) the bride. Her fitness and her beauty are alike due to His sacrifice of Himself.

παραστ....ἔνδ. τὴν ἐκκλ....] present the Church—the one Church—to Himself

in glorious majesty, without one trace of defilement or one mark of age.

παραστήσῃ] So 2 Cor. xi. 2 παρθένον ἁγνὴν παραστῆσαι τῷ χριστῷ. Comp. Rom. vi. 13 ; xii. 1 ; Col. i. 22, 28.

ἀλλ᾽ ἵνα ᾖ] *and not only without spot or wrinkle* for the marriage; *but that it should be* abidingly *holy and blameless.* For ἁγία καὶ αμωμος see c. i. 4 note.

28—30. The love of Christ for the Church is the pattern and measure of the husband's love for his wife. He loved the Church not because it was holy, but in order to make it holy by union with Himself. The husband's love must bear the same test, and overcome all failings in the wife. She is part of him, as Christians are of Christ, and claims the same tender affection which Christ bestows on the Church.

28. οὕτως...] *Even so ought husbands also....* For ὀφείλουσιν see Hebr. ii. 17 note.

τὰς ἑαυτ. γυν.] answering to τοῖς ἰδίοις ἀνδράσιν in v. 22. Notice the repetition : τὰς ἑαυτῶν γ., τὰ ἑαυτῶν σ., τὴν ἑαυτοῦ γ., τὴν ἑαυτοῦ σ.

ὡς τὰ ἑ. σώμ.] *as being their own bodies,* not 'as they love their own bodies.' As the Church is Christ's body, so in a true sense the wife is the husband's body. Through her he extends his life.

29. οὐδεὶς γάρ...] The conclusion which follows from the last verse is assumed but not expressed : The husband therefore must love his wife, *for no one ever....*

τὴν ἑαυτοῦ σ.] The words quoted in v. 31 are already in the Apostle's mind.

χριστὸς τὴν ἐκκλησίαν, ³⁰ὅτι μέλη ἐσμὲν τοῦ σώματος
αὐτοῦ. ³¹ἀντὶ τούτου καταλείψει ἄνθρωπος [τὸν]
πατέρα καὶ [τὴν] μητέρα καὶ προσκολληθήσεται
⌐πρὸς τὴν γυναῖκα⌐ αὐτοῦ, καὶ ἔσονται οἱ δύο εἰς
σάρκα μίαν. ³²τὸ μυστήριον τοῦτο μέγα ἐστίν, ἐγὼ δὲ
λέγω εἰς Χριστὸν καὶ [εἰς] τὴν ἐκκλησίαν. ³³πλὴν καὶ

30 τοῦ σώματος αὐτοῦ] + ἐκ τῆς σαρκὸς αὐτοῦ καὶ ἐκ τῶν ὀστέων αὐτοῦ אᶜD₂E₃G₃L₂P₂
al vg syrr Iren-gr lat Chrys Theod-Mops Victor Ambst al.   Text Bא A 17 67 me aeth
Meth Euthal cod : item (ut videtur) Or. Cant. (lat. Ruf.)

31 τῇ γυναικί

31 καὶ προσκολληθήσεται πρὸς τὴν γυναῖκα αὐτοῦ] om ? Marcion Tert (ut vid) Cyp
Hier.   Text BאAD₂G₃K₂L₂P₂ cuᵒᵐⁿ vvᵒᵐⁿ Or. Cels.   v. App.

ἐκτ. καὶ θ.] The words answer to
the elementary needs of food and
raiment. Ἐκτρέφειν occurs again in
c. vi. 4 ; and θάλπειν in 1 Thess. ii. 7.
ὁ χριστός] as in vv. 23, 25, 32.
30. ὅτι μέλη ἐσμέν...] The change
of form is most significant. St Paul
does not say simply, following the
language of the preceding sentence,
'because the Church is His body,'
but he appeals to the personal experience of Christians, 'because we
are members of His body and know
the power of His love.'
The words that follow in the common text are an unintelligent gloss,
in which an unsuccessful endeavour
is made to give greater distinctness
to the Apostle's statement. [v. inf.
p. 91, Addit. Note.]
31. ἀντὶ τούτου...] For this cause,
in consideration of this unique connexion of the husband and the wife,
a man shall leave.... The words are
to be understood literally as in Gen.
ii. 24. At the same time the union
of husband and wife points to that of
Christ and the Church and suggests
what Christ gave up for the accomplishment of His work.
ἔσονται...εἰς σ. μ.] Latt. erunt duo
in carne una.
32. τὸ μυστήριον τοῦτο...] This
revelation of the unity of man and
woman in one complex life is of great

moment. It opens before us a vision
of a higher form of existence, and
enables us to feel how parts which
at present are widely separated may
be combined into some nobler whole
without ceasing to be what they are.
But I speak looking to Christ and
to the Church. In this final union
we can see that humanity reaches its
consummation.
After writing the words τὸ μυστήριον
τοῦτο μέγα ἐστίν, St Paul seems to
pause for a while and contemplate
the manifold applications of the primitive ordinance (comp. 1 John iii. 1) ;
and then he marks the greatest of all.
ἐγὼ δέ...] Other thoughts may occur to reverent students of the Divine
word, but I—as indeed I have already
shewn—speak looking to....
λέγω εἰς...] Latt. in Christo (-um)
et in ecclesia (-am).
The exact form of expression εἰς
Χριστὸν καὶ εἰς τὴν ἐκκλησίαν [if notwithstanding B and the early patristic
evidence for omission of the εἰς we
accept the reading which retains it]
is significant. St Paul, speaking of
'Christ and the Church,' has regard
not to their connexion only, he thinks
also of each in its distinctness.
Χριστόν] It will be observed that
here, as in v. 21, St Paul uses the personal Name, not τὸν χριστόν.
It will be noticed that in this last

ὑμεῖς οἱ καθ᾽ ἕνα ἕκαστος τὴν ἑαυτοῦ γυναῖκα οὕτως
ἀγαπάτω ὡς ἑαυτόν, ἡ δὲ γυνὴ ἵνα φοβῆται τὸν ἄνδρα.

VI. ¹ Τὰ τέκνα, ὑπακούετε τοῖς γονεῦσιν ὑμῶν [ἐν
κυρίῳ], τοῦτο γάρ ἐστιν δίκαιον· ² τίμα τὸν πατέρα

1 ἐν κυρίῳ] om BDG₃ non hab Cl-Al 308 Tert (vel Marc ?) adv Marc Cypr. Ins.
אAD°K₂L₂P₂ vg syrr me Or

image of marriage the relation of
Christ to the Church is presented
somewhat differently from the view
given in c. i. 22 f. and c. iv. 15 f. In
the image of the body of which Christ
is the head the Church has, so to
speak, no completeness as a Church ;
but as the bride of Christ the Church
has her own perfect beauty. Yet this
is not apart from Christ : the Church
is still in a true sense His body, and
believers are members of it. The
complex thought is summed up in
earlier words of St Paul : Gal. iii. 28
εἶς ἐστὲ ἐν Χριστῷ Ἰησοῦ. There is
the personality of the body (εἶς) and
it is realised in fellowship with Christ.
Here, as it appears, we attain to the
final conception which we can reach
of life in the unseen order: τὸ μυστήριον τοῦτο μέγα ἐστίν.
Compare ' The Gospel of Creation,'
Epistles of St John, p. 309.
It is scarcely necessary to remark
that this passage does not in any way
support the opinion that marriage is
a sacrament, a conclusion which has
been drawn from the rendering in the
Vulgate Hoc sacramentum magnum
est. Μυστήριον is commonly rendered
by sacramentum in that version.

33. πλὴν καὶ ὑμεῖς...] However,
not to pursue this overwhelming subject, do ye also severally each in his
humble position, as Christ in His
majesty, love his own wife as himself.
For πλήν see 1 Cor. xi. 11 (πλὴν οὔτε
γυνὴ χωρὶς ἀνδρὸς οὔτε ἀνὴρ χωρὶς γυναικὸς ἐν κυρίῳ) ; Phil. iii. 16 ; iv. 14.
ὡς ἑαυτόν] as himself, not as his
body or as his own flesh : the personal
feeling is supreme (v. 28).

ἡ δὲ γ. ἵνα φοβ.] and let the wife see
that she fear....
In such fear there is nothing servile.

Children and parents (vi. 1—4).
vi. ¹ Children, obey your parents
in the Lord; for this is just. ² Honour thy father and mother—seeing
it is the first commandment with
promise—³ that it may be well with
thee and so thou shalt live long
upon the land. ⁴ And, ye fathers,
provoke not your children to wrath;
but nurture them in discipline and
admonition of the Lord.

1—4. The exposition of the relation of the wife to the husband is
followed naturally by an exposition
of the relation of children to parents.
Obedience (1—3) is met by loving
education (4).

1. τὰ τ. ὑπακ. τ. γ.] Obedience is
substituted for subjection (v. 22 f.)
here and in v. 5, parallel with Col. iii.
20, 22. For ὑπακούειν, ὑπακοή, compare Rom. vi. 16 f. ; Hebr. v. 8 f.
ἐν κυρίῳ] The child can recognise
his spiritual relation to Christ in
the earliest years, before doctrine is
grasped intellectually. There is from
the first a Divine element in all the
parts of human life, and St Paul
assumes the ideal as the standard.
[Origen, Cat. Cr. Eph. 208 observes
ἀμφίβολόν ἐστι τὸ ῥητόν· ἤτοι γὰρ τοῖς
ἐν κυρίῳ γονεῦσιν χρὴ ὑπακούειν τὰ
τέκνα ῆ ἐν κυρίῳ δεῖ ὑπακούειν τὰ τέκνα
τοῖς γονεῦσιν.]
δίκαιον] The obligation lies in the
nature of the relation. Compare
Acts iv. 19 ; Phil. i. 7 ; 2 Thess. i. 6 ;
2 Pet. i. 13.

ϲογ καὶ τὴν μητέρα, ἥτις ἐστὶν ἐντολὴ ⌐πρώτη ἐν
ἐπαγγελίᾳ, ³ἵνα⌐ εῢ ϲοι γένηται καὶ ἔϲη μακροχρό-
νιοϲ ἐπὶ τῆϲ γῆϲ. ⁴Καὶ οἱ πατέρες, μὴ παροργίζετε
τὰ τέκνα ὑμῶν, ἀλλὰ ἐκτρέφετε αὐτὰ ἐν παιδείᾳ καὶ

2, 3 πρώτη, ἐν ἐπαγγελίᾳ ἵνα

2. τίμα] Obedience must be founded on honour and find expression,
not only in act but in feeling. The
general command (ὑπακούετε) is sup-
plemented by the personal command
(τίμα) from the Decalogue (Ex. xx. 12).
[Cf. Deut. v. 16 τίμα τ. πατέρα σου κ. τ.
μητέρα σου, ὃν τρόπον ἐνετείλατό σοι
Κύριος ὁ θεός σου, ἵνα κ.τ.λ.] The commandment (ἐντολή) is quoted [but
without the promissory clause] in the
Gospels : Matt. xv. 4; xix. 19 and
parallels (Mk. vii. 10; Lk. xviii. 20).
For τιμᾶν see 1 Tim. v. 3 ; 1 Pet. ii.
17 (πάντας τιμήσατε, τ. βασιλέα τιμᾶτε).
ἥτις] c. iii. 13 ; seeing it is and
therefore claims regard. The interpretation of ἐντολὴ πρώτη ἐν ἐπαγγελίᾳ
is extremely uncertain. The words
may mean 'seeing it is a commandment of primary importance accompanied also by a promise' (comp. Matt.
xxii. 38 αὕτη ἐστὶν ἡ μεγ. καὶ πρώτη ἐντ.,
cf. Mk. xii. 28); or, as Chrysostom appears to take it, 'seeing it is a commandment preeminent in the promise
which is attached to it' (οὐ τῇ τάξει
εἶπεν αὐτὴν πρώτην ἀλλὰ τῇ ἐπαγγελίᾳ).
Others take it as 'the first commandment in the Law to which a promise
is attached,' or, since the words are
addressed to children, 'the first, earliest, commandment to be learnt....'
No explanation seems to be wholly
satisfactory. [The alternative punc-
tuation πρώτη, ἐν ἐπαγγελίᾳ ἵνα (Westcott and Hort marg.) leads to a
slightly modified form of the first of
the interpretations here recognised :
'a primary commandment, carrying
with it the promise—the offer and
the benediction—that it may be well
with thee and that thou shalt live
long upon the land.']

3. ἵνα...γένηται καὶ ἔσῃ...] A similar combination of moods with ἵνα in
the reversed order is found in Apoc.
xxii. 14, and ἵνα occurs elsewhere with
the future: 1 Cor. ix. 18; Gal. ii. 4.
The difference between the moods is
preserved: that it may be well...and
so thou shalt be....
ἐπὶ τῆς γῆς] upon the land. The
remainder of the quotation is assumed
to be known.

4. καὶ οἱ πατέρες...] The duty of
parents is connected closely with the
duty of children (so v. 9). There is
no καί in c. v. 25. 'Fathers' stand in
place of 'parents' (v. 1), because the
government and discipline of the
house rest with them.

μὴ παροργίζετε] Latt. nolite ad
iracundiam provocare. The verb
occurs Rom. x. 19 (a citation from
the LXX. Deut. xxxii. 21). In c. iv. 26
we have παροργισμός. In Col. iii. 21
the word used is ἐρεθίζετε. Even in
children there is a keen sense of
injustice and inconsiderateness.

ἐκτρέφετε] V. educate, V. L. nutrite
(enutrite): cf. c. v. 29. The ἐκ- is in-
tensive as in ἐκπειράζειν, ἐκπληροῦν,
ἐκτελεῖν &c.

ἐν παιδ. καὶ νουθεσίᾳ τ. κ.] Latt. in
disciplina et correptione domini, in
discipline and admonition not self-
chosen or self-invented but answering
to the mind of the Lord, administered through them. Bengel says truly
'harum altera occurrit ruditati, altera
oblivioni et levitati.' Παιδεία is discipline generally (2 Tim. iii. 16 πρὸς
παιδείαν τὴν ἐν δικαιοσύνῃ; Hebr. xii.
5 ff.); νουθεσία special admonition (1
Cor. x. 11 ἐγράφη δὲ πρὸς νουθεσίαν
ἡμῶν; Tit. iii. 10 μετὰ μίαν καὶ δευτέραν
νουθεσίαν).

ΝΟΥΘΕCΙΑ ΚΥΡΙΟΥ.   ⁵ Οἱ δοῦλοι, ὑπακούετε τοῖς κατὰ
σάρκα κυρίοις μετὰ φόβου καὶ τρόμου ἐν ἁπλότητι τῆς
καρδίας ὑμῶν ὡς τῷ χριστῷ, ⁶μὴ κατ᾽ ὀφθαλμοδουλίαν
ὡς ἀνθρωπάρεσκοι ἀλλ᾽ ὡς δοῦλοι Χριστοῦ ποιοῦντες τὸ
θέλημα τοῦ θεοῦ, ἐκ ψυχῆς ⁷μετ᾽ εὐνοίας δουλεύοντες, ὡς

Servants (slaves) and masters (5—9).

⁵ *Servants (slaves), be obedient to them that according to the flesh are your masters, with fear and trembling, in singleness of heart as unto Christ;* ⁶ *not in the way of eye-service, as men-pleasers; but as servants of Christ, doing the will of GOD;* ⁷ *doing service from the heart with good-will, as to the Lord and not to men;* ⁸ *knowing that whatsoever good thing each one doeth, this shall he receive again from the Lord, whether he be bond or free.* ⁹ *And, ye masters, do the same things in dealing with them, and forbear threatening; knowing that both their Master and yours is in heaven, and there is no respect of persons with Him.*

5—9. The third typical relation in the household was that of servants (slaves) and masters. The servant must remember that he renders his service to Christ (5—7), and that he will receive his reward from Him (8). The master must remember that in heaven the servant's Master is his own also (9).

The position of slaves (δοῦλοι) is touched on in 1 Tim. vi. 1 f.; Tit. ii. 9 f.; and 1 Pet. ii. 18 (οἰκέται).

In the Pastoral Epistles and 1 Peter the master of the slave is δεσπότης.

5. τοῖς κ. σ. κ.] Earthly relations are not neutralised by heavenly (Rom. xiii. 7). At the same time κατὰ σάρκα suggests the limit of the authority of earthly masters.

On this Primasius remarks: Non venit Christus mutare conditiones sed mores.

μετὰ φ. καὶ τρ.] *with fear* lest any duty should be left undone *and*

trembling: the feeling and the sign of it. The phrase recurs in 2 Cor. vii. 15 ; Phil. ii. 12; comp. 1 Cor. ii. 3; and is not uncommon in the LXX.: Gen. ix. 2; Is. xix. 16; Ps. ii. 11.

Such feelings have a right place in the relations of men to men.

ἐν ἁπλ. τ. κ. ὑ.] *in singleness of heart*, without hypocrisy or one secondary or selfish thought. For ἁπλότης see Col. iii. 22; 2 Cor. i. 12. The obedience is to be rendered *as unto Christ*, 'Who knoweth the hearts of all men.'

ὡς τῷ χρ.] v. 7 δουλεύοντες ὡς τῷ κυρίῳ. Comp. Col. iii. 24.

6. μὴ κατ᾽ ὀφθ. ὡς ἀνθρ.] Latt. non ad oculum servientes....

κατ᾽ ὀφθ.] Col. iii. 22 ἐν ὀφθαλμοδουλίαις. The word is not quoted from any earlier writer.

ἀνθρωπάρεσκοι] Col. iii. 22. The word is found in Ps. lii. (liii.) 6 (LXX.); Ps. Sol. iv. 8, 10, 21.

ὡς δοῦλοι Χρ.] Comp. 1 Cor. vii. 22; 1 Pet. ii. 16 ὡς δοῦλοι θεοῦ. The phrase in a spiritual sense is the chosen title of apostles : Rom. i. 1 ; James i. 1 ; 2 Pet. ii. 1 ; Jude 1 ; Apoc. i. 1.

ποι. τὸ θ. τ. θ.] Mk. iii. 35 ; John vii. 17 ; ix. 13 ; Hebr. x. 36; xiii. 21 ; 1 John ii. 17. Comp. Matt. vii. 21 ; xii. 50; xxi. 31 ; Lk. xii. 47; John iv. 34. The absolute use of the phrase in these passages suggests that it is so used here, and that ἐκ ψυχῆς is to be joined with the words which follow. True service bears two marks. It is rendered under a sense of a personal relation to Christ, and with a recognition of the Divine law written in the heart.

7. (ἐκ ψυχῆς) μετ᾽ εὐ. δουλ.] The

τῷ κυρίῳ καὶ οὐκ ἀνθρώποις, ⁸ εἰδότες ὅτι ἕκαστος, ἐάν
τι ποιήσῃ ἀγαθόν, τοῦτο κομίσεται παρὰ κυρίου, εἴτε
δοῦλος εἴτε ἐλεύθερος. ⁹ Καὶ οἱ κύριοι, τὰ αὐτὰ ποιεῖτε
πρὸς αὐτούς, ἀνιέντες τὴν ἀπειλήν, εἰδότες ὅτι καὶ αὐτῶν
καὶ ὑμῶν ὁ κύριός ἐστιν ἐν οὐρανοῖς, καὶ προσωπολημψία οὐκ ἔστιν παρ' αὐτῷ.

9 καὶ αὐτῶν καὶ ὑμῶν] B (אֵ ἑαυτῶν) ADP₂ 17 37 vg Cl-Al ; καὶ ὑμῶν καὶ αὐτῶν (אᶜ
ἑαυτῶν) L₂ m syr-hcl Petr-Al Cypr ; καὶ αὐτῶν ὑμῶν Dᶜ₂G₃ ; καὶ ὑμῶν αὐτῶν K₂ syr-vg rec

connexion of ἐκ ψ. with this verse is
supported by the parallel in Col. iii.
23 ; and the two phrases ἐκ ψ. and
μετ' εὐν. combine to characterise the
service completely, in relation to the
servant (ἐκ ψ.) and to the master
(μετ' εὐνοίας, V. cum bona voluntate,
V.L. cum benignitate). For ἐκ ψ. see
Col. iii. 23 ὃ ἐὰν ποιῆτε, ἐκ ψυχῆς ἐργάζεσθε, ὡς τῷ κυρίῳ καὶ οὐκ ἀνθρώποις ;
1 Macc. viii. 25, 27 ; Mk. xii. 30 (not 33).
Εὔνοια occurs here only in N.T. Kindly
feeling must underlie loyal service.

ὡς τῷ κυρίῳ] The change of the
title here (ὁ χρ. v. 23, 24, 25, 29 ;
v. 5 ; Χρ. v. 32 ; v. 6) is natural. Stress
is laid on the thought of sovereignty.

8. εἰδότες...] The Divine judgment
lies essentially in each deed of man.
The good which we do remains ours
still ; and the evil (Col. iii. 25) also.
The doer in each case will receive
what he has done. Cf. 2 Cor. v. 10
ἵνα κομίσηται ἕκαστος τὰ διὰ τοῦ σώματος πρὸς ἃ ἔπραξεν, εἴτε ἀγαθὸν εἴτε
φαῦλον ; Col. iii. 25 ; 2 Pet. ii. 12 f.
Comp. Job xxxiv. 11 ἀλλὰ ἀποδιδοῖ
ἀνθρώπῳ καθὰ ποιεῖ ἕκαστος αὐτῶν.
This thought gives final expression
to the truth of proportionate retribu-
tion : Matt. xvi. 27 καὶ τότε ἀποδώσει
ἑκάστῳ κατὰ τὴν πρᾶξιν αὐτοῦ, Rom. ii.
6 ὃς ἀποδώσει ἑκάστῳ κατὰ τὰ ἔργα
αὐτοῦ (Ps. lxii. 12 ; Prov. xxiv. 12), 1
Pet. i. 17 τὸν ἀπροσωπολήμπτως κρίνοντα
κατὰ τὸ ἑκάστου ἔργον, Apoc. xxii. 12
ἀποδοῦναι ἑκάστῳ ὡς τὸ ἔργον ἐστὶν
αὐτοῦ (cf. Ps. xxviii. 4 ; Jer. xvii. 10).

κομίσεται] receive again as his own.
See Hort on 1 Pet. i. 9.

9. καὶ οἱ κ....] And ye masters do
the same things—fulfil your obligations with the same sincerity—in
dealing with them : recognise their
equality with you as men in virtue of
their nature and in regard to one
sovereign Lord. Τὰ αὐτὰ ποιεῖν expresses identity of spirit and not
identity of outward action.

ποιεῖτε πρὸς αὐ.] in regard to, in
dealing with them. The construction
appears to be unique in the N. T.
Comp. 1 Thess. iv. 10 ποιεῖτε αὐτὸ εἰς
πάντας τοὺς ἀδελφούς....

ἀνιέντες τ. ἀ.] Latt. remittentes
minas (laxantes iracundiam): forbearing to use the habitual threatening.
This clause applies τὰ αὐτὰ ποιεῖτε.
Earthly law allows you to exercise
practically irresponsible power : to
enforce your will by fear of punishment. For ἀνιέντες cf. Thuc. iii. 10, 2.

εἰδότες] answering to εἰδότες in v. 8.
An appeal is made to conscience to
witness to two truths: 'there shall
never be one lost good'; no wrong
is condoned.

αὐτῶν καὶ ὑ. ὁ κ.] their Lord and
yours.... Comp. Rom. xvi. 13 τὴν
μητέρα αὐτοῦ καὶ ἐμοῦ.

προσωπολημψία] Comp. Rom. ii. 11
οὐ γάρ ἐστιν προσωπολημψία παρὰ τῷ
θεῷ ; Col. iii. 25 ὁ γὰρ ἀδικῶν κομίσεται
ὃ ἠδίκησεν, καὶ οὐκ ἔστιν προσωπολημψία ; James ii. 1 μὴ ἐν προσωπολημ-
ψίαις ἔχετε τὴν πίστιν τ. κ. ἡμῶν Ἰ.
Χ. τ. δόξης. Προσωπολημπτεῖν occurs
James ii. 9 ; προσωπολήμπτης Acts x.
34 (cf. Deut. x. 17); and ἀπροσωπολήμπτως 1 Pet. i. 17.

Additional Notes on v. 14, v. 30, and v. 31.

v. 14 ἐπιφαύσει σοι ὁ χριστός] ἐπιψαύσεις τοῦ χριστοῦ Western (Gr. Lat.); incl. MSS mentioned by Theod.mops.lat by Chr and by Thdt (the two latter probably not independently) Orig. *Jos.* lat. Ruf; *Cant.* lat. Ruf; not G₃ Marcion (ap. Epiph) Naasseni (ap. Hipp) Clem Orig. *loc.*; *Ps²* Hipp. *Ant* Amb Hier 'Vig'. The supposed intermediate reading ἐπιψαύσει σοι ὁ χριστός appears to be due to the transcribers of Chr, though Aug once, at least as edited, and Ambst. cod have *continget te Christus*. The two imperatives doubtless suggested that the following future would be in the second person, the required c stood next after ἐπιφαύσει, easily read as ἐπιψαύσει, and then the rest would be altered accordingly.

v. 30 τοῦ σώματος αὐτοῦ]+ἐκ τῆς σαρκὸς αὐτοῦ καὶ ἐκ τῶν ὀστέων αὐτοῦ Western and Syrian (Gr. Lat. Syr. Arm.); incl. Iren. gr. lat. Text א* AB 17 67** me aeth Meth (anon. [?Tit. bost] *Lc.* 88 Cramer) Euthal. cod: also probably Orig. *Cant.* lat. Ruf, who quotes nothing after σώματος αὐτοῦ. From Gen. ii. 23.

v. 31 καὶ προσκολληθήσεται πρὸς τὴν γυναῖκα αὐτοῦ] < (Marcion, see below) Orig. *loc.* expressly (the scholium, though anonymous, is certainly his) Tert (apparently, as well as Marcion) Cyp. *Ep.* 52. codd. opt Hier. *loc* (doubtless from Orig). Text אABD₂G₃K₂L₂P₂ cuᵒᵐⁿ vvᵒᵐⁿ Orig. *Cels*; (?*Mt.* gr. lat) Meth Victorin ppˡᵃᵗ· ˢᵉʳ. A singular reading, which would not be improbable if its attestation were not exclusively patristic: the words might well be inserted from Gen. ii. 24. They are absent from the quotation as it occurs in the true text of Mc. x. 7; but were there inserted so early and so widely that the only surviving authorities for omission are אB lt 48 go.

¹⁰ Τοῦ λοιποῦ ⌈ἐνδυναμοῦσθε⌉ ἐν κυρίῳ καὶ ἐν τῷ κράτει
τῆς ἰσχύος αὐτοῦ. ¹¹ἐνδύσασθε τὴν πανοπλίαν τοῦ θεοῦ

10 δυναμοῦσθε

10 τοῦ λοιποῦ] (v. τὸ λοιπον)+ἀδελφοι Α𝕏ᶜG₃ 37 47 vg syrr.   Text Β𝕏 17 (D₂)
Luc Cal   δυναμοῦσθε] Β 17 Or (?) Cat-Gr

III. THE CHRISTIAN WARFARE (vi.
10—20).

The general survey of the conditions of social life which St Paul
has now completed leads him to consider the whole range of the Christian
conflict. This deals with the unseen
as well as with the seen. In order to
understand its character we must
take account of spiritual hosts of
wickedness by which we are assailed
and of the heavenly forces which are
within our reach. He first shews our
actual position (10—12); and then
describes in detail the Divine equipment of the Christian soldier (13—17)
passing to the duties of intercession
(18—20).

10—12. The Christian position.
Claim all the help which GOD offers
you. Your enemies are not men only
but the whole hierarchy of evil. We
must face the stern, tragic view of
life.
¹⁰ *In the future, be made powerful
in the Lord, and in the might of His
strength.* ¹¹ *Put on the whole armour
of GOD, that ye may be able to stand
against the wiles of the devil.* ¹² *Because our wrestling is not against
blood and flesh, but against the principalities, against the powers, against
the world-rulers of this darkness,
against the spiritual forces of wickedness in the heavenly order.*

10. τοῦ λοιποῦ] Latt. *de cetero.*
This phrase occurs again Gal. vi. 17,
in the future. We should expect τὸ
λοιπόν (which is less well supported)
for the future (2 Thess. iii. 1; 1 Cor.
vii. 29; Phil. iv. 8; Hebr. x. 13).
Perhaps both here and in Galatians
the thought is turned to special crises
of trial.

ἐνδυναμοῦσθε...] Latt. *confortamini
(confirmamini): be made powerful
for your work in the Lord and,
through fellowship with Him, in the
might of His strength.* Ἐνδυναμοῦσθε is certainly passive (Acts ix.
22; Rom. iv. 20; Hebr. xi. 34. Comp.
Col. i. 11; Lk. i. 80; ii. 40. The
active occurs Phil. iv. 13; 1 Tim. i. 12;
2 Tim. iv. 17), and has respect to the
work to be done. Ἰσχύς expresses
strength positively: κράτος *might* as
abundantly effective for the end contemplated. Τὸ κρ. τῆς ἰσχ. occurs
again *c.* i. 19 note. Ἐν τῷ κράτει
answers to ἐν κυρίῳ: by fellowship
with Him we share in all that is His.

11. ἐνδύσασθε τὴν παν....] Armour
represents the aspect of Divine help
in reference to the Christian warfare.
The image occurs in each group of
St Paul's Epistles: 1 Thess. v. 8; 2
Cor. vi. 7; x. 4; Rom. vi. 13; xiii. 12.
Comp. Wisd. v. 17 ff. λήψεται πανοπλίαν τὸν ζῆλον αὐτοῦ κ.τ.λ.; Is. lix.
16 f.

τὴν παν. τ. θ.] V. *arma (omnia
arma)*, V.L. *armaturam: the full,
complete, armour of God,* that is,
which GOD supplies (*v.* 13; comp. Lk.
xi. 22). Ἡ πανοπλία was properly the
equipment of the heavy-armed soldier.
Polyb. vi. 23, 2 ff. Ἔστι δ᾽ ἡ Ῥω-
μαϊκὴ πανοπλία πρῶτον μὲν θυρεός....
ἅμα δὲ τῷ θυρεῷ μάχαιρα·...πρὸς δὲ
τούτοις ὑσσοὶ δύο, καὶ προσκεφαλαία
χαλκῆ, καὶ προκνημίς...Οἱ μὲν οὖν πολ-
λοὶ προσλαβόντες χάλκωμα σπιθαμιαῖον
πάντη πάντως, ὃ προστίθενται μὲν πρὸ
τῶν στέρνων, καλοῦσι δὲ καρδιοφύλακα,
τελείαν ἔχουσι τὴν καθόπλισιν· οἱ δὲ
ὑπὲρ τὰς μυρίας τιμώμενοι δραχμὰς ἀντὶ
τοῦ καρδιοφύλακος σὺν τοῖς ἄλλοις ἀλυ-
σιδωτοὺς περιτίθενται θώρακας.

πρὸς τὸ δύνασθαι ὑμᾶς στῆναι πρὸς τὰς μεθοδίας τοῦ
διαβόλου· ¹²ὅτι οὐκ ἔστιν ⌜ἡμῖν⌝ ἡ πάλη πρὸς αἷμα καὶ
σάρκα, ἀλλὰ πρὸς τὰς ἀρχάς, πρὸς τὰς ἐξουσίας, πρὸς

12 ὑμῖν

12 ὑμῖν] BDG₃ m syr-vg go aeth Luc-Cal

πρὸς τὸ δύν....] that ye may be—
with a view to your being—able to
stand.... The conflict is regarded
from afar. Contrast v. 13 ἵνα δυνηθῆτε
which expresses the immediate object.
στῆναι πρὸς...] to stand—hold your
position—against, in face of. Comp.
John vi. 52 ; Hebr. xii. 4 οὔπω μέχρις
αἵματος ἀντικατέστητε πρὸς τὴν ἁμαρτίαν ἀνταγωνιζόμενοι.
τὰς μεθ. τ. δ.] Latt. adversus
insidias (machinationes, nequitias,
versutias): the wiles of the devil,
the supreme leader of the powers of
evil (c. iv. 27 note).
Μεθοδεία (c. iv. 14) is not found in
class. writers or in the LXX. though
μεθοδεύω occurs. Ἀs μεθοδεία describes
the general system, μεθοδεῖαι are the
many forms in which it is embodied.
Compare Polycarp, ad Phil. 7 (ed.
Lightfoot, p. 918) καὶ ὃς ἂν μὴ ὁμολογῇ
τὸ μαρτύριον τοῦ σταυροῦ, ἐκ τοῦ διαβόλου ἐστίν· καὶ ὃς ἂν μεθοδεύῃ τὰ λόγια
τοῦ Κυρίου πρὸς τὰς ἰδίας ἐπιθυμίας καὶ
λέγει [?λέγῃ] μήτε ἀνάστασιν εἶναι μήτε
κρίσιν, οὗτος πρωτότοκός ἐστι τοῦ Σατανᾶ,
and Lightfoot's note (ad loc.) on μεθοδεύῃ ; for which he cites Polybius
xxxviii. 4, 10 πολλὰ πρὸς ταύτην τὴν
ὑπόθεσιν ἐμπορεύων καὶ μεθοδευόμενος
and Philo Vit. Moys. iii. 27 ὅπερ
μεθοδεύουσιν οἱ λογοθῆραι καὶ σοφισταί.
[The verb occurs in the LXX. of 2 Sam.
xix. 27 μεθώδευσεν ἐν τῷ δούλῳ σου,
but not in the N.T. Commenting on
μεθοδεία here Chrysostom says μεθο-
δεῦσαί ἐστι τὸ ἀπατῆσαι καὶ διὰ συντό-
μου ἑλεῖν. For μέθοδος in this sense
cf. Plutarch, Moral. 176A ἐθαύμαζε
τὴν μέθοδον τοῦ ἀνθρώπου (quoted by
Lightfoot l. c.) and 2 Macc. xiii. 18
κατεπείρασε διὰ μεθόδων τοὺς τόπους.]
12. ὅτι οὐκ ἔστιν ἡ π....] Latt.

quia non est nobis colluctatio (lucta,
pugna). Because our wrestling....
The order throws emphasis on ἡμῖν.
All life is a struggle, but our struggle
is....
The metaphor (πάλη here only in
N. T.) is changed in order to bring
out the personal individual conflict.
Comp. 2 Tim. ii. 4 f.
αἷμα καὶ σ.] blood and flesh. This
unusual order is found also in Hebr.
ii. 14. Perhaps αἷμα is placed first as
representing the vital principle in
man.
ἀλλὰ πρὸς τὰς ἀρχάς...] but against
the principalities.... All is definite
and organised in the array of our
spiritual enemies. Each is to be
dealt with severally : πρός...πρός...
πρός...πρός. Compare John xvi. 8
περί...περί...περί. The three classes
distinguished all belong to 'this darkness.'
The forces with which we have to
contend are not ultimately human.
Our earthly adversaries are stirred by
powers of another order (John xiii. 2 ;
Acts v. 3). Comp. August. de verbo
Dom. 8 Vasa sunt, alius utitur :
organa sunt, alius tangit (Meyer).
τοὺς κοσμοκρ.] Latt. mundi rectores : the world-rulers. The title
stands in significant contrast with
παντοκράτωρ (2 Cor. vi. 18 ; Apoc. i. 8,
iv. 8, xi. 17, xv. 3, xvi. 7, 14, xix. 6, 15,
xxi. 22). Compare John xii. 31 ὁ ἄρχων τοῦ κόσμου τούτου ; xiv. 30 ὁ τοῦ
κόσμου ἄρχων ; 2 Cor. iv. 4 ὁ θεὸς τοῦ
αἰῶνος τούτου. The Tempter speaks of
his power over the world as 'delivered
unto him' (Lk. iv. 6 ἐμοὶ παραδέδοται).
The word κοσμοκράτωρ was transliterated and used by Rabbinical writers
for 'ruler of world-wide power.'

τοὺς κοσμοκράτορας τοῦ σκότους τούτου, πρὸς τὰ πνευ-

12 τοῦ σκότους] + τοῦ αἰῶνος אᶜD₂K₂L₂P₂ Or semel (codd) Did Chrys Theod-Mops-
lat ; om. BאAD₂G₃ 17 67ᶜ 80 m vg syr-vg me Cl-Al (bis) Or (bis v. ter) Tert Cypr Vict

See also Iren. i. 1. 10 Ἐκ δὲ τῆς
λύπης τὰ πνευματικὰ τῆς πονηρίας διδά-
σκουσι (sc. οἱ Οὐαλεντίνου μαθηταὶ) γε-
γονέναι· ὅθεν τὸν διάβολον τὴν γένεσιν
ἐσχηκέναι, ὃν καὶ κοσμοκράτορα καλοῦσι,
καὶ τὰ δαιμόνια, καὶ τοὺς ἀγγέλους, καὶ
πᾶσαν τὴν πνευματικὴν τῆς πονηρίας
ὑπόστασιν.
Test. xii. Patr. Sym. (περὶ φθόνου)
§ δ. Καὶ ὑμᾶς οὖν, τέκνα μου ἀγαπητά,
ἀγαπήσατε ἕκαστος τὸν ἀδελφὸν αὐτοῦ
ἐν ἀγαθῇ καρδίᾳ καὶ ἀποστήσατε ἀφ'
ὑμῶν τὸ πνεῦμα τοῦ φθόνου, ὅτι ἀγριοῖ
τοῦτο τὴν ψυχὴν καὶ φθείρει τὸ σῶμα,
ὀργὴν καὶ πόλεμον παρέχει τὸ διαβούλιον
(v. l. τῷ διαβουλίῳ) καὶ εἰς αἵματα παρο-
ξύνει καὶ εἰς ἔκστασιν ἄγει τὴν διάνοιαν
καὶ οὐκ ἐᾷ τὴν σύνεσιν ἀνθρώποις ἐνερ-
γεῖν· ἀλλὰ καὶ τὸν ὕπνον ἀφαιρεῖ καὶ
κλόνον παρέχει τῇ ψυχῇ καὶ τρόμον τῷ
σώματι· ὅτι καίγε ἐν ὕπνῳ τις ζῆλος
κακίας αὐτὸν φαντάζουσα κατεσθίει καὶ
ἐν πνεύματι πονηροῖς διαταράσσει τὴν
ψυχὴν αὐτοῦ καὶ ἐκθροεῖσθαι τὸ σῶμα
ποιεῖ καὶ ἐν ταραχῇ διυπνίζεσθαι τὸν νοῦν
καὶ ὡς πνεῦμα πονηρὸν καὶ ἰοβόλον ἔχων
οὕτως φαίνεται τοῖς ἀνθρώποις.
[Harvey (on Irenaeus l. c.) quotes
also Didascalia Orientalis (ad calc.
Clem. Al. Hypotypos.) § 48. Καὶ ποιεῖ
ἐκ τῶν ὑλικῶν τὸ μὲν ἐκ λύπης οὐσιῶδες,
κτίζων πνευματικὰ τῆς πονηρίας πρὸς ἃ
ἡ πάλη ἡμῖν.]
τοῦ σκότους τούτου] Comp. c. v. 11 ;
Lk. xxii. 53 ; 1 Cor. iv. 5 ; Rom. ii. 19;
xiii. 12 ; Col. i. 13 ; 1 John i. 6 ; and
σκοτία John i. 5 ; viii. 12 ; xii. 46 ;
1 John ii. 8 f. ; 11.
The phrase τὸ σκότος τοῦτο is
moulded on ὁ αἰὼν οὗτος, ὁ κόσμος οὗτος.
πρὸς τὰ πν. τ. π. ἐν τ. ἐπ.] against the
spiritual forces of wickedness in the
heavenly order. This clause sums up
in an abstract form all the powers of
evil which work in the unseen order.
Man's conflict, in man's life, is partly
on earth and partly in 'the heavenly
realm.' He is met by spiritual enemies

in both. We are not to conceive of
this heavenly realm as properly local,
though we are constrained so to represent it. The term describes rather
a mode of existence than a place.
Comp. i. 3 note.
There appears to be no force in the
combination of ἐν τ. ἐπ. with τὰ πν. τ.
πον. as if the heavenly realm were
their dwelling-place (comp. c. ii. 6).
It will be noticed that 'the world'
itself is not spoken of as our antagon-
ist, but the evil powers which have
usurped the rule over it. We must
'overcome' the world (1 John v. 5)
even as Christ 'overcame' it (John
xvi. 33) by suffering. Compare Ruskin,
Modern Painters, v. p. 385 (small
edition).
'I do not know what my England
desires, or how long she will choose
to do as she is doing now ; with her
right hand casting away the souls of
men and with her left the gifts of
God. In the prayers which she dic-
tates to her children, she tells them
to fight against the world, the flesh,
and the devil. Some day, perhaps, it
may also occur to her as desirable to
tell those children what she means by
this. What is the world which they
are to "fight with," and how does it
differ from the world which they are
to "get on in"? The explanation
seems to me the more needful, because
I do not, in the book we profess to
live by, find anything very distinct
about fighting with the world. I find
something about fighting with the
rulers of its darkness, and something
also about overcoming it ; but it does
not follow that this conquest is to be
by hostility, since evil may be overcome
with good. But I find it written very
distinctly that God loved the world,
and that Christ is the light of it.'
When does 'the world, the flesh,
and the devil' first appear ?

ματικὰ τῆς πονηρίας ἐν τοῖς ἐπουρανίοις.   ¹³διὰ τοῦτο
ἀναλάβετε τὴν πανοπλίαν τοῦ θεοῦ, ἵνα δυνηθῆτε ἀντιστῆναι ἐν τῇ ἡμέρᾳ τῇ πονηρᾷ καὶ ἅπαντα κατεργασά-
μενοι στῆναι.   ¹⁴στῆτε οὖν περιζωϲάμενοι τὴν ὀϲφὺν
ὑμῶν ἐν ἀληθείᾳ, καὶ ἐνδυϲάμενοι τὸν θώρακα τῆϲ

The Christian armour (13—17).

¹³ For this reason take up the whole armour of GOD, that ye may be able to withstand in the evil day and, having accomplished all, to stand.   ¹⁴ Stand therefore having girded your loins with truth, and having put on the breastplate of righteousness, ¹⁵ and having shod your feet in the preparedness of the gospel of peace, ¹⁶ in all taking up the shield of faith, in which ye shall be able to quench all the darts of the evil one that are set on fire. ¹⁷ And receive the helmet of salvation, and the sword of the Spirit, which is the word of GOD.

13. διὰ τοῦτο] For this reason, that our conflict is essentially spiritual. There is a perceptible difference in tone between διὰ τοῦτο and διό : the former appears to point to a specific, the latter to a general reason. See also iii. 1 τούτου χάριν.

ἀναλάβετε τ. π.] v. 16 (Acts vii. 43), opposed to καταθέσθαι. The armour is laid at the feet of the warrior.

ἵνα δυν.] the conflict is imminent : the adversaries are on the field (ἀντι-στῆναι). Ἀντιστῆναι is not used absolutely elsewhere in the N. T.

ἐν τ. ἡ. τ. π.] the day preeminently evil in evil days (c. v. 16): in the most violent outbreak of the powers of evil. Comp. Lk. iv. 13 ; John xiv. 20.

ἅπαντα κατεργ. στ.] V. in omnibus perfecti stare : having accomplished all, to stand, having accomplished all that belongs to your duty and to your position, still to hold your ground. Κατεργάζεσθαι implies the accomplishment of something grave and difficult : Phil. ii. 12 ; Rom. vii. 15, 17, 20

(κατεργάζεσθαι, πράσσειν, ποιεῖν). The Christian has not only to repel assaults but also to achieve great results. The rendering 'having overcome' is un-Pauline.

For στῆναι see Apoc. vi. 17 καὶ τίς δύναται σταθῆναι; (Lk. xxi. 36).

14—16. στῆτε οὖν...] stand therefore.... In this confidence take up the position which you will be enabled to maintain to the end, having duly equipped yourselves (περιζωσάμενοι, ἐνδυσάμενοι, ὑποδησάμενοι, ἀναλαβόν-τες).

περιζωσάμενοι ... ἀναλαβόντες] As the first preparation for the conflict the combatant braces up himself. The value of his arms must depend on his own vigour. Truth, perfect sincerity, perfect reality, is the stay of the Christian character. Hypocrisy or falsehood paralyses one who is strong as a believer. Before all things the Christian warrior is true. Such a man applies truth to life. In his dealings with others he aims at intellectual and moral rectitude. He puts on the breastplate of righteousness, which guards the heart.

Yet further (v. 15) he secures his foothold and power of vigorous advance, having shod his feet with the preparedness of the gospel of peace. And, as affecting all he has to do, he takes up the shield of faith, to be a protection against spiritual assaults.

14. περιζωσάμενοι] Comp. Lk. xii. 35, 37 ; xvii. 8 ; 1 Pet. i. 13 (ἀναζωσ.).

Isaiah (xi. 5 καὶ ἔσται δικαιοσύνη ἐζωσμένος τὴν ὀσφὺν αὐτοῦ καὶ ἀληθείᾳ εἰλημένος τὰς πλευράς) indicates the close connexion between righteousness and truth.

τὸν θώρ. τῆς δικ.] the breastplate of

Δικαιοcγνнс, ¹⁵καὶ ὑποδησάμενοι τοΥc πόδαc ἐν ἑτοιμασίᾳ τοῦ εὐαγγελίοΥ τῆc εἰρήνнc, ¹⁶ἐν πᾶσιν ἀναλαβόντες τὸν θυρεὸν τῆς πίστεως, ἐν ᾧ δυνήσεσθε πάντα
τὰ βέλη τοῦ πονηροῦ [τὰ] πεπυρωμένα σβέσαι· ¹⁷καὶ

righteousness, truth applied to our relations with others (Acts x. 35), illuminated, purified, strengthened by the grace of Christ. Comp. Is. lix. 17 ἐνεδύσατο δικαιοσύνην ὡς θώρακα ; Wisd. v. 19 ἐνδύσεται θώρακα δικαιοσύνην. In 1 Thess. v. 8 St Paul speaks of 'faith and love' as the Christian breastplate. The two statements are completely harmonious. By faith we are able to realise the Divine will and the Divine power and by love to embody faith in our dealings with men : this is righteousness. The gen. τῆς δικαιοσύνης describes that which constitutes the breastplate, just as in *v.* 17 (τὴν περικεφ. τοῦ σωτηρίου) salvation is the helmet. Comp. ii. 14 τὸ μεσότοιχον τοῦ φραγμοῦ ; iv. 3 ἐν τῷ συνδέσμῳ τῆς εἰρήνης ; Rom. iv. 11 σημεῖον—περιτομῆς ; Col. iii. 24 τὴν ἀνταπόδοσιν τῆς κληρονομίας.

15. ὑποδησάμενοι τ. π....] *having shod your feet in*.... Comp. Acts xii. 8 ζῶσαι καὶ ὑπόδησαι τὰ σανδάλιά σου.

ἐν ἑτοιμ. τ. εὐ. τ. εἰρ.] *in the preparedness of the gospel of peace.* In the midst of the conflict that which brings alacrity at once and firmness is the consciousness of a message of peace for the world. Warfare is the work of an enemy whom our Lord has overcome.

Ἑτοιμασία occurs in the LXX. in the sense of 'preparedness' in Ps. x. 17 (ix. 38 LXX.) τὴν ἑτοιμασίαν τῆς καρδίας αὐτῶν : but more commonly in the sense of 'preparation,' as Wisd. xiii. 12 εἰς ἑτοιμασίαν τροφῆς, or 'prepared foundation,' as Ps. lxxxix. 14 (lxxxviii. 15) δικαιοσύνη καὶ κρίμα ἑτοιμασία τοῦ θρόνου σου ; Ezra ii. 68 τοῦ στῆσαι αὐτὸν ἐπὶ τὴν ἑτοιμασίαν αὐτοῦ (cf. Dan. xi. 7, Theodot.).

τοῦ εὐαγγ. τῆς εἰρ.] The phrase is

unique, but the thought is given in Nahum i. 15 οἱ πόδες εὐαγγελιζομένου καὶ ἀπαγγέλλοντος εἰρήνην ; Is. lii. 7 ; *c.* ii. 17 καὶ ἐλθὼν εὐηγγελίσατο εἰρήνην ὑμῖν τοῖς μακρὰν καὶ εἰρήνην τοῖς ἐγγύς ; Rom. x. 15. Compare Lk. ii. 14 ; John xiv. 27 ; Acts x. 36.

Similar titles are found : Acts xx. 24 τὸ εὐαγγ. τῆς χάριτος τοῦ θεοῦ. 2 Cor. iv. 4 τὸ εὐαγγ. τῆς δόξης τοῦ χριστοῦ. 1 Tim. i. 11 τὸ εὐαγγ. τῆς δόξης τοῦ μακαρίου θεοῦ. *c.* i. 13 τὸ εὐαγγ. τῆς σωτηρίας ὑμῶν.

Compare ὁ θεὸς τῆς εἰρήνης 1 Thess. v. 23 (2 Cor. xiii. 11) ; Rom. xv. 33 ; xvi. 20 ; Phil. iv. 9 ; Hebr. xiii. 20 ; 2 Thess. iii. 16 ὁ κύριος τῆς εἰρ.

16. ἐν πᾶσιν ἀναλ.] *in all*—as affecting your whole action—*having taken up the shield of faith*.... For ἀναλαβόντες see *v.* 13. The θυρεός (*scutum*) was a large oblong shield capable of being used as a protection for every part. This is the quality of faith, and specially *in this* the Christian is *able to quench all the darts of the evil one that are set on fire* (as they strike harmlessly upon it).

τὰ β....τὰ πεπυρ.] Such πυρφόροι ὀϊστοί (Thuc. ii. 75), *malleoli* (Amm. Marcell. 23, 4) were used in Greek and Roman warfare : see also Ps. vii. 13 and Hupfeld. The image describes vividly the manifold and deadly malignity of the attack of the Evil One.

τοῦ πονηροῦ] Latt. *nequissimi* (*maligni*). This title is not found elsewhere in St Paul. It is characteristic of the first Epistle of St John (ii. 13 f. ; iii. 12 ; v. 18 f.). It occurs also in Matt. v. 37 ; vi. 13 ; xiii. 19, 38 (not Lk. xi. 4) ; John xvii. 15.

17. When the Christian soldier has taken his stand, well-girt with

τὴν περικεφαλαίαν τοῦ cωτηρίου δέξασθε, καὶ τὴν
μάχαιραν τοῦ πνεύματος, ὅ ἐστιν ρῆμα θεοῦ, ¹⁸διὰ
πάσης προσευχῆς καὶ δεήσεως, προσευχόμενοι ἐν παντὶ

breastplate, shoes, shield, he yet needs
helmet and sword. So St Paul continues, changing the construction, καὶ
...δέξασθε.

τὴν περικ. τοῦ σωτ. δέξασθε] receive
—accept from GOD—the helmet of
salvation.... Δέξασθε suggests a personal welcome of GOD's gift, and a
glad appropriation of it: 2 Cor. vi. 1 ;
viii. 17 ; 2 Thess. ii. 10.
The helmet guards the centre of
life. The sense of salvation puts life
beyond all danger.
For the image compare Is. lix. 17
καὶ περιέθετο περικεφαλαίαν σωτηρίου
ἐπὶ τῆς κεφαλῆς. In 1 Thess. v. 8 St
Paul describes 'the hope of salvation'
(ἐλπ. σωτηρίας) as our helmet.
Τὸ σωτήριον is used frequently in
the LXX. for salvation.
In the N. T. it occurs (τὸ σωτ. τοῦ
θεοῦ) Lk. ii. 30 ; iii. 6 (Is. xl. 5); Acts
xxviii. 28. The phrase expresses
rather 'that which brings salvation'
than 'salvation' itself.

τὴν μάχ. τοῦ πν.] the sword which
the Spirit provides and through which
it acts.

ρῆμα θεοῦ] a definite utterance of
GOD: Matt. iv. 4 ; John vi. 63. Comp.
c. v. 26 note. The ρήματα are manifold expressions of the λόγος: Hebr.
iv. 12.

The Christian spirit (18—20).
¹⁸ In all prayer and supplication
praying at every season in spirit,
and watching thereunto in all perseverance and supplication for all
the saints ; ¹⁹ and on my behalf,
that utterance may be given me in
opening my mouth to make known
with boldness the revelation (mystery)
of the gospel, ²⁰ for which I am
an ambassador in chains ; that in it
I may speak boldly, as I ought to
speak.

The description of the armour of
the warrior is followed by the description of his spirit. He must use
the vital powers and the instruments
of service which he has received in
unceasing prayer for all his fellow-
believers. Prayer is naturally connected with action.

διὰ πάσης...] V. in omni instantia
et obsecratione pro omnibus. The
universality of the duty as to mode,
time, persons, is enforced by πάσης,
παντί, πάσῃ, πάντων. Προσευχή is
addressed to GOD only and includes
the element of devotion: δέησις is
general in its application and includes
some definite request. The words
occur together Phil. iv. 6 (see Lightfoot's note) ; 1 Tim. ii. 1 ; v. 5.
Διά marks the condition 'in every
prayer,' that is, while you use every
prayer: compare 2 Cor. ii. 4 διὰ πολλῶν
δακρύων.
It appears to be most natural to
connect διὰ π. προσ. καὶ δεήσ. with
προσευχόμενοι, and not to take them
absolutely : 'using every kind of
prayer and supplication, praying....'
ἐν π. κ.] 1 Thess. v. 17 (ἀδιαλείπτως);
Rom. xii. 12 (προσκαρτεροῦντες) ; Phil.
iv. 6 (ἐν παντί).
ἐν πνεύματι] in spirit, not in form
or in word only, but in that part of
our being through which we hold
communion with GOD. Thus praying
in spirit, when viewed from the other
side, is 'praying in the Holy Spirit'
(Jude 21). Comp. c. ii. 22 note ; iii. 5
note.
καὶ...ἀγρυπ.] not merely praying
under the influence of a natural desire, but also watching thereunto with
resolute effort. Ἀγρυπνεῖν is found
in N.T., Mark xiii. 33 ; Lk. xxi. 36 ;
Hebr. xiii. 17 αὐτοὶ γὰρ ἀγρυπνοῦσιν
ὑπὲρ τῶν ψυχῶν ὑμῶν ὡς λόγον ἀποδώ-
σοντες : and in the LXX., Ps. cxxvii.

καιρῷ ἐν πνεύματι, καὶ εἰς αὐτὸ ἀγρυπνοῦντες ἐν πάσῃ
προσκαρτερήσει καὶ δεήσει περὶ πάντων τῶν ἁγίων,
¹⁹καὶ ὑπὲρ ἐμοῦ, ἵνα μοι δοθῇ λόγος ἐν ἀνοίξει τοῦ στόματός μου, ἐν παρρησίᾳ γνωρίσαι τὸ μυστήριον [τοῦ
εὐαγγελίου] ²⁰ὑπὲρ οὗ πρεσβεύω ἐν ἁλύσει, ἵνα ἐν αὐτῷ
παρρησιάσωμαι ὡς δεῖ με λαλῆσαι.

(cxxvi.) 1 ἐὰν μὴ ὁ κύριος φυλάξῃ πόλιν,
εἰς μάτην ἠγρύπνησεν ὁ φυλάσσων,
Wisd. vi. 15 ὁ ἀγρυπνήσας δι' αὐτὴν
ταχέως ἀμέριμνος ἔσται. Compare Col.
iv. 2 (γρηγοροῦντες).

εἰς αὐτό] The power of prayer is
gained by systematic discipline.

ἐν πάσῃ προσκ....] in all perseverance, steadfastness.... The word
προσκαρτέρησις is found here only.
Προσκαρτερεῖν is used in connexion
with prayer: Acts i. 14; vi. 4; Rom.
xii. 12; Col. iv. 2.

περὶ π. τ. ἁγ.] in close connexion
with προσευχόμενοι. The words between define the nature of the prayer
as constant, spiritual, resolute, manifold.

The combatant even in the stress of
personal conflict thinks of all with
whom he is united (ἁγίων); and in
this way—to regard the truth from
the other side — the weakest and
simplest Christian can take part in
the efforts of the strongest. There is
now no difference of Jew and Gentile.
Comp. v. 24; c. i. 15; iii. 18.

19, 20. Specially the Apostle asks
for prayer on his own behalf, that he
may declare his message boldly.

19. καὶ ὑπὲρ ἐμοῦ] and on my
behalf.... More direct and definite
than for, v. 18 (περί).

ἵνα μοι δοθῇ...] The one thing
which St Paul asks is, not success,
not deliverance, but simply boldness
to deliver the Gospel which had been
revealed to him. The first was an
encouragement but not a ground for
self-confidence. Day by day he looked
for a new gift through the prayers of
Christians. For λόγος see 1 Cor. xii. 8
ᾧ μὲν γὰρ διὰ τοῦ πνεύματος δίδοται

λόγος σοφίας, ἄλλῳ δὲ λόγος γνώσεως
κατὰ τὸ αὐτὸ πνεῦμα.

ἐν ἀνοίξει τ. στ. μ.] in opening my
mouth, that is probably 'when I open
my mouth to speak'; or the words
may be closely connected with δοθῇ
λόγος in the sense 'that utterance
may be given me by GOD when He
opens my mouth.' This interpretation
is suggested by Col. iv. 3 (ἵνα ὁ θεὸς
ἀνοίξῃ ἡμῖν θύραν τοῦ λόγου, λαλῆσαι
τὸ μυστήριον τοῦ χριστοῦ), though the
image there is different. In either
case ἀνοίγειν τὸ στόμα marks some
weighty deliverance: Matt. v. 2; Acts
viii. 32, 35.

ἐν παρρ. γν.] The structure of the
sentence no less than the sense favours
the connexion of ἐν παρρησίᾳ with
γνωρίσαι and not with the preceding
words. That which was before 'spoken
in proverbs' is now 'spoken plainly'
(John xvi. 25).

τὸ μυστ. τοῦ εὐαγγ.] the revelation
of the gospel, the revelation contained
in the gospel. The phrase is unique.

20. πρεσβ. ἐν ἁλ.] Latt. legatione
fungor in catena. The words are an
oxymoron. The dignity of the ambassador of the great king remains,
though he is a prisoner and bearing
the marks of bondage. Compare the
language of Philemon 9 τοιοῦτος ὢν ὡς
Παῦλος πρεσβύτης νυνὶ δὲ καὶ δέσμιος
Χριστοῦ Ἰησοῦ, and Lightfoot's note.

For ἅλυσις see Acts xxi. 33; xxviii.
20; 2 Tim. i. 16.

ἵνα ἐν αὐ. παρρησ.] This clause is
parallel with ἵνα μοι δοθῇ λόγος (compare Gal. iii. 14). For παρρησιάσωμαι
see Acts ix. 27 f.; xiii. 46 παρρησιασά-
μενοί τε ὁ Παῦλος καὶ ὁ Βαρνάβας εἶπαν
κ.τ.λ.; xix. 8 ἐπαρρησιάζετο ἐπὶ μῆνας

²¹ "ἵνα δὲ ⌜εἰδῆτε καὶ ὑμεῖς⌝ τὰ κατ' ἐμέ, τί πράσσω,
πάντα γνωρίσει ὑμῖν Τύχικος ὁ ἀγαπητὸς ἀδελφὸς καὶ
πιστὸς διάκονος ἐν κυρίῳ, ²² ὃν ἔπεμψα πρὸς ὑμᾶς εἰς
αὐτὸ τοῦτο ἵνα γνῶτε τὰ περὶ ἡμῶν καὶ παρακαλέσῃ
τὰς καρδίας ὑμῶν.

21 καὶ ὑμεῖς εἰδῆτε

τρεῖς διαλεγόμενος καὶ πείθων περὶ τῆς
βασιλείας τοῦ θεοῦ ; 1 Thess. ii. 2 ἐπαρ-
ρησιασάμεθα ἐν τῷ θεῷ ; and for ἐν
αὐτῷ compare Col. iv. 2 ; 1 Tim. iv. 15
ἐν τούτοις ἴσθι.
    ὡς δεῖ με λαλ.] So Col. iv. 4 ἵνα
φανερώσω αὐτὸ ὡς δεῖ με λαλῆσαι.
    δεῖ] cf. Hebr. ii. 1 διὰ τοῦτο δεῖ
περισσοτέρως προσέχειν ἡμᾶς τοῖς
ἀκουσθεῖσιν.

21, 22. Personal tidings.

²¹ *But that ye also may know my
circumstances, how I fare, Tychicus
the beloved brother and faithful
minister in the Lord shall make
known to you all things,* ²² *whom I
sent to you for this very purpose,
that ye may know our affairs and
that he may comfort your hearts.*

21. καὶ ὑμεῖς] ye also as others.

τὰ κατ' ἐμέ...] my circumstances,
how I fare.... Col. iv. 7 ; Phil. i. 12.
The next verse suggests (παρακ. τ. κ.
ὑ.) that disquieting rumours had
reached them.

πάντα...Τυχικός...] There is no
reserve in his communication. For
Tychicus (Acts xx. 4 Ἀσιανοὶ δὲ Τυχι-
κὸς καὶ Τρόφιμος ; 2 Tim. iv. 12 Τυχικὸν
δὲ ἀπέστειλα εἰς Ἔφεσον ; Tit. iii. 12
ὅταν πέμψω Ἀρτεμᾶν πρός σε ἢ Τυχι-
κόν) see Lightfoot on Col. iv. 17.
This is the single personal reference
in the Epistle, as is the reference to
Timothy in the Epistle to the Hebrews
(c. xiii. 23). The words ὁ ἀγαπ....ἐν
κυρίῳ form one compound clause. The
spiritual kinsmanship of Tychicus with
St Paul and his service were alike
realised in fellowship with the Lord
(cf. Rom. xvi. 8 f.). This interpretation

appears to be more consonant with
St Paul's manner than to confine ἐν
κυρίῳ to πιστὸς διάκονος.

22. εἰς αὐτὸ τ. ἵνα...] Comp. 2 Cor.
ii. 9 ; Rom. xiv. 9 ; 1 Pet. iii. 9 ; 1 John
iii. 8.
    ἵνα γνῶτε...καὶ παρακαλέσῃ] For the
change of person compare Col. iv. 8 ἵνα
γνῶτε—καὶ παρακαλέσῃ (as here), Phil.
ii. 28 ἵνα ἰδόντες αὐτὸν πάλιν χαρῆτε
κἀγὼ ἀλυπότερος ὦ.
    τὰ περὶ ἡμῶν] St Paul now joins his
companions with himself : compare
Col. iv. 10 f. ; Philemon 23 f. Ἐπαφρᾶς
ὁ συναιχμάλωτός μου ἐν Χριστῷ Ἰησοῦ,
Μάρκος, Ἀρίσταρχος, Δημᾶς, Λουκᾶς, οἱ
συνεργοί μου.
    The words παρακαλέσῃ τὰς καρδίας
ὑμῶν imply that the readers had been
troubled by news which had reached
them perhaps as to St Paul's approach-
ing trial : comp. c. iii. 13. The phrase
is found again in Col. iv. 8.

²³ *Peace be to the brethren and love
with faith from* GOD *the Father and
the Lord Jesus Christ.* ²⁴ *Grace be
with all them that love the Lord
Jesus Christ in incorruption.*
    A double salutation and blessing.
    23, 24. St Paul first addresses the
special society (οἱ ἀδελφοί) ; and then
'all that love the Lord Jesus.' The
variation εἰρήνη τοῖς...ἡ χάρις μετά...
is to be noticed. Peace is GOD's gift
complete in itself : grace is realised
through man's cooperation. Yet in
the opening salutations St Paul writes
χάρις ὑμῖν. In this connexion χάρις is
always anarthrous.
    The form of the salutation in the
third (not the second) person differs

²³ Εἰρήνη τοῖς ἀδελφοῖς καὶ ἀγάπη μετὰ πίστεως ἀπὸ θεοῦ πατρὸς καὶ κυρίου Ἰησοῦ Χριστοῦ. ²⁴ Ἡ χάρις μετὰ πάντων τῶν ἀγαπώντων τὸν κύριον ἡμῶν Ἰησοῦν Χριστὸν ἐν ἀφθαρσίᾳ.

from St Paul's usual manner. But compare Gal. vi. 16.

23. εἰρήνη τ. ἀ. καὶ ἀγ. μ. π.] 'With faith' is to be taken with 'peace' and 'love,' since 'from GOD' belongs to both. Peace and love are GOD'S gifts, and faith is the condition of appropriating them. 'Love' occurs in benedictions 1 Cor. xvi. 24 (ἡ ἀγ. μου); 2 Cor. xiii. 13 (ἡ ἀγ. τ. θεοῦ); and 'peace' 2 Thess. iii. 16; Gal. vi. 16 (cf. Rom. xv. 33); 1 Pet. v. 14.

τοῖς ἀδ.] here only in the Epistle (v. 10 a false reading). Comp. v. 21 ὁ ἀδελφός. It occurs in Col. i. 2 ; iv. 15.

ἀπὸ θ. π.] Gal. i. 3 v. l.; 2 Tim. i. 2 ; Tit. i. 4.

24. ἡ χ. μ. π.] Ἡ χάρις stands thus absolutely in benedictions : Col. iv. 18 ; 1 Tim. vi. 21 ; 2 Tim. iv. 22 ; Tit. iii. 15 ; Hebr. xiii. 25. Elsewhere

St Paul writes ἡ χάρις τοῦ κυρίου Ἰ. [Χρ.]. It is uniformly followed by μετά. Comp. v. 23 note.

π. τῶν ἀγ....Ἰ. Χρ.] Compare 1 Pet. i. 8 ὃν οὐκ ἰδόντες ἀγαπᾶτε, James i. 12, John viii. 42, xiv. 15, 23.

ἐν ἀφθαρσίᾳ] with a love free from every element liable to corruption. The Lord 'brought incorruption (ἀ-φθαρσίαν) to light' (2 Tim. i. 10). Thus He revealed the eternal in things perishable in form. The Christian realises this in his love for his Lord. He knows Him no more after the flesh (2 Cor. v. 16). His love is directed to that which is beyond change, and is itself unchangeable. Primasius describes in part the character of such believers : in quorum corde nullo adulterino saeculi amore Christi dilectio violatur.

USE OF THE OLD TESTAMENT IN THE EPISTLE.

QUOTATIONS AND REMINISCENCES.

[The passages are given in full on pp. 200, 201.]

EPISTULA AD EPHESIOS

LATINE

INTERPRETE HIERONYMO

E CODICE AMIATINO

INCIPIUNT CAPITULA

EXPLICIUNT CAPITULA

INCIPIT EPISTULA AD EPHESIOS

I.

1 [1]Paulus apostolus Christi Iesu per voluntatem dei sanctis omnibus qui sunt Ephesi et fidelibus in Christo Iesu. [2]Gratia vobis et pax a deo patre nostro et domino Iesu Christo. [3]Benedictus deus et pater domini nostri Iesu Christi, qui benedixit nos in omni benedictione spiritali in caelestibus in Christo, [4]sicut elegit nos in ipso ante mundi constitutionem, ut essemus sancti et immaculati in conspectu eius in caritate, [5]qui praedestinavit nos in adoptionem filiorum per Iesum Christum in ipsum, secundum propositum voluntatis suae, [6]in laudem gloriae gratiae suae, in qua gratificavit nos in dilecto, [7]in quo habemus redemptionem per sanguinem eius, remissionem peccatorum, secundum divitias gratiae eius, [8]quae superabundavit in nobis in omni sapientia et prudentia, [9]ut notum faceret nobis sacramentum voluntatis suae, secundum bonum placitum eius quod proposuit in eo [10]in dispensationem plenitudinis temporum, instaurare omnia in Christo, quae in caelis et quae in terra sunt, in ipso, [11]in quo etiam sorte vocati sumus, praedestinati secundum propositum eius qui omnia operatur secundum consilium voluntatis suae ; [12]ut simus in laudem gloriae eius, qui ante speravimus in Christo, [13]in quo et vos, cum audissetis verbum veritatis, evangelium salutis vestrae, in quo credentes signati estis spiritu promissionis sancto, [14]qui est pignus hereditatis nostrae in redemptionem adquisitionis, in laudem gloriae eius. 2 [15]Propterea et ego, audiens fidem vestram quae est in domino Iesu et dilectionem in omnes sanctos, [16]non cesso gratias agens pro vobis, memoriam vestri faciens in orationibus meis, [17]ut deus domini nostri Iesu Christi, pater gloriae, det vobis spiritum sapientiae et revelationis in agnitione eius, [18]inluminatos oculos cordis vestri, ut sciatis quae sit spes vocationis eius, quae divitiae gloriae hereditatis eius in sanctis, [19]et quae sit supereminens magnitudo virtutis eius in nos qui credidimus secundum operationem potentiae virtutis eius, [20]quam operatus est in Christo, suscitans illum

a mortuis et constituens ad dexteram suam in caelestibus [21]supra
omnem principatum et potestatem et virtutem et dominationem et
omne nomen quod nominatur non solum in hoc saeculo sed et in
futuro, [22]et omnia subiecit sub pedibus eius, et ipsum dedit caput
supra omnia ecclesiae, [23]quae est corpus ipsius, plenitudo eius quia
omnia in omnibus adimpletur.

II.

3 [1]Et vos, cum essetis mortui delictis peccatis vestris, [2]in quibus
aliquando ambulastis secundum saeculum mundi huius, secundum
principem potestatis aeris huius, spiritus qui nunc operatur in filios
diffidentiae; [3]in quibus et nos omnes aliquando conversati sumus in
desideriis carnis nostrae, facientes voluntatem carnis et cogitationem,
et eramus natura filii irae sicut et ceteri. 4 [4]Deus autem qui dives est
in misericordiam, propter nimiam caritatem suam qua dilexit nos, [5]et
cum essemus mortui peccatis, convivificavit nos Christo, gratia estis
salvati, [6]et conresuscitavit et consedere fecit in caelestibus in Christo
Iesu, [7]ut ostenderet in saeculis supervenientibus abundantes divitias
gratiae suae in bonitate super nos in Christo Iesu. 5 [8]Gratia enim estis
salvati per fidem; et hoc non ex vobis, dei enim donum est : [9]non ex
operibus, ut ne quis glorietur: [10]ipsius enim sumus factura, creati in
Christo Iesu in operibus bonis, quae praeparavit deus ut in illis ambu-
lemus. 6 [11]Propter quod memores estote quod aliquando vos gentes in
carne, qui dicimini praeputium ab ea quae dicitur circumcisio in carne
manu facta, [12]quia eratis illo in tempore sine Christo, alienati a con-
versione Israhel et hospites testamentorum promissionis, spem non
habentes et sine deo in mundo: 7 [13]nunc autem in Christo Iesu vos qui
aliquando eratis longe, facti estis prope in sanguine Christi. [14]Ipse
est enim pax nostra, qui fecit utraque unum, et medium parietem
macheriae solvens, [15]inimicitias in carne sua, legem mandatorum de-
cretis evacuans, ut duos condat in semet ipsum in unum novum
hominem, faciens pacem, [16]et reconciliet ambos in uno corpore deo
per crucem, interficiens inimicitiam in semet ipso. [17]Et veniens evan-
gelizavit pacem vobis qui longe fuistis et pacem his qui prope, [18]quoniam
per ipsum habemus accessum ambo in uno spiritu ad patrem. 8 [19]Ergo
iam non estis hospites et advenae, sed estis cives sanctorum et domestici
dei, [20]superaedificati super fundamentum apostolorum et prophetarum,
ipso summo angulari lapide Christo Iesu, [21]in quo omnis aedificatio
constructa crescit in templum sanctum in domino, [22]in quo et vos
coaedificamini in habitaculum dei in spiritu.

III.

9 [1]Huius rei gratia ego Paulus vinctus Christi Iesu pro vobis gentibus, [2]si tamen audistis dispensationem gratiae dei quae data est mihi
in vobis, [3]quoniam secundum revelationem notum mihi factum est
sacramentum, sicut supra scripsi in brevi, [4]prout potestis legentes
intellegere prudentiam meam in mysterio Christi, [5]quod aliis genera-
tionibus non est agnitum filiis hominum, sicuti nunc revelatum est
sanctis apostolis eius et prophetis in spiritu, [6]esse gentes coheredes
et concorporales et conparticipes promissionis in Christo Iesu per evangelium, [7]cuius factus sum minister secundum donum gratiae dei, quae
data est mihi secundum operationem virtutis eius. [8]Mihi omnium
sanctorum minimo data est gratia haec, in gentibus evangelizare investigabiles divitias Christi, [9]et inluminare omnes quae sit dispensatio
sacramenti absconditi a saeculis in deo qui omnia creavit; [10]ut innotes-
cat principibus et potestatibus in caelestibus per ecclesiam multiformis
sapientia dei, [11]secundum praefinitionem saeculorum quam fecit in
Christo Iesu domino nostro; [12]in quo habemus fiduciam et accessum
in confidentia per fidem eius. 10 [13]Propter quod peto ne deficiatis in
tribulationibus meis pro vobis, quae est gloria vestra. 11 [14]Huius rei
gratia flecto genua mea ad patrem domini nostri Iesu Christi, [15]ex
quo omnis paternitas in caelis et in terra nominatur, [16]ut det vobis
secundum divitias gloriae suae virtute conroborari per spiritum eius in
interiore homine, [17]habitare Christum per fidem in cordibus vestris,
[18]in caritate radicati et fundati, ut possitis conpraehendere cum omnibus sanctis quae sit latitudo et longitudo et sublimitas et profundum,
[19]scire etiam supereminentem scientiae caritatem Christi, ut impleamini
in omnem plenitudinem dei. 12 [20]Ei autem qui potens est omnia facere
superabundanter quam petimus aut intellegimus secundum virtutem
quae operatur in nobis, [21]ipsi gloria in ecclesia et in Christo Iesu in
omnes generationes saeculis saeculorum, amen.

IV.

13 [1]Obsecro itaque vos ego vinctus in domino ut digne ambuletis
vocatione qua vocati estis, [2]cum omni humilitate et mansuetudine,
cum patientia, subportantes invicem in caritate, [3]solliciti servare unitatem spiritus in vinculo pacis. [4]Unum corpus et unus spiritus, sicut
vocati estis in una spe vocationis vestrae. 14 [5]Unus dominus, una fides,
unum baptisma, [6]unus deus et pater omnium, qui super omnes et per
omnia et in omnibus nobis. 15 [7]Unicuique autem nostrum data est
gratia secundum mensuram donationis Christi. [8]Propter quod dicit

Ascendens in altum captivam duxit captivitatem, dedit dona hominibus.
⁹Quod autem ascendit, quid est nisi quod et descendit in inferiores
partes terrae? ¹⁰Qui descendit, ipse est et qui ascendit super omnes
caelos, ut impleret omnia. ¹¹Et ipse dedit quosdam quidem prophetas,
quosdam quidem apostolos, alios evangelistas, alios autem pastores et
doctores, ¹²ad consummationem sanctorum, in opus ministerii, in aedificationem corporis Christi, ¹³donec occuramus omnes in unitatem fidei
et agnitionis filii dei, in virum perfectum, in mensuram aetatis plenitudinis Christi, ¹⁴ut iam non simus parvuli fluctuantes et circum-
feramur omni vento doctrinae in nequitia hominum, in astutia ad
circumventionem erroris, ¹⁵veritatem autem facientes in caritate crescamus in illo per omnia, qui est caput, Christus, ¹⁶ex quo totum
corpus conpactum et conexum per omnem iuncturam subministrationis
secundum operationem in mensuram uniuscuiusque membri augmentum
corporis facit in aedificationem sui in caritate. 16 ¹⁷Hoc igitur dico et
testificor in domino, ut iam non ambuletis sicut gentes ambulant in
vanitate sensus sui, ¹⁸tenebris obscuratum habentes intellectum, alienati a vita dei, per ignorantiam quae est in illis, propter caecitatem
cordis ipsorum, ¹⁹qui desperantes semet ipsos tradiderunt impudicitiae
in operationem inmunditiae omnis in avaritia. 17 ²⁰Vos autem non ita
didicistis Christum, ²¹si tamen illum audistis et in ipso edocti estis
sicut est veritas in Iesu, ²²deponere vos secundum pristinam conver-
sationem veterem hominem, qui corrumpitur secundum desideria erroris: ²³renovamini autem spiritu mentis vestrae, ²⁴et induite novum
hominem qui secundum deum creatus est in iustitia et sanctitate
veritatis. ²⁵Propter quod deponentes mendacium loquimini veritatem
unusquisque cum proximo suo, quoniam sumus invicem membra.
18 ²⁶Irascimini et nolite peccare: sol non occidat super iracundiam vestram. ²⁷Nolite locum dare diabulo. ²⁸Qui furabatur, iam non furetur,
magis autem laboret operando manibus quod bonum est, ut habeat
unde tribuat necessitatem patienti. 19 ²⁹Omnis sermo malus ex ore vestro
non procedat, sed si quis bonus ad aedificationem oportunitatis, ut
det gratiam audientibus. ³⁰Et nolite contristare spiritum sanctum dei,
in quo signati estis in die redemptionis. ³¹Omnis amaritudo et ira et
indignatio et clamor et blasphemia tollatur a vobis cum omni malitia:
³²estote autem invicem benigni, misericordes, donantes invicem sicut et
deus in Christo donavit nobis.

V.

20 ¹Estote ergo imitatores dei, sicut filii carissimi, ²et ambulate in
dilectionem, sicut et Christus dilexit nos et tradidit se ipsum pro nobis

oblationem et hostiam deo in odorem suavitatis.   21 [3]Fornicatio autem
et omnis inmunditia aut avaritia nec nominetur in vobis, sicut decet
sanctos,   [4]aut turpitudo aut stultiloquium aut scurrilitas, quae ad rem
non pertinent, sed magis gratiarum actio.   [5]Hoc enim scitote intellegentes, quod omnis fornicator aut inmundus aut avarus, quod est
idolorum servitus, non habet hereditatem in regno Christi et dei.
22 [6]Nemo vos seducat inanibus verbis: propter haec enim venit ira dei
in filios diffidentiae.   [7]Nolite ergo effici participes eorum.   [8]Eratis enim
aliquando tenebrae, nunc autem lux in domino: ut filii lucis ambulate;
[9]fructus enim lucis est in omni bonitate et iustitia et veritate;   [10]pro-
bantes quod sit beneplacitum deo,   [11]et nolite communicare operibus
infructuosis tenebrarum, magis autem et redarguite.   [12]Quae enim in
occulto fiunt ab ipsis, turpe est et dicere: [13]omnia autem quae argu-
untur a lumine manifestantur: omne enim quod manifestatur, lumen
est.   [14]Propter quod dicit Surge qui dormis et exurge a mortuis, et
inluminabit tibi Christus.   23 [15]Videte itaque, fratres, quomodo caute
ambuletis, non quasi insipientes, sed ut sapientes,   [16]redimentes tempus,
quoniam dies mali sunt.   [17]Propterea nolite fieri inprudentes, sed
intellegentes quae sit voluntas dei.   [18]Et nolite inebriari vino, in quo
est omnis luxuria, sed implemini spiritu,   [19]loquentis vosmet ipsis in
psalmis et hymnis et canticis spiritalibus, cantantes et psallentes in
cordibus vestris domino,   [20]gratias agentes semper pro omnibus in
nomine domini nostri Iesu Christi deo et patri,   [21]subiecti invicem
in timore Christi.   24 [22]Mulieres viris suis subiectae sint sicut domino,
[23]quoniam vir caput est mulieris, sicut Christus caput est ecclesiae,
ipse salvator corporis.   [24]Sed ut ecclesia subiecta est Christo, ita et
mulieres viris suis in omnibus.   25 [25]Viri, diligite uxores vestras, sicut
et Christus dilexit ecclesiam et se ipsum tradidit pro ea,   [26]ut illam
sanctificaret mundans lavacro aquae in verbo,   [27]ut exhiberet ipse sibi
gloriosam ecclesiam, non habentem maculam aut rugam aut aliquid
eiusmodi, sed ut sit sancta et immaculata.   [28]Ita et viri debent diligere
uxores suas ut corpora sua.   Qui suam uxorem diligit, se ipsum diligit:
[29]nemo enim umquam carnem suam odio habuit, sed nutrit et fovet
eam, sicut et Christus ecclesiam,   [30]quia membra sumus corporis eius,
de carne eius et de ossibus eius.   [31]Propter hoc relinquet homo patrem
et matrem suam et adherebit uxori suae, et erunt duo in carne una.
[32]Sacramentum hoc magnum est, ego autem dico in Christo et in
ecclesia.   [33]Verum tamen et vos singuli unusquisque suam uxorem
sicut se ipsum diligat, uxor autem ut timeat virum.

VI.

26 [1]Filii, oboedite parentibus vestris in domino: hoc enim iustum est. [2]Honora patrem tuum et matrem, quod est mandatum primum in promissione, [3]ut bene sit tibi et sis longevus super terram. 27 [4]Et patres, nolite ad iracundiam provocare filios vestros, sed educate illos in disciplina et correptione domini. 28 [5]Servi, oboedite dominis carnalibus cum timore et tremore, in simplicitate cordis vestri, sicut Christo, [6]non ad oculum servientes quasi hominibus placeatis, sed ut servi Christi facientes voluntatem dei ex animo, [7]cum bona voluntate servientes sicut domino et non hominibus, [8]scientes quoniam unusquisque quodcumque fecerit bonum hoc percipiet a domino, sive servus sive liber. 29 [9]Et domini, eadem facite illis, remittentes minas, scientes quia et illorum et vester dominus est in caelis et personarum acceptio non est apud eum. 30 [10]De cetero, fratres, confortamini in domino et in potentia virtutis eius. [11]Induite vos arma dei, ut possitis stare adversus insidias diaboli; [12]quia non est nobis conluctatio adversus carnem et sanguinem, sed adversus principes et potestates, adversus mundi rectores tenebrarum harum, contra spiritalia nequitiae in caelestibus. [13]Propterea accipite arma dei, ut possitis resistere in die malo et in omnibus perfecti stare. [14]State ergo succincti lumbos vestros in veritate, et induti lorica iustitiae, [15]et calciati pedes in praeparatione evangelii pacis, [16]in omnibus sumentes scutum fidei, in quo possitis omnia tela nequissimi ignea extinguere. [17]Et galeam salutis adsumite, et gladium spiritus, quod est verbum dei, [18]per omnem orationem et obsecrationem orantes omni tempore in spiritu, et in ipso vigilantes in omni instantia et obsecratione pro omnibus sanctis, [19]et pro me, ut detur mihi sermo in apertione oris mei cum fiducia notum facere mysterium evangelii, [20]pro quo legatione fungor in catena, ita ut in ipso audeam prout oportet me loqui. 31 [21]Ut autem et sciatis vos quae circa me sunt, quid agam, omnia nota vobis faciet Tychicus carissimus frater et fidelis minister in domino, [22]quem misi ad vos in hoc ipsum, ut cognoscatis quae circa nos sunt et consoletur corda vestra. [23]Pax fratribus et caritas cum fide a deo patre et domino Iesu Christo. [24]Gratia cum omnibus qui diligunt dominum Iesum Christum in incorruptione.

EXPLICIT AD EPHESIOS.

EPISTLE TO THE EPHESIANS

EPISTLE TO THE EPHESIANS

1. POUL the apostle of ihesus crist, bi the wille of god, to alle seyntis that ben at effecie, and to the feithful men in ihesus crist, [2] grace be to ʒou and pees of god oure fadir and oure lord ihesus crist. [3] Blessid be god and the fadir of oure lord ihesus crist : that hath blessid us in al spiritual blessynge in heuenli thingis in crist, [4] as he hath chosun us in hym silf, bifor the makynge of the world : that we weren holi and without wemme in his siʒt in charite, [5] whiche hath bifore ordeyned us in to adopcioun of sones bi ihesus crist in to him, bi the purpos of his wille [6] in to the heryinge of the glorie of his grace, in which he hath glorified us in his dereworthe sone,

[7] in whom we han redempcioun bi his blood : forʒeuenesse of synnes, aftir the richessis of grace, [8] that aboundid gretli in us, in al wisdom and prudens : [9] to make knowe to us the sacrament of his wille, bi the good pleasaunce of hym the whiche sacramente he purposid in hym : [10] in to dispensacioun of plente of tymes, to enstore alle thingis in crist : whiche ben in heuenes & which ben in erthe in hym,

[v. supr. Preface, p. ix.]

1. PAUL an Apostle of Iesu Christ, by the will of God.

To the saynctes which are at Ephesus, and to them which beleve on Iesus Christ. [2] Grace be with you and peace from God oure father, and from the Lorde Iesus Christ. [3] Blessed be God the father of oure lorde Iesus Christ, which hath blessed vs with all maner of spirituall blessinges in hevenly thynges by Chryst, [4] accordynge as he had chosen vs in him, before the foundacion of the worlde was layde, that we shuld be saintes, and without blame before him, thorow loue. [5] And ordeyned vs before thorow Iesus Christ to be heyres vnto him silfe, accordinge to the pleasure of his will, [6] to the prayse of the glorie of his grace where with he hath made vs accepted in the beloved.

[7] By whom we have redemption thorow his bloude euen the forgevenes of synnes, accordynge to the riches of his grace, [8] which grace he shed on vs aboundantly in all wisdome, and perceavaunce. [9] And hath openned vnto vs the mistery of his will according to his pleasure, and purposed the same in hym silfe [10] to have it declared when the tyme were full come, that all thynges, bothe the

WICLIF—1380.

[11] in whom we ben clepid bi sorte bifor ordeyned, bi the purpos of him that worchith alle thingis : bi the counceil of his wille, [12] that we be in to the heriynge of his glorie : we that han hopid bifor in crist, [13] in whom also ȝe weren clepid, whanne ȝe herden the word of truthe, the gospel of ȝoure helthe, in whom ȝe bileuynge ben markid, with the holi goost of biheest. [14] whiche is the ernes of ȝoure eritage : in to the redempcioun of purchasynge in to heryinge of his glorie,

[15] therfor I herynge ȝoure feith that is in crist ihesus, and the loue in to al seintis : [16] ceese not to do thankingis for ȝou, makynge mynde of ȝou in my preyers, [17] that god of oure lord ihesus crist, the fadir of glori : ȝeue to ȝou the spirit of wisdom and of reuelacioun in to the knowynge of hym, [18] that the iȝen of ȝoure herte lyȝtned : that ȝe wite whiche is the hope of his clepynge, and whiche ben the richessis of the glorie of his eritage in seyntis, [19] and whiche is the excellent greetnesse of his vertu in to us that han bileued bi the worchynge of the myȝt of his vertu, [20] whiche he wrouȝte in crist reisynge hym fro deeth, and settynge him on his riȝthalf in heuenli thingis : [21] aboue eche principat and potestat, and vertu & domynacioun and *aboue* eche name that is named, not oonli in this world : but also in the world to comynge, [22] and made alle thingis suget vndir his feet : & ȝaf hym to be heed ouer al the chirche [23] that is the bodi of hym, & the plente of hym whiche is al thingis : in alle thingis fulfillide.

TYNDALE—1534.

thynges which are in heven, and also the thynges which are in erthe, shuld be gaddered togedder, even in Christ : [11] that is to saye, in him in whom we are made heyres, and were therto predestinate accordynge to the purpose of him which worketh all thinges after the purpose of his awne will : [12] that we which before beleved in Christ shuld be vnto the prayse of his glory.

[13] In whom also ye (after that ye hearde the worde of trueth, I meane the gospell of youre saluacion, wherin ye beleved) were sealed with the holy sprete of promes, [14] which is the ernest of oure inheritaunce, to redeme the purchased possession and that vnto the laude of his glory.

[15] Wherfore even I (after that I hearde of the fayth which ye have in the lorde Iesu, and love vnto all the saynctes) [16] cease not to geve thankes for you, makynge mencion of you in my prayers, [17] that the God of oure lorde Iesus Christ and the father of glory, myght geve vnto you the sprete of wisdome, and open to you the knowledge of him silfe, [18] and lighten the eyes of your myndes, that ye myght knowe what that hope is, where vnto he hath called you, and what the riches of his glorious inheritaunce is apon the sainctes, [19] and what is the excedynge greatnes of his power to vs warde which beleve accordynge to the workynge of that his mighty power, [20] which he wrought in Christ, when he raysed him from deeth, and set him on his right honde in hevenly thynges, [21] above all rule, power, and myght and dominacion, and above all names that are named, not in this worlde only, but also in the worlde to come : [22] and hath put all thynges vnder his fete, and hath made him aboue all thynges, the heed of

the congregacion [23] which is his body
and the fulnes of him that filleth all
in all thynges.

2. AND whanne ȝe weren deed in
ȝoure giltis : and synnes [2] in whiche
ȝe wandriden sumtyme, aftir the
couris of this world, aftir the prince
of the power of this eire, of the spirit
that worchith now in to the sones of
vnbileue, [3] in whiche also we alle
lyueden sumtyme in the desiris of
oure fleisch, doynge the willis of the
fleisch & of thouȝtis, and we weren bi
kynde the sones of wraththe as other
men,

[4] but god that is riche in merci : for
his ful myche charite in whiche he
loued us, [5] ȝe whanne we weren deed
in synnes, quykened us to gidre in
crist, bi whos grace ȝe ben saued,
[6] and aȝenreisid to gidre : and made
to gidre to sitte in heuenly thingis in
crist ihesus, [7] that he schulde schewe
in the worldis aboue comyng : the
plenteuous richessis of his grace in
goodnes on us in crist ihesus, [8] for bi
grace ȝe ben saued bi feith : and this
not of ȝou, for it is the ȝifte of god,
[9] not of werkis : that no man haue
glorie, [10] for we ben the makynge of
hym made of nouȝt in crist ihesus
in good werkis whiche god hath
ordeyned : that we go in tho werkis,

[11] for whiche thing be ȝe myndeful :
that sumtyme ȝe weren hethen in
fleisch, whiche weren seide prepucie :
fro that that is seide circumcisioun
made by hond in fleisch, [12] & ȝe weren
in that tyme without crist, alienede
fro the lyuynge of israel and gestis of
testamentis, not hauynge hope of
biheest : and withouten god in this

2. AND hath quickened you also
that were deed in treaspasse and synne,
[2] in the which in tyme passed ye
walked, accordynge to the course of
this worlde, and after the governor
that ruleth in the ayer, the sprete
that now worketh in the children of
vnbelefe, [3] amonge which we also had
oure conversacion in tyme past, in the
lustes of oure flesshe, and fulfilled the
will of the flesshe and of the mynde :
and were naturally the children of
wrath, even as wel as other.

[4] But God which is rich in mercy
thorow his greate love wherwith he
loved vs, [5] even when we were deed
by synne, hath quickened vs together
in Christ (for by grace are ye saved)
[6] and hath raysed vs vp together and
made vs sitte together in hevenly
thynges thorow Christ Iesus, [7] for to
shewe in tymes to come the excedynge
ryches of his grace, in kyndnes to vs
warde in Christ Iesu. [8] For by grace
are ye made safe thorowe fayth, and
that not of youre selves. For it is the
gyfte of God, [9] and commeth not of
workes, lest eny man shuld bost him
silfe. [10] For we are his worckman-
shippe, created in Christ Iesu vnto
good workes, vnto the which god
ordeyned vs before, that we shuld
walke in them.

[11] Wherfore remember that ye beynge
in tyme passed gentyls in the flesshe,
and were called vncircumcision to
them which are called circumcision
in the flesshe, which circumcision is
made by hondes : [12] Remember I saye,
that ye were at that tyme with oute
Christ, and were reputed aliantes
from the commen welth of Israel, and

WICLIF—1380.

world, [13] but now in crist ihesus, ȝe that weren sumtyme fer, ben made nyȝ in the blood of crist, [14] for he is oure pees, that made bothe oon, & vnbindynge the myddil walle [15] of a wal with out morter enemytees in his fleisch, and a voidide the lawe of maundementis, bi domes : that he make .ij. in hym silf in to o newe man, makynge pees : [16] to recounceile bothe in o bodi to god bi the cros, sleynge the enemytees in hym silf, [17] and he comynge prechid pees to ȝou, that weren fer : and pees to hem that weren nyȝ, [18] for bi hym we bothe han nyȝ comynge : in o spirit to the fadir.

[19] therfor now ȝe ben not gestis, and straungers : but ȝe ben citeseynes of seintis : & housholde meyne of god, [20] aboue bildid on the foundement of apostlis & of profetis, vpon that hiȝist corner stoon crist ihesus, [21] in whom eche bildynge made : wexeth in to an holi temple in the lord, [22] in whom also ȝe be bildid to gidre in to the habitacle of god in the hooli gooste.

3. FOR the grace of this thing, I poul the bounden of crist ihesus for ȝou hethen men : [2] if netheles ȝe han herde the dispensacioun of goddis grace that is ȝouun to me in ȝou, [3] for bi reuelacioun the sacrament is made knowun to me, as I aboue wrote in schort thing : [4] as ȝe moun rede and vndurstonde my prudence in the mynysterie of crist, [5] whiche was not knowun to othere generaciouns to the sones of men : as it is now schewid to

TYNDALE—1534.

were straungers from the testamentes of promes, and had no hope, and were with out god in this worlde. [13] But now in Christ Iesu, ye which a whyle agoo were farre of, are made nye by the bloude of Christ.

[14] For he is oure peace, whych hath made of both one, and hath broken doune the wall that was a stoppe bitwene vs, [15] and hath also put awaye thorow his flesshe, the cause of hatred (that is to saye, the lawe of commaundementes contayned in the lawe written) for to make of twayne one newe man in him silfe, so makynge peace : [16] and to reconcile both vnto god in one body thorow his crosse, and slewe hatred therby : [17] and came and preached peace to you which were a farre of, and to them that were nye : [18] For thorow him we both have an open waye in, in one sprete vnto the father.

[19] Now therfore ye are no moare straungers and foreners : but citesyns with the saynctes, and of the housholde of god : [20] and are bilt apon the foundacion of the apostles and prophetes, Iesus Christ beynge the heed corner stone, [21] in whom every bildynge coupled togedder, groweth vnto an holy temple in the lorde, [22] in whom ye also are bilt togedder, and made an habitacion for god in the sprete.

3. FOR this cause I Paul am in the bondes of Iesus christ for youre sakes which are hethen : [2] Yf ye have hearde of the ministracion of the grace of god which is geven me to you warde. [3] For by revelacion shewed he this mistery vnto me, as I wrote above in feawe wordes, [4] wher by when ye rede ye maye knowe myne vnderstondynge in the mistery of Christ, [5] which mistery in tymes passed was not opened vnto the sonnes of men, as it is nowe de-

WICLIF—1380.

hise holi apostlis and profetis, in the spirit, ⁶that hethen men ben euen eiris, and of o bodi : and parteneris to gidre, of his biheest in crist ihesus bi the euangeli, ⁷ whos mynystre I am made by the ȝifte of goddis grace : whiche is ȝouun to me bi the worchynge of his vertu,

⁸ to me leest of alle seyntis, this grace is ȝouun to preche among hethen men, the vnserchable richessis of crist, ⁹ & to liȝtene alle men whiche is the dispensacioun of sacramente hidde fro worldis in god : that made alle thingis of nouȝt, ¹⁰ that the myche foold wisdom of god be knowun to princis & potestatis in heuenli thingis, bi the chirch : ¹¹ bi the bifor ordenaunce of worldis whiche he made in crist ihesus oure lord, ¹² in whom we han trist and nyȝ comynge : in tristenynge bi the feith of hym. ¹³ for whiche thing I axe : that ȝe faile not in my tribulaciouns for ȝou whiche is ȝoure glorie,

¹⁴ for grace of this thing I bowe my knees to the fadir of oure lord ihesus crist, ¹⁵ of whom eche fadirheed in heuenes and in erthe is named, ¹⁶ that he ȝeue to ȝou aftir the richessis of his glorie : vertu to be strengthid bi his spirit in the ynner man, ¹⁷ that crist dwelle bi feith in ȝoure hertis, that ȝe rootid, and groundid in charite : ¹⁸ moun comprehende with alle seyntis whiche is the breed and ¹⁹ the lengthe, and the hiȝist and the depnesse, also to wite the charite of crist more excellent thanne science : that ȝe be fillid in al the plente of god, ²⁰ and to hym that is myȝti to do alle thingis more plenteuousli thanne we axen, or vndirstonde bi the vertu

TYNDALE—1534.

clared vnto his holy apostles and prophetes by the sprete : ⁶that the gentyls shuld be inheritours also, and of the same body, and partakers of his promis that is in Christ, by the meanes of the gospell, ⁷ wherof I am made a minister, by the gyfte of the grace of god geven vnto me thorow the workynge of his power.

⁸ Vnto me the lest of all sayntes is this grace geven, that I shuld preache amonge the gentyls the vnsearchable ryches of Christ, ⁹ and to make all men se what the felyshippe of the mistery is, which from the begynnynge of the worlde hath bene hid in God which made all thynges thorow Iesus Christ, ¹⁰ to the intent, that now vnto the rulars and powers in heven myght be knowen by the congregacion the many folde wisdome of god, ¹¹ accordinge to the eternall purpose, which he purposed in Christ Iesu oure lorde, ¹² by whom we are bolde to drawe nye in that trust, which we have by faith on him. ¹³ Wherfore I desire that ye faynt not because of my trybulacions for youre sakes : which is youre prayse.

¹⁴ For this cause I bowe my knees vnto the father of oure lorde Iesus Christ, ¹⁵ which is father over all that ys called father In heven and in erth, ¹⁶ that he wolde graunt you acordynge to the ryches of his glory, that ye maye be strenghted with myght by his sprete in the inner man, ¹⁷ that Christ maye dwell in youre hertes by fayth, that ye beynge roted and grounded in loue, ¹⁸ myght be able to comprehende with all sayntes, what ys that bredth and length, deepth and heyth : ¹⁹ and to knowe what is the love of Christ, which love passeth knowledge : that ye might be fulfilled with all manner of fulnes which commeth of God.

WICLIF—1380.

that worchith in us : [21] to hym be glorie in the chirche, and in crist ihesus in to alle the generaciouns of the worldis Amen.

4. THERFOR I bounden for the lord bisech ʒou, that ʒe walke worthili in the clepynge in which ʒe ben clepid, [2] with al mekenesse, and myldenesse : with pacience, supportinge eche other in charite, [3] bisie to kepe vnyte of spirit : in the boond of pees, [4] o bodi and o spirit : as ʒe ben clepid in oon hope of ʒoure clepinge, [5] o lord, o feith, o baptym, [6] o god, and fadir of alle, whiche is aboue alle *men*, and bi alle thingis and in us alle,

[7] but to eche of us grace is ʒouun : bi the mesure of the ʒeuynge of crist, [8] for whiche thing he seith, he stiynge an hiʒ : ledde caitifte caitif, he ʒaf ʒiftis to men,

[9] but what is it that he stied up : no but also that he cam doun first in to the lower partis of the erthe. [10] he it is that cam doun and that stied on alle heuenes : that he schulde fille alle thingis, [11] and he ʒaf summe apostlis : summe profetis, other euangelistis, other schepardis, and techers :

[12] to the ful endynge of seyntis, in to the werke of mynysteri : in to edificacioun of cristis bodi, [13] til we rennen alle in to vnyte of feith, and of knowynge of goddis sone : in to a perfiʒt man, aftir the mesure of age of the plente of crist, [14] that we be not now litil children mouynge as wawis : & be not borun aboute with eche wynde of techynge, in the weywardnesse of

TYNDALE—1534.

[20] Vnto him that is able to do excedynge aboundantly aboue all that we axe or thynke, accordynge to the power that worketh in us, [21] be prayse in the congregacion by Iesus Christ, thorowout all generacions from tyme to tyme Amen.

4. I therfore which am in bondes for the lordes sake, exhorte you, that ye walke worthy of the vocacion wherwith ye are called, [2] in all humblenes of mynde, and meknes, and longe sufferynge, forbearinge one another thorowe love, [3] and that ye be dyligent to kepe the vnitie of the sprete in the bonde of peace, [4] beynge one body, and one sprete, even as ye are called in one hope of youre callynge. [5] Let ther be but one lorde, one fayth, one baptim : [6] one god and father of all, which is aboue all, thorow all and in you all.

[7] Vnto every one of vs is geven grace acordinge to the measure of the gyft of christ. [8] Wherfore he sayth : He is gone vp an hye, and hath ledde captivitie captive, and hath geven gyftes vnto men. [9] That he ascended : what meaneth it, but that he also descended fyrst into the lowest parties of the erth ? [10] He that descended, is even the same also that ascended vp, even above all hevens, to fulfill all thinges.

[11] And the very same made some Apostles, some prophetes, some Evangelistes, some Sheperdes, some Teachers : [12] that the sainctes might have all thinges necessarie to worke and minister with all, to the edifyinge of the body of christ, [13] tyll we every one (in the vnitie of fayth, and knowledge of the sonne of god) growe vp vnto a parfayte man, after the measure of age of the fulnes of Christ. [14] That we hence forth be no moare chyldren, wauerynge and caryed with every

WICLIF—1380.

men, in sutil witte, to the disceyuynge of errour,

¹⁵ but do we truthe in charite and wexe in him bi alle thingis, that is crist oure hed, ¹⁶ of whom al the bodi sette to gidre, and bounden to gidre bi eche ioynture of vndir seruynge bi worchynge in to the mesure of eche membre : makith encreesynge of the bodi in to edificaciouns of it silf in charite. ¹⁷ therfor I seie and witnesse this thing in the lord : that ȝe walke not now, as hethen men walken in the vanyte of her wit, ¹⁸ that han vndirstondynge derkned with derknessis, and ben aliened fro the liif of god, bi ygnoraunce that is in hem : for the blyndenesse of her herte, ¹⁹ whiche dispeirynge bitoken hem silf to vnchastite : in to the worchynge of alle vnclennesse in coueitise, ²⁰ but ȝe han not so lernd crist : ²¹ if netheles ȝe herden hym, and ben tauȝte in hym : as is truthe in ihesus, ²² do ȝe awey bi the oold lyuynge, the oolde man that is corrupt bi the desiris of errour, ²³ And be ȝe renewid in the spirit of ȝoure soule : ²⁴ and clothe ȝe the newe man whiche is made aftir god in riȝtwisnesse and holynesse of truthe, ²⁵ for whiche thing ȝe putte aweye lesynge : and speke ȝe truthe eche man with his neiȝbore, for we ben membris eche to othir, ²⁶ be ȝe wrooth, and nyle ȝe do synne, the sunne falle not doun on ȝoure wraththe ; ²⁷ nyle ȝe ȝeue stede to the deuel, ²⁸ he that stal, now stele he not, but more traueile he in worchynge with hise hondis, that that is gode, that he haue wherof he schal ȝeue to the nedy,

TYNDALE—1534.

wynde of doctryne, by the wylynes of men and craftynes, wherby they laye a wayte for vs to deceave vs.

¹⁵ But let vs folowe the trueth in loue, and in all thynges growe in him which is the heed, that ys to saye Christ, ¹⁶ in whom all the body ys coupled and knet togedder in every ioynt wherwith one ministreth to another (accordinge to the operacion as every parte hath his measure) and increaseth the body, vnto the edyfyinge of it silfe in love. ¹⁷ This I saye therfore and testifie in the lorde, that ye hence forth walke not as other gentyls walke, in vanitie of their mynde, ¹⁸ blynded in their vnderstondynge, beynge straungers from the lyfe which is in god thorow the ignorancy that is in them, because of the blyndnes of their hertes : ¹⁹ which beynge past repentaunce, have geven them selves vnto wantannes, to worke all manner of vnclennes, even with gredynes. ²⁰ But ye have not so learned Christ, ²¹ if so be ye have hearde of him, and are taught in him, even as the trueth is in Iesu. ²² So then as concernynge the conversacion in tyme past, laye from you that olde man, which is corrupte thorow the deceavable lustes ²³ and be ye renued in the sprete of youre myndes, ²⁴ and put on that newe man, which after the ymage of God is shapen in ryghtewesnes and true holynes. ²⁵ Wherfore put awaye lyinge, and speake every man truth vnto his neghbour, for as moche as we are members one of another. ²⁶ Be angrye but synne not let not the sonne go doune apon youre wrathe ²⁷ nether geue place vnto the backbyter. ²⁸ Let him that stole, steale no moare, but let him rather laboure with his hondes some good thinge that he maye have to geve vnto him that nedeth.

WICLIF—1380.

29 eche yuel word go not of 30ure mouth, but if ony is good to the edificacioun of feith, that it 3eue grace to men that heren, 30 and nyle 3e make the holi goost of god sorie : in whiche 3e ben markid in the dai of redempcioun, 31 alle bittirnesse & wraththe and indignacioun, and crie and blasfemy, be takun aweye fro 30u, with al malice, 32 and be 3e to gidre benyngne, merciful, for3euynge to gidre as also god for3af to 30u in crist.

5. THERFOR be 3e folowers of god : as moost dereworthe sones, 2 and walke 3e in loue : as crist loued us, and 3af hym silf for us an offrynge and a sacrifice to god : in to the odour of swetnesse, 3 and fornycacioun and al vnclennes or auarice be not named among 30u : as it bicometh hooly men, 4 ethere filthe or foli speche or harlotrie that perteyneth not to profi3t : but more doynge of thankyngis, 5 for wite 3e this and vndirstonde that eche lecchour, or vnclene man or coueitous, that serueth to mawmetis : hath not eritage in the kyngdom of crist & of god,

6 no man disceyue 30u bi veyn wordis, for whi for these thingis : the wraththe of god cam on the sones of vnbileue, 7 therfor nyle 3e be made parteners of hem, 8 for 3e weren sumtyme derknessis, but now li3t in the lord, walke 3e as the sones of li3t : 9 for the fruit of li3t is in alle goodnes and ri3twisnesse and truthe, 10 and preue 3e what thing is wel plesynge to god, 11 & nyle 3e comyne to vnfruytuous werkis of derknessis : but more repreue 3e, 12 for what thingis ben don of hem in pryuy : it is foule 3e to speke, 13 and alle thingis that ben repreued of the li3t : ben opunly schewid, for al thing that

TYNDALE—1534.

29 Let no filthy communicacion procede out of youre mouthes : but that whych is good to edefye with all, when nede ys : that it maye have faveour with the hearers. 30 And greve not the holy sprete of God, by whome ye are sealed vnto the daye of redempcion. 31 Let all bitternes fearsnes and wrath, rorynge and cursyd speakynge, be put awaye from you, with all maliciousnes. 32 Be ye courteouse one to another, and mercifull, forgevynge one another, even as god for Christes sake forgave you.

5. BE ye folowers of god as dere children, 2 and walke in love even as Christ loved vs and gave him silfe for vs, an offerynge and a sacrifyce of a swete saver to god. 3 So that fornicacion and all vnclennes, or coveteousnes be not once named amonge you, as it be commeth saynctes : 4 nether filthynes, nether folishe talkyng, nether gestinge which are not comly : but rather gevynge of thankes 5 For this ye knowe, that no whormonger, other vnclene person, or coveteous person which is the worshipper of ymages, hath eny inheritaunce in the kyngdome of Christ and of God.
6 Let no man deceave you with vayne wordes. For thorow soche thinges commeth the wrath of God vpon the chyldren of vnbelefe. 7 Be not therfore companions with them. 8 Ye were once dercknes, but are now light in the Lorde.
Walke as chyldren of light. 9 For the frute of the sprete is in all goodnes, rightewesnes and trueth. 10 Accept that which is plesinge to the Lorde : 11 and have no fellishippe with the vnfrutfull workes of dercknes : but rather rebuke them. 12 For it is shame even to name those thinges which are done of them in secrete :

WICLIF—1380.

is schewid : is li3t, [14] for whiche thing he seith, rise thou that slepist rise up fro deeth, and crist schal li3tne thee,

[15] therfor britheren se 3e : hou warli 3e schuln go, not as vnwise men, [16] but as wise men a3enbiynge tyme, for the daies ben yuel, [17] therfor nyle 3e be made vnwise : but vndirstondynge, whiche is the wille of god, [18] and nyle 3e be drunken of wyne in whiche is leccherie : but be 3e fillid with the holi goost, [19] and speke 3e to 3ou silf in salmes & ympnes and spiritual songis syngynge, and seiynge salme in 3oure hertis to the lord, [20] euer more doynge thankyngis for alle thingis in the name of oure lord ihesus crist : to god and to the fadir, [21] be 3e suget to gidre in the drede of crist,

[22] wymmen be thei suget to her housbondis, as to the lord, [23] for the man is heed of the woman : as crist is heed of the chirche, he is sauyour of his bodi, [24] but as the chirche is suget to crist so and wymmen to her housbondis in alle thingis. [25] Men loue 3e 3oure wyues : as crist loued the chirche, and 3af hym silf for it, [26] to make it holi, and clensid it with the waischynge of watir, in the word of liif ? [27] to 3eue the chirche glorious to him silf, that it hadde no wemme ne reuelynge, or ony suche thing, but that it be holi & vndefoulid,

[28] so & men loue thei her wyues, as her owne bodies, he that loueth his wiif : loueth him silf, [29] for no man hatid euer his owne fleisch : but

TYNDALE—1534.

[13] but all thinges, when they are rebuked of the light, are manifest. For whatsoever is manifest, that same is light. [14] Wherfore he sayth : awake thou that slepest, and stond vp from deeth, and Christ shall geve the light. [15] Take hede therfore that ye walke circumspectly : not as foles : but as wyse [16] redemynge the tyme : for the dayes are evyll. [17] Wherfore, be ye not vnwyse, but vnderstonde what the will of the Lorde is, [18] and be not dronke with wyne, wherin is excesse : but be fulfilled with the sprete, [19] speakynge vnto youre selves in psalmes, and ymnes, and spretuall songes, synginge and makinge melodie to the Lorde in youre hertes, [20] gevinge thankes all wayes for all thinges vnto God the father, in the name of oure Lorde Iesu Christ : [21] submittinge youre selves one to another in the feare of God.

[22] Wemen submit youre selves vnto youre awne husbandes, as vnto the Lorde. [23] For the husbande is the wyves heed, even as Christ is the heed of the congregacion, and the same is the saveoure of the body. [24] Therfore as the congregacion is in subieccion to Christ, lykwyse let the wyves be in subieccion to their husbandes in all thinges. [25] Husbandes love youre wyves, even as Christ loved the congregacion, and gave him silfe for it, [26] to sanctifie it, and clensed it in the fountayne of water thorow the worde, [27] to make it vnto him selfe, a glorious congregacion with oute spot or wrynckle, or eny soche thinge : but that it shuld be holy and with out blame. [28] So ought men to love their wyves, as their awne bodyes. He that loveth his wyfe, loveth his sylfe. [29] For no man ever yet, hated his awne flesshe :

WICLIF—1380.

nurischith and fosterith it, as crist doith the chirche, ³⁰ and we ben membris of his bodi : of his fleisch, and of his boonys, ³¹ for this thing a man schal forsake his fadir and modir : and he schal drawe to his wiif, and thei schuln be tweyne in o fleisch, ³² this sacrament is greet, ȝe I seie in crist, and in the chirche, ³⁸ netheles ȝe alle, eche man loue his wiif as hym silf, & the wiif drede hir housbonde.

6. SONES obeisch ȝe to ȝoure fadir and modir in the lord, for this thing is riȝtful, ² onoure thou thi fadir and thi modir, that is the first maundement in biheest, ³ that it be wel to thee, & that thou be long lyuynge on erthe, ⁴ and fadris nyle ȝe terre ȝoure sones to wraththe : but nurische ȝe hem in the techynge and chastisynge of the lord. ⁵ Seruauntis obeische ȝe to fleischli lordis with drede and tremblynge in symplenesse of ȝoure herte as to crist, ⁶ not seruynge at the iȝe, as plesyng to men : but as seruauntis of crist, doynge the wille of god bi discrescioun ⁷ with good wille : seruynge as to the lord : and not as to men, witynge that eche man ⁸ what euer good thing he schal do : he schal resceyue this of the lord, whether seruaunt whether fre man, ⁹ & ȝe lordis to do the same thingis to hem : forȝeuynge manassis, witynge that bothe her lord and ȝoure is in heuenes : and the takynge of persouns is not anentis god.

¹⁰ here aftirward britheren be ȝe counfortide in the lord : and in the myȝt of his vertu, ¹¹ clothe ȝou with the armure of god, that ȝe moun stonde aȝens aspiyngis of the deuel, ¹² for why stryuynge is not to us aȝens fleisch and blood but aȝens the princis and potestis, aȝens gouernouris of

TYNDALE—1534.

but norissheth and cherisseth it even as the lorde doth the congregacion. ³⁰ For we are members of his body, of his flesshe, and of his bones. ³¹ For this cause shall a man leave father and mother, and shall continue with his wyfe, and two shalbe made one flesshe. ³² This is a great secrete, but I speake bitwene Christ and the congregacion. ³³ Neverthelesse do ye so that every one of you love his wyfe truely even as him silfe. And let the wyfe se that she feare her husbande.

6. CHYLDREN obey youre fathers and mothers in the Lorde : for so is it right. ² Honoure thy father and mother, that is the fyrst commaundement that hath eny promes, ³ that thou mayst be in good estate, and lyve longe on the erthe. ⁴ And ye fathers, move not your children to wrath : but bringe them vp with the norter and informacion of the Lorde. ⁵ Servauntes be obedient vnto youre carnall masters, with feare and trimblinge, in singlenes of youre hertes, as vnto Christ : ⁶ not with service in the eye sight, as men pleasars : but as the servauntes of Christ, doynge the will of God from the herte ⁷ with good will servinge the Lorde, and not men. ⁸ And remember that whatsoever good thinge eny man doeth, that shall he receave agayne of the Lorde, whether he be bonde or fre. ⁹ And ye masters, do even the same thinges vnto them, puttinge awaye threateninges : and remember that even youre master also is in heven, nether is ther eny respecte of person with him. ¹⁰ Finally my brethren, be stronge in the Lorde, and in the power of his myght. ¹¹ Put on the armour of God, that ye maye stonde stedfast agaynst the crafty assautes of the devyll. ¹² For we wrestle not agaynst flesshe and bloud : but agaynst rule, agaynst power, and agaynst worldly rulars of

WICLIF—1380.

the world of these derknessis, a3ens spiritual thingis of wickidnesse, in heuenli thingis,

[13] therfor take 3e the armure of god, that 3e moun a3enstonde in the yuel dai, and in alle thingis stonde parfi3t, [14] therfor stonde 3e and be 3e girde aboute 3oure leendis in sothfastnesse, and clothid with the haburioun of ri3twisnesse, [15] and 3oure feet schode in makynge redi of the gospel of pees, [16] in alle thingis take 3e the scheeld of feith in whiche 3e moun quenche alle the firi dartis of the worst, [17] and take 3e the helme of helthe, and the swerde of the goost, that is the word of god, [18] bi alle preier and bisech-ynge preie 3e al tyme in spirit : and in hym wakynge in al bisynesse, and bisechyng, for alle holi men [19] and for me, that word be 3ouun to me in openynge of my mouth : with trist to make knowun the mysterie of the gospel

[20] for whiche I am sette in message in a chayne, so that in it y be hardi to speke, as it bihoueth me, [21] and 3e wite, what thingis ben about me, what I do : titicus my moost dere brother, and trewe mynystre in the lord schal make alle thingis knowen to 3ou, [22] whom I sente to 3ou for this same thing : that 3e knowe what thingis ben aboute us, & that he com-forte 3oure hertis, [23] pees to britheren and charite with feith of god oure fadir, & of the lord ihesus crist, [24] grace with alle men : that louen oure lord ihesus crist in vncorrup-cioun Amen.

TYNDALE—1534.

the darckenes of this worlde, agaynst spretuall wickednes for hevenly thinges. [13] For this cause take vnto you the armoure of God, that ye maye be able to resist in the evyll daye, and to stonde perfect in all thinges. [14] Stonde therfore and youre loynes gyrd aboute with veritie, havinge on the brest plate of rightewesnes, [15] and shood with showes prepared by the gospell of peace. [16] Above all take to you the shelde of fayth, wherwith ye maye quenche all the fyrie dartes of the wicked. [17] And take the helmet of salvacion, and the swearde of the sprete, which is the worde of God. [18] And praye all wayes with all manner prayer and supplicacion : and that in the sprete : and watch thervnto with all instance and supplicacion for all saynctes, [19] and for me, that vttraunce maye be geven vnto me, that I maye open my mouth boldly, to vtter the secretes of the gospell, [20] wherof I am a messenger in bondes, that therin I maye speake frely, as it be-commeth me to speake.

[21] But that ye maye also knowe what condicion I am in and what I do, Tichicus my deare brother and fayth-full minister in the Lorde, shall shewe you of all thinges, [22] whom I sent vnto you for the same purpose, that ye myght knowe what case I stonde in, and that he myght comfort youre hertes. [23] Peace be with the brethren, and love with fayth, from God the father and from the Lorde Iesu Christ. [24] Grace be with all them which love oure lorde Iesus Christ in puernes. Amen.

APPENDIX

HEADS OF DOCTRINE
ADDITIONAL NOTES
VOCABULARY OF THE EPISTLE

HEADS OF DOCTRINE IN THE EPISTLE

THEOLOGY OF THE EPISTLE TO THE EPHESIANS

God the Father.
Christ.
The Holy Spirit.
Doctrine of the Holy Trinity.
The Will of God.
The World and Creation.
Man :—Body—Soul—Spirit.
The Heart.
The Unseen World.
Angels—Evil Powers.
The Devil.
Sin.
Predestination and Divine Purpose.
Redemption—Atonement.
Forgiveness.
Grace.
Peace—Righteousness—Truth.
Revelation.
Knowledge and Wisdom.
Faith—Hope—Love.
Light—Life.
Good Works.
Thanksgiving—Prayer.
The Church.
The Communion of Saints.
Christian Sacraments.
The Christian Ministry.

THEOLOGY OF THE EPISTLE TO THE EPHESIANS

God the Father. (i. 2.)

'The Father, from whom every family in heaven and on earth derives its name'—derives that which gives it a right to the title—and—that which truly makes it what it is. (iii. 14 and notes.)

'The Father of glory'—the source and the object of all revelation—'the God of our Lord Jesus Christ'—the God whom He acknowledges and at the same time reveals. (i. 17 and notes.)

'One God and Father of all (εἷς θεὸς καὶ πατὴρ πάντων), Who is over all and through all and in all.' (iv. 6.)

[The notes on this verse, as left by Dr Westcott, are probably to be regarded as incomplete.—More particularly the note on the words ὁ ἐπὶ πάντων καὶ διὰ πάντων καὶ ἐν πᾶσιν would probably have been longer, had the Commentary received the author's final revision, and would have contained some further explanation of the statement that in these words 'the reference is not to the Person of the Father, but to the triune God—.' Comparison of *c.* v. 20, cited in the previous note on εἷς θεὸς κ. πατὴρ πάντων, indicates that here, as there, God the Father is contemplated as revealed by, and approached through, 'our Lord Jesus Christ,' the 'one Lord' of iv. 5.]

Cf. *The Historic Faith*, Lect. IX. p. 52, 1904 ed.:—'Looking then to this trust in a common redemption, let us hold fast our belief in one Church, in one Body of Christ knit together by the rites which He Himself appointed, one in virtue of the One Spirit Who guides each member severally as He will, of the One Saviour Who fulfils Himself in many ways, of the *One God and Father of all, Who is over all and through all and in all.*'

See also *Gospel of St John*, p. 3, note on Jo. i. 1: 'Thus we are led to conceive that the Divine nature is essentially in the Son and at the same time that the Son can be regarded, according to that which is His peculiar characteristic, in relation to God as God. He is the "image of God" (εἰκὼν τοῦ θεοῦ) and not simply of the Father.'

'Giving thanks always for all things in the name of our Lord Jesus Christ to our God and Father' (τῷ θεῷ καὶ πατρί). (v. 20.)

Christ.

(*a*) 'Grace to you and peace from God our Father and our Lord Jesus Christ.' (i. 2.)

'Blessed be the God and Father of our Lord Jesus Christ.' (i. 3.)

'He chose us in Him before the foundation of the world—having fore-ordained us unto adoption as sons through Jesus Christ unto Himself.' (i. 4, 5.)

'The Son of God.' (iv. 13.)

(*b*) The Divine counsel—now revealed—according to His gracious purpose—'to sum up all things in the Christ, the things in the heaven and the things in the earth.' (i. 10.)

'In Him' and 'through Him' and 'unto Him' (Col. i. 16) were all things made.

He is the 'first-born,' 'the beginning' of all creation. Man was formed in His Image; and in Him men find their consummation. The forces of Nature, so to speak, are revealed to us in the Bible as gathered together and crowned in man, and the diversities of men as gathered together and crowned in the Son of Man; and so we are encouraged to look forward to the end, to a unity of which every imaginary unity on earth is a phantom or a symbol, when the Will of the Father shall be accomplished and He shall *sum up all things in Christ*—all things and not simply all persons—both *the things in the heavens and the things upon the earth.* (Eph. i. 10.)

We see, inscribed upon the age-long annals in which the prophetic history of the world and of humanity has been written, the sentence of inextinguishable hope 'From God unto God.' We see when we look back upon the manifestation of the Divine plan that the order which we trace—nature, humanity, Christ—corresponds inversely with our earnest expectation of its fulfilment. Christ, the sons of God, nature. We see, in short, while we thus regard the universe, as we must do, under the limitation of succession, from first to last a supreme harmony underlying all things—a holy unity which shall hereafter crown and fulfil creation as one revelation of Infinite Love.

(*Christus Consummator*, pp. 103, 108, 111.)

'One Lord.' (iv. 5.)

(*c*) 'His grace, which He freely bestowed upon us in the Beloved.' (i. 6.)

'In Whom we have our redemption through His blood, the forgiveness of our trespasses.' (i. 7.)

'In the blood of Christ' (ii. 13) the Gentiles, once afar, were made near.

'For He,'—uniting—and reconciling—Jew and Gentile—'in one body—to God—proclaimed Peace'—glad tidings of peace—'to all far and near.' (ii. 14—17.)

'Through Him we have our access—to the Father' (ii. 18)—'freedom of access' ($\pi\rho\sigma\alpha\gamma\omega\gamma\dot{\eta}\nu$) and 'freedom of address' ($\pi\alpha\rho\rho\eta\sigma\dot{\iota}\alpha\nu$)—and thus personal communion with God. (iii. 12.)

And an eternal purpose was thus fulfilled. The same Lord, Who is the stay of our faith and hope, is also the crown of the whole development of the world.

Through all the changes of time God prepared the way to the fulfilment of His counsel;—all creation and life tending to one end, now made manifest by the coming of the Son of God (iii. 11).

'Even as God also in Christ forgave—dealt graciously with ($\dot{\epsilon}\chi\alpha\rho\dot{\iota}\sigma\alpha\tau o$)—you.' (iv. 32.)

The thought of the lovingkindness of God in Christ leads St Paul to speak of the self-sacrifice of Christ.

'Walk in love, even as Christ also loved you and gave Himself up for you.' (v. 1.)

'Christ loved the Church and gave Himself up for it.' (v. 25.)

'The love of Christ which passeth knowledge' (iii. 19)—a love—answering to His very nature—including His love both for the Church and for the believer.

(d) The work 'which He wrought in the Christ, when He (1) raised Him from the dead and (2) set Him at His right hand in sovereign power. (i. 20 f.)

Exalted to the Heavens—invested with universal sovereignty (i. 22)—He is even now Head of His Church on earth (*ib.*)—and has exercised His sovereignty by the gift of His quickening grace. (ii. 1 f.)

The Christological passages in the Epistle [declare] that God is the God and Father of our Lord Jesus Christ (i. 3), that Jesus Christ is the Son of God (iv. 13), the Beloved (i. 6), the centre and source of blessing, sanctification, adoption, grace, redemption to believers (i. 3 ff.). One Lord (iv. 15), to Whom God has given universal dominion (i. 21 f.). He is the Head of the Church, His Body (i. 22 f., v. 23). In Him we were quickened, raised, set in heaven (iv. 5 f.), created 'for good works' (ii. 10). In Him the Gentiles are united with Israel in one body and reconciled

(ii. 13 f.).   He is the chief corner-stone of the spiritual sanctuary (ii. 20): in Him and in the Church God's glory is revealed through all the ages (ii. 21).   The Ascended Christ (i. 20) endows His Church (iv. 7 f.), which in and through Him reaches its completeness (iv. 16).   In Him (Jesus) is Truth (iv. 21): He communicates Himself to His people (iv. 24).   In Christ God forgives (iv. 32, cf. i. 7).   Christ gave Himself an offering and a sacrifice to God for us (v. 2), gave Himself for the Church, to sanctify it (v. 25), is to it as husband to wife (v. 32).   He is the source of light (v. 14), the saviour of the Body (v. 23).

Present to God before Creation (i. 4), He took flesh (ii. 5). By His Blood (i. 7) and Cross (ii. 6) He is to men the source of peace with God (i. 2, vi. 23).   The Ascended Christ fills all things (iv. 10); in Him is the fulfilment of God's purpose (iii. 11):—the future kingdom is the 'kingdom of Christ and God' (v. 5): 'the wealth of Christ' is unsearchable (iii. 8).   He dwells in the hearts of His people (iii. 17); our progress in the faith is measured by increasing knowledge of 'the Son of God' (iv. 13).

The Holy Spirit.

'Sealed with the Spirit of promise, the Holy Spirit.'   (i. 13.)

The 'spirit of wisdom and revelation' (cf. i. 17) is a gift of the Paraclete.

'In one Spirit.'   (ii. 18.)

The Spirit—the surrounding, sustaining power.

'Revealed to Christ's holy apostles and prophets in the Spirit.'
(iii. 5).

'That ye may be strengthened with power through His Spirit in the inward man.'   (iii. 16.)

'Giving diligence to keep the unity of the Spirit in the bond of peace.'   (iv. 3.)   [But see note *ad loc.*]

'One body and one spirit, even as also ye were called in one hope of your calling.'   (iv. 4.)

Here a *personal* reference to the Holy Spirit seems to be foreign to the context, though His work is recognised in the formation of the Church, and the informing spirit of the Christian Society is necessarily in fellowship with the Holy Spirit.

'And grieve not the Holy Spirit of God, in whom ye were sealed (cf. i. 13, Apoc. vii. 3 ff.) unto a day of redemption.'   (iv. 30.)

'The sword of the Spirit.'   (vi. 17.)

The sword which the Spirit provides and through which it acts.

With these Ephesian passages are to be compared

1 Thess. i. 5 ἐν πνεύματι ἁγίῳ καὶ πληροφορίᾳ πολλῇ.

1 Cor. vi. 11 ἐν τῷ πνεύματι τοῦ θεοῦ ἡμῶν.

„   xii. 3 ἐν πνεύματι θεοῦ λαλῶν—ἐν πν. ἁγίῳ.

„   13 ἐν ἑνὶ πνεύματι—πάντες εἰς ἓν σῶμα ἐβαπτίσθημεν.

2 Cor. vi. 6 ἐν πνεύματι ἁγίῳ, ἐν ἀγάπῃ ἀνυποκρίτῳ (cf. Gal. v. 22).

Rom. viii. 9 οὐκ ἐστὲ ἐν σαρκί, ἀλλ' ἐν πνεύματι, εἴπερ πνεῦμα θεοῦ οἰκεῖ ἐν ὑμῖν.

„   ix. 1, xiv. 17, xv. 16 ἐν πν. ἁγίῳ.

Phil. i. 27 ὅτι στήκετε ἐν ἑνὶ πνεύματι.

Col. i. 8 τὴν ὑμῶν ἀγάπην ἐν πνεύματι.

1 Tim. iii. 16 ἐδικαιώθη ἐν πνεύματι.

1 Pet. i. 12 τ. εὐαγγελισαμένων ὑμᾶς πνεύματι ἁγίῳ ἀποσταλέντι ἀπ' οὐρανοῦ.

Jude 20 ἐν πνεύματι ἁγίῳ προσευχόμενοι.

Apoc. i. 10, iv. 2, xvii. 3, xxi. 10.

Doctrine of the Holy Trinity.

By St John glimpses are opened to us of the absolute tri-personality of God. From the statement that 'God is Love' —Love involving a subject, and an object, and that which unites both—we gain the idea of a tri-personality in an Infinite Being. In the Unity of Him, Who is One, we acknowledge the Father, the Son, and the Holy Spirit, in the interrelation of Whom we can see Love fulfilled.

Other Apostolic writers, as St John elsewhere, deal with the Trinity revealed in the work of Redemption—the 'Economic Trinity.'

St Paul, in 1 Cor. xii. 4–6 had written : διαιρέσεις δὲ χαρισμάτων εἰσίν, τὸ δὲ αὐτὸ πνεῦμα· καὶ διαιρέσεις διακονιῶν εἰσίν, καὶ ὁ αὐτὸς κύριος· καὶ διαιρέσεις ἐνεργημάτων εἰσίν, ὁ δὲ αὐτὸς θεὸς ὁ ἐνεργῶν τὰ πάντα ἐν πᾶσιν, in 2 Cor. xiii. 13 ἡ χάρις τ. κυρίου ἡμῶν 'Ι. Χρ. κ. ἡ ἀγάπη τ. θεοῦ κ. ἡ κοινωνία τ. ἁγίου πνεύματος μετὰ πάντων ὑμῶν, and in Rom. xv. 30 παρακαλῶ δὲ ὑμᾶς, διὰ τ. κυρίου ἡμῶν 'Ι. Χρ. κ. διὰ τ. ἀγάπης τοῦ πνεύματος συναγωνίσασθαί μοι ἐν τ. προσευχαῖς ὑπὲρ ἐμοῦ πρὸς τ. θεόν.

In the Epistle to the Ephesians the doctrine of the Holy Trinity is brought into sight in more than one passage.

First in the Hymn of Praise (i. 3–14) which immediately

follows the opening salutation, the work of each Person of the
Holy Trinity is shewn :—of the Father (ὁ θεὸς καὶ πατὴρ τοῦ κυρίου
ἡμῶν Ἰ. Χρ.) in the eternal purpose of His love (*vv.* 4–6): of the
Son (τ. ἠγαπημένῳ) in His Incarnation (*vv.* 7–12): of the Holy
Spirit (τῷ πνεύματι τῆς ἐπαγγελίας τῷ ἁγίῳ) giving to believers the
pledge of a larger hope.

Then in the passage (ii. 11–22) describing the union of Jews
and Gentiles in one Divine Body, the doctrine of the Holy Trinity
is based upon facts of Christian experience, St Paul declaring the
message of Peace brought by Christ to be universally effective
'because (ii. 18) through Him (Christ Jesus) we have our access
in one Spirit (ἐν ἑνὶ πνεύματι) to the Father (πρὸς τὸν πατέρα).'

And in the parenthetical view (iv. 4–14) of the unity and
manifold endowment of the Christian Society there is reference
(*vv.* 4–6) to the Triune God, ruling, pervading, sustaining all ;
and the work is recognised of a Holy Spirit, of Christ Jesus our
Lord, and of 'One God and Father of all,' made known by the
Incarnate Son.

The Will of God.

(*a*) 'Paul by the will of God an apostle of Christ Jesus.' (i. 1.)

(*b*) 'According to the good pleasure of His Will' (i. 5):—
where we see God's Will as the expression of a gracious purpose.

'Having made known the mystery of His Will' (τὸ μυστήριον
τοῦ θελήματος αὐτοῦ):—that is, the Divine counsel now revealed,
which expressed His Will. (i. 9.)

'According to the purpose of Him, Who worketh all things
after the counsel of His Will.' (i. 11.)

[*v. inf.* on 'Predestination and Divine Purpose.']

(*c*) 'Doing *the will of God*—as servants of Christ.' (vi. 6.)

The phrase 'the will of the Lord (τ. κυρίου)' occurs at v. 17
διὰ τοῦτο μὴ γίνεσθε ἄφρονες, ἀλλὰ συνίετε τί τὸ θέλημα τοῦ κυρίου, —
and elsewhere only in Acts xxi. 14.

The World (ὁ κόσμος, ὁ αἰών).

Αἰών describes an age marked by a particular character: κόσμος
the whole constitution of things.

(*a*) 'He chose us in Him before the foundation of the world'
(πρὸ καταβολῆς κόσμου). (i. 4.)

The members of Christ are placed in an eternal relation to
Christ their Head—beyond time, before all time.

(b) 'Without God (ἄθεοι) in the world (ἐν τῷ κόσμῳ). (ii. 12.)
'The world'—the order of the physical universe.

(c) 'Not only in this world—or age—(ἐν τούτῳ τῷ αἰῶνι), but 'also in that which is to come.' (i. 21.)

'That in the ages to come (ἐν τοῖς αἰῶσιν τοῖς ἐπερχομένοις) He might shew the exceeding wealth of His grace.' (ii. 7.)

The Apostle looks forward to a succession of ages—units of the great age (iii. 21 εἰς πάσας τὰς γενεὰς τοῦ αἰῶνος τῶν αἰώνων).

(d) 'According to the course of this world' (κατὰ τὸν αἰῶνα τοῦ κόσμου τούτου). (ii. 2.)

Creation.

The phrase πρὸ καταβολῆς κόσμου is used also in 1 Pet. i. 20 of the work of Redemption in the Son (προεγνωσμένου μὲν πρὸ καταβολῆς κόσμου, φανερωθέντος δὲ ἐπ' ἐσχάτων τῶν χρόνων δι' ὑμᾶς) and in Jo. xvii. 24 of the love of the Father for the Son (ὅτι ἠγάπησάς με πρὸ καταβολῆς κόσμου). This is 'the only place where St Paul has it': but 'the idea of the designation of Messiah in the counsel of God before all worlds is expressed more or less distinctly in other language in Eph. i. 9, 10; iii. 9–11; Col. i. 26, 27; 2 Tim. i. 9; cf. 1 Cor. ii. 7; Rom. xvi. 25' (Hort on 1 Pet. i. 20). The phrase is not used in the LXX. or elsewhere than in the N.T.

[Hort, however, *l.c.* compares Plutarch, *Moral.* ii. 956 A τὸ ἐξ ἀρχῆς καὶ ἅμα τῇ πρώτῃ καταβολῇ τῶν ἀνθρώπων.]

The corresponding phrase ἀπὸ καταβολῆς κόσμου, likewise not found in the LXX., is used in Heb. iv. 3 (τῶν ἔργων ἀπὸ καταβολῆς κόσμου γενηθέντων), ix. 26; Apoc. xiii. 8; xvii. 8 (ὧν οὐ γέγραπται τὸ ὄνομα ἐπὶ τὸ βιβλίον τῆς ζωῆς ἀπὸ καταβολῆς κόσμου); Mt. xxv. 34; Lk. xi. 50.

'In God, Who created all things (τῷ τὰ πάντα κτίσαντι)' has been hidden (iii. 9) from all time (ἀπὸ τῶν αἰώνων) an eternal purpose now made manifest and fulfilled by the coming of the Incarnate Son :—in Him, in the Christ, it was the purpose and good pleasure of God to sum up all things (i. 9 f.)—'the things in the heavens and the things upon the earth.'

Man in himself.

Body. Soul. Spirit.

Man's body : v. 29 ὡς τὰ ἑαυτῶν σώματα.

Man's soul : vi. 7 ἐκ ψυχῆς μετ' εὐνοίας δουλεύοντες.

Man's spirit : the highest part of his nature, by which he holds fellowship with God.

ii. 22. 'The Lord, in Whom ye also are builded together for a dwelling-place of God *in the spirit* (ἐν πνεύματι)' : cf. iii. 5.

iv. 23. 'And that ye be renewed *in the spirit of your mind* (τῷ πνεύματι τοῦ νοὸς ὑμῶν).

Contrast iv. 17 ἐν ματαιότητι τοῦ νοὸς αὐτῶν (of the Gentiles) and Col. ii. 18.

v. 18. 'But *be filled in spirit* (πληροῦσθε ἐν πνεύματι) : where ἐν πνεύματι is opposed to ἐν σαρκί.

vi. 18. 'Praying at every season *in spirit*.'

The Heart (καρδία).

(*a*) 'To the end that, having the eyes of your heart (τοὺς ὀφθαλμοὺς τῆς καρδίας) enlightened, ye may know....' (i. 18.)

(*b*) The heart—the seat of character.
'That Christ may dwell in your hearts through faith.' (iii. 17.)
'Because of the hardening of their heart.' (iv. 18.)
'In singleness (ἁπλότητι) of heart (τῆς καρδίας ὑμῶν) as unto Christ'—*i.e.* without hypocrisy, as unto Christ, Who knoweth the hearts of men. (vi. 5.) So Col. iii. 22.

(*c*) 'Singing and making melody with your heart to the Lord.' (v. 19.)

The outward music to be accompanied by the inward music of the heart. So Col. iii. 16.

'That He may comfort (παρακαλέσῃ) your hearts.' So Col. iv. 8, ii. 2. (vi. 22.)

In Col. iii. 15 ἡ εἰρήνη τοῦ χριστοῦ βραβευέτω ἐν ταῖς καρδίαις ὑμῶν.

The Unseen World.

Of the relation of Man to the Unseen St Paul speaks

(*a*) in earlier Epistles:

1 Cor. ii. 9 f.: 'things which eye saw not and ear heard not.' (Is. lxiv. 4.)

2 Cor. iv. 18: 'while we look not at the things which are seen (τὰ βλεπόμενα), but at the things which are not seen (τὰ μὴ βλεπόμενα): for the things which are seen are temporal; but the things which are not seen are eternal.'

Rom. i. 20: 'For the invisible things (τὰ—ἀόρατα) of Him from the Creation of the world are clearly seen (καθορᾶται), being understood (νοούμενα) by means of the things that are made (τοῖς ποιήμασιν), even His everlasting power and Godhead.'

(b) in the Colossian and Ephesian Epistles.

Col. i. 15 ff.: 'things visible and things invisible—thrones or dominions or principalities or powers.'

Eph. i. 3 : 'The God and Father of our Lord Jesus Christ, Who blessed us in all spiritual blessing in the heavenly order (ὁ εὐλογήσας ἡμᾶς ἐν πάσῃ εὐλογίᾳ πνευματικῇ ἐν τοῖς ἐπουρανίοις) in Christ.'

Eph. i. 20 : 'when He raised Him from the dead and made Him to sit at His right hand in the heavenly order (ἐν τ. ἐπουρανίοις).'

Eph. ii 6 : 'raised us up with Him and made us to sit with Him in the heavenly order.'

Eph. iii. 10 : 'to the intent that now to the principalities and the powers in the heavenly order may be made known through the church the manifold wisdom of God.'

Eph. vi. 12 : 'our wrestling is—against the principalities, against the powers, against the world-rulers of this darkness, against the spiritual forces of wickedness in the heavenly order.'

Cf. Phil. iii. 20 ἡμῶν γὰρ τὸ πολίτευμα ἐν οὐρανοῖς ὑπάρχει, ἐξ οὖ καὶ σωτῆρα ἀπεκδεχόμεθα κ.τ.λ. and 2 Tim. iv. 18 ῥύσεταί με ὁ κύριος ἀπὸ παντὸς ἔργου πονηροῦ, καὶ σώσει εἰς τὴν βασιλείαν αὐτοῦ τὴν ἐπουράνιον.

The expression τὰ ἐπουράνια [v. Add. Note, p. 152] is characteristic of the Epistle to the Ephesians.

At iii. 10 (v. supr.) we have reference to intelligences of the heavenly order, to whom 'the manifold wisdom of God' should be made known through the Church; while at ii. 2 is indicated organisation of powers of evil (κατὰ τὸν ἄρχοντα τῆς ἐξουσίας τοῦ ἀέρος), to whose assaults we are exposed, and at vi. 12 man's connexion with another—a spiritual—order, in which work powers of evil (πρὸς τὰ πνευματικὰ τῆς πονηρίας ἐν τ. ἐπουρανίοις).

The devil (ὁ διάβολος).

(a) 'Nor give place to the devil' (iv. 27)—'the devil'—the Tempter [to whom] unchecked passion leaves open the way.

(b) 'That ye may be able to stand against the wiles of the devil'—'the devil'—the supreme leader of the powers of evil.

The *word* does not occur elsewhere in St Paul except in the Pastoral Epistles (1 Tim. iii. 6, 7; 2 Tim. ii. 26).

(c) The title 'the Evil One' (ὁ πονηρός), occurring in Mt. v. 37, vi. 13, xiii. 19, 38; Jo. xvii. 15, and characteristic of the First Epistle of St John (ii. 13 f., iii. 12, v. 18 f.), is found Eph. vi. 16,—'the shield of faith,' whereby the Christian is 'able to quench all the darts of *the evil one* that are set on fire,'—but not elsewhere in St Paul.

(*d*) 'The prince of the power of the air' (ii. 2)—a temporary and contingent power—is the 'god of this world' (ὁ θεὸς τοῦ αἰῶνος τούτου) of 2 Cor. iv. 4—a personal power [to whom] is subordinate the spirit which is active (τοῦ ἐνεργοῦντος) in the sons of disobedience—'the prince (or ruler) of this world' (ὁ ἄρχων τοῦ κόσμου τούτου) of Jo. xii. 31, xiv. 30, xvi. 11, [is] the one great enemy [of whom] all other enemies are, as it were, instruments.

Sin.

'You, when you were dead through your trespasses (παραπτώμασιν) and sins (ἁμαρτίαις), wherein aforetime ye walked according to the course of this world.......' (ii. 1.)

'Us, when we were dead through our trespasses, God quickened together with the Christ.' (ii. 5.)

'In Whom we have our redemption through His blood, the forgiveness of our trespasses.' (i. 7.)

'Be ye angry and sin not.' (iv. 26, from Ps. iv. 5, LXX.)

[See Addit. Note.]

Predestination and Divine Purpose.

'Having foreordained (προορίσας) us unto adoption as sons through Jesus Christ unto Himself.' (i. 5.)

'In Whom we were also made God's portion, having been foreordained' (προορισθέντες, praedestinati) to occupy this position 'according to the purpose of Him, Who worketh all things after the counsel of His Will.' (i. 11.)

The word προορίζειν occurring in these two verses of the Ephesian Letter, had previously been used by St Paul in two passages only of his Epistles, namely once in the First Epistle to the Corinthians (1 Cor. ii. 7) 'But we speak a wisdom of God in a mystery, the wisdom which has been hidden, which God *fore-ordained* (προώρισεν) before the ages unto our glory,' and twice, in one context, in the Epistle to the Romans (Rom. viii. 29 f.) 'Because whom He foreknew (προέγνω), them He also *foreordained* (προώρισεν, praedestinavit) to be conformed to the image of His Son, that He might be the firstborn among many brethren : and whom He *foreordained*, them He also called : and whom He called, them He also justified; and whom He justified, them He also glorified.'

It occurs in no other Epistle.

But it is used in Acts iv. 28: 'to do whatsoever Thy hand and Thy counsel (ἡ χείρ σου κ. ἡ βουλὴ) foreordained to come to pass.' The word πρόθεσις, used of 'purpose' generally Acts xi. 23, xxvii. 13, 2 Tim. iii. 10, is found (in connexion with προορίζειν) of God's eternal purpose in both the Roman and the Ephesian Epistles, and in no other excepting the Second Epistle to Timothy: and the verb προέθετο likewise occurs only in Romans and Ephesians.

In Rom. iii. 25 St Paul writes (ἐν Χρ. Ι.) ὃν προέθετο ὁ θεὸς ἱλαστήριον, 'Whom God set forth (R.V. marg. purposed) to be a propitiation': in viii. 28 'And we know that to them that love God all things work together for good, even to them that are called according to His purpose (τοῖς κατὰ πρόθεσιν κλητοῖς οὖσιν)': and in ix. 11 'that the purpose of God according to election (ἡ κατ᾽ ἐκλογὴν πρόθεσις τοῦ θεοῦ) might stand.'

Here in the Epistle to the Ephesians we have i. 9 'according to His good pleasure, which He purposed (προέθετο) in Him,' i.e. in accordance with the gracious purpose which He set before Himself to accomplish in Him (sc. ἐν τῷ ἠγαπημένῳ): then i. 11 'foreordained according to the purpose (κατὰ πρόθεσιν) of Him, Who worketh all things after the counsel of His will (κατὰ τ. βουλὴν τοῦ θελήματος αὐτοῦ): and lastly iii. 11 'according to a purpose of the ages (κατὰ πρόθεσιν τῶν αἰώνων) which He accomplished in the Christ, even Jesus our Lord.'

The word βουλή is used of God in Luke vii. 30, Acts ii. 23, xiii. 36, xx. 27, and in Heb. vi. 17 τὸ ἀμετάθετον τῆς βουλῆς αὐτοῦ, as well as in the passage in Acts above quoted (iv. 28) where it occurs with the verb προώρισε, and in the verse of this Epistle just cited (i. 11) in connexion with πρόθεσις. The 'counsel' referred to in the Epistle to the Hebrews was that of bringing universal blessing to men through the seed of Abraham: and so in this Epistle it is through Israel in old time, and now through the Christian Church, a new Israel, that the counsel of God is wrought out for the world.

Βούλεσθαι is used of the Divine purpose in 1 Cor. xii. 11 πάντα δὲ ταῦτα ἐνεργεῖ τὸ ἓν καὶ τὸ αὐτὸ πνεῦμα, διαιροῦν ἰδίᾳ ἑκάστῳ καθὼς βούλεται, Ja. i. 18, 2 Pet. iii. 9, Mt. xi. 27 (= Lk. x. 22), as well as in Heb. vi. 17 περισσότερον βουλόμενος ὁ θεὸς ἐπιδεῖξαι κ.τ.λ.

(*v. supr.*), where, as elsewhere, it regards a purpose with respect to something else—*God being minded to shew more abundantly* to man's apprehension—and not (like θέλειν) a feeling in respect of the person 'willing' himself (cf. Col. i. 27 οἷς ἠθέλησεν ὁ θεὸς γνωρίσαι, τί τὸ πλοῦτος τῆς δόξης τ. μυστηρίου τούτου ἐν τ. ἔθνεσιν). The verb (βούλεσθαι) does not occur in the Ephesian Epistle.

The Will of God is not arbitrary, but guided by a settled counsel (βουλή).

The revelation of this Divine counsel—or 'mystery'—is thus the expression of His Will.

To the fulfilment of His counsel God prepared the way through all the changes of time unceasingly, and now at length the steps towards it can be seen.

By the coming of the Son of God an eternal purpose was fulfilled—a purpose eternally designed, if only lately disclosed.

With the Father purpose and work are one.

Historically, the great counsel of God, interrupted by man's sin, was accomplished by the redemptive work of Christ.

Redemption.

The words connected with the idea of 'redemption,' found in the New Testament (for their use in the LXX. see Add. Note on Heb. ix. 12, *Hebrews*, p. 295) are λύτρον, ἀντίλυτρον, λυτροῦσθαι, λυτρωτής, λύτρωσις, ἀπολύτρωσις.

Of these λύτρον alone occurs in the Gospels, and only in Mt. xx. 28 (= Mk. x. 45) δοῦναι τὴν ψυχὴν αὐτοῦ λύτρον ἀντὶ πολλῶν : while λυτρωτής is found only in Acts vii. 35, of Moses.

With the exception of the single occurrence of λύτρον in the Synoptic narrative, the whole group of words is confined to the Epistles of St Paul and writings (including 1 Peter) which are strongly coloured by his language. They are entirely absent from the writings of St John.

Of one or other of the three words λυτροῦσθαι, 'to redeem,' λύτρωσις, ἀπολύτρωσις, we have the following instances :

(*a*) In earlier Epistles of St Paul :

1 Cor. i. 30 : 'in Christ Jesus, Who was made unto us (ἐγενήθη) wisdom from God, both righteousness and sanctification and *redemption*' (ἀπολύτρωσις).

Rom. iii. 24 : 'being justified freely by His grace through the *redemption* that is in Christ Jesus' (διὰ τῆς ἀπολυτρώσεως τῆς ἐν Χριστῷ Ἰησοῦ).

Rom. viii. 23 : 'the redemption of the body' (τ. ἀπολύτρωσιν τ. σώματος).

(b) In the Epistles of the Captivity :

Col. i. 14, and here in Eph. i. 7 : 'in Whom we have our *redemption*' (ἐν ᾧ ἔχομεν τὴν ἀπολύτρωσιν)—the redemption which is the outcome of our faith—a redemption wrought by Christ 'through His blood' (*v.* 7)—'our redemption which is nothing less than the remission of our sins' (Lightfoot, *Colossians*, p. 137).

Eph. i. 14 : 'unto the *redemption* of God's own possession' (εἰς ἀπολύτρωσιν τῆς περιποιήσεως)—this, and the consequent 'praise of His glory,' being the final cause of the work of Christ and of the Mission of the Spirit (*v.* 13).

Eph. iv. 30 : 'in Whom ye were sealed unto a day of *redemption*' (εἰς ἡμέραν ἀπολυτρώσεως).

The 'redemption' is of captives from bondage—from the bondage of sin.

(c) In the Pastoral Epistles λυτροῦσθαι occurs once: Tit. ii. 14 ἵνα λυτρώσηται ἡμᾶς ἀπὸ πάσης ἀνομίας, and ἀντίλυτρον once, 1 Tim. ii. 6 Χριστὸς Ἰησοῦς, ὁ δοὺς ἑαυτὸν ἀντίλυτρον ὑπὲρ πάντων.

(d) In 1 Peter i. 18 οὐ φθαρτοῖς...ἐλυτρώθητε ἐκ τῆς ματαίας ὑμῶν ἀναστροφῆς...ἀλλὰ τιμίῳ αἵματι—we have some 'words—apparently founded on Is. lii. 3 (οὐ μετὰ ἀργυρίου λυτρωθήσεσθε)': while 'the idea of the whole passage is—deliverance through the payment of a costly ransom by another' (Hort, *ad loc.*).

(e) In the Epistle to the Hebrews we have λύτρωσις at ix. 12 αἰωνίαν λύτρωσιν εὑράμενος and ἀπολύτρωσις at ix. 15 εἰς ἀπολύτρωσιν τῶν ἐπὶ τῇ πρώτῃ διαθήκῃ παραβάσεων as well as at xi. 35 οὐ προσδεξάμενοι τ. ἀπολύτρωσιν.

Christ 'entered in once for all into the Holy place, having obtained *an eternal Redemption*'—an eternal, not a temporary, deliverance for His people (οὐχ ἑαυτῷ, πῶς γὰρ ὁ ἀναμάρτητος ; ἀλλὰ τῷ λαῷ αὐτοῦ. Oecumenius). He is Mediator of a New Covenant, that a death having taken place '*for redemption from* the transgressions that were under the first covenant they that have been called may receive' what had been promised—an eternal inheritance.

(f) In the Synoptic Gospels, besides 'our Lord's saying in Mt. xx. 28 (= Mk. x. 45) "The Son of Man came not to be ministered unto, but to minister καὶ δοῦναι τὴν ψυχὴν αὐτοῦ λύτρον (a ransom) ἀντὶ πολλῶν "—the starting-point of this and all similar language in the Epistles' (Hort on ἐλυτρώθητε, 1 Pet. i. 18)— we have

Lk. i. 68 : ἐποίησεν λύτρωσιν τῷ λαῷ αὐτοῦ (from LXX. of Ps. cxi. 9 λύτρωσιν ἀπέστειλεν τῷ λαῷ αὐτοῦ).

Lk. ii. 38 : τοῖς προσδεχομένοις λύτρωσιν Ἰσραήλ.

Lk. xxi. 28 : ἀρχομένων δὲ τούτων γίνεσθαι ἀνακύψατε κ. ἐπάρατε τ. κεφαλὰς ὑμῶν, διότι ἐγγίζει ἡ ἀπολύτρωσις ὑμῶν.

Lk. xxiv. 21 : ἠλπίζομεν ὅτι αὐτός ἐστιν ὁ μέλλων λυτροῦσθαι τὸν Ἰσραήλ.

In the Epistle to the Ephesians *Redemption* (ἀπολύτρωσις) is presented

(1) as wrought by Christ, Whose 'blood' in relation to the redemption and salvation of men, appears at i. 7 as that *by means of* which (διὰ τοῦ αἵματος αὐτοῦ) and at ii. 13 as that *in* which (ἐν τ. αἵμ. τ. χ.), as in an encompassing life and atmosphere, the believer is ransomed and lives;

(2) as made known by God to Christians in its universal power and as commensurate with the whole of Creation (i. 10, 21 : cf. Col. i. 20, Phil. ii. 9, 10);

(3) in connexion with the gift of the Holy Spirit, whereby believers are 'sealed' (i. 13, iv. 30).

Further :

(4) in Eph. i. 7 'the Apostle defines τὴν ἀπολύτρωσιν as τὴν ἄφεσιν τῶν παραπτωμάτων' (Lightfoot on Col. i. 14). The past with its results is that which holds us in bondage. Not unlikely that some false interpretation of 'redemption' as a deliverance from the fetters of physical law caused the Apostle to emphasise its moral nature.

Atonement (Reconciliation).

In earlier Epistles (1 Cor., 2 Cor., Rom.) the words καταλ- λάσσειν and καταλλαγὴ are used in connexion with the death of Christ.

'The reconciliation is always represented as made to the Father. The reconciler is sometimes the Father Himself (2 Cor. v. 18, 19 ἐκ τοῦ θεοῦ τοῦ καταλλάξαντος ἡμᾶς ἑαυτῷ διὰ Χριστοῦ... θεὸς ἦν ἐν Χριστῷ κόσμον καταλλάσσων ἑαυτῷ), sometimes the Son (Rom. v. 10, 11 : cf. Eph. ii. 16).' (Lightfoot on Col. i. 20.)

'In the Colossian and Ephesian Epistles the double compound ἀποκαταλλάσσειν is used...in place of the usual καταλλάσσειν. It may be compared with ἀποκατάστασις, Acts iii. 21.—The word ἀποκαταλλάσσειν corresponds to ἀπηλλοτριωμένους... implying a *restitution* to a state from which they had fallen, or which was potentially theirs, or for which they were destined.' (*id. ib.*) As in Col. i. 19-22: 'For it was the good pleasure of the Father that in Him should all the fulness dwell, and through Him to *reconcile* (ἀποκαταλλάξαι) all things unto Himself, having made peace (εἰρηνοποιήσας) through the blood of His cross; through Him—whether things upon the earth or things in the heavens;—and you, though ye were once estranged, and enemies in your mind in (the midst of) your evil works; yet now *hath he reconciled* (ἀποκατήλλαξεν: v.l. ἀποκατηλλάγητε) in the body of His flesh through death,'—so here in Eph. ii. 16, the *reconciliation* of humanity to God by the Cross is expressed in the words καὶ ἀποκαταλλάξῃ...τῷ θεῷ διὰ τοῦ σταυροῦ, and Christ, Who thus Himself *is* our Peace (*v.* 14 αὐτὸς γάρ ἐστιν ἡ εἰρήνη ἡμῶν), and, after His victory, 'proclaimed peace' (*v.* 17) to all far and near, [is presented as] uniting and reconciling both Jew and Gentile in one body to God, abolishing the enmity, the twofold enmity, which the Fall had brought to men and the Law had fixed and revealed between themselves and towards God.

Forgiveness.

'In Whom we have our redemption through His blood, the forgiveness of our trespasses' (τὴν ἄφεσιν τῶν παραπτωμάτων). (i. 7.)

The word ἄφεσις occurs in the Pauline Epistles only here and in the parallel Col. i. 14 (τ. ἄφεσιν τ. ἁμαρτιῶν).

The verb ἀφιέναι in the sense of 'forgive' is not found in St Paul's writings except (Rom. iv. 7) in a quotation from LXX. Ps. xxxii. 1.

But the verb χαρίζεσθαι, 'deal graciously with' is used by St Paul in eight Epistles (1 Cor., 2 Cor., Gal., Rom., Phil., Col., Eph. and Philem.) and in some of these passages (as in Lk. vii. 42 f.) 'forgiving' is [the bounty] specially [intended], namely in 2 Cor. ii. 7 ὥστε τοὐναντίον ὑμᾶς χαρίσασθαι, 10 ᾧ δέ τι χαρίζεσθε, κἀγώ· καὶ γὰρ ἐγὼ ὃ κεχάρισμαι, εἴ τι κεχάρισμαι, δι' ὑμᾶς ἐν προσώπῳ Χριστοῦ, in Col. ii. 13 χαρισάμενος ἡμῖν πάντα τὰ παραπτώματα, *ib.* iii. 13 χαριζόμενοι ἑαυτοῖς.. καθὼς καὶ ὁ κύριος ἐχαρίσατο ὑμῖν οὕτως καὶ ὑμεῖς; and in this Epistle twice in the verse iv. 32 : 'Be ye kind one to another, tender-hearted, *forgiving each other even as God also in Christ forgave* (ἐχαρίσατο) you.'

Grace (χάρις).

(a)   The grace—the free and bounteous goodness—of God.

'Grace to you and peace from God our Father and the Lord Jesus Christ.' (i. 2.)

'To the praise of the glory of His grace, which He freely bestowed upon us in the Beloved, in Whom we have our redemption through His blood, forgiveness of our trespasses, according to the riches of His grace.' (i. 7.)

'The exceeding riches of His grace.' (ii. 8.)

'By grace have ye been saved' (ii. 5)—'by grace—through faith' (v. 7).

(b)   Apostleship—a stewardship of the Grace of God.

'The administration (stewardship) of the grace of God which was given me to you-ward." (iii. 2.)

'The gift of the grace of God that was given to me.' (iii. 7.)

'To me—was this grace given.' (v. 8.)

(c)   Specific grace given to each member of the Christian Society.

'But to each one of us was the grace given according to the measure of the gift of Christ.' (iv. 7.)

'Grace be with all them that love the Lord Jesus Christ in incorruption.' (vi. 24.)

That which is elsewhere a Divine prerogative is, however, once (in iv. 29) attributed to human speech : 'no corrupt speech …but whatever is good…that it may give grace to them that hear.'

Peace (εἰρήνη).

'Grace to you and *peace* from God our Father and the Lord Jesus Christ' (i. 2)—'*Peace* to the brethren—from God the Father and the Lord Jesus Christ' (vi. 23).

Cf. Phil. iv. 7 'the peace of God,' Col. iii. 15 'the peace of Christ.'

The Divine gift of peace which (Jo. xiv. 27) the Lord in departing left behind as His bequest to His disciples (εἰρήνην ἀφίημι ὑμῖν, εἰρήνην τὴν ἐμὴν δίδωμι ὑμῖν)—the realised confidence of faith and fellowship with God—attends the Church during the period of gradual revelation.

'For He'—He Himself and no other—'is our Peace' reconciling Jews and Gentiles in Himself—and both thus united in one body—to God (ii. 14). Thus 'making peace' (v. 15) He (v. 17) proclaimed 'Peace to all.'

'In preparedness of' this 'Gospel of Peace' Christian warriors will stand. (vi. 15.)

'To keep the unity of the spirit in the bond of peace.' (iv. 3.)

Righteousness (δικαιοσύνη).

The fulfilment of duties to others.

'The new man which has been created after God in *righteousness* and holiness of the truth.' (iv. 24.)

'For the fruit of light is—is shewn—in all goodness and *righteousness* and truth.' (v. 9.) Cf. Is. xi. 5, xxxii. 17.

'The breastplate of righteousness' (vi. 14)—righteousness, which guards the heart.

So Isaiah lix. 17 'And he put on righteousness as a breastplate' and Wisd. v. 19 'He shall put on righteousness (as) a breastplate' (ἐνδύσεται θώρακα δικαιοσύνην).

Truth (ἀλήθεια).

(a) 'The word—the message—of *the truth*—the Gospel of your salvation.' (i. 13.)

For τὸν λόγον τῆς ἀληθείας cf. 2 Tim. ii. 15.

(b) 'The new man, which hath been created after God *in righteousness and holiness of the truth.*' (iv. 24.)

(c) 'Wherefore putting away falsehood (τὸ ψεῦδος) speak ye *truth* each one with his neighbour.' (iv. 25.)

From Zech. viii. 16 sq. λαλεῖτε ἀλήθειαν ἕκαστος πρὸς τὸν πλησίον αὐτοῦ, ἀλήθειαν καὶ κρίμα εἰρηνικὸν κρίνατε ἐν ταῖς πύλαις ὑμῶν, καὶ ἕκαστος τὴν κακίαν τοῦ πλησίον αὐτοῦ μὴ λογίζεσθε ἐν ταῖς καρδίαις ὑμῶν, καὶ ὅρκον ψευδῆ μὴ ἀγαπᾶτε.

(d) 'For the fruit of light is—is shewn—in all—in every form of—goodness and righteousness and *truth.*' (v. 9.)

In Phil. i. 11 καρπὸν δικαιοσύνης (cf. Amos vi. 12, Prov. xi. 30, Ja. iii. 18 καρπὸς δὲ δικαιοσύνης ἐν εἰρήνῃ σπείρεται τοῖς ποιοῦσιν εἰρήνην), 'righteousness in Christ [is regarded as] in its very nature fruitful: it is indeed the condition of bearing fruit' (Lightfoot ad loc.)

(e) 'Stand ye therefore,—having girded your loins with *truth*' (vi. 14): truth—sincerity—the stay of the Christian character.

Revelation (ἀποκάλυψις).

'a spirit of wisdom and revelation' (i. 17).

'by revelation was made known unto me the mystery' (iii. 2).

'as now it was revealed (ἀπεκαλύφθη) unto His holy apostles and prophets' (iii. 5).

Knowledge and Wisdom.

The importance of Knowledge and Wisdom appears from the passages of the Epistle in which one or more of the words γνῶσις, ἐπίγνωσις [*v.* note on i. 17], σοφία, φρόνησις, or corresponding verbs or adjectives occur.

In addition to, and through the accomplishment of, his office of evangelising the Gentiles it was given to St Paul 'to bring to light what is the dispensation of the mystery which from all ages has been hid in God Who created all things—hid, I say, to the intent that now to the principalities and the powers in the heavenly order *may be made known* (γνωρίσθη) through the Church *the manifold wisdom* (ἡ πολυποίκιλος σοφία) of God' (iii. 9 f.).

And his thanksgiving (i. 16) for the faith of the readers of the Epistle is combined with prayer 'that the God of our Lord Jesus Christ, the Father of glory, may give unto you a spirit of *wisdom and revelation in knowledge* (ἐπιγνώσει) *of Him*' (i. 17).

Ἐπίγνωσις recurs iv. 13 : 'till we all attain unto the unity of the faith and of the *knowledge* of the Son of God' (*v. inf. s.v. Faith*).

'In all wisdom and prudence' (i. 8) is the phrase (parallel to Col. i. 9 ἐν πάσῃ σοφίᾳ κ. συνέσει πνευματικῇ) describing the manner in which the grace of God was manifested in those on whom it was bestowed. Wisdom deals with principles : prudence with action. Through these gifts believers are enabled to trace (*a*) the connexion between successive revelations which He made 'by divers portions and in divers manners,' all leading up to the final revelation in His Son, (*β*) the complete and harmonious fulfilment of His earthly work in His Birth, Death, Resurrection, and Ascension, followed by the descent of the Holy Spirit, (γ) the signs of God's counsel in the training of 'the nations' and in the slow realisation of manifold lessons of the Gospel in post-Christian history. Φρόνησις occurs in N.T. only here and Lk. i. 17; but φρόνιμος frequently, viz. (*a*) in Pauline Epistles : 1 Cor. iv. 10, x. 15, 2 Cor. xi. 19, Rom. xi. 25, xii. 16; (*b*) in Synoptic Gospels, Mt. vii. 24, x. 16, xxii. 45, xxv. 2, 4, 8, 9, Lk. xii. 42, xvi. 8.

While in i. 16 ff. the Apostle's prayer began with the thought of personal enlightenment, his prayer in iii. 16 ff. begins with the thought of personal strengthening, but a strengthening which shall issue in fuller knowledge (iii. 18 f.) 'that ye may be strong to *apprehend* (καταλαβέσθαι) with all the saints what is the breadth and length and height and depth, *to know* (γνῶναι) the love of Christ which passeth *knowledge*, that ye may be filled with all the fulness of God.' [Γνῶσις here only in Eph.; Col. ii. 3, Phil. iii. 8.]

The other passages are :

v. 15 : 'Look therefore carefully how ye walk, not as unwise, but as wise (σόφοι).'

v. 17 : 'For this reason be not foolish, but *understand* (συνίετε) what the will of the Lord is.'

vi. 8 f.: '*Knowing* (εἰδότες) that whatever good thing each man doeth, that shall he receive again from the Lord.'

'*Knowing* that their Master and yours is in heaven.'

[See Additional Note on 'Intellectual claims and gifts of the Gospel.']

Faith (πίστις).

(*a*)   'The faith which is among you (καθ' ὑμᾶς) in (*i.e.* grounded and resting in) the Lord Jesus.'   (i. 15.)

(*b*)   'The faith shewn to all the saints' (*ib.*)—the practical expression of (*a*).

(*c*)   'Saved through faith (διὰ πίστεως)—by God's grace (τῇ χάριτι)—not of yourselves—not of works.'   (ii. 8.)

(*d*)   'Freedom of address and access to God through our faith in Christ (διὰ τῆς πίστεως αὐτοῦ).'   (iii. 12.)

(*e*)   'That Christ through faith (διὰ τῆς πίστεως) may dwell in your hearts.'   (iii. 17.)

(*f*)   'One faith' (μία πίστις)—in its objective sense.   (iv. 5.)

(*g*)   'The unity of the faith (τὴν ἑνότητα τῆς πίστεως) and of the knowledge (κ. τῆς ἐπιγνώσεως) of the Son of God'—the Son of God being the object of both—faith and knowledge.   (iv. 13.)
Faith is a principle of knowledge. The special object of Faith is a Divine Person made known to men and recognised by them.

(*h*)   'The shield of faith' (τ. θυρεὸν τῆς πίστεως).   (vi. 16.)

(*i*)   'Peace to the brethren and love with faith'—faith being the condition of appropriating God's gifts of peace and love.   (vi. 23.)

Hope (ἐλπίς).

'*The hope* of His calling'—the hope—kindled and sustained in us by the fact that God has called us to His presence—the call being a Divine invitation. (i. 18.)

'Even as also ye were called in *one hope* of your calling'—the hope being [here] coincident with the calling. (iv. 4.)

'Apart from Christ—strangers to the covenants of the promise —having no hope (ἐλπίδα μὴ ἔχοντες) and without God in the world'—face to face with the problems of nature and life, but without Him in Whose wisdom and righteousness and love they could find rest and hope.

Love (ἀγάπη).

(*a*)   'God—for *His great love* (διὰ τὴν πολλὴν ἀγάπην αὐτοῦ) wherewith He loved us—quickened us.' (ii. 4.)

(*b*)   'And to know *the love of Christ* which passeth knowledge' —"including both His love for the Church and for the believer." (iii. 19.)

(*c*)   'Peace be unto the brethren *and love* with faith from God the Father and Lord Jesus Christ'—peace and love being God's gifts and faith the condition of appropriating them. (vi. 23.)

(*d*)   'Be ye—imitators of God, as beloved children, and *walk in love*, even as Christ also loved you' (v. 1, 2)—the love of Christians answering to the love of Christ: cf. Jo. xiii. 34 ἐντολὴν καινὴν δίδωμι ὑμῖν, ἵνα ἀγαπᾶτε ἀλλήλους, καθὼς ἠγάπησα ὑμᾶς, ἵνα καὶ ὑμεῖς ἀγαπᾶτε ἀλλήλους (and xv. 12, and 1 Jo. iii. 16 sq.).

(*e*)   'That we should be holy and without blemish before Him *in love*'—love, which they have appropriated as God's great gift. (i. 4.)

(*f*)   'Forbearing one another *in love*.' (iv. 2.)

(*g*)   'Living the truth in love' (veritatem facientes): 'Christ —from Whom all the Body, fitly framed and knit together, through every contact, according to the effective working of that which is supplied in due measure by each several part, maketh for itself the growth of the Body, unto the building up of itself *in love*.' (iv. 15, 16.)

Truth and Love (2 Jo. 3) describe an intellectual harmony

and a moral harmony; and the two correspond with each other according to their subject-matter.

Love is truth in human action; and truth is love in regard to the order of things.

(*h*) 'Rooted and grounded in love.' Love—the source of growth and the stay of endurance.

Light (φῶς).

(*a*) 'For ye were once darkness (σκότος), but now are light (φῶς) in the Lord (ἐν Κυρίῳ)—light in fellowship with Him, Who is the Light of the World.' (v. 8.) Cf. v. 14, ἐπιφαύσει σοι ὁ χριστός.

'Walk as children of light.' (*ib.*)

'For the fruit of light is in all goodness and righteousness and truth.' (v. 9.)

On the other hand, 'with the unfruitful works of darkness' the Christians must 'have no fellowship.' (v. 11.)

Darkness perishes in the presence of light:

'All things, when they are shewn in their true nature by the light are made manifest:—for everything which is made manifest is light (φῶς ἐστίν).' (v. 13.)

(*b*) 'Having the eyes of your heart enlightened (πεφωτισμένους).' (i. 18.)

(*c*) In addition to preaching the Gospel to the Gentiles, St Paul was called 'to bring to light (φωτίσαι) what is the dispensation of the mystery which from all ages hath been hid in God.' (iii. 9.)

Life (ζωή).

'Alienated from the life of God (τῆς ζωῆς τοῦ θεοῦ) —that life which answers to the nature of God and which He communicates to His children. (iv. 18.)

'But God—even when we were dead through our trespasses quickened us together with (συνεζωοποίησε) the Christ.' (ii. 5, 6.)

The word θάνατος, 'death,' is not found in the Epistle. But νεκροὺς τ. παραπτώμασιν occurs ii. 1, 5 (*v. supr.*): while ἐκ νεκρῶν occurs i. 20, and ἐκ τῶν νεκρῶν (v. 14) in the Hymn 'Awake, thou that sleepest, and arise from the dead.'

Of the future resurrection of men nothing is [directly] said in the Epistle.

Good Works.

'For it is His workmanship we are, created in Christ Jesus for good works (ἐπὶ ἔργοις ἀγαθοῖς) which God afore prepared that in them we should walk.' (ii. 10.)

In Gal. v. 22, 23 'love, joy, peace, longsuffering, kindness, goodness, faithfulness (πίστις), meekness, temperance' are as 'fruit of the Spirit' contrasted with 'the works of the flesh.'

Here in Ephesians 'the fruit of light,' in contrast with 'the fruitless works of darkness' (v. 10), is said to be shewn 'in all goodness and righteousness and truth' (v. 9)—a classification of moral duties marking our obligation to self, our neighbour, God; while in another place (iv. 2) humility (ταπεινοφροσύνη), meekness (πραΰτης), and longsuffering (μακροθυμία) are named as graces, which Christians are bound to cultivate, 'forbearing one another in love' and living 'in the bond of peace.' Kindness (χρηστότης), joined with these in Col. iii. 12, stands in Ephesians (ii. 7) as a Divine attribute. But in iv. 32 St Paul speaks of the duty of Christians to be to one another kind (χρηστοί) and tender-hearted (εὔσπλαγχνοι), and thus (v. 1) 'imitators of God.'

Thanksgiving (εὐχαριστία).

'But rather giving of thanks' (v. 4)—our duty—recognising the signs of God's love in every good thing.

'Giving thanks (εὐχαριστοῦντες) always for all things in the name of our Lord Jesus Christ to our God and Father.' (v. 20.)

So St Paul's opening Hymn of Praise (i. 3—14) is followed by thanksgiving for the faith of the Ephesians :—

'For this cause I also, having heard of the faith which is among you in the Lord Jesus, and which ye shew toward all the saints, cease not to give thanks for you.'

Prayer (προσευχή).

(*a*) 'In all prayer (προσευχῆς) and supplication (δεήσεως), praying (προσευχόμενοι) at every season in spirit'—not in form or in word only, but in that part of our being through which we hold communion with God—and also 'watching thereunto (εἰς αὐτὸ ἀγρυπνοῦντες) in all perseverance and supplication for all the saints.'

(*b*) So at i. 16 in the Epistle—after thanksgiving Prayer :—
'making mention (of you) in my prayers (ἐπὶ τῶν προσευχῶν μου).

The Church.

(*a*) 'And He gave Him to be Head over all things to the Church, which is His body, the fulness of Him Who reaches His fulness through all things in all.' (i. 22 f.)

(*b*) 'That now to the principalities and the powers in the heavenly order may be made known through the Church the manifold wisdom of God.' (iii. 10.)

(*c*) 'To Him be the glory in the Church and in Christ Jesus unto all the generations of the age of the ages.' (iii. 21.)

(*d*) 'For a husband is head of the wife, as Christ also is Head of the Church, being Himself Saviour of the body. But as the Church is subject to Christ, so let the wives be to their husbands in everything. Husbands, love your wives even as Christ also loved the Church and gave Himself up for it;......that He might present the Church to Himself a glorious Church, not having spot or wrinkle or any such thing.......' (v. 23—27.)

Cf. v. 29, 'nourisheth and cherisheth it, even as Christ the Church.'

'But I speak looking to Christ and to the Church.' (v. 32.)

The Communion of Saints.

'That we should be holy (ἁγίους) and without blemish before Him in love.' (i. 4.)

'The faith which is among you in the Lord Jesus and which ye shew to all the saints.' (i. 15.)

'But ye are fellow-citizens (συμπολῖται) with the saints.' (ii. 19.)

'Which in other generations was not made known unto the sons of men as now it was revealed unto His holy apostles and prophets in the Spirit—that the Gentiles are fellow-partakers of the promise in Christ Jesus.' (iii. 5.)

'That being rooted and grounded in love ye may be strong enough to apprehend *with all the saints* what is the breadth......' (iii. 17 f.)

'With a view to the perfecting of the saints for a work of ministry.' (iv. 12.)

'Watching thereunto in all perseverance and supplication for all the saints.' (vi. 18.)

Christian Sacraments—
Baptism.

'One Lord, one Faith, one *Baptism*' (ἐν βάπτισμα). (iv. 5.)
'That He might sanctify it (the Church), having cleansed it by the bath of water accompanied by a confession of faith ('with a word': ἐν ῥήματι).' (v. 26.)

The ῥῆμα—the Baptismal Confession—was, there can be little doubt, the simple creed that 'Jesus is Lord' (Rom. x. 9 ἐὰν ὁμολογήσῃς τὸ ῥῆμα ἐν τῷ στόματί σου ὅτι κύριος Ἰησοῦς).

'Detrahe verbum et quid est aqua nisi aqua? Accedit verbum ad elementum et fit sacramentum.' (Aug. *in Joh.* lxxx. 3, on John xv. 3.)

[v. Add. Note on 'The Sacrament of Baptism.']

Holy Communion.

To the Sacrament of Holy Communion there is no reference in the Epistle.

The Christian Ministry.

Mention is made (in iv. 11) of (*a*) 'apostles,' (*b*) 'prophets,' (*c*) 'evangelists,' (*d*) 'pastors and teachers.'

But, while there is thus evidence of specialisation of functions, there is no sign in the Epistle of the existence of any outward organisation or ecclesiastical hierarchy.

[See Additional Notes on
    'The Christian Society and the Apostolic Ministry.'
    'The Church in the Epistle to the Ephesians.'
    'Prophets of the New Covenant.']

ADDITIONAL NOTES

On the expression τὰ ἐπουράνια.

Ἐνέργεια and ἐνεργεῖν in the N. T.

Wisdom and Revelation.

Intellectual claims and gifts of the Gospel.

The Sacrament of Baptism.

On 'Sin' in the Pauline Epistles.

The Fall of Man.

The Kingdom of God,—Kingdom of Christ.

The Christian Society, and the Apostolic Ministry.

'The Church' in the Epistle to the Ephesians.

Use of the word ἀποκάλυψις in the N. T.

On the use of the term μυστήριον in the N. T.

On the phrases ἐν Χριστῷ, ἐν Χριστῷ Ἰησοῦ, ἐν τῷ χριστῷ.

The expression τὰ πάντα.

Ἡ δόξα in the Epistle to the Ephesians.

Words in the N. T. denoting Resurrection or Raising from
    Death: ἐγείρειν, ἀναστῆναι, ἀνάστασις.

On the meaning of κυβεία (Eph. iv. 14).

Spiritual Powers.

Use of κατὰ c. acc. in the Epistle to the Ephesians.

Use of the phrase ἐν σαρκί.

Prophets of the New Covenant.

Ruskin on Eph. iv. 17 and on Conflict with Evil.

'The world, the flesh, and the devil.'

Use of the Old Testament in the Epistle.

On the expression τὰ ἐπουράνια.

The adjective ἐπουράνιος [apart from the particular phrase τὰ ἐπουράνια] is used

(a) by *St Paul*:

    1 Cor. xv. 40. 'celestial bodies.'

            48. 'the heavenly (man)......the heavenly (men).'

)(χοϊκὸς...χοϊκοί.

            49. 'the likeness of the heavenly (man).'

    Phil. ii. 10. 'of things in the heaven (ἐπουρανίων) and on the earth and under the earth.')(ἐπιγείων and καταχθονίων.

    2 Tim. iv. 18. κ. σώσει εἰς τὴν βασιλείαν αὐτοῦ τὴν ἐπουράνιον.

(β) by *other writers of the N. T.*:

    Mt. xviii. 35. A v. l. for οὐράνιος.

    Heb. iii. 1. κλήσεως ἐπουρανίου.

         vi. 4. τ. δωρεᾶς τ. ἐπουρανίου.

         xi. 16. κρείττονος (sc. πατρίδος)...τοῦτ' ἔστιν ἐπουρανίου.

         xii. 22. Ἰερουσαλὴμ ἐπουρανίῳ.

The phrase τὰ ἐπουράνια is used

(a) by *St Paul*: in the Epistle to the Ephesians only, viz.

    Eph. i. 3. ὁ εὐλογήσας ἡμᾶς—ἐν τ. ἐπουρανίοις.

         20. κ. καθίσας ἐν δεξιᾷ αὐτοῦ ἐν τ. ἐπ.

       ii. 6. συνήγειρεν κ. συνεκάθισεν ἐν τ. ἐπ.

      iii. 10. γνωρισθῇ—τ. ἀρχαῖς κ. τ. ἐξουσίαις ἐν τ. ἐπ.

      vi. 12. πρὸς τὰ πνευματικὰ τ. πονηρίας ἐν τ. ἐπ.

(β) in the Epistle to the Hebrews:

    viii. 5. ὑποδείγματι κ. σκιᾷ—τ. ἐπουρανίων.

    ix. 23. αὐτὰ—τὰ ἐπουράνια.

(γ) once by *St John*: Jo. iii. 12. ἐὰν εἴπω ὑμῖν τὰ ἐπουράνια.

The adj. οὐράνιος is used only by St Matthew and St Luke.

    Mt. v. 48.

      vi. 14, 26, 32.

      xv. 13.   In every case with ὁ πατήρ (μου v. ὑμῶν).

      xviii. 35.

      xxiii. 9.

    Lk. ii. 13. πλῆθος στρατιᾶς οὐρανίου.

    Acts xxv. 19. τῇ οὐρανίῳ ὀπτασίᾳ.

The phrase ἐν οὐρανοῖς or ἐν (once ἐπὶ) τοῖς οὐρανοῖς is used

(a) by St Paul in

2 Cor. v. 1.   αἰώνιον ἐν τ. οὐρανοῖς.

Phil. iii. 20.   ἡμῶν—τὸ πολίτευμα ἐν οὐρανοῖς ὑπάρχει.

Col. i. 5.   διὰ τ. ἐλπίδα τ. ἀποκειμένην ὑμῖν ἐν τοῖς οὐρανοῖς.

16.   τὰ ἐν τοῖς οὐρανοῖς κ. τὰ ἐπὶ τ. γῆς.

20.   εἴτε τὰ ἐπὶ τ. γῆς εἴτε τὰ ἐν τοῖς οὐρανοῖς.

Eph. i. 10.   τὰ ἐπὶ τοῖς οὐρανοῖς κ. τὰ ἐπὶ τῆς γῆς.

iii. 15.   ἐν οὐρανοῖς καὶ ἐπὶ γῆς.

vi. 9.   κ. αὐτῶν κ. ὑμῶν ὁ κύριός ἐστιν ἐν οὐρανοῖς.

(b) by St Peter : 1 Pet. i. 4.

,, the author of 'Hebrews': viii. 1, ix. 23, xii. 23.

,, St Matthew and St Mark, passim : they also use the sing.
ἐν (τῷ) οὐρανῷ.

,, St Luke once only (x. 20) : ἐγράφη ἐν τ. οὐρανοῖς.

In the Apocalypse and in the Gospel of St John only the singular is found.

The general idea of the phrase—which is not found in the LXX.—is that of 'the heavenly order,' the scene of the spiritual life with the realities which belong to it.

In Hebr. ix. 23 the phrase αὐτὰ τὰ ἐπουράνια expresses those things, answering to the sanctuary with all its furniture, which have their proper sphere in the heavenly order ; while at viii. 5 it means the realities of heaven generally, of which the Tabernacle presented the ideas in figures—copy and shadow.

By faith τὰ ἐπουράνια are in one sense realised on earth. τὰ ἡμέτερα (says Theophylact, following Chrysostom) ἐπουράνια· ὅταν γὰρ μηδὲν ἐπίγειον, ἀλλὰ πάντα πνευματικὰ ἐν τοῖς μυστηρίοις κ.τ.λ......ὅταν ἡμῶν τὸ πολίτευμα ἐν οὐρανοῖς ὑπάρχει, πῶς οὐκ ἐπουράνια τὰ καθ' ἡμᾶς;

So Primasius : cælestia, id est spiritalia quæ in veritate modo in ecclesia celebrantur.

In Jo. iii. 12, τὰ ἐπουράνια is used of the 'heavenly' in contrast with the 'earthly' elements of the Lord's teaching—of those truths which belong to the higher order—which are in heaven and are brought down thence to earth as they can become to men.

As used in Ephesians, the phrase is peculiar to the Epistle (cf., however, ὁ ἐπουράνιος, sc. ἄνθρωπος, of 1 Cor. xv. 48 f.), and describes the supra-mundane, supra-sensual, eternal order—'the spiritual world' generally, and not, as elsewhere, something which belongs to the spiritual order.

On the other hand, 'the metaphor of the heavenly citizenship' (Lightfoot on Phil. i. 27) occurs once in the Epistle to the Ephesians (ii. 19, συμπολῖται τ. ἁγίων) and twice in the Epistle to the Philippians, i. 27, πολιτεύεσθε ἀξίως τοῦ εὐαγγελίου τοῦ χριστοῦ (cf. Polyc. § 5), and iii. 20, where, after telling us that 'our citizenship is even now (ὑπάρχει) in heaven'—'for the Kingdom of Heaven is a present Kingdom' (Lightfoot ad loc.)—St Paul goes on to say, 'from heaven hereafter we look in patient hope (ἀπεκδεχόμεθα) for a deliverer' (id.)—'even the Lord Jesus Christ, who shall change the fashion of this body of our humiliation to be conformable to (σύμμορφον)—"take the abiding form of"—the body of His glory: "for such is the working of the mighty power whereby He is able to subdue all things alike unto Himself"' (id. ib.).

This universal sovereignty of the Lord Jesus Christ is again dwelt upon, in the same Epistle, at ii. 10, ἵνα ἐν τῷ ὀνόματι Ἰησοῦ πᾶν γόνυ κάμψῃ ἐπουρανίων καὶ ἐπιγείων καὶ καταχθονίων (cf. Ignat. Trall. § 9, βλεπόντων τῶν ἐπουρανίων κ. ἐπιγείων κ. ὑποχθονίων, and Polyc. Phil. § 2, ᾧ ὑπετάγη τὰ πάντα, ἐπουράνια καὶ ἐπίγεια), where ἐπουράνια, as contrasted with ἐπίγεια and καταχθόνια, is (acc. to Lightfoot) not to be explained of one of three 'different classes of intelligent beings' (e.g. of 'angels')—'limitation to intelligent beings is not required by the expression'—but rather of 'all created things in heaven' (Lightfoot, Philippians, p. 110 f.).

Man's life is partly on earth, partly in the 'heavenly' realm.

There is one life which finds expression in many forms, but that life is greater, deeper than all.

This vast life, which reaches through all time, is in its nature beyond time.

In itself the spiritual life—of which the Communion of Saints is the foretaste—belongs to another order.

Yet—eternal life is here. Our blessings and our struggles lie now 'in the heavenly realms' (ἐν τοῖς ἐπουρανίοις).

The power by which we grasp the unseen—the eternal—is Faith.

ἐνέργεια and ἐνεργεῖν in the N.T.

In the New Testament ἐνέργεια and ἐνεργεῖν are characteristically used of moral and spiritual working, whether Divine (Eph. i. 19, iii. 7, Col. i. 29, ii. 12, Phil. iii. 21) or Satanic (2 Th. ii. 9, 11).

(a) *Usage of St Paul.*

1 Th. ii. 13. λόγον θεοῦ, ὃς καὶ ἐνεργεῖται ἐν ὑμῖν τοῖς πιστεύουσιν.

2 Th. ii. 7. τὸ γὰρ μυστήριον ἤδη ἐνεργεῖται τῆς ἀνομίας.

9. οὗ ἐστιν ἡ παρουσία κατ᾽ ἐνέργειαν τοῦ σατανᾶ.

11. πέμπει αὐτοῖς ὁ θεὸς ἐνέργειαν πλάνης.

1 Cor. xii. 6. καὶ διαιρέσεις ἐνεργημάτων εἰσίν, ὁ δὲ αὐτὸς θεὸς ὁ ἐνεργῶν τὰ πάντα ἐν πᾶσιν. (Cf. v. 10 ἄλλῳ δὲ ἐνεργήματα δυνάμεων.)

1 Cor. xii. 11. πάντα δὲ ταῦτα ἐνεργεῖ τὸ ἓν καὶ τὸ αὐτὸ πνεῦμα.

2 Cor. i. 6. ὑπὲρ τῆς ὑμῶν παρακλήσεως τῆς ἐνεργουμένης ἐν ὑπομονῇ τῶν αὐτῶν παθημάτων.

2 Cor. iv. 12. ὥστε ὁ θάνατος ἐν ἡμῖν ἐνεργεῖται, ἡ δὲ ζωὴ ἐν ὑμῖν.

Gal. ii. 8. ὁ γὰρ ἐνεργήσας Πέτρῳ εἰς ἀποστολὴν τῆς περιτομῆς ἐνήργησεν ἐμοὶ εἰς τὰ ἔθνη.

Gal. iii. 5. ὁ οὖν ἐπιχορηγῶν ὑμῖν τὸ πνεῦμα καὶ ἐνεργῶν δυνάμεις ἐν ὑμῖν.

Gal. v. 6. πίστις δι᾽ ἀγάπης ἐνεργουμένη.

Rom. vii. 5. τὰ παθήματα τῶν ἁμαρτιῶν τὰ διὰ τοῦ νόμου ἐνηργεῖτο ἐν τοῖς μέλεσιν ἡμῶν.

Phil. ii. 13. ὁ θεὸς—ὁ ἐνεργῶν ἐν ὑμῖν καὶ τὸ θέλειν καὶ τὸ ἐνεργεῖν ὑπὲρ τῆς εὐδοκίας.

Phil. iii. 21. κατὰ τὴν ἐνέργειαν τοῦ δύνασθαι αὐτὸν καὶ ὑποτάξαι αὐτῷ τὰ πάντα.

Col. i. 29. κατὰ τὴν ἐνέργειαν αὐτοῦ τὴν ἐνεργουμένην ἐν ἐμοὶ ἐν δυνάμει.

Col. ii. 12. διὰ τῆς πίστεως τῆς ἐνεργείας τοῦ θεοῦ τοῦ ἐγείραντος αὐτὸν ἐκ νεκρῶν.

Eph. i. 11. τοῦ τὰ πάντα ἐνεργοῦντος κατὰ τὴν βουλὴν τοῦ θελήματος αὐτοῦ.

Eph. i. 19 f. κατὰ τὴν ἐνέργειαν τοῦ κράτους τῆς ἰσχύος αὐτοῦ, ἣν ἐνήργηκεν ἐν τῷ χριστῷ ἐγείρας αὐτὸν ἐκ νεκρῶν.

Eph. ii. 2. τοῦ πνεύματος τοῦ νῦν ἐνεργοῦντος ἐν τοῖς υἱοῖς τῆς ἀπειθίας.

Eph. iii. 7.   κατὰ τὴν ἐνέργειαν τῆς δυνάμεως.
    20.   κατὰ τὴν δύναμιν τὴν ἐνεργουμένην ἐν ἡμῖν.
  iv. 16.   τῆς ἐπιχορηγίας κατ᾽ ἐνέργειαν.

(β)   *Use in non-Pauline Books.*

Ja. v. 16.   δέησις δικαίου ἐνεργουμένη.
Mt. xiv. 2.   αἱ δυνάμεις ἐνεργοῦσιν ἐν αὐτῷ.   ‖ Mk. vi. 14.

According to Lightfoot (on Gal. v. 6) ἐνεργεῖσθαι 'is never passive in St Paul,' but 'the Spirit of God or the spirit of evil ἐνεργεῖ; the human agent or the human mind ἐνεργεῖται' (middle). The adjective ἐνεργής occurs 1 Cor. xvi. 6, Philem. 6, and Hebr. iv. 12.

Divine working is denoted in

1 Th. ii. 13.   'Ye accepted it not as the word of men, but, as it is in truth, the word of God, which also *worketh* in you that believe.'

1 Cor. xii. 6.   'And there are diversities of workings (ἐνεργη-μάτων), but the same God, who worketh (ὁ ἐνεργῶν) all things in all.' (Cf. *v.* 10 'workings of miracles.')

ib. v. 11.   'But all these *worketh* the one and the same Spirit, dividing to each one severally even as He will.'

2 Cor. i. 6.   'Or whether we be comforted, it is for your comfort, which *worketh* (ἐνεργεῖται) in the patient enduring of the same sufferings which we also suffer.'

Gal. ii. 8.   'For He that *wrought* for Peter (ὁ ἐνεργήσας Πέτρῳ) unto the apostleship of the circumcision wrought for me also unto the Gentiles.'

Gal. iii. 5.   'He that supplieth to you the Spirit and worketh miracles among you.'

Phil. ii. 13.   'God it is Who "*worketh* in you both to will and to *work*" in fulfilment of His good pleasure' ('His benevolent purpose,' Lightfoot, *q.v.*):

where 'the θέλειν and the ἐνεργεῖν correspond respectively to the "gratia praeveniens" and the "gratia cooperans" of a later theology' (Lightfoot *ad loc.*).

Phil. iii. 21.   'According to *the working* (*i.e.* by 'the exercise of the power,' Lightfoot *ad loc.*) whereby He is able also to subject all things unto Himself':

where, as in 'Eph. i. 19 τὴν ἐνέργειαν τοῦ κράτους τῆς ἰσχύος αὐτοῦ [and iii. 7 τὴν ἐνέργειαν τῆς δυνάμεως αὐτοῦ], the expression τὴν ἐνέργειαν τοῦ δύνασθαι involves the common antithesis of δύναμις and ἐνέργεια᾽ (Lightfoot ad loc.).

Col. ii. 12. 'Through your faith *in the working* (τῆς ἐνεργείας) of God, Who raised Him from the dead.'

Eph. i. 11. 'Of Him, Who *worketh* all things after the counsel of His Will':

where the verb ἐνεργεῖν brings out the idea of the personal power which is operative rather than the result produced.

ib. v. 19. 'According to the working of the might of His strength.'

Eph. iii. 7. 'Whereof I became a minister according to the working of His power.'

ib. v. 20. 'According to the power that worketh in us.'

[where, as in Col. i. 29, 1 Th. ii. 13, and Gal. v. 6, the middle ἐνεργουμένην is used, apparently because there is a human agent transmitting the Divine energy.]

On the other hand *Satanic* working is denoted in

2 Th. ii. 7. 'For the mystery of lawlessness doth already work.'

ib. v. 9. 'Whose coming is according to the working of Satan with all power and signs and wonders of falsehood.' Cf. *v.* 11.

Eph. ii. 2. 'Of the spirit that now worketh in the sons of disobedience.'

Of the Ephesian passages [the first (i. 11) recalls] 1 Cor. xii. 6, 11 (*v. supr.*); [the next (i. 19) refers to] the active exercise of the power of God in the exaltation of Christ, [a third (iii. 7) shews how] the continuous working of His Power in the Apostle was a determining condition of his ministry, [another (iii. 20) tells us] that His power working in believers generally is the measure of that which He does. In ii. 2 the Ephesians [are reminded that] resisting the Will of God lays 'the sons of disobedience' open to the working of a personal power of evil. [For the meaning of κατ᾽ ἐνεργείαν in iv. 16, *v.* note *ad loc.*].

Wisdom and Revelation (Eph. i. 17).

'These Ephesian Christians had already received Divine illumination, or they would not have been Christians at all; but Paul prayed that the Divine Spirit who dwelt in them would make their vision clearer, keener, stronger, that the Divine power and love and greatness might be revealed to them far more fully. And perhaps in these days in which men are making such rapid discoveries in inferior provinces of thought, discoveries so fascinating and so exciting as to rival in interest, even for Christian men, the manifestation of God in Christ, there is exceptional need for the Church to pray that God would grant it "*a spirit of wisdom and revelation*"; if He were to answer that prayer, we should no longer be dazzled by the knowledge which relates to "things seen and temporal," it would be outshone by the transcendent glory of "things unseen and eternal."'

(Dale: *The Epistle to the Ephesians: Its Doctrine and Ethics*, p. 133.)

'By the inspiration which was granted to Jewish prophets they saw in the history of their nation—as their uninspired contemporaries did not see—the Divine laws which the history illustrated.

.   .   .   .

The inspiration which was granted to apostles enabled them to discover what was already contained in the life, teaching, death and resurrection of the Lord Jesus Christ. Special revelations were given to them: .   .   .   . but the main substance of what they knew about God and the Divine method of human redemption they discovered in the history and teaching of Christ. Their inspiration enabled them to see what that revelation of God really meant.   .   .   . The great *revelation* was made in Christ; the *inspiration* of the apostles enabled them to see the truths and laws which the revelation contained.

.   .   .   .

And so the "spirit of wisdom" may also be called the "spirit of revelation"; for until the spirit of wisdom is given, the revelation is unintelligible. It becomes an actual revelation when it is understood.

To the apostles inspiration was given in an exceptional measure. They were appointed by the Lord Jesus Christ to lay the foundations of the Christian Church. They had authority to teach all nations in

His name.   Later ages were to learn His mind from their lips . . .
. . . .
But in kind the inspiration of the apostles was the same as that which
St Paul prayed might be granted to the Christians at Ephesus, the
same as that which we ourselves may hope to receive from God.'

(id. ib. pp. 135 ff.)

'Perhaps the safest description of the gift which is promised to
all Christians is that which is contained in the text.   It is the "spirit
of wisdom."   It is not a blind impulse, resulting in a conviction having
no intelligible grounds ; it is not an impression having nothing to
justify it except the obstinacy with which we hold to it.   When the
Spirit of God illuminates the mind, we see the meaning of what Christ
said and of what Christ did.   We simply find what was in the
Christian revelation from the beginning.'

(id. ib. p. 142.)

'If I am asked how we are to distinguish between what is revealed
to us by the Spirit of God and what we discover by the energy and
penetration of our own thought, I can only reply that the question
seems to me to rest on a misconception of the nature of spiritual
illumination.   The "wisdom" which the Spirit grants us is not a
"wisdom" separable from the ordinary activity and discernment of
our own minds ; it is not something alien to our own higher life ; it
becomes our own wisdom, just as the vision which Christ miraculously
restored to blind men was not something foreign to them, but their
own.   They saw what before they had only handled, and the nobler
sense revealed to them what the inferior sense could not make known ;
they saw for themselves what they had only heard of from others.
The reality of the supernatural work was ascertained by the new
discoveries it enabled them to make of the world in which they were
living.   Analogous effects follow the illumination of the Holy Spirit.
When the "*spirit of wisdom and revelation*" is granted to us, "*the eyes*"
of our heart, to use Paul's phrase in the next verse, are "enlightened"
—*our own eyes*,—and we see the glory of God.'

(id. ib. p. 142 f.)

Intellectual claims and gifts of the Gospel.

In 1 Cor. ii.—the main Pauline passage—St Paul has spoken of a 'wisdom—not of this world (οὐ τοῦ αἰῶνος τούτου) nor of the rulers of this world' (*v.* 6)—a wisdom 'that hath been hidden'—'God's wisdom' which 'we speak—in a mystery'—wisdom 'which God preordained before the world unto our glory' (*v.* 7). For 'unto us God through the Spirit revealed—even the deep things of God' (*v.* 11)—things 'which eye saw not, and ear heard not (Is. lxiv. 4) and which came not up into man's heart' (*v.* 9)—things which 'God prepared for them that love Him.'

'Through the Spirit.' For 'the Spirit searcheth (ἐραυνᾷ) all things': and as none 'knoweth the things of a man, save the spirit of the man which is in him, so none knoweth the things of God save the Spirit of God' (*v.* 10) Now '*we*, that we may know the things freely given us by God,' have received—not the spirit of the world (τοῦ κόσμου), but—the Spirit which is from God (τὸ πνεῦμα τὸ ἐκ τοῦ θεοῦ). Now a '*natural* man' (ψυχικὸς ἄνθρωπος) receiveth not the things of the Spirit of God—they are foolishness to him—he cannot know them—because they are judged spiritually. But the spiritual man (ὁ πνευματικὸς) judgeth all things.'

This 'wisdom'—God's wisdom—'we speak (says St Paul in *v.* 6) among the full-grown' (ἐν τοῖς τελείοις).

In the Epistle to the Ephesians St Paul tells of God's grace abounding (cf. i. 8) 'in all wisdom and prudence':—and (v. i. 17) of his prayers to God—'making mention of you in my prayers'—for 'a spirit of wisdom and revelation in the knowledge of Him'—'having the eyes of your *heart* enlightened (*v.* 18) that ye may *know*.'

At ii. 6 he contemplates Christians 'saved by grace' in contact with the heavenly order; and then (*v.* 11) all, that is realised in time through faith, is seen to be of God's ordering. Among the great mysteries of the faith, which he has prayed that the Ephesians may be enabled to understand, is that of the vital unity—the 'one man'— of ii. 10—wherein Christ, by the assumption of human nature, by His death, united in one body and 'reconciled' to God, Jews and Gentiles.

But '*to comprehend* (καταλαβέσθαι) what is the breadth and length and height and depth, and to *know* the love of Christ'—a 'love which passeth knowledge (iii. 18)—to know that which never can be known—the co-operation of all is required (σὺν πᾶσι τ. ἁγίοις). Consecration is the condition of such knowledge. There is need of effort. And there is a corresponding power—God's gift : His 'power working in us' (iii. 20 f.).

In the unity of the Christian body each of its members has his part, a special function and a special endowment. (iv. 7. 'But to each one of us was the grace given according to the measure of the gift of the Christ').

Yet unity of knowledge, as of faith,—of the faith and knowledge of the Son of God—is the final issue and limit of the work and manifold ministry of all.

Appropriation of the truth is not intellectual only, but is expressed in character and action (iv. 15, ἀληθεύοντες ἐν ἀγάπῃ).

The spring of all error is ignorance, or forgetfulness, of God. So it was with 'the Gentiles' (τὰ ἔθνη). And this 'ignorance (ἄγνοια) which was in them' was due to moral conditions (διὰ τ. πώρωσιν τ. καρδίας αὐτῶν).

The Christian is to have [in him], and to be, light (φῶς)—light is fellowship with Him, Who is the Light of the World (Jo. viii. 12 : cf. Mt. v. 14). And the life in light is shewn in moral duties— 'in every form of goodness and righteousness and truth'—the good, the right, the true.

In action—there is need of moral discrimination (v. 10 δοκιμάζοντες τί ἐστιν εὐάρεστον τῷ κυρίῳ), and of effort and carefulness in wise conduct, (15 f.) μὴ ὡς ἄσοφοι, ἀλλ' ὡς σόφοι), need to 'understand (συνίετε) what the will of the Lord is.'

In the imperfect, transitory relations of earthly life (vi. 6 ff.) higher duties are involved :—'servants' must remember (εἰδότες) that service is rendered to Christ, 'masters' must remember (εἰδότες) that in heaven the servants' Master is their own also.

In conflict with the spiritual hosts of wickedness (vi. 12 f.) the Christian warrior stands having his 'loins girded with truth.' He applies truth to life.

Religion includes thought or knowledge, as well as feeling and action. Each of these three implies, needs, and is strengthened by the other two. Knowledge in excess leads to Gnosticism or to dead orthodoxy. But realisation in thought of absolute Truth as revealed in the Incarnation is apprehension of a fact, which can be made the basis of a Science and yet is not for speculation only or for aesthetic contemplation only, but is essentially ethical.

The Sacrament of Baptism.

The rite of Baptism was connected with the work of Messiah by the prophets Ezekiel and Zechariah.

Ezek. xxxvi. 25 f. : 'And I will sprinkle clean water upon you, and ye shall be clean : from all your filthiness and from all your idols will I cleanse you. A new heart also will I give you, and a new spirit will I put within you : and I will take away the stony heart out of your flesh, and I will give you an heart of flesh.'

Zech. xiii. 1 : 'In that day there shall be a fountain opened to the house of David and to the inhabitants of Jerusalem for sin and for uncleanness.'

(Cf. Is. lii. 15.)

We cannot but believe that Christ, when (Jo. iii. 22, 25) He administered a baptism through His disciples (iv. 2), explained to those, who offered themselves, the new birth which John's baptism and this preparatory cleansing typified. At the same time He may have indicated, as to Nicodemus (iii. 5 f.), the future establishment of Christian Baptism, the sacrament of the new birth.

The *sacrament* of Baptism presupposes the Death and Resurrection of Christ.

In St John's record of the incident of the 'feet-washing' (Jo. xiii. 4—14), where the symbolic meaning of the act as a process of cleansing is introduced at *v.* 10; 'He that is *bathed* needs not save to wash his feet,' it seems impossible not to see a foreshadowing of the idea of Christian Baptism in the word '*bathed*' (Jo. xiii. 8 ὁ λελουμένος) as contrasted with 'wash' (*id. ib.* νίψασθαι).

There is, however, no evidence to shew that the Apostles themselves were baptized unless with John's baptism. The 'bathing' in their case consisted in direct intercourse and union with Christ (cf. Jo. xv. 3, 'Already ye are clean because of the word which I have spoken unto you').

It was His office to baptize with the Spirit. So Jo. i. 33 : 'the same is He which baptizeth with (or 'in') the Holy Spirit': the Holy Spirit being the atmosphere, the element of the new life. The transference of the image of baptism to the impartment of the Holy Spirit was prepared by such passages as Joel ii. 28 (quoted in Acts ii. 17), 'and it shall come to pass afterward that *I will pour out* of my Spirit upon all flesh.'

In Jo. iii. 5, 'Except a man be born of water and (the) Spirit (ἐξ ὕδατος κ. πνεύματος)' the preposition used (ἐξ) recalls the phrase (Mt.

iii. 11) 'I baptize (plunge) you *in* water; *He* shall baptize you *in* Holy Spirit and fire,'—so that the image suggested is that of rising, reborn, out of the water and out of the spiritual element, so to speak, to which the water outwardly corresponds. The combination of the words *water* and *spirit* suggests a remote parallel and a marked contrast. They carry back the thoughts of hearer and reader to the narrative of Creation (Gen. i. 2), when the Spirit of God brooded on the face of the waters. But (2) *Water* symbolizes purification and *Spirit* quickening : the one implies a definite external rite, the other indicates an energetic internal operation. The two are co-ordinate, correlative, complementary. Interpretations, which treat the term *water* here as simply figurative, are essentially defective. The words, taken in their immediate meaning, set forth as required before entrance into the Kingdom of God the acceptance of the preliminary rite Divinely sanctioned—John's baptism—which was the seal of repentance (Mt. iii. 11, εἰς μετάνοιαν) and so of forgiveness, and, following on this, the communication of a new life, resulting from the direct action of the Holy Ghost through Christ. But they have also a fuller sense, a final and complete sense for us. They look forward to the fulness of the Christian dispensation.

After the Resurrection the baptism of water was no longer separated from, but united with, the baptism of the Spirit—united with it in the "laver of regeneration" (Titus iii. 5 ἔσωσεν ἡμᾶς διὰ λουτροῦ παλιγγενεσίας καὶ ἀνακαινώσεως πνεύματος ἁγίου), even as the outward and the inward are united generally in a religion which is sacramental and not only typical.

Christian baptism, the outward act of faith welcoming the promise of God, is incorporation into the Body of Christ [cf. 1 Cor. xii. 13, Gal. iii. 27]; and so being born (the birth) 'of the Spirit' is potentially united with being born (the birth) 'of water.' The general inseparability of these two is indicated (in Jo. iii. 5) by the form of the expression 'born of water and Spirit' (ἐξ ὕδατος καὶ πνεύματος) as distinguished from the double phrase 'born of water and of Spirit' (καὶ ἐκ πνεύματος).

With the διὰ λουτροῦ παλιγγενεσίας of Tit. iii. 5 may be compared τῷ λουτρῷ τοῦ ὕδατος of Eph. v. 26. Here the initiatory sacrament of Baptism is the hallowing of the Bride. In this she is at once cleansed and hallowed (ἵνα αὐτὴν ἁγιάσῃ καθαρίσας). The actions are coincident.

To the Corinthians St Paul had written (1 Cor. vi. 11): 'But ye were washed (ἀπελούσασθε), but ye were sanctified (ἡγιάσθητε), but ye were justified in the name of the Lord Jesus Christ and in the Spirit of our God'; and (xii. 13) 'For in one Spirit we all were baptized into one Body.'

And to the Romans (Rom. vi. 3) : 'all we who were baptized into Christ Jesus were baptized into His death. We were buried therefore with Him through our Baptism (διὰ τοῦ βαπτίσματος) into death : that like as Christ was raised from the dead through the glory of the Father, so we might also walk in newness of life.'

In the Epistle to the Colossians these 'two complementary aspects of baptism' (Lightfoot ad loc.) appear in the passage ii. 18 (parallel to Eph. ii. 45) : 'being buried with Him (συνταφέντες αὐτῷ) in the act of baptism (ἐν τῷ βαπτισμῷ), in Whom also ye were raised together with Him (συνηγέρθητε) through your faith in the operation (the working) of God, Who raised Him from the dead and quickened together with Him you, that were dead by reason of your transgressions' [v. Lightfoot's note].

Here in the Epistle to the Ephesians St Paul (at iv. 4—6) lays open a view of the *unity* of the whole Christian Society in its objective foundation : and while (a) its unity is established by the acknowledgment of *one Lord* : and (b) in proclaiming that 'Jesus is Lord,' it confesses *one Faith* : (c) it is entered by *one Baptism*. [Cf. 1 Cor. xii. 13.]

And of this 'material act' that confession (ῥῆμα) is the spiritual accompaniment, a Confession involved in, and implying the acceptance of, the Baptismal formula (Mt. xxviii. 19) 'Into the name of the Father and of the Son and of the Holy Ghost.'

The 'teaching of baptisms' (βαπτισμῶν διδαχὴν) of Heb. vi. 2, where the plural and the peculiar form seem used to include Christian Baptism and other lustral rites, would naturally be directed to shew their essential difference. And the 'different washings' (διαφόροις βαπτισμοῖς) to which reference is made in the same Epistle (ix. 10) as accompaniments of the Levitical offerings (cf. Ex. xxix. 4, Lev. xi. 25 ff., xvi. 4, 24 f., Num. viii. 7, xix. 17) recall the 'washings, or baptizings, of cups and pots and brazen vessels' (βαπτισμοὺς ποτηρίων καὶ ξεστῶν καὶ χαλκίων) and other ceremonial lustrations (κ. ἀπ' ἀγορᾶς ἐὰν μὴ ῥαντίσωνται—v. l. βαπτίσωνται—οὐκ ἐσθίουσιν) of Mk. vii. 4 [v. Swete ad loc.].

The outward rite draws its virtue from the action of the Spirit.

[Cf. 1 Pet. iii. 21 : δι' ὕδατος· ὃ καὶ ὑμᾶς ἀντίτυπον νῦν σώζει βάπτισμα, οὐ σαρκὸς ἀπόθεσις ῥύπου ἀλλὰ συνειδήσεως ἀγαθῆς ἐπερώτημα εἰς θεόν, δι' ἀναστάσεως Ἰησοῦ Χριστοῦ.]

On 'Sin' in the Pauline Epistles.

Apostolic writers distinguish clearly between 'sin,' the principle, and 'sins,' specific acts.

1. *Sin* (ἁμαρτία, ἡ ἁμαρτία).

The singular is found (apart from 2 Th. ii. 3, where B has ἀνομίας) in four only of the Pauline Epistles, namely those of the second group, 1 and 2 Corinthians, Galatians, and Romans:

1 Cor. xv. 56. τὸ δὲ κέντρον τ. θανάτου ἡ ἁμαρτία, ἡ δὲ δύναμις τῆς ἁμαρτίας ὁ νόμος.

2 Cor. v. 21. τὸν μὴ γνόντα ἁμαρτίαν ὑπὲρ ἡμῶν ἁμαρτίαν ἐποίησεν.

2 Cor. xi. 7. ἢ ἁμαρτίαν ἐποίησα ἐμαυτὸν ταπεινῶν......;

Gal. ii. 17. ἆρα Χριστὸς ἁμαρτίας διάκονος;

iii. 22. συνέκλεισεν ἡ γραφὴ τὰ πάντα ὑπὸ ἁμαρτίαν.

Rom. iii.—viii. *passim.*

xiv. 21. πᾶν δὲ ὃ οὐκ ἐκ πίστεως ἁμαρτία ἐστίν.

Neither ἁμαρτία, nor ἡ ἁμαρτία, in the singular occurs in the Epistle to the Ephesians or any of the Epistles of the Captivity, nor yet in the Pastoral Epistles.

2. *Sins* (ἁμαρτίαι).

The plural is found in all groups of the Pauline Epistles.

(*a*) 1 Th. ii. 16. εἰς τὸ ἀναπληρῶσαι αὐτῶν τὰς ἁμαρτίας πάντοτε.

1 Cor. xv. 3. Χριστὸς ἀπέθανεν ὑπὲρ τῶν ἁμαρτιῶν ἡμῶν κατὰ τὰς γραφάς.

1 Cor. xv. 17. ἔτι ἐστὲ ἐν ταῖς ἁμαρτίαις.

Gal. i. 4. τοῦ δόντος ἑαυτὸν ὑπὲρ τῶν ἁμαρτιῶν ἡμῶν.

(*b*) Col. i. 14. τὴν ἄφεσιν τῶν ἁμαρτιῶν.

Eph. ii. 1. νεκροὺς τοῖς παραπτώμασιν καὶ ταῖς ἁμαρτίαις ὑμῶν.

(*c*) 1 Tim. v. 22. ἁμαρτίαις ἀλλοτρίαις.

v. 24. τινῶν ἀνθρώπων αἱ ἁμαρτίαι πρόδηλοί εἰσιν, προάγουσαι εἰς κρίσιν, τισὶν δὲ καὶ ἐπακολουθοῦσιν.

2 Tim. iii. 6. γυναικάρια σεσωρευμένα ἁμαρτίαις.

3. The word ἁμάρτημα occurs 1 Cor. vi. 18 πᾶν ἁμάρτημα ὃ ἐὰν ποιήσῃ ἄνθρωπος, Rom. iii. 25 διὰ τὴν πάρεσιν τ. προγεγονότων ἁμαρτημάτων, —and Rom. v. 16.

The verb ἁμαρτάνειν, ἁμαρτεῖν is used by St Paul as follows :

(a) 1 Cor. vi. 18, vii. 28, 36, viii. 12, xv. 34.
Rom. ii. 12, iii. 23, v. 12, 14, 16, vi. 15.

(b) Eph. iv. 26. ὀργίζεσθε καὶ μὴ ἁμαρτάνετε.

(c) 1 Tim. v. 20. τοὺς ἁμαρτάνοντας ἐνώπιον πάντων ἔλεγχε.
Tit. iii. 11. εἰδὼς ὅτι ἐξεστράπται ὁ τοιοῦτος κ. ἁμαρτάνει.

The word παράπτωμα, 'trespass,' bringing out the idea of violation of a definite law, occurs

(a) repeatedly in Romans, iv. 25, v. 15—29, xi. 11, 12, as well as in 2 Cor. v. 19 and Gal. vi. 1.

(b) in the Epistles of the Captivity, Col. ii. 13, where παραπτώματα are 'actual definite transgressions' (Lightfoot ad loc.), Eph. i. 7 τ. ἄφεσιν τ. παραπτωμάτων, ii. 1 τ. παραπτώμασιν κ. τ. ἁμαρτίαις (v. supr.), and ii. 5.

The word παράβασις, 'transgression,' occurs Gal. iii. 19 τῶν παραβάσεων χάριν, Rom. ii. 23 τῆς παραβάσεως τ. νόμου, iv. 15 οὗ γὰρ οὐκ ἔστι νόμος, οὐδὲ παράβασις, v. 14 τ. π. Ἀδάμ, and 1 Tim. ii. 14.

The Fall of Man.

The story of the Fall is the Divine parable of the origin of sin ; implying self-assertion and violation of dependence,—seeking not a wrong end, but a right end in a wrong way.

We know so little of our spiritual relations one to another that there is no greater difficulty in supposing that the earthly destiny of humanity was imperilled in a representative than in believing (as we do) that the restoration of humanity was obtained by the Son of Man.

In any case this is the simplest way of presenting a fact which is universal.

The consequence of self-assertion necessarily descended to all generations. (See Hegel's analysis of the Fall in his 'Logic.')

It is most important to notice that it is not 'death' as the passage to another order, but the circumstances of death, which are due to sin.

The effects of an act may be retrospective as well as prospective ; that is to say, the certainty that something will be modifies what goes before.

The Kingdom of God,—Kingdom of Christ.

A. Usage of St Paul.

(a) 1 Th. ii. 12. ἀξίως τ. θεοῦ τοῦ καλοῦντος ὑμᾶς εἰς τὴν ἑαυτοῦ βασιλείαν κ. δόξαν.

2 Th. i. 5. εἰς τὸ καταξιωθῆναι ὑμᾶς τῆς βασιλείας τοῦ θεοῦ.

1 Cor. iv. 20. οὐ γὰρ ἐν λόγῳ ἡ βασιλεία τοῦ θεοῦ, ἀλλ' ἐν δυνάμει.

1 Cor. vi. 9. ἢ οὐκ οἴδατε ὅτι ἄδικοι θεοῦ βασιλείαν οὐ κληρονομήσουσιν; (Cf. v. 10.)

1 Cor. xv. 24. εἶτα τὸ τέλος, ὅταν παραδιδοῖ τὴν βασιλείαν τῷ θεῷ καὶ πατρί.

1 Cor. xv. 50. σὰρξ καὶ αἷμα βασιλείαν θεοῦ κληρονομῆσαι οὐ δύναται.

Gal. v. 21. οἱ τοιαῦτα πράσσοντες βασιλείαν θεοῦ οὐ κληρονομήσουσιν.

Rom. xiv. 17. οὐ γάρ ἐστιν ἡ βασιλεία τ. θεοῦ βρῶσις καὶ πόσις, ἀλλὰ δικαιοσύνη καὶ εἰρήνη καὶ χαρὰ ἐν πνεύματι ἁγίῳ.

(b) Col. i. 13. ὃς ἐρύσατο ἡμᾶς ἐκ τῆς ἐξουσίας τοῦ σκότους καὶ μετέστησεν εἰς τὴν βασιλείαν τοῦ υἱοῦ τῆς ἀγάπης αὐτοῦ.

Col. iv. 11. συνεργοὶ εἰς τὴν βασιλείαν τοῦ θεοῦ.

Eph. v. 5. ἐν τῇ βασιλείᾳ τοῦ χριστοῦ καὶ θεοῦ.

(c) 2 Tim. iv. 1. Χριστοῦ Ἰησοῦ, τοῦ μέλλοντος κρίνειν ζῶντας κ. νεκρούς, καὶ τὴν ἐπιφάνειαν αὐτοῦ καὶ τὴν βασιλείαν αὐτοῦ.

2 Tim. iv. 18. ῥύσεταί με ὁ κύριος ἀπὸ παντὸς ἔργου πονηροῦ κ. σώσει εἰς τὴν βασιλείαν αὐτοῦ τὴν ἐπουράνιον.

B. Use in other Epistles.

(a) Heb. i. 8. ἡ ῥάβδος τῆς βασιλείας (from LXX. of Ps. xlv. 7).

xii. 28. βασιλείαν ἀσάλευτον παραλαμβάνοντες.

(b) Ja. ii. 5. κληρονόμους τῆς βασιλείας ἧς ἐπηγγείλατο τοῖς ἀγαπῶσιν αὐτόν.

(c) 2 Pet. i. 11. εἰς τὴν αἰώνιον βασιλείαν τοῦ κυρίου ἡμῶν καὶ σωτῆρος Ἰησοῦ Χριστοῦ.

C. Use in the Synoptic Gospels and in 'Acts.'

(a) In the Synoptists, besides ἡ βασιλεία σου of the Lord's Prayer, the expression ἡ βασιλεία τοῦ θεοῦ is of constant occurrence, except in the Gospel of St Matthew, where it is found four times only (vi. 33, xii. 28, xix. 24, xxi. 43), being elsewhere replaced by the phrase ἡ β. τῶν οὐρανῶν. Three times in St Matthew (iv. 23, ix. 35, xxiv. 14) we have τὸ εὐαγγέλιον τῆς βασιλείας,—'the Gospel of the Kingdom'—and once (xiii. 19) τὸν λόγον τῆς βασιλείας— 'the word of the Kingdom.'

[Note especially Lk. xxii. 29 κἀγὼ διατίθεμαι ὑμῖν, καθὼς διέθετό μοι ὁ πατήρ μου βασιλείαν, ἵνα ἔσθητε καὶ πίνητε ἐπὶ τῆς τραπέζης μου ἐν τῇ βασιλείᾳ μου, καὶ καθῆσθε ἐπὶ θρόνων τὰς δώδεκα φυλὰς κρίνοντες τοῦ Ἰσραήλ.

(b) In 'Acts' the phrase τὰ περὶ τῆς βασιλείας τ. θεοῦ occurs thrice (i. 3, viii. 12, xix. 8). The other references to 'the Kingdom of God' are xiv. 22 εἰσελθεῖν εἰς τ. βασιλείαν τ. θ., xxviii. 23 διαμαρτυρόμενος τ. βασιλείαν τ. θ., ib. 31 κηρύσσων τ. β. τ. θ.: in xx. 25 κηρύσσων τ. βασιλείαν (om. τ. θεοῦ) is read:—cf. i. 6.

D. Use in Johannine writings.

(a) Apoc. i. 6. κ. ἐποίησεν ἡμᾶς βασιλείαν ἱερεῖς τῷ θεῷ κ. πατρὶ αὐτοῦ.

Apoc. i. 9. συνκοινωνὸς ἐν τῇ θλίψει κ. βασιλείᾳ κ. ὑπομονῇ ἐν Ἰησοῦ.

Apoc. v. 10. ἐποίησας αὐτοὺς τῷ θεῷ ἡμῶν βασιλείαν κ. ἱερεῖς, καὶ βασιλεύσουσιν ἐπὶ τῆς γῆς.

Apoc. xi. 15. ἐγένετο ἡ βασιλεία τοῦ κόσμου τοῦ κυρίου ἡμῶν καὶ τοῦ χριστοῦ αὐτοῦ, κ. βασιλεύσει εἰς τοὺς αἰῶνας τῶν αἰώνων.

Apoc. xii. 10. ἡ βασιλεία τοῦ θεοῦ ἡμῶν κ. ἡ ἐξουσία τοῦ χριστοῦ αὐτοῦ.

(b) Jo. iii. 3. ἐὰν μή τις γεννηθῇ ἄνωθεν, οὐ δύναται ἰδεῖν τὴν βασιλείαν τοῦ θεοῦ.

Jo. iii. 5. εἰσελθεῖν εἰς τὴν βασιλείαν τοῦ θεοῦ.

Jo. xviii. 36. ἡ βασιλεία ἡ ἐμὴ οὐκ ἔστιν ἐκ τοῦ κόσμου τούτου· εἰ ἐκ τοῦ κόσμου τούτου ἦν ἡ βασιλεία ἡ ἐμή, οἱ ὑπηρέται οἱ ἐμοὶ ἠγωνίζοντο ἄν, ἵνα μὴ παραδοθῶ τοῖς Ἰουδαίοις· νῦν δὲ ἡ βασιλεία ἡ ἐμὴ οὐκ ἔστιν ἐντεῦθεν.

'The Kingdom' [implies] 'a Sovereign of whose Personal Rule His subjects would be conscious and by Whose Will they would be guided, an organization, by which the relative functions and duties and stations of those included within it would be defined and sustained, a common principle of action, and common rights of citizenship.'

(Gospel of the Resurrection, p. 195.)

The Christian Society, and the Apostolic Ministry.

'Our bodies (1 Cor. vi. 15) are members of Christ' (μέλη Χριστοῦ); and conversely (1 Cor. xii. 27) a Christian society is 'a body of Christ' (σῶμα Χριστοῦ)—[a body of which Christ is the Head].—[Such is] *each* Christian society—'a body of Christ,' of which the members are charged with various functions and gifts. And these 'bodies' again are 'members' of other 'bodies' wider and greater, and thus at last 'members' of that universal Church which is the 'fulness of Christ,' its Heavenly Head. (*G. of R.* pp. 177—182.)

In the providential ordering of the Christian Society these various functions and graces have been variously concentrated; but all belong alike to the new life, which the Risen Christ breathed into His Church.

To this Body, as a whole, the Risen Lord communicated the virtue of His glorified Life.

For it is a fact of the highest importance and clearly established by the documents—that the commission given on the evening of the first Easter Day—the 'Great Commission'—was given to the Church and not to any class in the Church—to the whole Church—and not to any part of it, primarily.

The Commission and the Promise, like the Pentecostal blessing which they prefigured, were given to the Christian Society, and not to any special order in it.

Not that every member of the Church has in virtue of the corporate gift a right to exercise it *individually*.

The very fact that the commission is given to the body renders it impossible for any member to exercise it except by the authority of the body.

When the Body is quickened and endowed, then the Spirit works out its purpose through the several *parts*.

It is indeed a general law of life that differentiation of organs answers to [the] increasing fulness of life. The particular power of the living being finds expression through the organs. The specialisation of functions required for the permanent well-being of the Church [appears, when] in Eph. iv. 7—11 St Paul marks the types of ministry with which the Church is endowed. He states the fact of the individual endowment of the several members of the Christian Society (*v.* 7); and (*v.* 11) notes that certain special gifts have been made for its government.

'Receive ye the Holy Ghost; whosesoever sins ye forgive, they are forgiven unto them; whosesoever sins ye retain, they are retained.' (Jo. xx. 22 f.)

The words are the Charter of the Christian Church, and not simply the Charter of the Christian Ministry.

The gift is conveyed once for all. It is made part of the life of the whole Society, flowing from the relation of the body to the Risen Christ.

Before His Passion Christ had given to His disciples

(a) the power of the keys to open the treasury of the Kingdom of Heaven and *dispense* things new and old;

(b) power to bind and to loose, to fix and to unfix ordinances for the government of the new Society.

Now (c) as Conqueror He added the authority to deal with sins.

The message of the Gospel is the glad tidings of sin conquered. To apply this to each man severally is the office of the Church and so of each member of the Church. To embrace it personally is to gain absolution.

He to whom the word comes can appropriate or reject the message of deliverance which we as Christians are authorised to bear. As he does so, we, speaking in Christ's name, either remove the load by which he is weighed down or make it more oppressive.

To this end all the sacraments and ordinances of Christianity combine, to deepen the conviction of sin and to announce forgiveness of sin.

In the first age, however, it is perfectly clear from the Pauline Epistles, that the Christian Society was not as yet under any rigid organisation; there was not as yet a recognised ecclesiastical hierarchy.

In some of these Epistles, particularly in 1 Cor. xii. 28 and Eph. iv. 11, specific offices are named.

Thus in 1 Cor. xii. 27 St Paul says to the Church of Corinth, 'Ye are a body of Christ, and members in particular'; and then in *v.* 28 'God—set ($\check{\epsilon}\theta\epsilon\tau o$)—in the Church first apostles, secondly prophets, thirdly teachers,—then miracles, then gifts of healings, helps, governments, divers kinds of tongues.'

And in Eph. iv. 11 he writes, 'And He Himself gave some as Apostles, and some as prophets, and some as evangelists, and some as pastors and teachers.'

But the offices named are not parts of a hierarchy. They are related to *personal* gifts.

The language of the verse in the Ephesian Epistle, indeed, clearly *excludes* the idea of the existence, at that time, of any Divinely ordered hierarchy.

The gift which Christ 'gave' to the Church was a gift of 'men.' It was a double gift. He first endowed the men, and then gave them, endowed, to the Church.

Through their work the character of permanent offices became revealed.

There is in the New Testament no trace of any rigid universal constitution of the Christian Society.

Divine gifts for its edification are recognised.

These appear to be general, and stand prominent.

There are also ecclesiastical offices.

The presbyterate, as yet identical with the episcopate, is practically universal.

Deacons are treated of by St Paul as universal : though there is no trace of any perpetuation of 'the seven.'

There is no definition of the respective duties of presbyters or of deacons.

Timothy appears to have apostolic functions by ordination[1].

The Church appears guided by a self-widening ministry—apostles and prophets.

Of a primitive hierarchical ministry there is no record or tradition.

And there is no provision for all time. The provision of a permanent and universal organisation of the Church was, in fact, wholly alien from the thought of the first age. The vision was closed by 'the Coming.' At the close of it the Lord was to come Himself.

---

[1] 1 Tim. iv. 14 τοῦ ἐν σοὶ χαρίσματος, ὃ ἐδόθη σοι διὰ προφητείας μετὰ ἐπιθέσεως τ. χειρῶν τοῦ πρεσβυτερίου.

2 Tim. i. 6 τὸ χάρισμα τοῦ θεοῦ, ὅ ἐστιν ἐν σοὶ διὰ τῆς ἐπιθέσεως τῶν χειρῶν μου.

'The Church' in the Epistle to the Ephesians.

The word ἐκκλησία occurs in the Gospels in two places only (Mt. xvi. 18; xviii. 17): in the former place in the sense of the universal Church (καὶ ἐπὶ ταύτῃ τῇ πέτρᾳ οἰκοδομήσω μου τὴν ἐκκλησίαν), and in the latter of a special Church (ἐὰν δὲ παρακούσῃ αὐτῶν, εἰπὸν τῇ ἐκκλησίᾳ, ἐὰν δὲ καὶ τῆς ἐκκλησίας παρακούσῃ, ἔστω σοι ὥσπερ ὁ ἐθνικὸς καὶ ὁ τελώνης).

Both senses are found in the Acts.

In the Apocalypse, as also in St James (v. 14) and in 3 Jo. 6, 9, 10, the word is used in the special sense only.

In the Epistles of St Paul both senses are found.

In the Epistle to the Ephesians the Christian Society—the Church —is a commonwealth, but it is more than a commonwealth.

The Church is a spiritual building—the temple of the Spirit.

    „   „   a living organism—the Body of Christ.

    „   „   the Bride of Christ.

The word ἐκκλησία is used nine times in the Epistle to the Ephesians. But of these instances six occur in one and the same context in the fifth chapter, and the nine occurrences of the word are thus practically reducible to four.

(1) i. 22 f. καὶ αὐτὸν ἔδωκεν κεφαλὴν ὑπὲρ πάντα τῇ ἐκκλησίᾳ, ἥτις ἐστὶν τὸ σῶμα αὐτοῦ, τὸ πλήρωμα τοῦ τὰ πάντα ἐν πᾶσιν πληρουμένου.

Not only was Christ Himself exalted to the heavens:

(a) He is invested with universal sovereignty (cf. Mt. xxvii. 28 ἐδόθη μοι πᾶσα ἐξουσία ἐν οὐρανῷ καὶ ἐπὶ τῆς γῆς).

(b) He is even now Head of His Church on earth:

    'Head over all things to the Church, which is His body'— and

(c) He has already exercised His sovereignty by the gift of His quickening grace.

So in the parallel passage, Col. i. 18: καὶ αὐτός ἐστιν ἡ κεφαλη τοῦ σώματος, τῆς ἐκκλησίας (cf. v. 24), i.e. (as Lightfoot paraphrases) 'not only does He hold this position of absolute priority and sovereignty over the Universe—the natural creation—He stands also in the same relation to the Church—the new spiritual creation. He is its head, and it is His body.'

'The Creator of the World is also the Head of the Church'—'*the head*, the inspiring, ruling, guiding, combining, sustaining power, the mainspring of its activity and the centre of its unity, and the seat of its life.'

The image (of Christ as the Head) occurs in a different yet cognate application in 1 Cor. xi. 3 παντὸς ἀνδρὸς ἡ κεφαλὴ ὁ χριστός ἐστιν, κεφαλὴ δὲ τ. χριστοῦ ὁ θεός.

Moreover the relations of the Church to Christ are (as Lightfoot points out) described—by St Paul—in his earlier Epistles—under the same image : 1 Cor. xii. 12—27 : 'For, as the body is one and hath many members, and all the members of the body, being many, are one body ; so also is Christ. For in one Spirit were we all baptized into one body, whether Jews or Greeks, whether bond or free ; and were all made to drink of one Spirit. For the body is not one member, but many. . . . . Now ye are the body of Christ, and severally members thereof (ὑμεῖς—ἐστὲ σῶμα Χριστοῦ καὶ μέλη ἐκ μέρους).'

1 Cor. vi. 15. 'Know ye not that your bodies are members of Christ.' Cf. x. 17.

Rom. xii. 4 sq. 'For even as we have many members in one body, and all the members have not the same office ; so we, who are many, *are one body in Christ* and severally members one of another' (ἓν σῶμά ἐσμεν ἐν Χριστῷ).

But the Apostle there takes as his starting-point the various functions of the members, and not, as in these later Epistles, 'the originating and controlling power of the Head.' (*Col.* p. 157.)

Here (in Ephesians i. 22) 'the thought of *sovereignty*, already given, is now connected with that of *vital union with a glorious organism* which draws its life from Him,—that one Divine society,—the Body of Christ,—to which the life of every individual believer is a contributory element and in which every individual life finds its consummation.' (*Revelation of the Risen Lord*, Pref. p. xxvi.)

And while, on the one side, Christ by His Presence gives to all things their true being and Christians in a special sense reach their 'fulness,' their full development, in Him, on the other side—He Himself finds His fulness in the sum of all things that He thus brings into living union with Himself.

(2) iii. 10. ἵνα γνωρισθῇ νῦν ταῖς ἀρχαῖς καὶ ταῖς ἐξουσίαις ἐν τοῖς ἐπουρανίοις διὰ τῆς ἐκκλησίας ἡ πολυποίκιλος σοφία τοῦ θεοῦ.

In the Church humanity advances towards its true unity.

And 'the display of God's wisdom before the intelligences of the heavenly order......was......the work of the Church.'

'The effect of the Gospel reaches through all being,—and we are allowed to see......how other rational creatures follow the course of its fulfilment.'

The *manifold wisdom of God* is seen in the adaptation of the manifold capacities of man and the complicated vicissitudes of human life to minister to the one end to which "all creation moves."

(3) iii. 21. αὐτῷ ἡ δόξα ἐν τῇ ἐκκλησίᾳ καὶ ἐν Χριστῷ Ἰησοῦ εἰς πάσας τὰς γενεὰς τοῦ αἰῶνος τῶν αἰώνων· ἀμήν.

The contemplation of the glorious fulness of Divine blessing in the Gospel—closes with a Doxology—in which God's work in man is regarded as issuing in His glory 'in the Church and in Christ Jesus' to the last development of life in time.

The glory of God is shewn, as the Universe moves forward to its end, by the fulfilment of God's Will in man and by the offering of man's service to God.

(4) v. 23 f. ἀνήρ ἐστιν κεφαλὴ τῆς γυναικὸς ὡς καὶ ὁ χριστὸς κεφαλὴ τῆς ἐκκλησίας, αὐτὸς σωτὴρ τοῦ σώματος.

ἀλλὰ ὡς ἡ ἐκκλησία ὑποτάσσεται τῷ χριστῷ, οὕτως καὶ κ.τ.λ.

οἱ ἄνδρες, ἀγαπᾶτε τὰς γυναῖκας, καθὼς καὶ ὁ χριστὸς ἠγάπησεν τὴν ἐκκλησίαν καὶ ἑαυτὸν παρέδωκεν ὑπὲρ αὐτῆς, ἵνα αὐτὴν ἁγιάσῃ καθαρίσας τῷ λουτρῷ τοῦ ὕδατος ἐν ῥήματι, ἵνα παραστήσῃ αὐτὸς ἑαυτῷ ἔνδοξον τὴν ἐκκλησίαν, μὴ ἔχουσαν σπίλον ἢ ῥυτίδα ἤ τι τῶν τοιούτων, ἀλλ' ἵνα ᾖ ἁγία καὶ ἄμωμος.

The Apostle—points out that the wife is to the husband *as the Church to Christ*.

The relation of husband to wife, *like that of Christ to the Church*, points to a unity included in the idea of creation. And of the primitive ordinance that 'a man shall leave father and mother and shall cleave to his wife, and the twain shall become one flesh' (*v.* 31, from Gen. ii. 24), the greatest of all the manifold applications is [and the highest fulfilment is] the union of Christ and the Church:

τὸ μυστήριον τοῦτο μέγα ἐστίν, ἐγὼ δὲ λέγω εἰς Χριστὸν καὶ [εἰς] τὴν ἐκκλησίαν.

The marriage-relation of 'the Lord' to Israel runs through the Old Testament.

And the application of this relation to Christ and the Church—the spiritual Israel—implies His Divinity.

Christ offers to the Church the devotion of love. And such is the duty of the husband to the wife. The Church offers to Christ the devotion of subjection, as is the duty of the wife to the husband.

Christ loved the Church (v. 25 : Acts xx. 28) not because it was perfectly lovable, but in order to make it such; not because it was holy, but in order to make it holy by union with Himself.

The love of Christ—for the Church—was crowned by His sacrifice of Himself.

And the purpose of the self-sacrifice of Christ for the Church is ⟨1⟩ to hallow it, (2) to present it to Himself—glorious—without spot or wrinkle, (3) that it may continue—holy and blameless ('without blemish ').

Further in ii. 20 ff. [though the *word* ἐκκλησία does not occur] the new Society of believers is a fabric, destined to become a sanctuary :

ἐποικοδομηθέντες ἐπὶ τῷ θεμελίῳ τῶν ἀποστόλων καὶ προφητῶν, ὄντος ἀκρογωνιαίου αὐτοῦ Χριστοῦ Ἰησοῦ, ἐν ᾧ πᾶσα οἰκοδομὴ συναρμολογουμένη αὔξει εἰς ναὸν ἅγιον ἐν κυρίῳ, ἐν ᾧ καὶ ὑμεῖς συνοικοδομεῖσθε εἰς κατοικητήριον τοῦ θεοῦ ἐν πνεύματι.

To the Corinthians St Paul had said (1 Cor. iii. 17) 'Ye are a temple of God (ναὸς θεοῦ) and the Spirit of God dwelleth in you'; and also (*ib.* xii. 28), 'And some God set in the Church, first apostles, secondly prophets, thirdly teachers'; and again (2 Cor. vi. 16), 'For we are a temple of the living God (ναὸς θεοῦ ἐσμὲν ζῶντος).'

Now in Ephesians he writes (ii. 19—22): 'Ye are fellow-citizens with the saints and of the household of God, being built upon the foundation of the apostles and prophets, Christ Jesus himself being the chief corner stone; in Whom each several building, fitly framed together, groweth into a holy temple in the Lord; in Whom ye also are builded together for a habitation of God in the Spirit.'

We see then that in the Epistle in which he opens the widest prospect of the being and destiny of the Church, St Paul uses two images [besides that of the Bride] to describe it,—that of a 'body'— a body of which Christ is the Head (i. 22 f.)—and that of a spiritual building or 'sanctuary ' (ii. 20 f.).

At the same time he combines the two images together. Thus in the passage cited, ii. 21 f. (*v. supr.*), the many buildings are said to grow into a sanctuary—a 'holy temple': and on the other hand the body is built: the body, 'fitly framed and knit together'—maketh 'increase unto the building up of itself in love' (iv. 16). The body is built; the temple grows.

We need both images, of building and of growth, in order to
understand our position socially and personally. The progress which
we observe in human society and in our own several lives is due in
part to human effort and in part to vital forces, which lie beyond our
reach. Everywhere we find this twofold action of 'building' and of
'growth.'

Thus in the material building we have to notice the influence of
natural powers which we cannot control. The sunshine and the rain ;
—the silent, ceaseless action of the air,—bring to the fabric some of
its greatest charms.

In the body again there is room for the effects of care and discipline.
We grow by a force which is independent of our will : but of ourselves
we can within certain measure retard or hasten or guide the growth.

So God Himself works, and He works also through us. As His
fellow-workers we recognise on the one side inexorable laws, on the
other the results of personal endeavour.

This thought applies alike to the individual Christian and to the
Church.

It applies, I say, to the Church, the Society of Christian men.
For the Church is built and yet it grows. Human endeavour and
Divine energy co-operate in its development.

The Church a Temple.

The Church is 'a structure complex and multiform—a dwelling-
place of the Holy Spirit'—a temple 'reared through long ages, each
stone of which fills its special place and contributes its share to the
grace and stability of the fabric.' It includes many buildings, but all
equally parts of the sanctuary (ναός). Of this temple Christ Himself
is the corner-stone ; Apostles and Prophets, united with and having
authority from Him, form its foundation (cf. Apoc. xxi. 14).

The Church the Body of Christ.

Again, the Church is 'a Body, where a royal will directs and
disciplines and uses the functions of every member'—Christ being 'the
Head, from which the body receives its divine impulse.'

'The Body is one : it is multiform ; and it is quickened by a power
which is not of itself but from above.'

'For unity is not uniformity. Differences of race, class, social
order obviously have no influence upon it. They are of earth only.
But more than this, it is consistent with serious differences in the
apprehension of the common faith in which it reposes....The Unity of

the whole is consistent with a wide variety of parts, each having to a certain degree a corresponding unity in itself.'

'And the essential bond of union is not external but spiritual; it consists not in one organization. but in a common principle of life.'

'It follows—that external, visible unity is not required for the essential unity of the Church.'

'But though the principle of the unity of the Christian Church is spiritual and not necessarily connected with uniformity of constitution or even with intercommunion, it by no means follows that the outward organization of the whole of the constituent Churches is a matter of indifference.'

'The range of variation in the constitution of the Christian societies must be limited by their fitness to embody the fundamental ideas of Christianity.'

'Divisions, as we see them, are' indeed 'a witness to human imperfection.' But, 'if we regard the imperfection of our nature,— division appears to be the preliminary of that noblest catholicity, which will issue from the separate fulfilment by each part in due measure (Eph. iv. 16) of its proper function towards the whole. Thus the material unity of Judaism is transformed into the moral unity of the Apocalypse.'

The Church the Bride of Christ.

The image used in prophetical books of the Old Testament (Hos. ii. 19, Ezek. xvi., Mal. ii. 11) to describe the relation between Jehovah and His people, is in the New Testament applied to Christ and the Church. Suggested, in the Synoptic Gospels, by the imagery of the Parables of the Marriage-feast (Mt. xxii. 1 ff.) and of the Ten Virgins (id. xxv. 1 ff., also Mt. ix. 15) is signified in the Gospel of St John by the language of the Baptist (Jo. iii. 29 f.): 'He that hath the bride is the bridegroom : but the friend of the bridegroom, which standeth and heareth him rejoiceth greatly because of the bridegroom's voice : this my joy therefore is fulfilled. He must increase, but I must decrease.' The Christ was gathering round Him the disciples who were the beginnings of His Church—representatives of the spiritual Israel—the divine Bride—brought by the forerunner to Christ—the Bridegroom.

In 2 Cor. xi. 2 ζηλῶ γὰρ ὑμᾶς θεοῦ ζήλῳ, ἡρμοσάμην γὰρ ὑμᾶς ἑνὶ ἀνδρὶ παρθένον ἁγνὴν παραστῆσαι τῷ χριστῷ, St Paul applies the figure to the connexion of Christ with a particular body of Christians ; even as in Ephesians (v. 32 ff.) he uses it (v. supr.) of the relation of Christ to

His Church as a whole,—the Church 'contemplated as distinct from Christ, though most closely bound to Him as His bride.' In the Apocalypse (xix. 7, xxi. 2, 9, xxii. 17) the Holy City, the New Jerusalem is seen 'as a bride adorned for her husband': and 'the bride' is 'the wife of the Lamb.'

The Church Universal.

'Every Family,' every Fatherhood, derives that, in virtue of which it is what it is, from the One Father (Eph. iii. 15); from Him comes all fellowship and unity in heaven and on earth.

The Church, of which the Family is the type and monument, is the herald and witness of the revelation of a living God,—'the interpreter of the world in the light of the Incarnation,'—'the appointed organ of the gifts of Christ.'

And it is in the Epistle to the Ephesians that the idea of the One Church, having a mission thus manifold and universal, is first developed.

'Here, for the first time, we hear Christians throughout the world described as together making up a single Ecclesia, a single assembly of God, or Church' (Hort: *Prolegomena*, p. 128).

Use of the word ἀποκάλυψις in the N.T.

A. Pauline usage :—

2 Th. i. 7.   ἐν τῇ ἀποκαλύψει τ. κυρίου Ἰησοῦ ἀπ' οὐρανοῦ.

1 Cor. i. 7.   τὴν ἀποκάλυψιν τ. κυρίου ἡμῶν Ἰ. Χριστοῦ.

xiv. 6.   ἢ ἐν ἀποκαλύψει ἢ ἐν γνώσει ἢ ἐν προφητείᾳ ἢ ἐν διδαχῇ.

26.   ψαλμὸν—διδαχὴν—ἀποκάλυψιν.

2 Cor. xii. 1.   ὀπτασίας καὶ ἀποκαλύψεις κυρίου.

7.   τῇ ὑπερβολῇ τῶν ἀποκαλύψεων.

Gal. i. 12.   δι' ἀποκαλύψεως Ἰησοῦ Χριστοῦ.

ii. 2.   ἀνέβην δὲ κατὰ ἀποκάλυψιν.

Rom. ii. 5.   ἐν ἡμέρᾳ ὀργῆς καὶ ἀποκαλύψεως δικαιοκρισίας τοῦ θεοῦ.

viii. 19.   τὴν ἀποκάλυψιν τῶν υἱῶν τοῦ θεοῦ.

xvi. 25.   κατὰ ἀποκάλυψιν μυστηρίου.

Eph. i. 17.   πνεῦμα σοφίας κ. ἀποκαλύψεως.

iii. 3.   κατὰ ἀποκάλυψιν ἐγνωρίσθη μοι τὸ μυστήριον.

B. Use by other writers :—

1 Pet. i. 7.   ἐν ἀποκαλύψει Ἰησοῦ Χριστοῦ.   So again *v.* 13.

iv. 13.   ἐν τῇ ἀποκαλύψει τῆς δόξης.

Lk. ii. 32.   εἰς ἀποκάλυψιν ἐθνῶν.

Apoc. i. 1.   ἀποκάλυψις Ἰησοῦ Χριστοῦ.

The verb ἀποκαλύπτειν is used :—

(A) by St Paul (13 times) in six Epistles (2 Th., 1 Cor., Gal., Rom., Phil., Eph.),

(B) in the First Epistle of St Peter, and in the Gospels of St Matthew and St Luke.
Except in a citation (xii. 38) from the LXX. of Is. liii. 1, it is not used by St John.

Revelation, in the New Testament, is

(a) of Jesus Christ.
2 Th. i. 7, 1 Cor. i. 7, Gal. i. 16 (cf. 2 Cor. xii. 1).
1 Pet. i. 7, 13 ; Lk. xvii. 30.
Apoc. i. 1 (v. Hort on 1 Pet. i. 7).

(b) of the Father. Mt. xi. 27 ‖ Lk. x. 22.

(c) of 'the righteous judgment of God.' Rom. ii. 5: 'wrath' ib. i. 18.

(d) of 'the sons of God.' Rom. viii. 19.

(e) of a 'glory.' Rom. viii. 18, 1 Pet. iv. 13, v. 1.

(f) of a salvation and deliverance. 1 Pet. i. 5.

(g) of an evil power. 2 Th. ii. 3, 6, 8.

(h) of a faith. Gal. iii. 23. εἰς τ. μέλλουσαν πίστιν ἀποκαλυφθῆναι.

(i) of whatever is covered (κεκαλυμμένον). Mt. x. 26 ‖ Lk. xii. 2.

(k) of heavenly truths. 1 Cor. ii. 10. τὰ βάθη τοῦ θεοῦ.
Rom. xvi. 25. μυστηρίου χρόνοις αἰωνίοις σεσιγημένου.
Eph. iii. 3, 5. τὸ μυστήριον.
Mt. xi. 25 ‖ Lk. x. 21. ὅτι ἔκρυψας ταῦτα ἀπὸ σοφῶν κ. συνετῶν καὶ ἀπεκάλυψας αὐτὰ νηπίοις. (Cf. Phil. iii. 15.)
Mt. xvi. 17. σὰρξ κ. αἷμα οὐκ ἀπεκάλυψέν σοι ἀλλ᾽ ὁ πατήρ μου ὁ ἐν τ. οὐρανοῖς. (Cf. v. 16.)

With Revelation is co-ordinated 'knowledge,' 'prophecy' and 'teaching.' 1 Cor. xiv. 6.

With Revelation is co-ordinated 'wisdom.' Eph. i. 17 (v. supr. p. 158, Dale on 'Wisdom and Revelation').

'Revelation is always (probably even in Gal. iii. 23) in the strictest sense an unveiling of what already exists, not the coming into existence of that which is said to be revealed.' (Hort on 1 Pet. i. 5.)

On the use of the term μυστήριον in the N. T.

The word μυστήριον (which in the LXX. occurs Judith ii. 2, Wisd.
vi. 24, Ecclus. xxii. 22, Tob. xii. 7, 21, 2 Macc. xiii. 21 and elsewhere ;
also in Theodotion's version of Dan. ii. 18 ff., Ps. xxv. 14 and Prov. xx.
19) is found, in the Synoptic Gospels in the parallel texts (Mt. xiii. 11,
Mk. iv. 11, Lk. viii. 10) of the Parable of the Sower, but elsewhere in
the N. T. only in the Epistles of St Paul and in the Apocalypse.

It is used (1) comprehensively of the Christian Revelation or of the
central truth of the universality of the Gospel, (2) of special truths in
that revelation.

But always in the N. T. the fact of revelation, actual or imminent,
is implied.

(1)   In the comprehensive meaning the word is used 13 times by
St Paul and once in the Apocalypse.

A. (a) 1 Cor. ii. 1.   καταγγέλλων ὑμῖν τὸ μυστήριον τοῦ θεοῦ.

6 f.   σοφίαν δὲ λαλοῦμεν ἐν τοῖς τελείοις (those who
are fully initiate), σοφίαν δὲ οὐ τοῦ αἰῶνος τούτου οὐδὲ κ.τ.λ....
ἀλλὰ λαλοῦμεν θεοῦ σοφίαν ἐν μυστηρίῳ.

Rom. xvi. 25 f.   κατὰ ἀποκάλυψιν μυστηρίου χρόνοις αἰωνίοις
σεσιγημένου φανερωθέντος δὲ νῦν διά τε γραφῶν προφητικῶν
κατ᾽ ἐπιταγὴν τοῦ αἰωνίου θεοῦ εἰς ὑπακοὴν πίστεως εἰς πάντα
τὰ ἔθνη γνωρισθέντος.

(b) Col. i. 26 f.   τὸ μυστήριον τὸ ἀποκεκρυμμένον ἀπὸ τῶν αἰώνων κ.

ἀπὸ τῶν γενεῶν, νῦν δὲ ἐφανερώθη τοῖς ἁγίοις, οἷς ἠθέλησεν ὁ
θεὸς γνωρίσαι τί τὸ πλοῦτος τῆς δόξης τοῦ μυστηρίου τούτου ἐν
τοῖς ἔθνεσιν, ὅ ἐστιν Χριστὸς ἐν ὑμῖν, ἡ ἐλπὶς τῆς δόξης.
(v. Lightfoot's note.)

Col. ii. 2.   εἰς ἐπίγνωσιν τοῦ μυστηρίου τοῦ θεοῦ Χριστοῦ ἐν ᾧ
εἰσὶν πάντες οἱ θησαυροὶ τῆς σοφίας καὶ γνώσεως ἀπόκρυφοι—
'God's mystery, which is nothing else than Christ—Christ
containing in Himself all the treasures of wisdom and
knowledge hidden away.' (Lightfoot, *ad loc.*)

Col. iv. 3 f.   ἵνα ὁ θεὸς ἀνοίξῃ ἡμῖν θύραν τοῦ λόγου, λαλῆσαι τὸ
μυστήριον τοῦ χριστοῦ, διὸ καὶ δέδεμαι· ἵνα φανερώσω αὐτό, ὡς
δεῖ με λαλῆσαι.

Eph. i. 9.   γνωρίσας ἡμῖν τὸ μυστήριον τοῦ θελήματος αὐτοῦ—
'the mystery of His will'—the Divine counsel now revealed, expressing God's Will.

Eph. iii. 3. κατὰ ἀποκάλυψιν ἐγνωρίσθη μοι τὸ μυστήριον.

4. ἐν τῷ μυστηρίῳ τοῦ χριστοῦ. The 'mystery of the Christ' was (*v.* 6) the truth, revealed to the Apostles, that the Gentiles, by incorporation in Christ, were, equally with Jews, heirs of all the hopes of the people of God, members of one Divine society, and partakers of the gift of the Holy Spirit.

Eph. iii. 9. ἡ οἰκονομία τοῦ μυστηρίου τοῦ ἀποκεκρυμμένου ἀπὸ τῶν αἰώνων ἐν τῷ θεῷ τῷ τὰ πάντα κτίσαντι. The words recall the language of Rom. xvi. 25 f. (*v. supr.*)

Eph. vi. 19. ἐν παρρησίᾳ γνωρίσαι τὸ μυστήριον τοῦ εὐαγγελίου —'the mystery of the Gospel'—the revelation contained in the Gospel.

(*c*) 1 Tim. iii. 9. ἔχοντας τὸ μυστήριον τῆς πίστεως ἐν καθαρᾷ συνειδήσει—'holding the mystery of the faith in a pure conscience.

1 Tim. iii. 16. κ. ὁμολογουμένως μέγα ἐστὶν τὸ τῆς εὐσεβείας μυστήριον—'the mystery of godliness.'

B. Apoc. x. 7. καὶ ἐτελέσθη τὸ μυστήριον τοῦ θεοῦ, ὡς εὐηγγέλισεν τοὺς ἑαυτοῦ δούλους τοὺς προφήτας—where 'the mystery of God' is a revelation now imminent (*v.* 6 'there shall be delay no longer': cf. Dan. xii. 7) and the language is that of Amos iii. 7 'Surely the Lord God will do nothing, but He revealeth his secret unto His servants the prophets.'

(2) In the sense of a particular truth, or detail, of the Christian revelation, the word occurs seven times in St Paul, and three times in the Apocalypse.

A. (*a*) 2 Th. ii. 7. τὸ γὰρ μυστήριον ἤδη ἐνεργεῖται τῆς ἀνομίας.

1 Cor. iv. 1. ὑπηρέτας Χριστοῦ κ. οἰκονόμους μυστηρίων θεοῦ.

xiii. 2. κἂν ἔχω προφητείαν καὶ εἰδῶ τὰ μυστήρια πάντα.

xiv. 2. πνεύματι δὲ λαλεῖ μυστήρια.

xv. 51. ἰδού, μυστήριον ὑμῖν λέγω—'a mystery'—a heavenly truth—revealed to me.

Rom. xi. 25. οὐ γὰρ θέλω ὑμᾶς ἀγνοεῖν τὸ μυστήριον τοῦτο—ὅτι πώρωσις ἀπὸ μέρους τῷ Ἰσραὴλ γέγονεν ἄχρι οὗ τὸ πλήρωμα τῶν ἐθνῶν εἰσέλθῃ κ.τ.λ.

(*b*) Eph. v. 32. τὸ μυστήριον τοῦτο μέγα ἐστίν, ἐγὼ δὲ λέγω εἰς Χριστὸν καὶ [εἰς] την ἐκκλησίαν—'this mystery'—this revealed truth of a unique relationship.

'The law of marriage laid down in Genesis as given to Adam was for St Paul a preliminary indication of a hidden Divine purpose or ordinance, the full meaning of which was to be revealed only by the revealing of Christ as the Head of His spouse the Church' (Hort: *Prolegomena to Romans and Ephesians*, p. 160).

B.   Mt. xiii. 11. ὑμῖν δέδοται γνῶναι τὰ μυστήρια τῆς βασιλείας τ. οὐρανῶν, ἐκείνοις δὲ οὐ δέδοται (Lk. viii. 10 τοῖς δὲ λοίποις ἐν παραβολαῖς).

[Mk. iv. 11 has ὑμῖν τὸ μυστήριον δέδοται, where perhaps the singular may be regarded as = γνῶναι τὰ μυστήρια of Mt. and Lk., and, for the second clause, ἐκείνοις δὲ τοῖς ἔξω ἐν παραβολαῖς τὰ πάντα γίνεται.]

Apoc. i. 20. τὸ μυστήριον τῶν ἑπτὰ ἀστέρων—'the mystery of [the inner meaning of the truth signified by] the seven stars.'

Apoc. xvii. 5. κ. ἐπὶ τὸ μέτωπον αὐτῆς ὄνομα γεγραμμένον, μυστήριον, Βαβυλών κ.τ.λ.—where μυστήριον = 'name significant of a spiritual truth.'

Apoc. xvii. 7. ἐγὼ ἐρῶ σοι τὸ μυστήριον [the mystery—the inner significance of—the unseen fact signified by] τῆς γυναικὸς κ. τοῦ θηρίου.

[The history of the use of the term in pre-Christian Greek deserves further study. Already in Plato, *Theaet.* 156 a, ἄλλοι δὲ κομψότεροι, ὧν μέλλω σοι τὰ μυστήρια λέγειν the word is used metaphorically, not, that is, of the actual, ceremonial, 'mysteries' or mystic implements, but of philosophical doctrines belonging to men of a particular School and expounded with authority by them alone, though the exposition may be subsequently transmitted by a hearer to others. Already the idea of secrecy is subordinate to that of special discovery or possession.]

"But, when adopted into the Christian vocabulary by St Paul, the word signifies simply 'a truth which was once hidden, but now is revealed,' 'a truth which without special revelation would have been unknown.' Hence μυστήριον is almost universally found in connexion with words denoting revelation or publication; *e.g.* ἀποκαλύπτειν, ἀποκάλυψις, Rom. xvi. 25, Eph. iii. 3, 5, 2 Th. ii. 7; γνωρίζειν, Rom. xvi. 26, Eph. i. 9, iii. 3, 10, vi. 19; φανεροῦν, Col. iv. 3, Rom. xvi. 26, 1 Tim. iii. 16; λαλεῖν Col. iv. 3, 1 Cor. ii. 7, xiv. 2; λέγειν 1 Cor. xv. 51." (Lightfoot on Col. i. 26.)

The word is characteristic of the Epistle to the Ephesians.

On the phrases ἐν Χριστῷ, ἐν Χριστῷ Ἰησοῦ, ἐν τῷ χριστῷ.

The phrases ἐν Χριστῷ Ἰησοῦ and ἐν Χριστῷ (without Ἰησοῦ) are found in the Epistles of St Paul as follows:

ἐν Χριστῷ Ἰησοῦ	ἐν Χριστῷ
(a) 1 Th. ii. 14	(a) 1 Th. iv. 16 οἱ νεκροὶ ἐν Χ.
v. 18	1 Cor. iii. 1
1 Cor. i. 2, 4, 30	iv. 10, 15, 17
iv. 15	xv. 18 οἱ κοιμηθέντες
xv. 31	ἐν Χ.
xvi. 24	19 ἠλπικότες ἐν Χ.
Gal. ii. 4	2 Cor. ii. 17
iii. 14 (W.H. mg.)	iii. 14 ἐν Χ. καταργεῖται
28 πάντες—ὑμεῖς εἰς	v. 17 εἴ τις ἐν Χ.
ἐστὲ ἐν Χ. Ἰ.	19 θεὸς ἦν ἐν Χριστῷ
v. 6	κόσμον καταλ-
Rom. iii. 24	λάσσων ἑαυτῷ
vi. 11, 23	xii. 2, 19
viii. 2, 39	Gal. i. 22
xv. 17	ii. 17
xvi. 3 συνεργούς μου ἐν	Rom. ix. 1
Χ. Ἰ.	xii. 5 ἓν σῶμά ἐσμεν ἐν Χ.
	xvi. 7, 9
(b) Phil. i. 1	(b) Phil. i. 13
ii. 5, 19	ii. 1
iii. 3, 14	iv. 19, 21
iv. 7	Col. i. 2 τ. ἐν Κολ. ἁγίοις καὶ
Col. i. 4	πιστοῖς ἀδελφοῖς ἐν Χ.
Eph. i. 1	28
ii. 6, 7, 10, 13	Eph. i. 3
iii. 6, 11, 21	iv. 32
Philem. 23	Philem. 8 πολλὴν ἐν Χ. παρ-
	ρησίαν ἔχων
(c) 1 Tim. i. 14	20 ἀνάπαυσόν μου τὰ
iii. 13	σπλάγχνα ἐν Χ.
2 Tim. i. 1, 9, 13	
ii. 1, 10	
iii. 12, 15	

Outside the Pauline Epistles there is no instance of ἐν Χριστῷ Ἰησοῦ. But ἐν Χριστῷ is found in

1 Pet. iii. 16.

    v. 10 [with v. l. ἐν τῷ χριστῷ].

      14.

It is also the reading of A in Apoc. i. 9.

The phrase ἐν τῷ χριστῷ is found only in

2 Cor. ii. 14.   τῷ πάντοτε θριαμβεύοντι ἡμᾶς ἐν τῷ χριστῷ.
Eph. i. 10.   ἀνακεφαλαιώσασθαι τὰ πάντα ἐν τῷ χριστῷ.
    12.   τοὺς προηλπικότας ἐν τῷ χριστῷ.
    20.   ἣν ἐνήργηκεν ἐν τῷ χριστῷ.
    (ii. 5. W. & H. mg. and so also 1 Pet. v. 10.)

[In Gal. iii. 14 ἐν Ἰησοῦ Χριστῷ is read (W. H. text).]

In Eph. iv. 21 occurs the unique phrase ἐν τῷ Ἰησοῦ (v. Add. Note, p. 70); and in Apoc. i. 9 the reading of C [adopted by W. & H.] is ἐν τῇ θλίψει κ. βασιλείᾳ κ. ὑπομονῇ ἐν Ἰησοῦ.

None of the phrases ἐν Χριστῷ, ἐν Χριστῷ Ἰησοῦ and ἐν τῷ χριστῷ occur in Hebrews or in any (save 1 Pet.) of the Catholic Epistles. Apart from 1 Pet. (ll. cc.) they are exclusively Pauline.

It will be seen that the short phrase ἐν Χριστῷ does not occur in the Pastoral Epistles.

Otherwise ἐν Χριστῷ and ἐν Χριστῷ Ἰησοῦ occur with about equal frequency, both in the earlier Epistles and in the Epistles of the Captivity.

On the other hand the unusual phrase ἐν τῷ χριστῷ is characteristic of the Epistle to the Ephesians, occurring in other Epistles nowhere excepting 2 Cor. ii. 14.

In Ephesians c. i. and more especially in the great Hymn of Praise (i. 3—14) the three forms of expression all occur, and, besides the instances of actual occurrence above cited, one or other of them is implied also in v. 4 (ἐν αὐτῷ), v. 6 (ἐν τῷ ἠγαπημένῳ), v. 7 (ἐν ᾧ), v. 11 (ἐν αὐτῷ), v. 13 (ἐν ᾧ).

Indeed in the rhythmical passage i. 3—14 the relation of the believer to Christ is shewn by development of the expression ἐν Χριστῷ.

It is 'in Christ' (ἐν Χριστῷ) that the Divine blessing is bestowed upon us (i. 3). Eternal election 'in Him' is spoken of (v. 4) as resting on a predestination to sonship: in *Him* too grace (v. 6; ii. 7; iv. 32) and redemption (i. 7) are ours. In Him, the Incarnate Son, God's purpose (i. 9) was embodied and accomplished, and would (v. 10) find its consummation. In Him the faithful of Israel had found fulfilment of their hope (vv. 11, 12); in Him Gentiles received (v. 13) the glad tidings of salvation and the gift of the Holy Spirit.

In the passage (ii. 1—10) describing what God in His mercy and love has done for man, it is 'in Christ Jesus' that man is seen to be (ii. 6) quickened, restored, and exalted:—in Him it is (v. 7) that the wealth of God's grace and goodness is manifested; in Him that Christians, a new creation, can do the works which God has prepared for them.

The other instances of ἐν Χριστῷ Ἰησοῦ in this Epistle are:

ii. 13. νυνὶ δὲ ἐν Χριστῷ Ἰησοῦ ὑμεῖς οἵ ποτε ὄντες μακρὰν ἐγενήθητε ἐγγύς,—followed by κτίσῃ ἐν αὐτῷ εἰς ἕνα· ἄνθρωπον (v. 16).

iii. 6. εἶναι τὰ ἔθνη συνκληρονόμα καὶ σύνσωμα καὶ συνμέτοχα τῆς ἐπαγγελίας ἐν Χριστῷ Ἰησοῦ.

iii. 21. αὐτῷ ἡ δόξα ἐν τῇ ἐκκλησίᾳ καὶ ἐν Χριστῷ Ἰησοῦ [where see note ad loc.].

The only other occurrence of ἐν Χριστῷ in the Epistle is at iv. 32 καθὼς καὶ ὁ θεὸς ἐν Χριστῷ ἐχαρίσατο ὑμῖν,—which recalls 2 Cor. v. 19 (v. inf.).

In Eph. iii. 11 ἐν τῷ χριστῷ Ἰησοῦ τῷ κυρίῳ ἡμῶν we have the same combination and order of titles as in Col. ii. 6 ὡς οὖν παρελάβετε τὸν χριστὸν Ἰησοῦν τὸν κύριον, ἐν αὐτῷ περιπατεῖτε (cf. Eph. iv. 20, 21).

This twofold title brings together the confession τὸν χριστὸν Ἰησοῦν (Acts v. 42), implied in the τοῦ χριστοῦ Ἰησοῦ of Eph. iii. 1, with the confession Κύριος Ἰησοῦς (1 Cor. xii. 3, Rom. x. 9) implied in the ἐν τῷ κυρίῳ Ἰησοῦ of Eph. i. 15:—a phrase which occurs nowhere else in St Paul.

(The combination ἐν Χριστῷ Ἰησοῦ τῷ κυρίῳ ἡμῶν occurs 1 Cor. xv. 31, Rom. vi. 23, viii. 39.)

The simple phrase ἐν κυρίῳ is found

(a)	1 Th. iii. 8		1 Cor. xvi. 19
	v. 12		2 Cor. ii. 12
	2 Th. iii. 4		x. 17
	1 Cor. i. 31		Gal. v. 10
	iv. 7		Rom. xvi. 2, 8, 11 ff., 22
	vii. 22, 39	(b)	Phil. i. 14
	ix. 1 f.		ii. 19, 24, 29
	xi. 11		iii. 1 χαίρετε ἐν κ.
	xv. 58		iv. 2, 10

Col. iii. 18, 20
iv. 7, 17
Eph. ii. 21 αὔξει εἰς ναὸν ἅγιον
ἐν κυρίῳ
iv. 1 παρακαλῶ—ὁ δέσ-
μιος ἐν κ.
17 μαρτύρομαι ἐν κ.
v. 8 νῦν δὲ φῶς ἐν κ.

Eph. vi. 1 ὑπακούετε τ. γονεῦσιν ὑμῶν [ἐν κ.]
10 ἐνδυναμοῦσθε ἐν κ.
21 πιστὸς διάκονος ἐν
κυρίῳ
Philem. 16, 20
(c) nowhere in the Pastoral Epistles.

It does not occur in Hebrews or in any of the Catholic Epistles.
Outside St Paul's writings it is found only in Apoc. xiv. 13 μακάριοι
οἱ νεκροὶ οἱ ἐν κυρίῳ ἀποθνήσκοντες ἀπ' ἄρτι.

Both expressions ἐν Χριστῷ and ἐν κυρίῳ, signify fellowship and
vital union with Him, in Whom the life of the Christian is ideally
lived.

'The Christian lives—in Christ. It is from Christ that he draws
his energy—it is as a member of Christ that he fulfils his part in the
great economy of the world. By his faith in God Incarnate and Man
ascended he stands forth as a witness of the essential unity of the seen
and the unseen, of earth and of heaven.......Doubtless it is hard *to
endure as seeing the invisible*; but when the spiritual eyes grow dim,
the thought of Christ risen, *in Whom* we are, will remove the mists
which cloud them. If once we realize what these words 'we are in
Christ' mean, we shall know that beneath the surface of life lie depths
which we cannot fathom, full alike of mystery and of hope.'

(*The Christian Life*, pp. 34, 35.)

The expression τὰ πάντα.

τὰ πάντα occurs
A. in Epistles of St Paul
  (a) 1 Cor. viii. 6. εἷς κύριος 'Ι. Χρ. δι' οὗ (v. l. ὃν) τὰ πάντα.
      xi. 12. τὰ δὲ πάντα ἐκ τοῦ θεοῦ.
      xii. 6. θεὸς ὁ ἐνεργῶν τὰ πάντα ἐν πᾶσιν.
      xv. 27 f. τ. ὑποτάξαντος αὐτῷ τὰ πάντα.
    2 Cor. iv. 15. τὰ γὰρ πάντα δι' ὑμᾶς.
        v. 18. τὰ δὲ πάντα ἐκ τοῦ θεοῦ.
    Gal. iii. 22. συνέκλεισεν ἡ γραφὴ τὰ πάντα ὑπὸ ἁμαρτίαν.
      (In 1 Cor. xii. 19 the reading is doubtful.)
  (b) Phil. iii. 8. δι' ὃν τὰ πάντα ἐζημιώθην.
        21. κατὰ τὴν ἐνέργειαν τοῦ δύνασθαι αὐτὸν καὶ ὑποτάξαι
        αὐτῷ τὰ πάντα.

Col. i. 16.   ἐν αὐτῷ ἐκτίσθη τὰ πάντα—τὰ πάντα δι᾽ αὐτοῦ κ. εἰς αὐτὸν ἔκτισται.

17.   κ. τὰ πάντα ἐν αὐτῷ συνέστηκεν.

20.   κ. δι᾽ αὐτοῦ ἀποκαταλλάξαι τὰ πάντα.

iii. 8.   ἀπόθεσθε καὶ ὑμεῖς τὰ πάντα.

Eph. i. 10.   ἀνακεφαλαιώσασθαι τὰ πάντα ἐν τῷ χριστῷ.

11.   τοῦ τὰ πάντα ἐνεργοῦντος.

23.   τὸ πλήρωμα τοῦ τὰ πάντα ἐν πᾶσιν πληρουμένου.

iii. 9.   ἐν τῷ θεῷ τῷ τὰ πάντα κτίσαντι.

iv. 10.   ἵνα πληρώσῃ τὰ πάντα.

15.   αὐξήσωμεν ἐν αὐτῷ τὰ πάντα.

v. 13.   τὰ δὲ πάντα ἐλεγχόμενα ὑπὸ τοῦ φῶτος.

(c)   1 Tim. vi. 13.   τ. θεοῦ τ. ζωογονοῦντος τὰ πάντα.

B.   Elsewhere in the N. T.

Heb. i. 3.   φέρων—τὰ πάντα τῷ ῥήματι τῆς δυνάμεως αὐτοῦ.

ii. 10.   δι᾽ ὃν τὰ πάντα καὶ δι᾽ οὗ τὰ πάντα.

[In ii. 8 the πάντα of τὰ πάντα is a repetition of the word from the quotation preceding. 'The τὰ πάντα takes up the πάντα of the Psalm' (note ad loc.).]

Apoc. iv. 11.   ὅτι σὺ ἔκτισας τὰ πάντα καὶ διὰ τὸ θέλημά σου ἦσαν καὶ ἐκτίσθησαν.

Τὰ πάντα, signifying all things in their unity,—the sum of all things, seen and unseen, in the heavens and upon the earth, whatever their sphere of being, their mode of existence, or their relation of dependence upon God,—may be contrasted with πάντα, which denotes all things regarded severally.

For πάντα cf. 1 Cor. iii. 22, ix. 22, xv. 27, 28, Col. iii. 11, Eph. i. 22 (iii. 20, vi. 21), Heb. iii. 4, Jo. i. 3 (where see note).

In Eph. i. 22 πάντα ὑπέταξεν ὑπὸ τοὺς πόδας αὐτοῦ is a quotation from Ps. viii. 6, the same passage being cited [in close agreement with the LXX.] in Heb. ii. 8 (q. v.).

On the other hand τὰ πάντα stands in contrast with τὸ πᾶν,—a term familiar in Greek philosophy and implying a self-contained unity. Τὸ πᾶν is not Scriptural.

Ἡ δόξα in the Epistle to the Ephesians.

In the Epistle to the Ephesians

(a)   δόξα, without the article, is found three times:

i. 6.   εἰς ἔπαινον δόξης τῆς χάριτος αὐτοῦ.

12.   εἰς ἔπαινον δόξης αὐτοῦ [where see note].

iii. 13.   ἥτις ἐστὶ δόξα ὑμῶν
(cf. Col. iii. 4, Phil. i. 11, ii. 11, iv. 19).

(*b*)   ἡ δόξα is found five times :

i. 14.   εἰς ἔπαινον τῆς δόξης αὐτοῦ.

17.   ὁ πατὴρ τῆς δόξης.

18.   τίς ὁ πλοῦτος τῆς δόξης τ. κληρονομίας αὐτοῦ ἐν τ. ἁγίοις.

iii. 16.   κατὰ τὸ πλοῦτος τῆς δόξης αὐτοῦ.

21.   αὐτῷ ἡ δόξα ἐν τῇ ἐκκλησίᾳ κ. ἐν Ἰησοῦ Χριστῷ.

The other occurrences of ἡ δόξα in the Epistles of the Captivity are:

Col. i. 11.   κατὰ τὸ κράτος τῆς δόξης αὐτοῦ.

27.   τί τὸ πλοῦτος τῆς δόξης τ. μυστηρίου τούτου.

Phil. iii. 21.   σύμμορφον τῷ σώματι τῆς δόξης αὐτοῦ.

(Compare in contrast *v.* 19 ἡ δ. ἐν τ. αἰσχύνῃ αὐτῶν.)

iv. 20.   τῷ δὲ θεῷ καὶ πατρὶ ἡμῶν ἡ δόξα.

'*The glory of the Lord*'—is a key-word of Scripture.—The Bible is one widening answer to the prayer of Moses (Ex. xxxiii. 18) 'Shew me Thy glory.'—And God has been pleased to make Himself known in many parts and in many fashions—as man could bear the knowledge :

(*a*) by material symbol (Ex. xxiv. 16, Lev. ix. 23, Ex. xl. 35, 1 K. viii. 11, Ezek. xliii. 4 ff., Apoc. xxi. 22 f.),

(*β*) through human Presence :

(i) in the Messianic nation (Is. xl. 5),—and (*id.* xlii. ff., liii. 3 ff.) the Figure of the 'Servant of the Lord,'

(ii) finally in the Incarnation of the Son of God, in the Life and Resurrection of the Son of Man (Jo. i. 14, ii. 11), the perfect revelation on earth of the Glory of God.

(*Revelation of the Father*, pp. 164 f.)

The 'glory of God' is the full manifestation of His attributes according to man's power of apprehending them, 'all His goodness' (Ex. xxxiii. 19 ff.). Of it—under the Old Dispensation the Shekinah was the Symbol.   (Note on Heb. i. 3.)

'It is the majesty, or the power or the goodness, of God as *manifested* to men.'   (Lightfoot on Col. i. 11.)

It is the sum of His manifested perfections.

The 'glory of His grace' (Eph. i. 6) is the manifestation of the power of His free and bounteous goodness.

The 'Father of Glory' (Eph. i. 17) is He, Whom Our Lord Jesus Christ has revealed as Father,—from Whom all perfection proceeds— the source or subject of all revelation.

(In Acts vii. 2 the phrase 'the God of glory' recalls Ps. xxix. 3; while in 1 Cor. ii. 8 Our Lord Jesus Christ, Whom 'the rulers of this world crucified' is 'the Lord of glory': cf. Ja. ii. 1.)

'The wealth of the glory' of God (Eph. i. 18, iii. 16)—a phrase occurring also in Col. i. 27 and in Rom. ix. 23—signifies the inexhaustible fulness of His Majesty and abundant goodness, as revealed to man.

The Doxology in Eph. iii. 21: 'To Him be the glory in the Church and in Christ Jesus unto all the generations of the age of the ages' may be compared with the doxologies in

Gal. i. 5.   ᾧ ἡ δόξα εἰς τ. αἰῶνας τ. αἰώνων.

Rom. xi. 3 f.   αὐτῷ ἡ δόξα εἰς τ. αἰῶνας (cf. xvi. 27).

Phil. iv. 20.   τῷ δὲ θεῷ κ. πατρὶ ἡμῶν ἡ δόξα εἰς τ. αἰ. τ. αἰ.

Apoc. i. 6, v. 12 f., vii. 12, xix. 1.   κ.τ.λ.

In all these instances the Doxology is addressed to God the Father.

In 2 Tim. iv. 18 ᾧ ἡ δόξα εἰς τ. α. τ. α. the Doxology is addressed to Christ (ῥύσεταί με ὁ κύριος); and so in 2 Pet. iii. 18, and in Apoc. i. 6 :— possibly also in Heb. xiii. 21 (v. note), and 1 Pet. iv. 11.

The article in all these doxologies implies that to God only belongs that through which whatever is glorious gains its glory—His is 'the glory' (ἡ δόξα).

Words in the New Testament denoting resurrection or raising from death.

Ἐγείρειν, ἀναστῆναι, ἀνάστασις.

A. In the *Pauline Epistles.*

(a) ἐγείρειν, ἐγείρεσθαι, ἐγεῖραι, ἐγερθῆναι are used.

1 Th. i. 10.   ὃν ἤγειρεν ἐκ τῶν νεκρῶν.

1 Cor. vi. 14.   ὁ δὲ θεὸς καὶ τὸν κύριον ἤγειρεν καὶ ἡμᾶς ἐξεγερεῖ (v. l. ἐξήγειρεν) διὰ τῆς δυνάμεως αὐτοῦ.

xv. 4.   κ. ὅτι ἐγήγερται τῇ ἡμέρᾳ τῇ τρίτῃ.

12.   ὅτι ἐκ νεκρῶν ἐγήγερται.

13.   οὐδὲ Χριστὸς ἐγήγερται.

14.   εἰ δὲ Χριστὸς οὐκ ἐγήγερται (So v. 17.)

15.   ὅτι ἐμαρτυρήσαμεν κατὰ τοῦ θεοῦ ὅτι ἤγειρεν τὸν χριστόν, ὃν οὐκ ἤγειρεν, εἴπερ ἄρα νεκροὶ οὐκ ἐγείρονται.

16.   εἰ γὰρ νεκροὶ οὐκ ἐγείρονται, οὐδὲ Χριστὸς ἐγήγερται.

20.   νυνὶ δὲ Χριστὸς ἐγήγερται ἐκ νεκρῶν.

29.   εἰ—νεκροὶ οὐκ ἐγείρονται. (So v. 32.)

35.   πῶς ἐγείρονται οἱ νεκροί;

1 Cor. xv. 42 ff.   ἐγείρεται ἐν ἀφθαρσίᾳ—ἐ. ἐν δόξῃ—ἐ. ἐν δυνάμει—ἐ.
σῶμα πνευματικόν.

52.   οἱ νεκροὶ ἐγερθήσονται ἄφθαρτοι.

2 Cor. i. 9.   τῷ ἐγείροντι τοὺς νεκρούς.

iv. 14.   ὁ ἐγείρας τὸν κύριον Ἰησοῦν καὶ ἡμᾶς σὺν Ἰησοῦ ἐγερεῖ.

v. 15.   τῷ ὑπὲρ αὐτῶν ἀποθανόντι καὶ ἐγερθέντι.

Gal. i. 1.   κ. θεοῦ πατρὸς τοῦ ἐγείραντος αὐτὸν ἐκ νεκρῶν.

Rom. iv. 24.   τ. ἐγείραντα Ἰησοῦν τ. κύριον ἡμῶν ἐκ νεκρῶν.

25.   κ. ἠγέρθη διὰ τὴν δικαίωσιν ἡμῶν.

vi. 4.   ἠγέρθη Χριστὸς ἐκ νεκρῶν.

9.   Χρ. ἐγερθεὶς ἐκ ν.

vii. 4.   τῷ ἐκ ν. ἐγερθέντι.

viii. 10.   τ. ἐγείραντος τ. Ἰ. ἐκ ν.—ὁ ἐγείρας ἐκ ν. Χ. Ἰ.

34.   μᾶλλον δὲ ἐγερθείς.

x. 9.   ὅτι ὁ θεὸς αὐτὸν ἤγειρεν ἐκ ν.

Col. ii. 12.   τοῦ θεοῦ τοῦ ἐγείραντος αὐτὸν ἐκ νεκρῶν.

Eph. i. 20.   ἐγείρας αὐτὸν ἐκ νεκρῶν.

2 Tim. ii. 8.   Χριστὸν ἐγηγερμένον ἐκ νεκρῶν.

(β)   The verb ἀνίστασθαι, ἀναστῆναι, is used

1 Th. iv. 14.   ὅτι Ἰησοῦς ἀπέθανεν καὶ ἀνέστη.

16.   οἱ νεκροὶ ἐν Χριστῷ ἀναστήσονται πρῶτον.
(On Eph. v. 14, v. infr.)

The noun ἀνάστασις occurs

1 Cor. xv. 12.   λέγουσιν—ὅτι ἀνάστασις νεκρῶν οὐκ ἔστιν.

13.   εἰ δὲ ἀνάστασις ν. οὐκ ἔστιν.

21.   καὶ δι᾽ ἀνθρώπου ἀνάστασις ν.

42.   οὕτω καὶ ἡ ἀνάστασις τ. ν.

Rom. i. 4.   τ. ὁρισθέντος υἱοῦ θεοῦ—ἐξ ἀναστάσεως νεκρῶν.

vi. 5.   ἀλλὰ καὶ τῆς ἀναστάσεως ἐσόμεθα.

Phil. iii. 10.   τὴν δύναμιν τῆς ἀναστάσεως αὐτοῦ.

2 Tim. ii. 18.   λέγοντες ἀνάστασιν ἤδη γεγονέναι.

Also once ἐξανάστασις.

Phil. iii. 11.   εἰς τὴν ἐξανάστασιν τὴν ἐκ νεκρῶν.

B.   In *non-Pauline Epistles.*

(a)   ἐγείρειν κ.τ.λ. are found

Heb. xi. 19.   λογισάμενος ὅτι καὶ ἐκ νεκρῶν ἐγείρειν δυνατὸς ὁ θεός
(where see note).

1 Pet. i. 21.   θεὸν τὸν ἐγείραντα αὐτὸν ἐκ νεκρῶν.
[See Hort's note *ad loc.*]

(β) The verb ἀνίστασθαι κ.τ.λ. does not occur.

But ἀνάστασις is found :—

Heb. vi. 4. ἀναστάσεως νεκρῶν κ. κρίματος αἰωνίου.
xi. 35. ἔλαβον γυναῖκες ἐξ ἀναστάσεως τ. νεκροὺς αὐτῶν.
ib. ἵνα κρείττονος ἀναστάσεως τύχωσιν.
1 Pet. i. 3. ὁ κατὰ τὸ πόλυ ἑαυτοῦ ἔλεος ἀναγεννήσας ἡμᾶς εἰς
ἐλπίδα ζῶσαν δι᾽ ἀναστάσεως Ἰησοῦ Χριστοῦ ἐκ
νεκρῶν. [where see Hort's note.]
iii. 21. σώζει—δι᾽ ἀναστάσεως Ἰησοῦ Χριστοῦ.

C. Usage of *Synoptic Gospels* and *Acts*.

In the *Synoptic Gospels* both verbs—ἐγείρεσθαι (ἐγερθῆναι κ.τ.λ.) and
ἀνίστασθαι (ἀναστῆναι κ.τ.λ.) are used : also ἀνάστασις.

(a) Raising of the daughter of Jairus.

Mk. v. 41. ἔγειρε—ἀνέστη.
Mt. ix. 25. ἠγέρθη.
Lk. viii. 55. ἔγειρε—ἀνέστη.

(b) Charge to the disciples.

Mt. x. 8. νεκροὺς ἐγείρετε.

(c) Message to the Baptist.

Mt. xi. 5 = Lk. vii. 22. νεκροὶ ἐγείρονται.

(d) Herod and John the Baptist.

Mk. vi. 14 ff. ἐγήγερται ἐκ νεκρῶν—ἠγέρθη (v. 16).
Mt. xiv. 2. ἠγέρθη ἀπὸ τ. νεκρῶν.
Lk. ix. 7. ὅτι Ἰωάνης ἠγέρθη ἐκ νεκρῶν.
8. ὅτι προφήτης τις τ. ἀρχαίων ἀνέστη.

(e) Answer to the Sadducees.

Mk. xii. 26. περὶ δὲ τ. νεκρῶν ὅτι ἐγείρονται.
Lk. xx. 27. ὅτι δὲ ἐγείρονται οἱ νεκροί.

Here also the noun ἀνάστασις is used :—

Mk. xii. 18, 22, Mt. xxii. 23, 28, 30, 31, Lk. xx. 27, 33, 35, 36.
(It also occurs Lk. xiv. 14 ἐν τῇ ἀναστάσει τῶν δικαίων.)

(f) The Lord's predictions of His Passion and Resurrection.

Mk. ix. 31, x. 33, ἀναστήσεται, xiv. 28 ἐγερθῆναι.
Mt. xvi. 21 ἐγερθῆναι, xx. 19 ἐγερθήσεται (v. l. ἀναστήσεται), xvii. 9
ἐγερθῇ (v. l. ἀναστῇ).

Lk. ix. 22.   ἐγερθῆναι (v. l. ἀναστῆναι), xviii. 33 ἀναστήσεται.
Cf. Mt. xxvii. 63 f. ἐγείρομαι—ἠγέρθη.

(g)   Parable of Rich Man and Lazarus.

Lk. xvi. 31.   ἐάν τις ἐκ νεκρῶν ἀναστῇ.

(h)   Records of the Resurrection.

Mk. xvi. 6.   ἠγέρθη (cf. v. 9 ἀναστάς, v. 14 ἐγηγερμένον).
Mt. xxviii. 6.   ἠγέρθη, v. 7 ἠγέρθη ἀπὸ τ. νεκρῶν.
Lk. xxiv. 6.   ἠγέρθη, v. 7 ἀναστῆναι.
       34.   ὄντως ἠγέρθη.

The noun ἔγερσις occurs once, Mt. xxvii. 53 μετὰ τὴν ἔγερσιν αὐτοῦ.

In Acts again both verbs are used :—

(α)   ἤγειρεν (sc. ὁ θεὸς) in iii. 15, iv. 10, v. 30, x. 40, xiii. 30, 37 ;
       and ἐγείρει in xxvi. 8.

(β)   ἀνέστησεν or ἀναστήσας (sc. ὁ θεὸς) in ii. 24, 32, iii. 26, xiii. 33,
       34 (ἐκ ν.), xvii. 31 (ἐκ ν.).

The noun ἀνάστασις occurs 11 times in Acts, viz.:—

Acts i. 22.   μάρτυρα τῆς ἀναστάσεως αὐτοῦ.

   ii. 21.   τ. ἀν. τ. χριστοῦ, iv. 33 τ. ἀν. τ. κυρίου Ἰησοῦ.

   xvii. 18.   Ἰ. καὶ τὴν ἀνάστασιν.

   xxiii. 8.   μὴ εἶναι ἀνάστασιν.

   iv. 2.   τ. ἀνάστασιν τὴν ἐκ νεκρῶν.

   xvii. 32, xxiii. 6, xxiv. 15, 21, xxvi. 23.   ἀν. νεκρῶν.

D.   In St John.

(α)   ἐγείρειν κ.τ.λ. is used

Jo. ii. 19.   ἐν τρισὶν ἡμέραις ἐγερῶ αὐτόν, and v. 20 ἐγερεῖς.

      22.   ὅτε οὖν ἠγέρθη ἐκ νεκρῶν.

   v. 21.   ἐγείρει τοὺς νεκρούς.

   xii. 1, 9.   ὃν ἤγειρεν ἐκ νεκρῶν, and v. 17 (of Lazarus).

   xxi. 14.   ἐγερθεὶς ἐκ νεκρῶν.

(β)   ἀνιστάναι, ἀνίστασθαι, ἀναστῆναι occur

Jo. vi. 39.   ἀναστήσω αὐτὸ (vv. 40, 44, 54 ἀναστήσω αὐτὸν) τῇ
                  (vel ἐν τῇ) ἐσχάτῃ ἡμέρᾳ.

   xi. 23.   ἀναστήσεται ὁ ἀδελφός σου.

      24.   οἶδα ὅτι ἀναστήσεται—ἐν τ. ἐσχ. ἡμέρᾳ.

      31.   ἀνέστη κ. ἐξῆλθεν.

   xx. 9.   ὅτι δεῖ αὐτὸν ἐκ νεκρῶν ἀναστῆναι.

(γ) ἀνάστασις occurs

Apoc. xx. 5.   ἡ ἀνάστασις ἡ πρώτη, v. 6 ἐν τῇ ἀν. τ. π.

Jo. v. 29.   εἰς ἀνάστασιν ζωῆς—εἰς ἀν. κρίσεως.

xi. 24.   ἐν τῇ ἀναστάσει.

25.   Ἐγώ εἰμι ἡ ἀνάστασις κ. ἡ ζωή.

The phrases ἀνάστασις νεκρῶν and ἡ ἀνάστασις ἡ ἐκ νεκρῶν must be distinguished. And the contrast between ἀνάστασις ζωῆς and ἀνάστασις κρίσεως ('resurrection which issues in judgment') is to be noted. Cf. 2 Macc. vii. 9. ὁ δὲ τοῦ κόσμου βασιλεὺς ἀποθανόντας ἡμᾶς ὑπὲρ τῶν αὐτοῦ νόμων εἰς αἰώνιον ἀναβίωσιν ζωῆς ἡμᾶς ἀναστήσει. Also id. ib. v. 14. αἱρετὸν μεταλλάσσοντας ὑπ' ἀνθρώπων τὰς ὑπὸ τοῦ θεοῦ προσδοκᾶν ἐλπίδας πάλιν ἀναστήσεσθαι ὑπ' αὐτοῦ· σοὶ μὲν γὰρ ἀνάστασις εἰς ζωὴν οὐκ ἔσται.

Reference to this Maccabean history of the seven brethren is made in Heb. xi. 35 ἄλλοι δὲ ἐτυμπανίσθησαν, οὐ προσδεξάμενοι τὴν ἀπολύτρωσιν, ἵνα κρείττονος ἀναστάσεως τύχωσιν (v. supr.), 'where in κρείττονος comparison is made implicitly, though not directly, between resurrection to eternal life and resurrection to an earthly life.' (Note ad loc.)

The words 'shall raise us up—unto an eternal renewal of life' (in v. 7) and 'but as for thee, thou shalt have no resurrection unto life' (in v. 14) of the passage in 2 Maccabees [bring us near to the language of the New Testament]. See on Jo. v. 29.

Cf. Lightfoot on Phil. iii. 11 : "The 'resurrection from the dead' (τ. ἐξανάστασιν τὴν ἐκ νεκρῶν) is the final resurrection of the righteous to a new and glorified life. The general resurrection of the dead, whether good or bad, is ἡ ἀνάστασις τῶν νεκρῶν (e.g. 1 Cor. xv. 42); on the other hand the resurrection of Christ and of those who rise with Christ is generally [ἡ] ἀνάστασις [ἡ] ἐκ νεκρῶν (Luke xx. 35, Acts iv. 2, 1 Pet. i. 3). The former includes both the ἀνάστασις ζωῆς and the ἀνάστασις κρίσεως (Jo. v. 29); the latter is confined to the ἀνάστασις ζωῆς."

In *Ephesians* there is no direct reference to the future resurrection of men.

The words of c. v. 14 :

Ἔγειρε, ὁ καθεύδων,

καὶ ἀνάστα ἐκ τῶν νεκρῶν,

καὶ ἐπιφαύσει σοι ὁ χριστός

signify an awakening from the sleep of spiritual death (cf. ii. 1 f.) and an arising to spiritual life and action in the present.

The words, in fact, express a paradox—a present miracle of translation from death to life, such a rising, and restoration to life, of the dead as is signified in the miracles of Christ. We may compare the language of Jo. iii. 14 μεταβεβήκαμεν ἐκ τοῦ θανάτου εἰς τὴν ζωήν. The realisation of the eternal in the present dominates the thought of the Epistle.

On the meaning of κυβεία (Eph. iv. 14).

' Κυβεία from κύβος is properly 'dice-playing' and hence 'trickery, deceit.' Von Soden prefers to take it as expressing conduct void of seriousness; these persons 'play with' the conscience and the soul's health of Christians. But this is not the ordinary sense of the word. The ἐν is instrumental, the words expressing the means by which the περιφ. κ.τ.λ. is attained.'

(Dr T. K. Abbott, *International Critical Commentary on ' Ephesians,'* p. 122.)

[The foregoing explanation of κυβεία is taken, by kind permission of Professor T. K. Abbott of Dublin, from that scholar's admirable *Commentary on Ephesians* in the 'International Critical' Series.

Permission to do this was asked on the following grounds.

There is evidence (*a*) that Dr Westcott was at first uncertain as to the precise meaning of κυβεία in this passage, but (*b*) that he eventually came to the decision that it here means 'fraud.'

There is also evidence that during the last months of his life and while engaged on 'Ephesians' Dr Westcott, who seldom read modern commentaries, consulted this work of Prof. Abbott, some of the MS. notes of his own Commentary now published being found within the pages of a copy of the *International Critical Commentary.*

It is reasonable to infer that his 'Additional Note,' promised but never written, would have contained a reference to Prof. Abbott's note,—in which a meaning, practically identical with that finally accepted by Dr Westcott, is given to κυβεία. J. M. S.]

Spiritual Powers.

The existence of other orders of rational (spiritual) beings about us is most natural.

That it is possible for us to hold communication with them under certain circumstances is not unlikely.

That it is wrong for us to seek such intercourse is probable.

That we may be subject to their assaults seems to be justified by experience.

The statements of Holy Scripture, however, on this subject are marked by singular reserve.

Use of κατά c. acc. in the Epistle to the Ephesians.

(a) κατὰ θεόν. iv. 24.

,, τὴν δωρεὰν τῆς χάριτος τ. θεοῦ. iii. 7.

,, τὸ μέτρον τῆς δωρεᾶς. iv. 7.

,, τὸ πλοῦτος τῆς χάριτος αὐτοῦ. i. 7.

,, ,, ,, ,, δόξης αὐτοῦ. iii. 16.

,, τὴν εὐδοκίαν τοῦ θελήματος αὐτοῦ. i. 5.

,, ,, ,, αὐτοῦ. i. 9.

,, τὴν βουλὴν τοῦ θελήματος αὐτοῦ. i. 11.

,, πρόθεσιν τοῦ τὰ πάντα ἐνεργοῦντος. ib.

,, ,, τῶν αἰώνων. iii. 11.

,, τὴν ἐνέργειαν τοῦ κράτους τ. ἰσχύος αὐτοῦ. i. 19.

,, ,, ,, τῆς δυνάμεως αὐτοῦ. iii. 7.

(b) κατὰ τὸν ἄρχοντα τῆς ἐξουσίας τ. ἀέρος. ii. 2.

,, τὸν αἰῶνα τοῦ κόσμου τούτου. ib.

,, τὴν προτέραν ἀναστροφήν. iv. 22.

,, τὰς ἐπιθυμίας τῆς ἀπάτης. ib.

(c) κατὰ σάρκα. vi. 5.

κατ᾽ ὀφθαλμοδουλείαν. vi. 6.

κατ᾽ ἐνέργειαν. iv. 16.

καθ᾽ ὑμᾶς. i. 15.

κατ᾽ ἐμέ. vi. 21.

Use of the phrase ἐν σαρκί.

Gal. ii. 20. ὃ δὲ νῦν ζῶ ἐν σαρκί, ἐν πίστει ζῶ τῇ τ. υἱοῦ τ. θεοῦ.

vi. 12. ὅσοι θέλουσιν εὐπροσωπῆσαι ἐν σαρκί.

2 Cor. x. 3. ἐν σαρκὶ...περιπατοῦντες.

Rom. viii. 8 f. οἱ ἐν σαρκὶ ὄντες...οὐκ ἐν σαρκί, ἀλλ᾽ ἐν πνεύματι.

Phil. i. 22. εἰ δὲ τὸ ζῆν ἐν σαρκί, τοῦτό μοι καρπὸς ἔργου.

iii. 3 f. οἱ πνεύματι θεοῦ λατρεύοντες...οὐκ ἐν σαρκὶ πεποιθότες.

Col. ii. 1. ὅσοι οὐχ ἑωράκασι τὸ πρόσωπόν μου ἐν σαρκί.

Philemon 16. καὶ ἐν σαρκὶ καὶ ἐν κυρίῳ.

Eph. ii. 11. τὰ ἔθνη ἐν σαρκί...τ. λεγομένης περιτομῆς ἐν σαρκί.

1 Tim. iii. 16. ἐφανερώθη ἐν σαρκί, ἐδικαιώθη ἐν πνεύματι.

1 Pet. iv. 2. τ. ἐπίλοιπον ἐν σαρκὶ βιῶσαι χρόνον (cf. *v.* 1).

1 Jo. iv. 2. ὃ ὁμολογεῖ Ἰ. Χ. ἐν σαρκὶ ἐληλυθότα (cf. 2 Jo. 7).

Prophets of the New Covenant.

(a) προφήτης.

Mt. x. 41.   ὁ δεχόμενος προφήτην εἰς ὄνομα πρ. μισθὸν πρ. λήψεται.

Acts xi. 27.   κατῆλθον ἀπὸ Ἰερουσαλὴμ προφῆται.

  xiii. 1.   προφῆται κ. διδάσκαλοι.

  xv. 32.   καὶ αὐτοὶ προφῆται ὄντες.

  xxi. 10.   κατῆλθέν τις ἀπὸ τῆς Ἰουδαίας προφήτης.

1 Cor. xii. 28.   καὶ οὓς μὲν ἔθετο ὁ θεὸς ἐν τῇ ἐκκλησίᾳ πρῶτον
           ἀποστόλους, δεύτερον προφήτας, τρίτον διδασκάλους.

      29.   μὴ πάντες προφῆται;

  xiv. 29.   προφῆται δὲ δύο ἢ τρεῖς λαλείτωσαν.

      32.   πνεύματα προφητῶν προφήταις ὑποτάσσεται.

      37.   εἴ τις δοκεῖ προφήτης εἶναι ἢ πνευματικός.

Eph. ii. 20.   ἐπὶ τῷ θεμελίῳ τ. ἀποστόλων κ. προφητῶν.

  iii. 5.   τ. ἁγίοις ἀποστόλοις αὐτοῦ κ. προφήταις.

  iv. 11.   τοὺς μὲν ἀποστόλους, τοὺς δὲ προφήτας, τ. δὲ εὐαγγελιστάς.

Apoc. xviii. 20.   κ. οἱ ἅγιοι κ. οἱ ἀπόστολοι κ. οἱ προφῆται.

      24.   αἷμα προφητῶν καὶ ἁγίων (cf. xvi. 16, x. 7, xi. 18).

  xxii. 6.   ὁ θεὸς τῶν πνευμάτων τῶν προφητῶν (cf. xi. 10).

      9.   σύνδουλός σού εἰμι κ. τ. ἀδελφῶν σου τῶν προφητῶν.

(b) προφῆτις.   Apoc. ii. 20.   λέγουσα ἑαυτὴν προφῆτιν (cf. Lk. ii. 36).

(c) προφητεύειν.

1 Cor. xi. 4, 5, xiii. 9, xiv. 1, 3, 4, 5, 14, 31, 39 (ζηλοῦτε τὸ
           προφητεύειν).

Mt. vii. 22.   τῷ σῷ ὀνόματι ἐπροφητεύσαμεν.

Acts xix. 6.   ἐλάλουν τε γλώσσαις κ. ἐπροφήτευον (cf. ii. 17, xxi. 9).

Apoc. xi. 3.   δώσω τ. δυσὶν μάρτυσίν μου κ. προφητεύσουσιν (cf. x. 11).

(d) προφητεία.

1 Th. v. 20.   προφητείας μὴ ἐξουθενεῖτε.

1 Cor. xii. 10.   ἄλλῳ προφητεία.

  xiii. 2.   κἂν ἔχω προφητείαν κ. εἰδῶ τὰ μυστήρια πάντα.

      8.   προφητεῖαι καταργηθήσονται.

  xiv. 6.   ἢ ἐν προφητείᾳ ἢ ἐν διδαχῇ.

      22.   ἡ δὲ προφητεία οὐ τ. ἀπίστοις ἀλλὰ τ. πιστεύουσιν.

Rom. xii. 6.   χαρίσματα...εἴτε προφητείαν...εἴτε διακονίαν.

1 Tim. i. 18.   κατὰ τὰς προαγούσας ἐπὶ σὲ προφητείας.

  iv. 14.   ὃ ἐδόθη σοι διὰ προφητείας.

Apoc. i. 3.   τ. λόγους τῆς προφητείας (xxii. 7, 10, 18 f.).

  xi. 6.   τ. ἡμέρας τ. προφητείας αὐτῶν.

Ruskin on Eph. iv. 17, *and on Conflict with Evil.*

(*a*) [In the notes on Eph. iv. 17 reference is made to Ruskin's *Modern Painters*, Pt III. c. ii. § 8. The section is entitled 'Ideals of Beauty, how essentially moral.' The sentences quoted below are from the latter part of this section and from the beginning of § 9, 'How degraded by heartless reception.']

Having shewn that 'it is evident that the sensation of beauty is not sensual on the one hand, nor is it intellectual on the other, but is dependent on a pure, right, and open state of the heart: dependent both for its truth and for its intensity, insomuch that even the right after-action of the Intellect upon facts of beauty as apprehended is dependent on the acuteness of the heart-feeling about them,' Ruskin proceeds: 'And thus the Apostolic words come true, in this minor respect, as in all others, that men are "alienated from the life of God through the ignorance that is in them, having the *Understanding* darkened because of the hardness of their *hearts*, and so, being past feeling, give themselves up to lasciviousness." For we do indeed see constantly that men having naturally acute perceptions of the beautiful, yet not receiving it with a pure heart, nor into their hearts at all, never comprehend it, nor receive good from it; but make it a mere minister to their desires, and accompaniment and seasoning of lower sensual pleasures, until all their emotions take the same earthly stamp, and the sense of beauty sinks into the servant of lust. Nor is what the world commonly understands by the cultivation of "taste" anything more or better than this; at least in times of corrupt and over-pampered civilization, when men build palaces and plant groves and gather luxuries, that they and their devices may hang in the corners of the world like fine-spun cobwebs, with greedy, puffed-up, spider-like lusts in the middle. And this, which in Christian times is the abuse and corruption of the sense of beauty, was in that Pagan life, of which St Paul speaks, little less than the essence of it, and the best they had.'

(*b*) [A reference, in Dr Westcott's note on vi. 12, to Ruskin's *Modern Painters*, was for some time difficult to identify owing to an uncertainty as to the page-number. Ultimately the passage intended was discovered, beyond all doubt, to be a passage in Pt IX. c. xii. § 18; which has accordingly been printed in the Commentary *ad loc.* But the following two passages, which the Index to *Modern Painters* in the first instance suggested as perhaps intended, may be felt to be worth citing in addition to the other; which in one or two points they illustrate and supplement.]

'The reason of this I believe to be that the right faith of man is not intended to give him repose, but to enable him to do his work.

It is not intended that he should look away from the place he lives in now, and cheer himself with thoughts of the place he is to live in next, but that he should look stoutly into this world, in faith that, if he does his work thoroughly here, some good to others or himself, with which however he is not at present concerned, will come of it hereafter. And this kind of brave, but not very hopeful or cheerful, faith I perceive to be always rewarded by clear practical success and splendid intellectual power; while the faith which dwells on the future fades away into rosy mist and emptiness of musical air. That result indeed follows naturally enough on its habit of assuming that things must be right, or must come right, when probably the fact is that, so far as we are concerned, they are entirely wrong, and going wrong : and also on its weak and false way of looking on what these religious persons call "the bright side of things," that is to say, on one side of them only, when God has given them two sides and intended us to see both.'

(*Modern Painters*, vol. v. p. 229, small edition ; Pt IX. c. ii. § 11.)

'Now, as far as I have watched the main powers of human mind, they have risen first from the resolution to see fearlessly, pitifully and to its very worst, what those deep colours mean, wheresoever they fall ; not by any means to pass on the other side, looking pleasantly up to the sky, but to stoop to the horror, and let the sky, for the present, take care of its own clouds. However this may be in moral matters, with which I have nothing here to do, in my own field of inquiry the fact is so ; and all great and beautiful work has come of first gazing without shrinking into the darkness. If, having done so, the human spirit can by its courage and faith conquer the evil, it rises into conceptions of victorious and consummated beauty.'

(*id. ib.* v. p. 232; Pt IX. c. ii. § 13.)

The world, the flesh and the devil.

[The question raised by Dr Westcott, after quoting Ruskin, in his notes on vi. 12, 'When does "the world, the flesh and the devil" first appear?' remains unanswered.

There can indeed be little doubt that the actual co-ordination in English, and in this unqualified form, of the three familiar terms, as well as the introduction into the Baptismal Office of the same threefold classification, though in a different and more ancient order, of ultimate sources of evil, is due to Cranmer.

But on the other hand it is to be noted :—

(a) That although in the earlier English, as in the Roman, Offices 'the devil' or 'Satan' with 'his works' (operibus eius) and 'his pomps' (pompis eius) stood alone as the object of baptismal renunciation,—in the Gallican Office, as also (with slight variants) in Luther's *Taufbüchlein* and Hermann's *Consultation*, the 'pomps of the *world*' (pompis seculi) and 'its pleasures' (voluptatibus eius) are co-ordinated with 'Satan'—a collocation which, there is evidence, had very early authority, both Eastern and Western (cf. Cyprian, *ad Rogatianum*, Ambros. *de Initiatis*, c. 2, Macarius, *Hom.* 49).

(b) That in several ancient Litanies, Greek and Latin, 'deceits of the *world*' or 'desires of the *flesh*,' or the like, had been co-ordinated in deprecation with 'snares of the devil.'

(c) That S. Thomas Aquinas had explicitly (*Summa* II. 114, 3), discussed the question 'Utrum omnia peccata procedunt ex tentatione *diaboli*?' and had concluded that not all sins were committed at his instigation, but some 'ex libertate arbitrii et *carnis* corruptione'; and had also (I. 65, 1) explained that 'the devil' is said by St Paul to be 'the god of *this world*' (deus huius seculi) because 'seculariter viventes ei serviunt.'

(d) That in the *Imitatio Christi* (II. 12, 9) occurs the sentence : 'Si ad te ipsum respicis, nihil huiusmodi ex te poteris; sed si in domino confidis, dabitur tibi fortitudo de caelo, et subicientur ditioni tuae *mundus* et *caro*; sed nec inimicum *diabolum* timebis, si fueris fide armatus et cruce Jesu signatus.'

Rightly to examine and interpret these and other data involves argument which, if presented here, would constitute a material departure from the rule, adopted in the editing of this volume, that beyond statistics and matter of common knowledge no conclusions should be advanced other than such as have the authority of Bishop Westcott himself. J. M. S.]

Use of the Old Testament in 'Ephesians.'

Gen. ii. 24. ἔνεκεν τούτου καταλείψει ἄνθρωπος τὸν πατέρα αὐτοῦ καὶ τὴν μητέρα αὐτοῦ καὶ προσκολληθήσεται τῇ γυναικὶ (E πρὸς τ. γ.) αὐτοῦ· καὶ ἔσονται οἱ δύο εἰς σάρκα μίαν.

Eph. v. 31. ἀντὶ τούτου καταλείψει ἄνθρωπος [τὸν] πατέρα καὶ [τὴν] μητέρα καὶ προσκολληθήσεται πρὸς τὴν γυναῖκα [v. l. τῇ γυναικὶ] αὐτοῦ καὶ ἔσονται εἰς σάρκα μίαν.

Ex. xx. 12 (Deut. v. 16). τίμα τὸν πατέρα σου καὶ τὴν μητέρα σου.

ib. vi. 2. τίμα τὸν πατέρα σου καὶ τὴν μητέρα.

Deut. xxxiii. 2 f. κ. ἐπέφανεν ἐκ Σηεὶρ ἡμῖν κ. κατέσπευσεν ἐξ ὄρους Φαρὰν σὺν μυριάσι Κάδης (Heb. from the ten thousands of the holy ones, R. V.)...κ. ἐφείσατο τοῦ λαοῦ αὐτοῦ, καὶ πάντες οἱ ἡγιασμένοι ὑπὸ τὰς χεῖράς σου...κ. ἐδέξατο...νόμον, ὃν ἐνετείλατο ἡμῖν Μωσῆς, κληρονομίαν συναγωγαῖς Ἰσραήλ.

ib. i. 18. τίς ὁ πλοῦτος τῆς δόξης τῆς κληρονομίας αὐτοῦ ἐν τοῖς ἁγίοις.

Ps. iv. 4 (5). ὀργίζεσθε καὶ μὴ ἁμαρτάνετε (Heb. Stand in awe and sin not, E. V.).

ib. iv. 26. ὀργίζεσθε καὶ μὴ ἁμαρτάνετε.

ib. viii. 6 (7). καὶ κατέστησας αὐτὸν ἐπὶ τὰ ἔργα χειρῶν σου· πάντα ὑπέταξας ὑποκάτω τ. ποδῶν αὐτοῦ.

ib. i. 22. καὶ πάντα ὑπέταξεν ὑπὸ τοὺς πόδας αὐτοῦ, κ.τ.λ.

ib. xl. (xxxix.) 6 (7). θυσίαν καὶ προσφορὰν οὐκ ἠθέλησας, σῶμα δὲ κατηρτίσω μοι.

ib. v. 2. κ. παρέδωκεν ἑαυτὸν ὑπὲρ ἡμῶν προσφορὰν καὶ θυσίαν τῷ θεῷ.

ib. lxviii. (lxvii.) 18 (19). ἀναβὰς εἰς ὕψος ἠχμαλώτευσας αἰχμαλωσίαν, ἔλαβες δόματα ἐν ἀνθρώπῳ (BᵃℵRᵃ -οις). (Heb. Thou hast ascended on high, Thou hast led Thy captivity captive, Thou hast received gifts among men, R. V.)

ib. iv. 8. διὸ λέγει Ἀναβὰς εἰς ὕψος ἠχμαλώτευσεν αἰχμαλωσίαν [καὶ] ἔδωκεν δόματα τοῖς ἀνθρώποις.

ib. cx. (cix.) 1. Εἶπεν ὁ κύριος τῷ κυρίῳ μου Κάθου ἐκ δεξιῶν μου.

ib. i. 20. ἐγείρας αὐτὸν ἐκ νεκρῶν καὶ καθίσας ἐν δεξιᾷ αὐτοῦ.

Prov. ii. 2 (LXX.). κ. παραβαλεῖς καρδίαν σου εἰς σύνεσιν, παραβαλεῖς δὲ αὐτὴν ἐπὶ νουθέτησιν τῷ υἱῷ σου.

ib. vi. 4. ἐκτρέφετε αὐτὰ ἐν παιδείᾳ καὶ νουθεσίᾳ Κυρίου.

ib. 5. τότε συνήσεις φόβον κυρίου καὶ ἐπίγνωσιν θεοῦ εὑρήσεις.

ib. iii. 11. υἱέ, μὴ ὀλιγώρει παιδείας κυρίου (cf. Is. l. 5).

Prov. xxiii. 31 (LXX.). μὴ μεθύσκεσθε ἐν οἴνοις (Heb. Look not thou
upon the wine when it is red).

Eph. v. 18. μὴ μεθύσκεσθε οἴνῳ.

Is. xi. 4. κ. πατάξει γῆν τῷ λόγῳ
τοῦ στόματος αὐτοῦ, καὶ ἐν πνεύματι
διὰ χειλέων ἀνελεῖ ἀσεβῆ.

ἰϐ. vi. 17. καὶ τὴν μάχαιραν τοῦ
πνεύματος, ὅ ἐστιν ῥῆμα θεοῦ.

ἰϐ. xlix. 2. κ. ἔθηκεν τὸ στόμα μου
ὡς μάχαιραν ὀξεῖαν.

ἰϐ. xi. 5. καὶ ἔσται δικαιοσύνη ἐζωσμένος τ. ὀσφὺν αὐτοῦ, καὶ ἀληθείᾳ
εἰλημένος τὰς πλευράς.

ἰϐ. 14. περιζωσάμενοι τὴν ὀσφὺν ὑμῶν ἐν ἀληθείᾳ.

ἰϐ. xxviii. 16. διὰ τοῦτο οὕτως λέγει
κύριος Κύριος Ἰδοὺ ἐγὼ ἐμβάλλω εἰς τὰ
θεμέλια Σειὼν λίθον πολυτελῆ ἐκλεκτὸν
ἀκρογωνιαῖον ἔντιμον εἰς τὰ θεμέλια
αὐτῆς, καὶ ὁ πιστεύων οὐ μὴ καταισ-
χυνθῇ.

ἰϐ. ii. 20. ἐποικοδομηθέντες ἐπὶ τῷ
θεμελίῳ τῶν ἀποστόλων καὶ προφητῶν,
ὄντος ἀκρογωνιαίου αὐτοῦ Χριστοῦ
Ἰησοῦ, ἐν ᾧ κ.τ.λ.

ἰϐ. xl. 3. ἐτοιμάσατε τὴν ὁδὸν
Κυρίου (cf. v. 9, ὁ εὐαγγελιζόμενος).

ἰϐ. vi. 15. ὑποδησάμενοι τοὺς
πόδας ἐν ἑτοιμασίᾳ τοῦ εὐαγγελίου τῆς εἰρήνης.

ἰϐ. lii. 7. ὡς πόδες εὐαγγελιζομένου ἀκοὴν εἰρήνης κ.τ.λ.

ἰϐ. lvii. 19. εἰρήνην ἐπ᾽ εἰρήνην
τοῖς μακρὰν καὶ τοῖς ἐγγὺς οὖσιν.

ἰϐ. ii. 17. κ. ἐλθὼν εὐηγγελίσατο
εἰρήνην ὑμῖν τοῖς μακρὰν καὶ εἰρήνην
τοῖς ἐγγύς (cf. v. 13).

ἰϐ. lix. 17. καὶ ἐνεδύσατο δικαιοσύνην ὡς θώρακα, καὶ περιέθετο
περικεφαλαίαν σωτηρίου ἐπὶ τῆς
κεφαλῆς.

ἰϐ. vi. 14. καὶ ἐνδυσάμενοι τὸν
θώρακα τῆς δικαιοσύνης.

ἰϐ. 17. κ. τὴν περικεφαλαίαν τοῦ
σωτηρίου δέξασθε.

Ezek. xx. 41. ἐν ὀσμῇ εὐωδίας
προσδέξομαι ὑμᾶς.

ἰϐ. v. 2. προσφορὰν κ. θυσίαν τ. θεῷ
εἰς ὀσμὴν εὐωδίας.

Hos. vi. 5. ἀπέκτεινα αὐτοὺς ἐν
ῥήματι στόματός μου, κ. τὸ κρίμα μου
ὡς φῶς ἐξελεύσεται.

ἰϐ. vi. 17. τ. μάχαιραν τ. πνεύματος,
ὅ ἐστιν ῥῆμα θεοῦ.

Zech. viii. 16. λαλεῖτε ἀλήθειαν
ἕκαστος πρὸς τὸν πλησίον αὐτοῦ.

ἰϐ. iv. 25. λαλεῖτε ἀλήθειαν ἕκαστος
μετὰ τοῦ πλησίον αὐτοῦ.

VOCABULARY OF THE EPISTLE TO THE EPHESIANS.

* Signifies 'found nowhere in N. T. except in *Ephesians.*'
  †   „   'found (in N. T.) only in *Ephesians* and *Colossians.*'
  ‡   „   'found (in N. T.) only in *Pauline Epistles.*'

ἀγαθός ii. 10, iv. 28, 29, vi. 8
‡ἀγαθωσύνη v. 9
ἀγαπᾶν i. 6 (ἐν τῷ ἠγαπημένῳ), ii. 4,
    v. 2, 25, 28, 33, vi. 24
ἀγάπη i. 4, 15 (v. l.), ii. 4, iii. 18, 19,
    iv. 2, 15, 16, v. 2, vi. 23
ἀγαπητός v. 1, vi. 21
ἀγιάζειν v. 26 (-άσῃ)
ἅγιος i. 1, 4, 13, 15, 18 (τῷ πν.—τ. ἅγ.),
    ii. 19, 21, iii. 5, 8, 18, iv. 12, 30 (τὸ
    πν. τὸ ἅγ. τοῦ Θ.), v. 3, 27, vi. 18
ἄγνοια iv. 18
ἀγρυπνεῖν vi. 18
ἀδελφός vi. 21, 23 (-οῖς)
ἀήρ ii. 2
*ἄθεος ii. 12
αἷμα i. 7, ii. 13, vi. 12 (αἷ. κ. σάρκα)
αἴρειν iv. 31
‡αἰσχρός v. 12 (-όν ἐστι)
*αἰσχρότης v. 4: 'vox N. T. propria'
    (Bruder)
αἰτεῖσθαι iii. 13, 20
αἰχμαλωσία iv. 8 (LXX)
*αἰχμαλωτεύειν iv. 8 (LXX)
αἰών i. 21, ii. 2, 7 (pl.), iii. 9 (pl.), 11
    (pl.), 21 (τ. αἰῶνος τ. αἰώνων)
ἀκαθαρσία iv. 19, v. 3
ἀκάθαρτος v. 5
ἄκαρπος v. 11
ἀκούειν i. 13, 15, iii. 2, iv. 21, 29
ἀκριβῶς v. 15
ἀκροβυστία ii. 11
ἀκρογωνιαῖος ii. 20
ἀλήθεια i. 13, iv. 21, 24, 25, v. 9, vi. 14

‡ἀληθεύειν iv. 15
ἀλλά i. 21, ii. 19, iv. 29, v. 4, 15, 17,
    18, 24, 27, 29, vi. 4, 6, 12
ἀλλήλων iv. 2, 25, 32 (-ους), v. 21 (-οις)
ἄλυσις vi. 20
ἁμαρτάνειν iv. 26
ἁμαρτία ii. 1 (τ. ἁμαρτίαις)
ἀμήν iii. 21
ἀμφότεροι ii. 14 (-α), 16, 18
ἄμωμος i. 4, v. 27
ἀναβαίνειν iv. 8, 9, 10
ἀναγινώσκειν iii. 4
‡ἀνακεφαλαιοῦσθαι i. 10
ἀναλαβεῖν vi. 13, 16
*ἀνανεοῦσθαι iv. 23
ἀναστῆναι v. 14
ἀναστρέφειν ii. 3
ἀναστροφή iv. 22
ἄνεμος iv. 14
‡ἀνεξιχνίαστος iii. 8
ἀνέχεσθαι iv. 2
‡ἀνήκει v. 4 (ἀνῆκεν)
ἀνήρ iv. 13, v. 22, 23, 24, 25, 28, 33
†ἀνθρωπάρεσκος vi. 6
ἄνθρωπος ii. 15, iii. 5, 16, iv. 8, 14, 22,
    24, v. 31, vi. 7
ἀνιέναι vi. 9
*ἄνοιξις vi. 19
ἀντί v. 31
ἀντιστῆναι vi. 13
ἀξίως iv. 1
*ἀπαλγεῖν iv. 19 (-ηλγηκότες)
ἅπαντα vi. 13
ἀπατᾶν v. 6

ὕδωρ v. 26
‡υἱοθεσία i. 5
υἱός ii. 2, iii. 5, iv. 13 (τ. υἱοῦ τ. θ.), v. 6
ὑμεῖς (n.) i. 13, ii. 11, 13, 22, iv. 20,
　v. 33, vi. 21: other cases 37 times
†ὕμνος v. 19
ὑπακούειν vi. 2, 5
ὑπέρ c. gen. i. 16, iii. 1, 13, v. 2, 20, 25,
　vi. 19, 20: c. acc. i. 22, iii. 20
ὑπεράνω i. 21, iv. 10 (else only Heb. ix. 5)
‡ὑπερβάλλειν i. 19, ii. 7, iii. 19
‡ὑπερεκπερισσοῦ iii. 20
ὑπό c. gen. ii. 11, v. 12, 13: c. acc. i. 22
ὑποδεῖσθαι vi. 15
ὑποτάσσειν i. 22, v. 21, 22, 24
ὕψος iii. 18, iv. 8

φανεροῦν v. 13 (bis)
φθείρειν iv. 22
φοβεῖσθαι v. 33
φόβος v. 21, vi. 5
φραγμός ii. 14
φρόνησις i. 8
φύσις ii. 3 (-ει)
φῶς v. 8 (bis), 9, 13 (bis)
φωτίζειν i. 18, iii. 9

χαρίζεσθαι iv. 32 (bis)
χάριν (prep.) iii. 1, 14
χάρις i. 2, 6, 7, ii. 5, 7, 8, iii. 2, 7, 8, iv.
　7, 29, vi. 24
χαριτοῦν i. 6
χείρ iv. 28
χειροποίητος ii. 11
χρεία iv. 28, 29
χρηστός iv. 32
‡χρηστότης ii. 7
Χριστός (alone) i. 3 (ἐν Χρ.), iv. 15, 32
　(ἐν Χρ.), v. 21, 32, vi. 6 (δοῦλοι Χρ.).
　For use with Ἰησοῦς before and after
　v.s. Ἰησοῦς. Ὁ χριστὸς (v. on i. 12)
　occurs 20 times
χωρίς ii. 12

ψάλλειν v. 19
ψαλμός v. 19
ψεῦδος iv. 25
ψυχή vi. 6 (ἐκ ψυχῆς)

ᾠδή v. 19
ὡς ii. 3, iii. 5, v. 1, 8, 15, 22, 23 28, 33,
　vi. 5, 6, 7, 20
ὥσπερ v. 24

CORRIGENDA

p. 12, l. 32, col. 2, for 'he' read 'He'.

p. 66, note on τῇ ἀσελγείᾳ, after 'as' insert 'to'.

p. 72, col. 2, l. 3, 'us' should, to accord with text, be 'you'.

p. 85, l. 15, col. 2, for αμωμος read ἄμωμος.

p. 93, l. 27, col. 1, for 'p. 918' read 'Pt. ii. vol. iii. p. 334'.

„ „ l. 40, in 2 Sam. xix. 27 for 'ἐν τῷ δούλῳ' the reading in Prof. Swete's edition is ὁ δοῦλος.

p. 168, l. 10, after 'Ισραήλ insert]

INDEX OF SUBJECTS